Tradition and Experiment in Wordsworth's *Lyrical Ballads* (1798)

Tradition and Experiment in Wordsworth's *Lyrical Ballads* (1798)

MARY JACOBUS

CLARENDON PRESS · OXFORD
1976

Oxford University Press, Ely House, London W.1

GLASGOW   NEW YORK   TORONTO   MELBOURNE   WELLINGTON
CAPE TOWN   IBADAN   NAIROBI   DAR ES SALAAM   LUSAKA   ADDIS ABABA
DELHI   BOMBAY   CALCUTTA   MADRAS   KARACHI   LAHORE   DACCA
KUALA LUMPUR   SINGAPORE   HONG KONG   TOKYO

ISBN 0 19 812069 9

© *Oxford University Press 1976*

*Printed in Great Britain by
Butler & Tanner Ltd, Frome and London*

Contents

Acknowledgements

I am grateful to the Trustees of Dove Cottage for permission to quote from manuscript material preserved in Dove Cottage Library, and to the Fellows of Lady Margaret Hall for a Randall McIver research fellowship which helped me to complete an early draft. At different times I have received valuable information, encouragement, or criticism from Stephen Gill, Rachel Trickett, and Robert Woof, and I am indebted throughout to Mark Reed's *Wordsworth: The Chronology of the Early Years 1770–1799* (Cambridge, Mass., 1967). I am also grateful to Peggy Broadbent for her expert preparation of the typescript and to Jane Havell for helping to check the proofs. My greatest debt is to Jonathan Wordsworth, to whom this book owes its existence.

Part of Chapter X appeared as 'The Idiot Boy' in *Bicentenary Wordsworth Studies*, ed. Jonathan Wordsworth (Ithaca, N.Y., 1970) and part of the Conclusion as '*Peter Bell* the First' in *Essays in Criticism*, xxiv (1974); I am grateful for permission to incorporate them here.

Note on Quotations from Wordsworth

THE title *Lyrical Ballads* refers throughout to the 1798 volume, from which quotations are drawn; quotations from the second volume are from the 1800 edition. *Prelude* references are to the 1805 text. Quotations from MS. and Isabella Fenwick notes are accompanied by references to *The Poetical Works of William Wordsworth*, ed. Ernest de Selincourt and Helen Darbishire (5 vols., Oxford, 1940–9), but my text at times differs from theirs. In presenting MS. material, the original spelling has been preserved except in the case of obvious errors, and some additional punctuation supplied; with drafts I have tried to present the final version, and with fair copy, the first. A list of MSS. from which quotations are drawn appears on p. 289, below, accompanied by their Dove Cottage numbering.

Abbreviations

CCW	*The Collected Works of Samuel Taylor Coleridge*, ed. Kathleen Coburn and Bart Winer ([16] vols., London, 1969—).
CPW	*The Complete Poetical Works of Samuel Taylor Coleridge*, ed. E. H. Coleridge (2 vols., Oxford, 1912).
Curry	*New Letters of Robert Southey*, ed. Kenneth Curry (2 vols., New York and London, 1965).
DC	Dove Cottage.
DWJ	*Journals of Dorothy Wordsworth*, ed. Ernest de Selincourt (2 vols., London, 1941).
EC	*Essays in Criticism.*
ELH	*English Literary History.*
EY	*The Letters of William and Dorothy Wordsworth: The Early Years 1787–1805*, ed. Ernest de Selincourt, rev. C. L. Shaver (2nd edn., Oxford, 1967).
Griggs	*Collected Letters of Samuel Taylor Coleridge*, ed. E. L. Griggs (4 vols., Oxford, 1956–9).
Howe	*The Complete Works of William Hazlitt*, ed. P. P. Howe (21 vols., London, 1930–4).
I.F. note	Note dictated by Wordsworth to Isabella Fenwick in 1843 and transcribed by Dora and Edward Quillinan.
JEGP	*Journal of English and Germanic Philology.*
Lucas	*The Letters of Charles Lamb to which are added those of his sister Mary Lamb*, ed. E. V. Lucas (3 vols., London, 1935).
LY	*The Letters of William and Dorothy Wordsworth: The Later Years 1821–1850*, ed. Ernest de Selincourt (3 vols., Oxford, 1939).
MLN	*Modern Language Notes.*
MLQ	*Modern Language Quarterly.*
MLR	*Modern Language Review.*
MP	*Modern Philology.*
MY	*The Letters of William and Dorothy Wordsworth: The Middle Years 1806–1820*, ed. Ernest de Selincourt, rev. Mary Moorman and A. G. Hill (2nd edn., 2 vols., Oxford, 1969–70).
N & Q	*Notes and Queries.*

PMLA   *Publications of the Modern Language Association of America.*

PQ   *Philological Quarterly.*

Prelude   *William Wordsworth: The Prelude or Growth of a Poet's Mind,* ed. Ernest de Selincourt, rev. Helen Darbishire (2nd edn., Oxford, 1959).

Prose Works   *The Prose Works of William Wordsworth,* ed. W. J. B. Owen and Jane Worthington Smyser (3 vols., Oxford, 1974).

PW   *The Poetical Works of William Wordsworth,* ed Ernest de Selincourt and Helen Darbishire (5 vols., Oxford, 1940–9), vols. ii and iii rev. Helen Darbishire (2nd edn., Oxford, 1952–4).

Reed   Reed, M. L., *Wordsworth: The Chronology of the Early Years 1770–1799* (Cambridge, Mass., 1967).

REL   *Review of English Literature.*

RES   *Review of English Studies.*

SB   *Studies in Bibliography.*

SEL   *Studies in English Literature.*

Shawcross   *Biographia Literaria by S. T. Coleridge,* ed. J. Shawcross (2 vols., Oxford, 1907).

SP   *Studies in Philology.*

SR   *Studies in Romanticism.*

UTQ   *University of Toronto Quarterly.*

Introduction:
Tradition and Experiment

IN 1815, Wordsworth wrote that

The predecessors of an original Genius of a high order will have smoothed the way for all that he has in common with them;—and much he will have in common; but, for what is peculiarly his own, he will be called upon to clear and often to shape his own road:—he will be in the condition of Hannibal among the Alps.[1]

Wordsworth's recognition of 'what is peculiarly his own' is crucial to his emergence as an 'original Genius'. But there is no simple discarding of tradition. Indebtedness to the past coexists with the independence of a pioneer; his path is smoothed by his predecessors as well as having to be cleared and shaped for the first time. Hazlitt's portrait of a sublime solipsist does not suggest a poet open to literary influence: 'It is as if there were nothing but himself and the universe. He lives in the busy solitude of his own heart; in the deep silence of thought.'[2] But Wordsworth's encounters with other writers were at least as important as his immersion in self. His renewal of tradition and his experimentalism both reflect his alertness to the movements of his time, and in each case his achievement lay in redefinition —whether of his identity, values, and vision, or of poetry itself. The younger Wordsworth portrayed in *The Prelude* had been a poet whose imagination

> to the works of art,
> The notions and the images of books
> Did knowingly conform itself . . . [3]

The poet he became was no less responsive, but his responsiveness increasingly took the form of reassessment rather than imitation,

---

[1] 'Essay, Supplementary to the Preface', 1815 (*Prose Works*, iii. 80).

[2] 'Character of Mr. Wordsworth's New Poem, The Excursion', *Examiner*, 21 August 1814 (Howe, xix. 11).

[3] *Prelude*, viii. 516–18.

challenge rather than conformity. More than any other, he had —in Coleridge's phrase—to create the taste by which he was enjoyed,[1] forcing his readers to undergo the process of redefinition which is central to his poetry. As Wordsworth's first major statement of literary identity, *Lyrical Ballads* (1798) demands a special awareness of the relation between tradition and experiment.

Looking back from 1843, Wordsworth spoke as though *Lyrical Ballads* had grown directly out of his failure to collaborate with Coleridge on 'The Ancient Mariner'. The two poets made their first plan for joint publication in November 1797, at the start of a walking-tour: 'we went eight miles,' wrote Dorothy Wordsworth, 'William and Coleridge employing themselves in laying the plan of a ballad, to be published with some pieces of William's.'[2] According to Wordsworth's later account, the scheme broke down almost at once:

As we endeavoured to proceed conjointly (I speak of the same evening) our respective manners proved so widely different that it would have been quite presumptuous in me to do anything but separate from an undertaking upon which I could only have been a clog.[3]

'The Ancient Mariner', Wordsworth goes on, 'grew & grew', and the two poets began to talk of the volume which would eventually become *Lyrical Ballads*—a volume consisting of poems on supernatural subjects, on the one hand, and on the other, of poems on subjects 'taken from common life but looked at, as much as might be, through an imaginative medium'.[4] But between the beginnings of 'The Ancient Mariner' in the autumn of 1797 and the volume which finally went to press in the summer of 1798, Wordsworth and Coleridge made a number of alternative plans for both joint and independent publication. *Lyrical Ballads* emerged only at a comparatively late stage, and after a number of setbacks. They had tried and failed to get

---

[1] See 'Essay, Supplementary to the Preface', 1815 (*Prose Works*, iii. 80).

[2] *EY*, p. 194. 'Some pieces of William's' presumably refers to the self-contained poems of 1796–7 which eventually found their way into *Lyrical Ballads* (see Appendix I, pp. 273–4, below). For a general account of the volume's origins, see also M. L. Reed, 'Wordsworth, Coleridge, and the "Plan" of the *Lyrical Ballads*', *UTQ* xxxiv (1964–5), 238–53.

[3] I.F. note to 'We are seven' (*PW* i. 361).

[4] Ibid. (*PW* i. 361).

their plays—*The Borderers* and *Osorio*—either put on in London
or published by Cottle;[1] Coleridge had toyed with the idea of a
third edition of his *Poems* (1796), and Wordsworth had thought
of publishing his two long narrative poems of the period,
Salisbury Plain and 'The Ruined Cottage'.[2] It was not until
April 1798 that the volume which finally became *Lyrical
Ballads* began to take shape. On 12 April Wordsworth wrote to
Cottle, 'You will be pleased to hear that I have gone on very
rapidly adding to my stock of poetry', and by the end of the
month Dorothy spoke of two forthcoming volumes—one presumably still *Salisbury Plain* and 'The Ruined Cottage', the
other a volume described as 'nearly ready for publishing'.[3]
Early in May Wordsworth wrote excitedly to Cottle of finishing
Salisbury Plain and of having 'lately been busy about another
plan which I do not wish to mention till I see you; let this be
very, very, soon.' By the end of May Cottle had been and gone,
taking with him a collection of poems corresponding, in part at
least, to *Lyrical Ballads*, and Dorothy wrote that 'William has
now some poems in the Bristol press'.[4] But there were still
problems. Cottle clearly preferred the idea of publishing
Wordsworth's poems alone (including *Peter Bell*) in two volumes,
and in a letter of early June Coleridge had to defend both the
inclusion of his contributions and the anonymity of the joint
volume: 'I . . . simply state it as an unaltered opinion, that you
should proceed as before, with the ancient Mariner.'[5] With
some modifications, the volume seems then to have gone ahead;
early in July Dorothy writes that her brother's poems 'are now
printing', and finally, on 13 September 1798, '[William's
poems are] printed, but not published. [They are] in one small
volume, without the name of the author; their title is "Lyrical
Ballads, with other Poems".'[6]

Confronted by Southey's hostile verdict in the *Critical Review*
for October 1798, Wordsworth wrote bitterly: 'He knew that I
published those poems for money and money alone. He knew
that money was of importance to me.'[7] 'The Ancient Mariner'
had been conceived as a means to cover the expenses of a

[1] See *EY*, pp. 194–6, and Griggs, i. 357, 384–5, 400.
[2] See ibid. i. 387, 391, 400.   [3] *EY*, pp. 215, 216.   [4] Ibid., pp. 218, 219.
[5] Griggs, i. 412; for the date, see *EY*, p. 220n., and Reed, p. 319.
[6] *EY*, pp. 224, 227.   [7] [Summer?] 1799; *EY*, pp. 267–8.

walking-tour: *Lyrical Ballads* was conceived as one of a number of
ways to finance the more ambitious expedition to Germany that
was being talked of in spring 1798.[1] Wordsworth and Coleridge
had urgent practical reasons for wanting to go into print as and
when they could, and the volume which finally appeared represents a considerable degree of compromise, expediency, and
chance. Publication of *Salisbury Plain* went by the board, and
instead Wordsworth excerpted the story of the Female Vagrant
to pad out the joint collection; Coleridge, similarly, excerpted
'The Dungeon' and 'The Foster-Mother's Tale' from *Osorio*.
Both included poems earlier published in the *Morning Post*
('The Convict' and 'Lewti'),[2] and both kept back much of their
most important writing of the period—Wordsworth, for
instance, withheld 'The Discharged Soldier' and 'The Old
Cumberland Beggar', using only a fragment left over from the
latter in 'Old Man Travelling'; while Coleridge withheld the
great Conversation Poems of 1797–8 ('This Lime-Tree Bower
my Prison' and 'Frost at Midnight'), only at the last minute
substituting 'The Nightingale' for 'Lewti' in order to preserve
the volume's anonymity—and, perhaps, to balance Wordsworth's inclusion of 'Tintern Abbey' on its composition in
July.[3] With earlier pieces by Wordsworth ('Lines written near
Richmond' and 'Lines left upon a Seat in a Yew-tree'), all
these constituted the 'other Poems' of the title. But the nucleus
of the collection had very different origins.

  Lyrical Ballads was made possible by one of those bursts of
composition which characterize Wordsworth's career—his
sudden production of the short poems and ballads referred to in
his mid-April letter to Cottle ('I have gone on very rapidly
adding to my stock of poetry'). The early months of 1798 had
been occupied by work on 'The Discharged Soldier', 'The Old
Cumberland Begger', and 'The Ruined Cottage' (completed by
mid-March);[4] but with 'The Ancient Mariner' once more under
way,[5] Wordsworth seems to have turned again to the ballad-

[1] See *PW* i. 360, and *EY*, p. 213.

[2] *Morning Post*, 14 December 1797 and 13 April 1798 respectively.

[3] For the bibliographical complications of the 'Lewti' cancellation see D. F.
Foxon, 'The Printing of *Lyrical Ballads*, 1798', *Library*, 5th ser. ix (1954), 221–41.

[4] See Reed, pp. 27–9 *passim*, 339.

[5] The finished poem was brought over to Alfoxden towards the end of March
(see *DWJ* i. 13).

writing on which he and Coleridge had originally hoped to collaborate. It is only at this point that one is justified in invoking the famous *Biographia Literaria* account of the plan of *Lyrical Ballads*:

The thought suggested itself . . . that a series of poems might be composed of two sorts. In the one, the incidents and agents were to be, in part at least, supernatural; and the excellence aimed at was to consist in the interesting of the affections by the dramatic truth of such emotions, as would naturally accompany such situations, supposing them real. . . . For the second class, subjects were to be chosen from ordinary life; the characters and incidents were to be such, as will be found in every village and its vicinity, where there is a meditative and feeling mind to seek after them, or to notice them, when they present themselves.[1]

Wordsworth did his share by writing, in quick succession, 'Goody Blake, and Harry Gill', 'The Thorn', and 'The Idiot Boy', followed by *Peter Bell*, his counterpart to 'The Ancient Mariner'. But as Coleridge admits, the balance of the partnership was not maintained: 'Mr. Wordsworth's industry had proved so much more successful, and the number of his poems so much greater, that my compositions, instead of forming a balance, appeared rather an interpolation of heterogeneous matter.'[2] 'Christabel' remained unfinished, along with Coleridge's continuation of 'The Three Graves';[3] while *Peter Bell* itself did not appear for another twenty years. Properly speaking, the plan behind *Lyrical Ballads* was never fulfilled.

Yet Coleridge could defend the scheme to Cottle by claiming that it represented '*one work*, in *kind tho' not in degree*, as an Ode is one work—& that our different poems are as stanzas'.[4] His insistence on the spirit of collaboration is a reminder of the pooling of ideas and the shared aims which lie behind *Lyrical Ballads*. The first thing Wordsworth and Coleridge did when they met at Racedown in June 1797 was read one another their most recent work, *The Borderers*, 'The Ruined Cottage', and *Osorio*.[5] In July Coleridge wrote pointedly to Southey—for whom he had once felt something of what he now felt for

[1] Shawcross, ii. 5.   [2] Ibid. ii. 6.   [3] See pp. 228–32, below.
[4] [4 June 1798]; Griggs, i. 412.
[5] See *EY*, p. 189. The two poets had met briefly in the late summer of 1795 and, more recently, in the spring of 1797 (see Reed, pp. 167, 195).

Wordsworth—that he had found 'the only man, to whom *at all times* & in *all modes of excellence*' he knew himself inferior.[1] If Coleridge saw in Wordsworth the 'very great man' he needed to admire, the Wordsworths saw in Coleridge a poet uniquely inspired ('more of the "poet's eye in a fine frenzy rolling" than I ever witnessed', wrote Dorothy).[2] By August, the Wordsworths had moved from Racedown to Alfoxden in order to be near Coleridge at Stowey—'Our principal inducement was Coleridge's society', Dorothy told Mary Hutchinson.[3] The superficial results of their partnership are well documented; as well as the abortive collaboration on 'The Ancient Mariner' and 'The Wanderings of Cain',[4] there are the poems which Wordsworth handed over to Coleridge, either to help him fulfil his contract with the *Morning Post* ('The Convict' and the basis for 'Lewti' among them),[5] or simply because he felt unable to finish them himself ('The Three Graves'). More elusive, but vastly more important, is the intellectual exchange which took place during the period leading up to *Lyrical Ballads*—a developing debate between ideas that at times converged, at times diverged, and at times ran parallel. It is symptomatic that, while a shared preoccupation with guilt drew them together over 'The Ancient Mariner', their 'respective manners' forced them apart; Wordsworth could suggest the slaying of the albatross as the poem's starting-point,[6] but in the end each had to create his own kind of ballad. The relationship, in fact, provides the best possible illustration of Wordsworth's later theory about the poet's twofold debt to other writers. For all that they gave one another, the most important effect of the partnership was to make each more fully himself.

What Coleridge recognized in the Wordsworth of 1797, according to *Biographia Literaria*, was

the union of deep feeling with profound thought; the fine balance of truth in observing, with the imaginative faculty in modifying the

---

[1] Griggs, i. 334.   [2] [June 1797]; *EY*, p. 189.

[3] 14 August 1797; ibid., p. 190.

[4] See Reed, p. 208, for the probable date of 'The Wanderings of Cain' (early November 1797).

[5] See J. W. Smyser, 'Coleridge's Use of Wordsworth's Juvenilia', *PMLA* lxv (1950), 419–26, and R. S. Woof, 'Wordsworth's Poetry and Stuart's Newspapers: 1797–1803', *SB* xv (1962), 149–89.

[6] See I.F. note to 'We are seven' (*PW* i. 361).

objects observed; and above all the original gift of spreading the tone, the *atmosphere*, and with it the depth and height of the ideal world around forms, incidents, and situations, of which, for the common view, custom had bedimmed all the lustre, had dried up the sparkle and the dew drops.[1]

But if the essentials of Wordsworth's vision were already present, many of his most characteristic poetic modes were not. His earlier writing had been that of a major poet working within, and to some extent limited by, the terms he had inherited. *An Evening Walk* and *Descriptive Sketches* (both published in 1793), *Salisbury Plain* and the recently-completed *Borderers*, show Wordsworth using modes to which he never returned—a backward-looking, discursive couplet-poetry; humanitarian protest; gothic drama. Not until 'The Ruined Cottage', written during the early summer of 1797, just before he came to know Coleridge, can the later, mature Wordsworth be seen. It was the ensuing period that crystallized those aspects of his writing we now think of as distinctively Wordsworthian. 'The Ruined Cottage' shows him already as the poet of the everyday, of shared human experience; now under Coleridge's influence he becomes the poet whose greatest subject is the interpenetration of nature and the mind. In each case Wordsworth's vision is infused by that meditative 'union of deep feeling with profound thought' described in *Biographia Literaria*; but it had taken Coleridge and the Conversation Poem to reveal to him the possibility of writing about himself as he did, and it seems to have been Coleridge's supernaturalism that made him aware of his own stance as the poet of the human heart. The running debate helped Wordsworth to formulate his assumptions about the nature and function of poetry itself. The experimentalism of *Lyrical Ballads* is at once a critique of the poetry Wordsworth saw round him, and a manifesto for his own. It was this experimentalism—Hannibal's assault on the Alps— that for Wordsworth and Coleridge themselves, as for subsequent readers, came to be central to the volume as a whole.

Coleridge later blamed 'the critical remarks' appended to *Lyrical Ballads* as 'the true origin of the unexampled opposition which Mr. Wordsworth's writings have been since doomed to encounter'.[2] Certainly they distracted attention from other

[1] Shawcross, i. 59.   [2] Shawcross, i. 51.

aspects of the collection—from its contemporaneity, and even,
in some cases, its traditionalism. An awareness of the literary
context of the 1790s modifies the impression given by Wordsworth himself that his choice of subject and style was inherently
new.[1] For his theory, too, Wordsworth drew on ideas that had
been made current during the past forty years—notably by
Hugh Blair, whose definition of poetry as 'the language of
passion',[2] primitive and unliterary in its origins, underlies many
of the assumptions of the 1800 'Preface'. Contemporary sensibility, eighteenth-century primitivism, and the democratizing
impulse of a revolutionary period—the impulse which for
Hazlitt formed the basis of the Lake School[3]—all converge in
Lyrical Ballads. Yet this was the period denounced by the 1800
'Preface' for its 'degrading thirst after outrageous stimulation'
('The invaluable works of our elder writers . . . are driven into
neglect by frantic novels, sickly and stupid German Tragedies,
and deluges of idle and extravagent stories in verse').[4] Wordsworth clearly felt himself at odds with central elements in his
literary context—'the gaudiness and inane phraseology of many
modern writers'[5] and the sensationalism that had helped to
inspire 'The Ancient Mariner'. The 1798 'Advertisement'
admits that readers of *Lyrical Ballads*

will perhaps frequently have to struggle with feelings of strangeness
and aukwardness: they will look round for poetry, and will be
induced to enquire by what species of courtesy these attempts can be
permitted to assume that title.[6]

And to John Stoddart at least, reviewing the 1800 edition,
there could be no doubt that it stood apart from

the flood of poetry, which is poured forth in such profusion by the
modern Bards of Science, or their brethren, the Bards of Insipidity.

[1] See, for instance, the important article by Robert Mayo, 'The Contemporaneity of the *Lyrical Ballads*', *PMLA* lxix (1954), 486–522; the discussion is continued
by Charles Ryskamp, 'Wordsworth's *Lyrical Ballads* in Their Time', *From Sensibility to Romanticism: Essays Presented to Frederick A. Pottle*, ed. F. W. Hilles and
Harold Bloom (New York, 1965), pp. 357–72, and by J. E. Jordan, 'The Novelty
of the *Lyrical Ballads*', *Bicentenary Wordsworth Studies*, ed. Jonathan Wordsworth
(Ithaca, N.Y., 1970), pp. 340–58.

[2] See *Lectures on Rhetoric and Belles Lettres* (2 vols., London, 1783), ii. 312.

[3] See *Lectures on the English Poets*, 1818 (Howe, v. 161).

[4] *Prose Works*, i. 128–30.

[5] 1798 'Advertisement' (*Prose Works*, i. 116).   [6] *Prose Works*, i. 116.

The author has thought for himself; he has deeply studied human nature, in the book of human action; and he has adopted his language from the same sources as his feelings.[1]

Stoddart may be saying no more than that Wordsworth is a major poet, and one who had, in his own phrase, 'thought long and deeply'.[2] But *Lyrical Ballads* went further than this; it asked its readers to think too:

> while they are perusing this book, they should ask themselves if it contains a natural delineation of human passions, human characters, and human incidents; and if the answer be favourable to the author's wishes . . . they should consent to be pleased in spite of that most dreadful enemy to our pleasures, our own pre-established codes of decision.[3]

Wordsworth's handling of existing themes and genres constitutes a deliberate challenge to 'pre-established codes of decision'. His problem was twofold: to replace the values he criticized by his own belief in the importance of the human heart; and to do so in a way which did not signal his distance from the ordinary feelings which were his subject. The literary awareness which underlies his experiment had to be subsumed into an anti-literary mode. Optimistically, Wordsworth believed that he could revitalize poetry itself—breaking down the barriers between literature and life, recapturing the enduring relevance achieved by 'the invaluable works of our elder writers', and re-educating his readers. Language became his central weapon against literary convention. By the early summer of 1798, the volume was being represented to Hazlitt as 'an experiment . . . to see how far the public taste would endure poetry written in a more natural and simple style than had hitherto been attempt-ed',[4] and in the 1798 'Advertisement' Wordsworth defines this style, more specifically, as 'the language of conversation in the

---

[1] *British Critic*, xvii (February 1801), 125. See Mary Moorman, *William Words-worth: A Biography: The Early Years 1770–1803* (Oxford, 1957), p. 505n., for the identification of Stoddart as the author of this review—possibly nudged into existence by Wordsworth himself, whom he had visited while *Lyrical Ballads* (1800) was being prepared for the press; see R. S. Woof, 'John Stoddart, "Michael" and *Lyrical Ballads*', *Ariel*, i, no. 2 (April 1970), 7–22.

[2] 1800 'Preface' (*Prose Works*, i. 126).

[3] 1798 'Advertisement' (*Prose Works*, i. 116).

[4] 'My First Acquaintance with Poets', 1823 (Howe, xvii. 120).

middle and lower classes of society'.[1] For Coleridge, the experiment came to verge on 'ventriloquism';[2] but for Wordsworth, identification with the feelings of ordinary people justified his adoption of the non-literary idiom they actually used—'a selection of the real language of men in a state of vivid sensation'.[3] Intent on removing 'the film of familiarity' from the everyday,[4] he had to find new ways to shock his readers into response and recognition, but ways that were firmly anchored in common experience.

To Southey, Wordsworth's experiment seemed a failure, not because the language of conversation was unsuited to poetry, but because it had been applied to 'uninteresting subjects'.[5] Hazlitt showed a better understanding of 'the unaccountable mixture of seeming simplicity and real abstruseness in the *Lyrical Ballads*' when he wrote that

Fools have laughed at, wise men scarcely understand them. He takes a subject or a story merely as pegs or loops to hang thought and feeling on; the incidents are trifling, in proportion to his contempt for imposing appearances; the reflections are profound, according to the gravity and the aspiring pretensions of his mind.[6]

Everyday subjects and stories are transformed by the Wordsworthian imagination, used 'as pegs or loops to hang thought and feeling on'. Hence the power of *Lyrical Ballads* to win, not just readers, but converts; Coleridge describes the 'young men of strong sensibility and meditative minds' whose admiration 'was distinguished by its intensity, I might almost say, by its *religious* fervor'.[7] For the 17-year-old John Wilson, writing to Wordsworth in 1802, *Lyrical Ballads* was 'the book which I value next to my Bible',[8] and at the same age, in 1803, De Quincey told Wordsworth that 'from the wreck of all earthly things which belong to me, I should endeavour to save that work by an impulse second to none but that of self-preservation.'[9]

[1] *Prose Works*, i. 116.
[2] See Shawcross, ii. 109.
[3] 1800 'Preface' (*Prose Works*, i. 118).   [4] Shawcross, ii. 6.
[5] *Critical Review*, xxiv (October 1798), 204.
[6] *The Spirit of the Age*, 1825 (Howe, xi. 87).   [7] Shawcross, ii. 7.
[8] See Mary Wilson Gordon, '*Christopher North*', *A Memoir of John Wilson* (2 vols., Edinburgh, 1862), i. 39–48.
[9] J. E. Jordan, *De Quincey to Wordsworth: A Biography of a Relationship* (Berkeley and Los Angeles, Calif., 1962), pp. 33–4.

It is because the volume both requires and provokes such an unusual degree of involvement that critical unanimity is rare, even among Wordsworth's admirers. Coleridge wrote that he had heard 'at different times, and from different individuals every single poem *extolled* and *reprobated*';[1] and the debate goes on. In asking us to rethink our assumptions both about poetry and about the subjects he chose, Wordsworth made sure that— whatever the merits and idiosyncrasies of individual poems— his experiment would take life from the debate. The self-defining process which underlies *Lyrical Ballads* is also the process which has made it consistently challenging and original for its readers.

[1] Shawcross, i. 54. Cf. also the contrasting verdicts listed for Coleridge in a letter of 1801 (*EY*, pp. 319–20).

PART I

'THE SILENT HOUR OF INWARD THOUGHT'

('Lines left upon a Seat in a Yew-tree')

I Guilt and Alienation: The Godwinian Background

'You would make me very happy, if you think W. has no objection, by transcribing for me that inscription of his,' wrote Charles Lamb to Coleridge in July 1797.[1] The poem he refers to is Wordsworth's recently composed 'Lines left upon a Seat in a Yew-tree'. Its plea for self-acceptance in the face of adversity and disappointment would have had special meaning for the Lamb to whose 'sad yet bowed soul' Coleridge elsewhere pays tribute.[2] For Wordsworth himself, the poem was the culmination of themes and ideas which had preoccupied him since the mid-1790s. Alienation and moral philosophy come together in this study of a misanthropic recluse—a figure whose significance is covertly personal. Although dwarfed in retrospect by 'Tintern Abbey', written just over a year later, the Yew-tree lines represent a similar attempt to formulate a creed capable of sustaining the individual against suffering and loss. The differences between the two poems point to crucial changes in Wordsworth's thinking. One concerns isolation, the other, communion; one suggests that the individual can transcend himself through 'the labours of benevolence', the other, through 'seeing into the life of things'. Yet for all the philosophic gulf between them and 'Tintern Abbey', the Yew-tree lines are transitional, looking back to the Godwin-influenced Wordsworth of the mid-1790s, and forward to the period of Coleridge's strongest influence in 1797-8. Drawing on the eccentric and tortured poetry of previous years, the poem also attempts to resolve the discord, and does so in terms that are unexpectedly compatible with Coleridge's thinking. What distinguishes the Yew-tree lines most sharply from 'Tintern Abbey' and the Coleridgean Conversation Poem is the widely different literary traditions on which they draw. In the earlier poem,

[1] Lucas, i. 112.

[2] See p. 78, below.

inherited material provides Wordsworth with a vehicle for personal preoccupations, but it is a vehicle only partly adequate as a means of self-exploration; 'Tintern Abbey', by contrast, draws on a tradition which liberated the deepest sources of Wordsworth's imagination, allowing him to write about himself in an entirely new way, and in the context of an entirely different kind of poetry. The Yew-tree lines are of unexpected interest for what they tell us about the Wordsworth of 1797 and before; but they also tell us how much he changed, and in what direction, during the year of *Lyrical Ballads*.

I. MISANTHROPY AND MORAL PHILOSOPHY

← Godwin

Wordsworth tells us that he modelled the recluse of the Yew-tree lines on a real-life original, 'a gentleman of the neighbourhood' in which he spent his schooldays.[1] But the misanthrope is also a well-established figure in the eighteenth-century literature of sensibility. Thomas Warton, jun.'s 'The Suicide', for instance, presents a solitary driven from society by his overwrought feelings—

> Oft was he wont, in hasty fit,
> Abrupt the social board to quit,
> And gaze with eager glance upon the tumbling flood.[2]

—and propelled towards suicide by an imagination which morbidly multiplies his sufferings:

> To griefs congenial prone,
> More wounds than nature gave he knew,
> While misery's form his fancy drew
> In dark ideal hues, and horrors not its own.[3]

Although designed, in Richard Mant's words, 'to comfort the miserable, and to restrain the vicious, by enforcing the dictates of religion', 'The Suicide' inevitably came to be associated

---

[1] I.F. note to the Yew-tree lines (*PW* i. 329); according to Wordsworth's note, some lines in the poem also went back to this Hawkshead period. For a full account of the Revd. William Braithwaite, Wordsworth's 'gentleman', see T. W. Thompson, *Wordsworth's Hawkshead*, ed. Robert Woof (London, 1970), pp. 256 ff.

[2] *Poems, A New Edition* (London, 1777), p. 44.

[3] Ibid., p. 45. These lines were quoted by Goethe apropos of Werter's suicide; see *The Auto-biography of Goethe. Truth and Poetry: from my own life*, trans. John Oxenford (London, 1848), p. 507.

with the romantic despair of Chatterton's death.[1] In fiction, the figure of the disillusioned solitary has even stronger antecedents. Fielding with the Man of the Hill in *Tom Jones* (1749), or Smollett with Mathew Bramble in *Humphry Clinker* (1771), both use the misanthrope to define, by contrast, a benevolent and socialized sensibility; above all, Henry Mackenzie in *The Man of Feeling* (1771) celebrates the book's eponymous hero by juxtaposing him with 'the Misanthropist'—a man whose disillusion with society shows itself in the sterile withdrawal which is to be Wordsworth's subject:

'He entered into life with those ardent expectations by which young men are commonly deluded: in his friendships, warm to excess; and equally violent in his dislikes. He was on the brink of marriage with a young lady, when one of those friends, for whose honour he would have pawned his life, made an elopement with that very goddess, and left him besides deeply engaged for sums which that good friend's extravagance had squandered.

'The dreams he had formerly enjoyed were now changed for ideas of a very different nature. He abjured all confidence in any thing of human form; sold his lands ... came to town, and immured himself with a woman who had been his nurse, in little better than a garret; and has ever since applied his talents to the vilifying of his species.'[2]

The pattern is to recur in differing guises in the fiction and poetry of the 1790s.

Charles Lloyd's 'Oswald', published in 1795, gives a political slant to misanthropy. Coleridge's pupil and lodger of the following year was at this stage under the influence of Godwin[3] —an influence which transforms alienation into a comment on society's shortcomings. A descendant of the nature-loving Edwin in Beattie's *Minstrel* (1771–4), identified by Dorothy with the young Wordsworth himself,[4] Oswald is a victim of his own idealism:

---

1 See *The Poetical Works of the Late Thomas Warton*, ed. Richard Mant (5th edn., 2 vols., Oxford, 1802), i. clii, 146 app. crit., and Coleridge's letter to the *Monthly Magazine* in January 1798 (Griggs, i. 381–2).

2 *The Man of Feeling* (London, 1771), pp. 70–1.

3 Lloyd's domestication with Coleridge, from late 1796 to early 1797, was to produce the controversial portrait of Coleridge in his novel *Edmund Oliver* (1798)— itself a record of his changing political views (see p. 22n., below).

4 See *EY*, pp. 100–1.

The following P O E M was written with intention to trace the possible effect of the present abuses of the social system, on <u>a Youth more accustomed to *feel* than *reason*;</u> who is doom'd, when his sentiments had been raised to a high toned enthusiasm, by contemplating the wildest features of Nature, through the magnifying medium of sensibility, to view, not only the effects of the selfish principle in others, but to feel himself its unfortunate victim.[1]

'The dark abuses of the social plan'[2] outrage a sensibility which has been heightened by 'The love of Nature'; betrayed in love and friendship like Mackenzie's 'Misanthropist', Oswald collapses into 'sullen impotence of mind', even in nature 'doom'd . . . a ceaseless blank to find'.[3] The answer, for Lloyd, lies in a Godwinian millenium—social revolution inaugurated by the triumph of Reason:

> Oh! may the clouds that veil the moral world
>   Be swift dispell'd by Truth's resistless day!—
> May Liberty's high standard be unfurl'd,
>   And may mankind with one consent obey
> The *Rule of Reason*, not the uncertain sway
>   Of *mortal power*!—May they gladly join
> To hail Benevolence, thy genial ray!—
>   Then, if perchance another Oswald shine,
> That worth that prov'd a curse—the world shall deem *divine*.[4]

The difference between 'Oswald' and the Yew-tree lines is that by 1797 Wordsworth had undergone a partial reaction against Godwin.[5] Though Godwinian benevolence can be put forward as a cure for alienation, Godwinian reason has become suspect.

The most powerful study of misanthropy in the mid-1790s turns out to be Godwin's own. *Things as They Are: or, the Adventures of Caleb Williams* (1794) was announced in the suppressed preface to the first edition as an uncompromising indictment of society—'a general review of the modes of domestic and unrecorded despotism, by which man becomes the destroyer of

---

[1] *Poems on Various Subjects* (Carlisle, 1795), p. 67.   [2] Ibid., p. 78.
[3] Ibid., p. 83.
[4] Ibid., p. 87. Cf. the original closing stanza of *Salisbury Plain* (*PW* i. 340–1), quoted p. 22, below.
[5] As, in fact, had Lloyd himself; see p. 22n., below, and see also B. R. Pollin, 'Charles Lamb and Charles Lloyd as Jacobins and Anti-Jacobins', *SR* xii (1973), 633–47.

man'.[1] Godwin's much later account of the novel's composition, however, reveals that the impulse behind it was psychological as well as political:

I bent myself to the conception of a series of adventures of flight and pursuit; the fugitive in perpetual apprehension of being overwhelmed with the worst calamities, and the pursuer, by his ingenuity and resources, keeping his victim in a state of the most fearful alarm.[2]

Caleb Williams is not only an attack on 'Things as They Are', but a compulsively readable study of conflict, persecution, and despair—a record of neurosis written, as Godwin recalls, in a high state of excitement: 'I said to myself a thousand times, "I will write a tale, that shall constitute an epoch in the mind of the reader, that no one, after he has read it, shall ever be exactly the same man that he was before." '[3] Godwin began his book at the end and worked back, believing that 'An entire unity of plot would be the infallible result';[4] but the logic is that of obsession rather than cause and effect. His theme taps archetypal sources of conflict—between father and son, or tyrannical Calvinist God and inquisitive man.[5] Obsessed by the suspicion that his admired master, Falkland, is guilty of murder, Caleb provokes a resentment that takes on almost supernatural dimensions. Falkland drives him into despairing isolation, leaving him only one connection with another human being: Caleb is bound indissolubly to the man whose guilt he has discovered, taking on his shattered reputation and, finally, his remorse—'To his story the whole fortune of my life was linked; because he was miserable, my happiness, my name, and my existence have been irretrievably blasted.'[6] In a culminating reversal, however, the victim outdoes his oppressor through an innate moral superiority. Pushed beyond endurance by Falkland's apparently omniscient and omnipotent persecution,

[1] *Things as They Are: or, The Adventures of Caleb Williams* (2nd edn., 3 vols., London, 1796), i. vi. Godwin's preface, withdrawn from the first edition 'in compliance with the alarms of booksellers' (ibid. i. vi–vii), was reinstated in the second edition.

[2] Preface, *Fleetwood: or, The New Man of Feeling*, Standard Novels, No. xxii (London, 1832), p. vii.

[3] Ibid., p. ix.   [4] Ibid., p. viii.

[5] See R. F. Storch, 'Metaphors of Private Guilt and Social Rebellion in Godwin's *Caleb Williams*', *ELH* xxxiv (1967), 188–207.

[6] *Things as They Are; or, the Adventures of Caleb Williams* (3 vols., London, 1794), i. 18.

Caleb first denounces him publicly as a murderer, then turns on himself for what he sees as a repetition of Falkland's own crime:

> No penitence, no anguish can expiate the folly and the cruelty of this last act I have perpetrated. . . . I despaired, while it was yet time to have made the just experiment; but my despair was criminal . . . Never will I forgive myself the iniquity of this day. . . . In thus acting I have been a murderer, a cool, deliberate, unfeeling murderer. . . . It would have been merciful in comparison, if I had planted a dagger in his heart. . . . I wantonly inflicted on him an anguish a thousand times worse than death.[1]

All ordinary stores of rational benevolence have been consumed by Falkland's vindictiveness, and as a climax this is emotionally strained. But it neatly fulfils the pattern which dominates the novel. Before dying of chagrin, Falkland recognizes Caleb as the better man: 'Williams, said he, you have conquered! I see too late the greatness and elevation of your mind. I adore the qualities that you now display . . . '[2] Disinterested benevolence, the quality Falkland lacks, is the ultimate value put forward by *Caleb Williams*.

In Falkland, the misanthrope of the eighteenth-century novel achieves his most impressive form. Godwin alternates between presenting him as a monster of vengeful hate and a tragedy of waste ('Thy intellectual powers were truly sublime, and thy bosom burned with a godlike ambition'),[3] and the novel ends unconvincingly by blaming society for his moral collapse: 'of what use are talents and sentiments in the corrupt wilderness of human society? It is a rank and rotten soil from which every finer shrub draws poison as it grows.'[4] Though the recording consciousness of the novel belongs to Caleb, Falkland's predicament is ideologically central. His history is that of Mackenzie's 'Misanthropist' writ large. Long before Caleb appears on the scene, Falkland's early promise has been blasted by the public ignominy of a murder trial. But despite his acquittal,

---

[1] *Caleb Williams*, iii. 288, 295, 296, 300–1. The original ending—the madness and disintegration of Caleb—is more consistent with Godwin's portrayal of him as a victim of the social system; see D. G. Dumas, 'Things As They Were: the Original Ending of *Caleb Williams*', *SEL* vi (1966), 575–97.

[2] *Caleb Williams*, iii. 298.   [3] Ibid. iii. 302.   [4] Ibid. iii. 302.

His youth, distinguished in its outset by the most generous promise, is tarnished. His sensibility is shrunk up and withered by events the most disgustful to his feelings. His mind was fraught with all the rhapsodies of visionary honour; and in his sense nothing but the grosser part, the mere shell of Falkland, was capable to survive the wound that his pride has sustained.[1]

We first see him, dignified but withdrawn, through Caleb's eyes ('There was a solemn sadness in his manner, attended with the most perfect gentleness and humanity').[2] His inner disturbance, like that of Wordsworth's recluse, is mirrored by the natural surroundings he seeks out: 'Mr. Falkland was sometimes seen climbing among the rocks, reclining motionless for hours together upon the edge of a precipice, or lulled into a kind of nameless lethargy of despair by the dashing of the torrents.'[3] Only later do we discover, as Caleb does, that his despair is that of guilt rather than disillusion. Not merely has he committed the murder, after being humiliated by a bullying enemy—he has let two innocent men hang in his place. He compounds the first crime by the second because he is bound by an outmoded and inadequate ideal:

This it is to be a gentleman! a man of honour! I was the fool of fame. My virtue, my honesty, my everlasting peace of mind were cheap sacrifices to be made at the shrine of this divinity. But, what is worse, there is nothing that has happened that has in any degree contributed to my cure. I am as much the fool of fame as ever.[4]

Falkland is trapped within the terms of his original failure, committed to saving his good name at all costs, unable to conceive of an alternative in suffering and expiation. The same moral imprisonment—less malign but equally sterile—afflicts the recluse of the Yew-tree lines; his talents neglected by the world, he too 'with the food of pride sustain[s] his soul/In solitude' (ll. 20–1).

But between *Caleb Williams* and the Yew-tree lines stands Wordsworth's play. Completed in early 1797,[5] *The Borderers* is in some sense a critique of Godwinian thought, but it is also

---

[1] Ibid. i. 17.   [2] Ibid. i. 292.   [3] Ibid. ii. 54.   [4] Ibid. ii. 87.
[5] See *EY*, p. 177, and Reed, pp. 329–30. For the place of *The Borderers* in Wordsworth's literary and intellectual development, see also the interesting discussion by P. D. Sheats, in *The Making of Wordsworth's Poetry, 1785–1798* (Cambridge, Mass., 1973), pp. 120–35.

indebted to Godwin's novel for its central situation. *Macbeth* offered Wordsworth a study of guilt; *Othello* a study of temptation and manipulation; and gothic drama, a villain who usurps the hero's place as the centre of interest.[1] Only *Caleb Williams* provided the motif of a repeated crime springing from the intense relationship between two central protagonists, and a villain whose predicament is designed to reveal the limitations of his ideology.[2] Wordsworth's discussion of Godwinian thought is thus expressed in the fictional terms of Godwin's own novel. Like a number of his contemporaries—Charles Lloyd and Coleridge among them—Wordsworth had moved from an initial enthusiasm for *Political Justice* (1793) to questioning some of its central tenets.[3] It was probably in 1795 that Godwin, in his own words, converted Wordsworth 'from the doctrine of self-love to that of benevolence'.[4] In 1794 Godwinian reason had been invoked at the close of the first version of *Salisbury Plain*—

> Heroes of Truth, pursue your march, uptear
> Th'Oppressor's dungeon from its deepest base;
> High o'er the towers of Pride undaunted rear
> Resistless in your might the herculean mace
> Of Reason . . .[5]

[1] See P. L. Thorslev, 'Wordsworth's *Borderers* and the Romantic Villain–Hero' *SR* v (1966), 84–103.

[2] Wordsworth's use of *Caleb Williams* had been anticipated by George Colman the Younger's clumsy dramatization, *The Iron Chest* (1796); this play and its source are unfavourably compared by Hazlitt in *A View of the English Stage*, 1818 (see Howe, v. 343). For its stormy and much-publicized staging, see J. F. Bagster-Collins, *George Colman the Younger: 1762–1836* (New York, 1946), pp. 84–96, 99–102. With Kemble in the lead, the play was put on in London in March 1796, it was published in July. Wordsworth was meeting Godwin in London from June to early July (see Reed, pp. 182–5), and he is likely to have known *The Iron Chest*.

[3] For Coleridge's changing views, see pp. 35–6, below. Lloyd's are reflected in *Edmund Oliver*, where the misguided heroine, echoing *The Borderers*, has 'long since acknowledged, that we should be "governed by the light of circumstance flashed on an independent intellect;" and that . . . we should proceed boldly onward in the difficult and untried path of intellectual experiment'; *Edmund Oliver* (2 vols., Bristol, 1798), i. 124 (cf. *PW* i. 187, ll. 1494–6 and app. crit., quoted p. 29, below). Lloyd visited Wordsworth at Alfoxden during September 1797 for a promised reading of *The Borderers* (see Griggs, i. 345–6n.)

[4] See B. R. Schneider, *Wordsworth's Cambridge Education* (Cambridge, 1957), pp. 222–3; Reed, p. 164; and Mary Moorman, *William Wordsworth*, pp. 262–3.

[5] MS. 1: *PW* i. 340–1.

—and by the end of 1795, the humanitarian protest of the second version was strongly Godwinian in bias.[1] In 1796, Wordsworth was reading the newly-published second edition of *Political Justice*, and again met Godwin himself on a number of occasions.[2] His acceptance or rejection of Godwinian thought was probably never as thorough-going as has sometimes been claimed.[3] While Godwin's humanitarianism retained its appeal, some of the attitudes implicit in *Political Justice* were incompatible with his own emerging creed. Godwin's solution to the problem of whether to rescue Fénelon or his chamber-maid from a burning building must have become increasingly alien to Wordsworth in its disregard of felt relationships:

> Supposing the chambermaid had been my wife, my mother or my benefactor. This would not alter the truth of the proposition. The life of Fenelon would still be more valuable than that of the chamber-maid; and justice, pure, unadulterated justice, would still have preferred that which was most valuable. Justice would have taught me to save the life of Fenelon at the expence of the other. What magic is there in the pronoun 'my,' to overturn the decisions of everlasting truth?[4]

*extrem
of Godw
reaso*

But there had been a time when Wordsworth himself—if *The Prelude* is to be believed—had adopted as his guide '<u>the light of circumstances, flash'd/Upon an independent intellect</u>',[5] obeying Godwin's dictum that 'The genuine and whol[e]some state of mind is, to be unloosed from shackles, and to expand every fibre of its frame according to the independent and individual impressions of truth upon that mind':[6]

> I took the knife in hand
> And stopping not at parts less sensitive,
> Endeavoured with my best of skill to probe
> The living body of society

[1] See pp. 153–5, below.

[2] See *EY*, pp. 170–1; Reed, pp. 182–3; and Mary Moorman, p. 297.

[3] See Alan Grob, 'Wordsworth and Godwin: A Reassessment', *SR* vi (1967), 98–119 for a qualification of the one-sided views held by Ernest de Selincourt, *Prelude*, pp. 605–6, at one extreme, and G. W. Meyer, *Wordsworth's Formative Years* (Ann Arbor, Mich., 1943), p. 190, at the other.

[4] *An Enquiry Concerning Political Justice* (2 vols., London, 1793), i. 83. Godwin himself was to move during the 1790s to a position closer to Wordsworth's; see Basil Willey, *The Eighteenth Century Background* (London, 1940), pp. 235–9.

[5] *Prelude*, x. 829–30.   [6] *Political Justice*, ii. 569.

> Even to the heart; I push'd without remorse
> My speculations forward; yea, set foot
> On Nature's holiest places.[1]

Tragedy in *The Borderers* turns on just such an attempt to violate the sanctity of 'Nature's holiest places'. What *The Prelude* does not tell us is that the thinker who armed Wordsworth with his knife in the first place also provided him with the means to dramatize its potential for destruction.

II. 'THE BORDERERS' AND THE YEW-TREE LINES

Wordsworth's play is his most sustained and eccentric study of guilt. The states of mind on which it centres—moral and emotional upheaval, isolation, self-condemnation—are those explored elsewhere in his poetry during the mid-1790s. In the earliest surviving version of *Salisbury Plain*, he had fictionalized the desolation and revulsion against society which he himself experienced while crossing the plain in the summer of 1793.[2] A landscape of inhuman solitude and hallucinations of druidic savagery externalize his state of mind. In the enlarged version of 1795, Wordsworth extends his attack on contemporary social oppression to include specifically the penal system.[3] The anonymous traveller becomes a man on the run after committing a murder; his state of mind is now directly attributable to guilt, and his journey across the plain becomes a flight from the vengefulness of retributive justice—graphically represented by the spectacle of a gibbet and chained body. In the fragment which comes between *Salisbury Plain* and *The Borderers*, the 'Gothic Tale' of 1796,[4] Wordsworth returns to the theme of murder. An anonymous youth is tempted to take the life of a blind and helpless old man—impelled, it seems, not so much by the thought of robbing him as by the turmoil of his setting ('Up as they climbed, the precipice's ridge/Lessons of death at every step had given . . . ').[5] Mysterious comings and goings in a gothic ruin alternately prompt and inhibit the murder, and in his state of restless dread the youth responds guiltily to a succession of unexplained, quasi-supernatural interventions. His experience

---

[1] *Prelude*, x. 873–9.
[2] Both versions of *Salisbury Plain* are discussed on pp. 148–58, below.
[3] See Wordsworth's letter of November 1795 (*EY*, p. 159).
[4] See Reed, p. 344.   [5] DC MS. 2: *PW* i. 290, ll. 143–4.

becomes the basis for Wordsworth's account in *The Borderers* of the attempt to murder Herbert, also innocent, helpless, and old. This time, murder provides the focus for an ideological debate.

The Borderers centres on the process by which its hero, Mortimer, is tricked into committing a crime against humanity.[1] Impelled by loneliness, guilt, and the desire for revenge, the villain, Rivers, attempts to bind Mortimer to him by a repetition of the crime he has himself committed in his youth ('I've join'd us by a chain of adamant').[2] His manipulation re-creates the events which had originally led to the death of his own humanity—or, as (with Iago) he prefers to think of it, to his emancipation from conventional morality. During the course of the play, Mortimer is taught a version of Godwin's proposition about Fénelon and the chamber-maid—

> I would not give a denier for the man
> Who could not chuck his babe beneath the chin
> And send it with a fillip to its grave.[3]

—and Rivers works him up to commit a murder that requires him to overcome, in Godwin's phrase, the magic of 'my'; the victim is father to the girl he loves. But confronted by what he believes to be a rationally dictated act of justice, Mortimer revolts instinctively:

> Murder! asleep! blind! old! alone! betray'd!
> Drugg'd and in darkness! Here to strike the blow
> Visible only to the eye of God! (flings away his sword)
> Away! away![4]

At this moment the sight of a star serves to symbolize the order violated by such a murder. Back in the rationalist fold, Mortimer later contrasts the 'twinkling atom's eye' with Rivers's

[1] Mortimer becomes Marmaduke and Rivers becomes Oswald in the version of *The Borderers* published in 1842. A small but characteristic link between *Caleb Williams* and *The Borderers* is Wordsworth's use of Falkland's christian name, Ferdinand, for his Mortimer in an early draft (see *PW* i. 343); the name of Mortimer may have been derived from the Falkland of Colman's *Iron Chest* (see p. 22 n., above), there re-christened Sir Edward Mortimer.

[2] MS. B: *PW* i. 202, l. 1854; 201 app. crit. (cf. *Othello*, III. iii. 217). MS. B of *The Borderers* belongs to 1799 or 1800 (see Reed, p. 330); it must contain at least some revisions of the original draft of 1797, but probably approximates fairly closely to the version prepared for stage or publication later the same year.

[3] Ibid.: *PW* i. 177, ll. 1241–4 and app. crit.

[4] Ibid.: *PW* i. 164, ll. 901–3 and app. crit.

'creed built in the heart of things'.[1] Rivers's travesty of Godwin's disinterested rationalism is referred to in a phrase that perfectly evokes Wordsworth's alternative position. Unable to kill Herbert outright, Mortimer abandons him on a desolate heath. The old man's death by exposure, and the revelation of his innocence precipitate in Mortimer the redeeming remorse which Rivers is unable to feel. Like Caleb Williams, Mortimer is transfigured by his humanity, condemning himself to ceaseless lonely wandering ('A thing by pain and thought compelled to live')[2] in expiation of his crime.

Yet, in the end, it is not his suffering we remember, but Rivers's guilt, and it is Rivers's account of his own earlier betrayal that constitutes the most powerful piece of writing in the play. His confession re-creates a nightmare of anger and cruelty, delusion and remorse. Wordsworth combines elements of Bligh's account of the mutiny on the *Bounty*[3] with the Revd. John Newton's *Authentic Narrative* (1764)[4] to evoke the claustrophobic intensity of ship-bound emotion. It is Newton, a reformed slaver, whose experience seems to lie behind Rivers's brooding on an imagined conspiracy against him by the captain of his ship ('my pride at that time suggested that I had been injured, and this so far wrought upon my wicked heart, that I actually formed designs against his life . . . ').[5] Rivers's state of mind must surely have been in Coleridge's thoughts when he wrote 'The Ancient Mariner':

---

[1] MS. B: *PW* i. 176, ll. 1219–20 and app. crit. Cf. also the valuable comments on this passage by John Jones, *The Egotistical Sublime* (London, 1954), pp. 76–8, and Jonathan Wordsworth, *The Music of Humanity* (London, 1969), pp. 246–7.

[2] Ibid.: *PW* i. 225, l. 2319; 224 app. crit.

[3] Wordsworth's interest in the mutiny on the *Bounty* is revealed by his letter of 23 October 1796 in the *Weekly Entertainer*, xxviii (7 November 1796), 377 (*EY*, p. 171 and n.); see J. R. MacGillivray, 'An Early Poem and Letter by Wordsworth', *RES* N.S. v (1954), 62–6.

[4] Dorothy's notebook transcription in DC MS. 16 of a paragraph from *An Authentic Narrative of Some Remarkable and Interesting Particulars in the Life of* ******** (London, 1764), pp. 82–3, probably does not date from before early 1799 (see Reed, pp. 325–8), but there seems to be a reminiscence of the passage in MS. B of 'The Ruined Cottage' in early 1798 (see *PW* v. 384, ll. 192–7); see also Reed, p. 325n., and Bernard Martin, *The Ancient Mariner and the Authentic Narrative* (London, 1949), pp. 37–40. There is no reason why Wordsworth's familiarity with this well-known conversion narrative should not go back to the period of *The Borderers*.

[5] *An Authentic Narrative*, p. 58.

we were becalmed—
The water of the vessel was exhausted—
I felt a double fever in my veins;
My rage suppressed itself—to a deep stillness
Did my Pride tame my pride—for many days
Beneath the burning sky on the dead sea
I brooded o'er my injuries—deserted
By man and nature—if a breeze had blown
It might have found its way into my heart . . . [1]

Compare with Coleridge, cient Mariner

The barren island that comes in sight is an appropriate symbol of Rivers's alienation from humanity. His recollection has the vividness and pain of what is to come:

One day at noon we drifted silently
By a bare rock, narrow and white and bare;
There was no food, no drink, no grass, no shade,
No tree nor jutting eminence, nor form
Inanimate, large as the body of a man
Nor any living thing whose span of life
Might stretch beyond the measure of one moon.[2]

Improbably, a landing-party goes to look for water; Rivers and the captain quarrel, and the captain is left to die on the island, an agonized castaway. The earlier description recurs once more, this time with the island seen no longer in terms of its hostility to human life ('no food, no drink, no grass, no shade'), but—ironically—in terms of its swarming insect population:

'Twas a spot
Methinks I see it now—how in the sun
Its stony surface glittered like a shield:
It swarmed with shapes of life scarce visible
And in that miserable place we left him—
A giant body mid a world of beings
Not one of which could give him any aid
Living or dead.[3]

[1] MS. B: *PW* i. 195, ll. 1693–1701 and app. crit.
[2] Ibid.: *PW* i. 195–6, ll. 1705–11 and app. crit.
[3] Ibid.: *PW* i. 196, ll. 1721–7 and app. crit. See Z. S. Fink, *The Early Words-worthian Milieu* (Oxford, 1958), p. 51 for the suggestion that Wordsworth was partly inspired by the 'Description of a Person Left on a Desert Island' in Knox's *Elegant Extracts of Poetry*.

The remorseless island ('Its stony surface glittered like a shield') comes to express the unfeeling cruelty of Rivers and his companions. The captain is a vulnerable giant, 'standing, walking—stretching forth his arms'.[1] His groans of anguish and the mocking laughter of the crew produce an insupportable realization of human suffering and human pitilessness; the captain is, of course, innocent, and the crew have merely used Rivers to rid themselves of a hated master. Behind the torment of Rivers's 'I had been deceived . . . I had been betrayed',[2] one hears Fletcher Christian's famous 'I am in hell—I am in hell' as he abandons Captain Bligh.[3]

Like Falkland, Rivers—once similarly 'the pleasure of all hearts—the darling/Of every tongue'[4]—can resort only to murder when he thinks himself wronged, and can express his guilt only in further crimes. But he differs from Falkland in his spurious intellectual emancipation. He is not 'the slave of fame', but rather the spokesman for a new and plausible creed.[5] In his own terms, he is not so much perverted as liberated. Wordsworth makes his philosophic upheaval seem disconcertingly impressive:

> oft I left the camp
> When all that multitude of hearts was still,
> And followed on through woods of gloomy cedar
> Into deep chasms troubled by warring streams
> Or from the top of Lebanon surveyed
> The moonlight desert and the moonlight sea;
> In these my lonely wanderings I perceived
> What mighty objects do impress their forms
> To build up this our intellectual being . . . [6]

[1] MS. B: *PW* i. 196, l. 1729.   [2] Ibid.: *PW* i. 197, ll. 1753, 1755.

[3] William Bligh, *A Narrative of the Mutiny, on Board His Majesty's Ship 'Bounty'* (London, 1790), p. 8. In MS. A of *The Borderers* (presumably belonging to the earliest phase of composition; see Reed, p. 329) Christian's words, 'I am in hell', are actually given to the hero, Mortimer (see *PW* i. 350).

[4] MS. B: PW i. 195, ll. 1687–8; 194 app. crit.

[5] Cf. Geoffrey Hartman's interpretation of *The Borderers* as 'a myth of the birth of the modern intellectual consciousness' in *Wordsworth's Poetry 1787–1814* (New Haven, Conn., and London, 1964), pp. 125–35, and Roger Sharrock's contention that the play's starting-point 'lies in a state of disillusion with the liberal experience', '*The Borderers*: Wordsworth on the Moral Frontier', *Durham University Journal*, N.S. xxv (1964), 170–83. See also Robert Osborn, 'Meaningful Obscurity: the Antecedents and Character of Rivers', *Bicentenary Wordsworth Studies*, ed. Jonathan Wordsworth, pp. 393–424.

[6] MS. B: *PW* i. 199–200, ll. 1802–10 and app. crit.

As yet, however, the grandeur of Wordsworth's vision is without transcendental significance; the warring streams, the moonlight desert and sea suggest only the conflict and desolation from which Rivers's new code springs. His position, as he expounds it to Mortimer, is one of solitary enlightenment. He sees himself as a man of the future—a lonely explorer in uncharted regions:

> When from these forms I turned to contemplate
> The opinions and the uses of the world,
> I seemed a being who had passed alone
> Beyond the visible barriers of the world
> And travelled into things to come.[1]

Rivers offers as the basis of his creed a Godwinian emphasis on reason—

> the immediate law
> Flashed from the light of circumstances
> Upon an independent intellect . . . [2]

—but a rationality divorced from its Godwinian complement, benevolence. Reason is terrifyingly perverted—

> Benevolence that has not power to use
> The wholesome ministry of pain and evil
> Is powerless and contemptible . . . [3]

—and the dangers of Godwin's system are exposed. Rivers is impelled by the irrational motives (loneliness, hatred of society, revenge) that make the exercise of reason a treacherous route to morality in the real world of human feelings.

The achievement of *The Borderers* is to make Wordsworth's intellectual point without sacrificing dramatic intensity; the play fails, not because it is too theoretical, but because the trappings of gothic drama can only weaken its central concern with the beliefs and states of mind embodied by its villain. The extent of Wordsworth's preoccupation with Rivers can be seen in his remarkable explanatory essay, composed alongside or

[1] Ibid.: *PW* i. 200, ll. 1815–18 and app. crit.
[2] Ibid.: *PW* i. 187, ll. 1494–6 and app. crit. (cf. *Prelude*, xi. 829–30, and *Political Justice*, ii. 569, quoted p. 23, above).
[3] Ibid.: *PW* i. 152, ll. 618–20 and app. crit.

soon after the play itself.[1] Wordsworth's ostensible purpose is to explain the motives of a villain whom we have seen 'deliberately prosecuting the destruction of an amiable young man by the most atrocious means, & with a pertinacity, as it should seem, not to be accounted for but on the supposition of the most malignant injuries'.[2] In a passage that looks back to Falkland, the essay provides Rivers's case-history:

Let us suppose a young man of great intellectual powers, yet without any solid principles of genuine benevolence. His master passions are pride and the love of distinction—He has deeply imbibed a spirit of enterprize in a tumultuous age. He goes into the world and is betrayed into a great crime.—That influence on which all his happiness is built immediately deserts him. His talents are robbed of their weight—his exertions are unavailing, and he quits the world in disgust, with strong misanthropic feelings. In his retirement, he is impelled to examine the reasonableness of established opinions, & the force of his mind exhausts itself in constant efforts to separate the elements of virtue and vice.[3]

But Wordsworth is as much concerned to clarify the play's half-submerged dialectic as to develop the psychology of Rivers's destructiveness ('The general moral intended to be impressed by the delineation of such a character is obvious: it is to shew the dangerous use which may be made of reason when a man has committed a great crime').[4] Like Falkland, Rivers turns 'moral sceptic' in self-defence, rationalizing his position 'by assuming the character of a speculator in morals':[5]

It is his pleasure & his consolation to hunt out whatever is bad in actions usually esteemed virtuous, & to detect the good in actions which the universal sense of mankind teaches us to reprobate. . . . whenever, upon looking back upon past ages, or in surveying the practices of different countries in the age in which he lives, he finds such contrarieties as seem to affect the principles of *morals*, he exults

---

[1] See Reed, pp. 329–30. There is an interesting possibility that the essay post-dates Coleridge's arrival at Racedown in June 1797, and that Wordsworth's use of the word 'contempt' in describing Rivers ('he nourishes a contempt for mankind', 'his contempt of those whom he despises', 'a mind fond of nourishing sentiments of contempt', *Prose Works*, i. 77) reflects Coleridge's influence; see p. 36, below.

[2] DC MS. 23: *Prose Works*, i. 78–9.   [3] Ibid.: *Prose Works*, i. 76.
[4] Ibid.: *Prose Works*, i. 79.   [5] Ibid.: *Prose Works*, i. 78.

over his discovery, and applies it to his heart as the dearest of his consolations.[1]

As Wordsworth wrote in his incomplete 'Essay on Morals'—probably belonging to late 1798—it is chiefly when we are in the wrong 'that we repair to systems of morality for arguments in defence of ourselves; & sure enough are we to find them'.[2] This later essay contains the final verdict on Godwin:

I shall scarcely express myself too strongly when I say that I consider such books as Mr. Godwyn's, Mr. Paley's, & those of the whole tribe of authors of that class as impotent [?in *or* ?to] all their intended good purposes, to which I wish I could add that they were equally impotent to all bad one[s].[3]

Wordsworth's position may have been less clear-cut in *The Borderers* and the essay on Rivers, but the same mistrust of rationalism is implicit in both. It is from the other side of Godwin's thinking—benevolence—that the Yew-tree lines emerge, and it is in the light of Wordsworth's continuing concern with moral philosophy that the figure of the melancholy recluse takes on its full significance.

The Borderers had dramatized the problem: the Yew-tree lines attempt to resolve it. Wordsworth discards the gothic paraphernalia of crime and guilt, retaining only the theme of morbid disappointment:

> —Who he was
> That piled these stones, and with the mossy sod
> First covered o'er, and taught this aged tree,
> Now wild, to bend its arms in circling shade,
> I well remember.—He was one who own'd
> No common soul. In youth, by genius nurs'd,
> And big with lofty views, he to the world
> Went forth, pure in his heart, against the taint
> Of dissolute tongues, 'gainst jealousy, and hate,
> And scorn, against all enemies prepared,

[1] Ibid.: *Prose Works*, i. 76–7. Cf. Falkland's defence of Alexander the Great against Caleb ('it seems to me', argues Caleb, 'as if murder and massacre were but a very left-handed way of producing civilization and love'; *Caleb Williams*, ii. 17).

[2] DC MS. 19: *Prose Works*, i. 104.

[3] Ibid.: *Prose Works*, i. 103. See also Geoffrey Little, 'An incomplete Wordsworth Essay upon Moral Habits', *REL* ii (1961), 9–20, and Reed, p. 34 and n. Wordsworth's conclusions parallel the Hartleian Christianity of Coleridge's criticism of Godwin during the mid-1790s; see *CCW* i: *Lectures 1795 On Politics and Religion*, ed. L. Patton and P. Mann (London, 1971), pp. lxi, 162–4 and n.

> All but neglect: and so, his spirit damped
> At once, with rash disdain he turned away,
> And with the food of pride sustained his soul
> In solitude.   (ll. 8–21)

This must in some sense be a self-portrait of the poet who had put his faith in the Revolution, in a Godwinian millenium, or simply in his own intellectual power; he himself, after all, had retired to Racedown in 1795, even if he had taken Dorothy with him. The Yew-tree lines record Wordsworth's realization that withdrawal is no answer; like Godwin, and like Coleridge in 'Reflections on Entering into Active Life', he insists on the need for active participation in the social struggle.[1] Only 'the labours of benevolence' could make the human world as meaningful to the recluse as his natural setting:

> And lifting up his head, he then would gaze
> On the more distant scene; how lovely 'tis
> Thou seest, and he would gaze till it became
> Far lovelier, and his heart could not sustain
> The beauty still more beauteous. Nor, that time,
> Would he forget those beings, to whose minds,
> Warm from the labours of benevolence,
> The world, and man himself, appeared a scene
> Of kindred loveliness: then he would sigh
> With mournful joy, to think that others felt
> What he must never feel . . .   (ll. 30–40)

The recluse is not merely another study in wasted sensibility but the first of Wordsworth's explorations of the introspecting mind. Where Rivers and Falkland before him had been portraits of mental upheaval, he embodies a sadder, quieter unbalance. The poem's setting reflects withdrawal rather than turmoil, sterility rather than destructiveness:

>   here he loved to sit,
> His only visitants a straggling sheep,
> The stone-chat, or the glancing sand-piper;
> And on these barren rocks, with juniper,
> And heath, and thistle, thinly sprinkled o'er,
> Fixing his downward eye, he many an hour
> A morbid pleasure nourished, tracing here
> An emblem of his own unfruitful life . . .   (ll. 22–9)

[1] See pp. 76–7, below.

Isolation from the world of men is suggested by closeness to the animal world ('His only visitants a straggling sheep . . . '), and uncultivated humanity by the barren, heathy vegetation. The recluse himself traces in his surroundings 'An emblem of his own unfruitful life', making Wordsworth's point that nature is important to him only as it relates to his inner state; the closely observed details of birds and plants evoke the limited vision of the central figure. There is no sense that love of nature leads to love of man—rather, it is associated with inability to transcend the self.

Charles Lamb's allusion to the Yew-tree lines ('But above all, *that Inscription!*')[1] draws attention to their topicality. The inscription had recently been given fresh currency by Southey's *Poems* (1797).[2] Southey's advertised point of departure had been Akenside's inscriptions,[3] but his own are consciously brought up to date—celebrating the moral and political issues embodied in such figures as Rousseau or Henry Marten the Regicide. The meditative nature inscription which was Akenside's special achievement becomes a platform for social protest.[4] Wordsworth, similarly, is not concerned with nature for its own sake; the misanthrope's response to landscape merely accentuates a contrasting inability to feel for 'the world, and man himself' (l. 37). The lesson preached by the Yew-tree lines is a Godwinian one of altruistic, self-rewarding involvement with society—a belief that 'men are capable of understanding the beauty of virtue, and the claims of other men

[1] Lucas, i. 112.

[2] Giles Barber, '*Poems, by Robert Southey*, 1797', *Bodleian Library Record*, vi (1960), 620–4, shows that the volume was printed by late December 1796 (cf. Reed, p. 192n. for its advertised publication on 8 February 1797); see also Coleridge's letter to Southey of 27 December 1796 (Griggs, i. 290) and Southey's to Wynn of 26 January 1797 (Curry, i. 120). Wordsworth's links with Cottle make it possible that he too had early access to the volume; he evidently discussed it with Coleridge in late March or early April 1797 (see Reed, p. 195; Griggs, i. 320).

[3] See the preface to *Poems* (Bristol and London, 1797).

[4] Cf., for instance, the two posthumously published inscriptions VII and VIII in the 1772 edition of Akenside's poems; see also Geoffrey Hartman, 'Wordsworth, Inscriptions, and Romantic Nature Poetry', *From Sensibility to Romanticism*, pp. 389–413. Jonathan Wordsworth, *The Music of Humanity*, p. 196, suggests that Wordsworth owes a special debt to Southey's inscription 'For a Cavern that over-looks the River Avon', particularly to the lines:

> Gaze Stranger here!
> And let thy soften'd heart intensely feel
> How good, how lovely, Nature! (*Poems* (1797), pp. 57–8)

upon their benevolence'.[1] The concluding lines of the poem
seem to echo Godwin's definition in *Political Justice* of 'the truly
wise man':

> The truly wise man will be actuated neither by interest nor ambition,
> the love of honour nor the love of fame. He has no emulation. He is
> not made uneasy by a comparison of his own attainments with
> those of others, but by a comparison with the standard of right. . . .
> All men are his fellow labourers, but he is the rival of no man. Like
> Pedaretus in ancient story, he exclaims: 'I also have endeavoured to
> deserve; but there are three hundred citizens in Sparta better than
> myself, and I rejoice.'[2]

'No man therefore, so far as he is virtuous,' insists Godwin,
'can be in danger to become a prey to sorrow and discontent.'[3]
Godwin gives Wordsworth both the moral and the psychological basis on which to exhort self-acceptance in the face of the
world's neglect:

> If thou be one whose heart the holy forms
> Of young imagination have kept pure,
> Stranger! henceforth be warned; and know, that pride,
> Howe'er disguised in its own majesty,
> Is littleness; that he, who feels contempt
> For any living thing, hath faculties
> Which he has never used; that thought with him
> Is in its infancy. The man, whose eye
> Is ever on himself, doth look on one,
> The least of nature's works, one who might move
> The wise man to that scorn which wisdom holds
> Unlawful, ever. O, be wiser thou!
> Instructed that true knowledge leads to love,
> True dignity abides with him alone
> Who, in the silent hour of inward thought,
> Can still suspect, and still revere himself,
> In lowliness of heart.   (ll. 44–60)

In an impressively Wordsworthian phrase, the introspective
mood that has been the poem's subject becomes 'the silent hour
of inward thought'. By now the poem has moved beyond the
individual case to the general predicament from which it had
originally grown; the recluse is recognizable as one 'whose eye/

---

[1] *Political Justice*, i. 357.   [2] Ibid. i. 361.   [3] Ibid. i. 363.

Is ever on himself', but hardly as one 'who feels contempt/For any living thing'. Wordsworth may simply be looking back to Rivers. But it is tempting to see another influence at work altogether—that of Coleridge, whose arrival at Racedown in June 1797 must certainly post-date all but this concluding passage of the Yew-tree lines.[1]

Coleridge's engagement with Godwinian thought ran parallel to Wordsworth's in a number of ways. He too had been drawn to Godwin for his radical views, hailing him as an enemy of oppression in the sonnet published in the *Morning Post* on 10 January 1795. But—unlike Wordsworth—he had been brought into conflict with Godwin by his own Christianity, and in May of the same year the third of his 'Lectures on Revealed Religion' denounces

a book popular among the professed Friends of civil Freedom— a book which builds without a foundation, proposes an end without establishing the means, and discovers a total ignorance of that obvious Fact in human nature that in virtue and in knowledge we must be infants and be nourished with milk in order that we may be men and eat strong meat. Of this work it may be truly said, that whatever is just in it, is more forcibly recommended in the Gospel and whatever is new is absurd. Severe Moralist! that teaches us that filial Love is a Folly, Gratitude criminal, Marriage Injustice, and a promiscuous Intercourse of the Sexes our wisdom and our duty.[2]

Or, as he wrote in *Conciones ad Populum* (1795), 'Let us beware of that proud Philosophy, which affects to inculcate Philanthropy while it denounces every home-born feeling, by which it is produced and nurtured.'[3] A notebook entry of late 1795 or early 1796 attacks 'the Godwinian System of Pride',[4] while in

---

[1] See Reed, p. 192 and n., and cf. also S. M. Parrish, *The Art of the Lyrical Ballads* (Cambridge, Mass., 1973), pp. 67–70, for a discussion of Coleridge's possible influence. Jonathan Wordsworth, *The Music of Humanity*, pp. 206–7n., suggests that Wordsworth's reference to 'the holy forms/Of young imagination' (ll. 44–5)—not present in the Racedown drafts—could have been added still later, in 1798, reflecting his new transcendental beliefs; but the lines could equally belong to the summer of 1797 and allude back to the youthful idealism ('big with lofty views', l. 14) of the recluse before his disappointment.

[2] *CCW* i: *Lectures 1795 On Politics and Religion*, ed. L. Patton and P. Mann, p. 164. For an admirable account of Coleridge's relationship to Godwin, see ibid., pp. lxvii–lxxx.

[3] Ibid., p. 46.

[4] *The Notebooks of Samuel Taylor Coleridge: 1794–1808*, ed. K. Coburn (4 vols., London, 1957–62), i. 174 and n.

April 1796 the *Watchman* contained his public recantation: 'I do consider Mr. Godwin's Principles as vicious; and his book as a Pandar to Sensuality. Once I thought otherwise . . . '[1] Coleridge's projected work of late 1796 and early 1797— described variously as 'an Examination of Godwin's political Justice' and 'a book of Morals in answer to Godwin'[2]—would have been that of a Christian apologist. A letter of December 1796 to John Thelwall, an atheistic radical like Godwin, suggests the terms in which Coleridge would have defended religious morality; and it is interesting to find the word 'contempt' recurring, both in contrast to the personal benevolence which Coleridge opposes to Godwin's generalized concept, and in the context of the intellectual arrogance which dismisses Christian belief:

> My dear Thelwall! 'It is the principal felicity of Life, & the chief Glory of Manhood to speak out fully on all subjects.' I will avail myself of it—I will express *all* my feelings; but will previously take care to make my feelings benevolent. Contempt is Hatred without fear—Anger Hatred accompanied with apprehension. But because Hatred is always evil, Contempt must be always evil—& a good man ought to speak *contemptuously* of nothing. I am sure a wise man will not of opinions which have been held by men, in *other* respects at least, confessedly of more powerful Intellect than himself. 'Tis an assumption of *infallibility* . . . [3]

When Coleridge laughed at himself in July 1797—'I am as much a Pangloss as ever—only less *contemptuous*, than I used to be, when I argue how unwise it is to feel contempt for any thing'[4] —he was at once invoking his own much-proclaimed position, and echoing the Yew-tree lines. Wordsworth's poem marks the meeting-point of the two major intellectual influences on his work during the 1790s; a problem formulated in Godwinian terms can be resolved in the terms used by Coleridge to attack him. It is the first sign of the way in which Wordsworth and Coleridge were to work together during the coming year.

Significantly, the letter of July 1797 in which Coleridge echoes his own and Wordsworth's views on 'contempt' also

---

[1] *CCW* ii: *The Watchman*, ed. L. Patton (London, 1970), p. 196.
[2] Griggs, i. 247, 320.   [3] Ibid. i. 279–80.
[4] To Robert Southey (ibid. i. 334). Cf. also the references to pride and contempt in *Osorio*, cited by S. M. Parrish, *The Art of the Lyrical Ballads*, p. 68.

contains his study of self-pitying alienation, 'This Lime-Tree Bower my Prison'. Expressed in the overtly personal terms of the Conversation Poem is a solution quite distinct from that of the Yew-tree lines; the solitary's fruitless 'gazing' becomes the basis for a moment of communion, and landscape offers a way to transcend the self because it affirms the immanent presence of God. It is a belief that could hardly have been more different from Wordsworth's predominantly social morality; yet it proved deeply congenial to him. The poet of the mid-1790s, obsessively concerned with discord within the individual and society, becomes the poet of visionary insight—

> that blessed mood,
> In which the burthen of the mystery,
> In which the heavy and the weary weight
> Of all this unintelligible world
> Is lighten'd . . .   ('Tintern Abbey', ll. 38–42)

Coleridge has freed Wordsworth from his struggle with moral philosophy, allowing him to write about what can be felt but not explained, apprehended, but not analysed. He has also given him a personal voice. In the Yew-tree lines, Wordsworth neither engages our interest in the recluse for his own sake, nor offers us the help we need to see that his situation has autobiographical significance. In 'Tintern Abbey', by contrast, the poet moves us by seeming to commune with himself, exploring his own inner feelings. The difference is between a half-realized fiction, and the poetic introspection which is to be Wordsworth's most fruitful mode.

II *Nature, Self, and Imagination: The Eighteenth-Century Legacy*

THE BORDERERS and the Yew-tree lines show Wordsworth's fictionalizing mind at work, searching for literary counterparts to his own experience. What they do not show, for all their concern with inner states, is the meditative imagination of the following year. There is no interplay between the mind and nature, only a use of natural setting to externalize unbalance, while the mind itself is portrayed as indulging in destructive modes of thought rather than fruitful introspection. The difference between the poetry of 1797 and that of 1798 is in part a doctrinal one—Wordsworth has abandoned moral philosophy for a belief in the One Life shared by man and nature. But he has also rediscovered a tradition which he had hitherto largely ignored. It is difficult to be certain how far this tradition was refracted through Coleridge's poetry. But directly or indirectly, Wordsworth owes the three great themes of his mature writing—nature, self, and the imagination—to the major eighteenth-century poets of the natural world. In Thomson's *Seasons* (1730), he would have found poetry sustained, as was his own in 1798, by the vision of a natural universe animated by God; Cowper's *Task* (1785) contains the exploration of inner life and the feeling for nature which characterize his own meditative blank verse; Akenside's *Pleasures of Imagination* (1744) reflects the philosophic concern with the relationship between nature and the perceiving mind which is to be central to some of Wordsworth's greatest writing. Each of these poems provides specific source-material for 'Tintern Abbey';[1] but the influence of Thomson's vision, Cowper's introspectiveness, and Akenside's intellectuality pervades the blank verse of 1798. The debt is an important one because it offered Wordsworth a new language. More completely than in any of his eighteenth-century predecessors,

[1] See pp. 105–12, below.

nature becomes a way of writing about the mind, and landscape-poetry a vehicle for meditation.

I. THOMSON AND THE POETRY OF CELEBRATION

Speaking of Thomson, Wordsworth noted not simply his 'true love and feeling for Nature',[1] but his 'genius as an imaginative Poet'.[2] Natural description in *The Seasons* evokes divine power, and Thomson's sense of an immanent God in nature is communicated with the personal excitement that led Wordsworth to call it 'a work of inspiration'. 'Much of it', Wordsworth continued, 'is written from himself, and nobly from himself.'[3] The eighteenth century took it for granted (in the words of John Aikin) that 'THOMSON'S SEASONS is as eminently a religious, as it is a descriptive poem';[4] but as early as 1816 it had come to disturb the orthodox:

The Religion of the Seasons, is of that general kind which Nature's self might teach to those who had no knowledge of the God of Revelation. It is a lofty and complacent sentiment, which plays upon the feelings like the ineffable power of solemn harmony, but has no reference to the quality of our belief . . . still less does it involve a devotional recognition of the revealed character of the Divine Being.[5]

To fit in with changing religious attitudes, *The Seasons* had increasingly to be seen as a purely descriptive poem, its deism played down much as Wordsworth's pantheism was to be.[6] But in its own time, Thomson's displacement of religious feeling onto the natural world would have needed no apology and caused no surprise.[7] The single most important influence on *The Seasons* was of course Shaftesbury, whose prose-poems of

[1] 'Personal Reminiscences (1836), by the Hon. Mr. Justice Coleridge', *The Prose Works of William Wordsworth*, ed. A. B. Grosart (3 vols., London, 1876), iii. 431.

[2] 'Essay, Supplementary to the Preface', 1815 (*Prose Works*, iii. 74). Cf. Coleridge, as reported by Hazlitt, who in 1798 called Thomson 'a great poet, rather than a good one' (Howe, xvii. 120).

[3] Ibid. (*Prose Works*, iii. 72).

[4] Prefatory essay, *The Seasons* (London, 1778), p. xliv.

[5] Preface, *The Seasons* (London, 1816), p. x.

[6] See A. D. McKillop, *The Background of Thomson's Seasons* (Minneapolis, Minn., 1942), pp. 4–6.

[7] For the 'physico-theological' tradition from which *The Seasons* ultimately derives, see ibid., pp. 7–13, and Basil Willey, *The Eighteenth Century Background*, pp. 27–42.

rhapsodic devotion make the formal distinction between nature
and God, only to blur it by treating natural appearances as
inspiring in their own right, and by treating response to them as
an act of worship:

'O GLORIOUS *Nature*! supremely Fair, and sovereignly Good!
All-loving and All-lovely, All divine! Whose Looks are so becoming,
and of such infinite Grace; whose Study brings such Wisdom, and
whose Contemplation such Delight; whose every single Work
affords an ampler Scene, and is a nobler Spectacle than all that
ever Art presented!—O mighty *Nature*! Wise Substitute of *Providence*!
impower'd *Creatress*! or Thou impowering DEITY, Supreme Creator!
Thee I invoke, and Thee alone adore. To thee this Solitude, this
Place, these Rural Meditations are sacred; whilst thus inspir'd with
Harmony of Thought . . . I sing of Nature's Order in created Beings,
and celebrate the Beautys which resolve in Thee, the Source and
Principle of all Beauty and Perfection.'[1]

Thomson's preface to the second edition of *Winter* (1726) has
Shaftesbury's exclamatory prose behind it:

I know no Subject more elevating, more amusing; more ready to
awake the poetical Enthusiasm, the philosophical Reflection, and
the moral Sentiment, than the *Works of Nature*. Where can we meet
with such Variety, such Beauty, such Magnificence? All that
enlarges, and transports, the Soul? What more inspiring than a calm,
wide, Survey of Them? . . . How gay looks the *Spring*! how glorious
the *Summer*! how pleasing the *Autumn*! and how venerable the
Winter!—But there is no thinking of these Things without breaking
out into POETRY . . . [2]

The Seasons is a poem of celebration, its enthusiasm subsumed
into religious affirmation.

Thomson's ability to create a world of passionately em-
pathized natural life that is at the same time animated by God
can be seen at its most sustained in 'Spring'—the best-known
part of *The Seasons*, as well as the part to which Wordsworth and
Coleridge owe most.[3] Shaftesbury's rhetoric is used to release

[1] *Characteristicks of Men, Manners, Opinions, Times* (3 vols., ?London, 1711),
ii. 345. See also Basil Willey, pp. 61–5.
[2] *Winter* (2nd edn., London, 1726), pp. 15–16.
[3] Wordsworth remarked that 'In any well-used copy of the Seasons the book
generally opens of itself with the rhapsody of love' (i.e. 'Spring', ll. 1030–87);
'Essay, Supplementary to the Preface', 1815 (*Prose Works*, iii. 74).

the underlying excitement of Thomson's descriptive writing. 'HAIL, MIGHTY BEING! UNIVERSAL SOUL/Of heaven and earth!'¹ opens an extended celebration of spring, and fifty lines later a chorus of bird-song is brought to its close with the assertion: 'TIS love creates their gaiety, and all/This waste of music is the voice of love . . . ';² the concert implies the divine, unifying joy later expressed in Coleridge's 'Nightingale'³ and heard by Wordsworth's Pedlar:

> in all things
> He saw one life, & felt that it was joy.
> One song they sang . . . ⁴

The poetry moves towards its culminating affirmation while remaining firmly anchored within a naturalistic context—the love-sick bull, for instance, or the ungainly playfulness of sea-beasts:

> NOR, undelighted by the boundless SPRING,
> Are the broad monsters of the boiling deep:
> From the deep ooze, and gelid cavern rous'd,
> They flounce, and tumble in unweildy joy.⁵

In Hazlitt's words, Thomson's descriptions 'teem with life and vivifying soul';⁶ it is this that persuades one to ask, with him, 'WHAT is this MIGHTY BREATH . . . ?' and to accept his answer:

> WHAT is this MIGHTY BREATH, ye curious, say,
> Which, in a language rather felt than heard,
> Instructs the fowls of heaven; and thro' their breasts
> These arts of love diffuses? What, but GOD?
> Inspiring GOD! who boundless spirit all,
> And unremitted energy, pervades,
> Adjusts, sustains, and agitates the whole.⁷

¹ 'Spring', ll. 509–10, *The Seasons* (London, 1730). Subsequent references are to the 1730 edition unless specified.

² 'Spring', ll. 568–9.

³ 'The Nightingale' seems to draw on the bird-chorus in 'Spring', ll. 547–51; and cf. also the creaking rook in 'This Lime-Tree Bower my Prison' and the discordant jay, rook, and daw of 'Spring', ll. 564–6—similarly absorbed into the general harmony of nature.

⁴ 'The Ruined Cottage', MS. B: *PW* v. 385, ll. 251–3.

⁵ 'Spring', ll. 764–7.   ⁶ *Lectures on the English Poets* (Howe, v. 87).

⁷ 'Spring', ll. 796–802. Cf. the parallel passage in *The Castle of Indolence* (London, 1748), II. xlvii. 5–9. For a discussion of Thomson's 'cosmic vision', see P. M. Spacks, *The Varied God: A Critical Study of Thomson's The Seasons* (Berkeley and Los Angeles, Calif., 1959), pp. 70–100.

Thomson infuses new meaning into claims that are traditional in themselves, and his 'mighty breath' becomes in turn the transcendental wind that blows through the poetry of Wordsworth and Coleridge—at its most philosophical in 'The Eolian Harp' ('one intellectual Breeze,/At once the Soul of each, and God of all')[1] and at its most natural in the 'Tintern Abbey' benediction for Dorothy ('And let the misty mountain winds be free/To blow against thee', ll. 137–8). Wordsworth's rediscovery of the natural world may have been doctrinal in impulse, but *The Seasons* helped him to make the One Life a subject for poetry.

Thomson is a precursor, not only of the transcendental claims later made by Wordsworth and Coleridge, but of their poetry of meditative response. A passage from the enlarged 1744 edition of 'Spring' closely anticipates their later studies of 'wise passiveness':

> by the vocal Woods and Waters lull'd,
> And lost in lonely Musing, in a Dream,
> Confus'd, of careless Solitude, where mix
> Ten thousand wandering Images of Things,
> Soothe every Gust of Passion into Peace,
> All but the Swellings of the soften'd Heart,
> That waken, not disturb the tranquil Mind.[2]

The lines again look forward to Coleridge in 'The Nightingale', urging meditative calm and receptivity on the ambitious poet—

> he had better far have stretch'd his limbs
> Beside a brook in mossy forest-dell
> By sun or moonlight, to the influxes
> Of shapes and sounds and shifting elements
> Surrendering his whole spirit . . .   (ll. 25–9)

—and, in Wordsworth's poetry, to the first meditative climax of 'Tintern Abbey'. Both Wordsworth and Thomson link tranquillity with a heightened inner life, playing on the conventional

---

[1] *Poems on Various Subjects* (London, 1796), p. 99 (*CPW* i. 102, ll. 47–8). See also M. H. Abrams, 'The Correspondent Breeze: A Romantic Metaphor', *English Romantic Poets*, ed. M. H. Abrams (New York, 1960), pp. 37–54.

[2] 'Spring', ll. 458–64, *The Seasons* (London, 1744). Wordsworth probably knew both the 1730 and the 1744 versions. In 1841, he possessed a copy of the first edition interlined with the later alterations; see J. P. Muirhead, 'A Day with Wordsworth', *Blackwood's Magazine*, ccxxi (1927), 737.

terminology of sleep and wakefulness to evoke a state of mind
that defies verbal analysis. Wordsworth's 'laid asleep/In body,
and become a living soul' ('Tintern Abbey', ll. 46–7) is less fussy
than Thomson's 'That waken, not disturb the tranquil mind',
but it relies on the same subdued paradox. The association
between dreamy responsiveness and insight into an underlying
harmony is anticipated elsewhere in 'Spring', and, with it, the
language of sense-transference that reappears in 'Tintern
Abbey' and the Conversation Poems:

> Pure serenity apace
> Induces thought, and contemplation still.
> By small degrees the love of nature works,
> And warms the bosom; till at last arriv'd
> To rapture, and enthusiastic heat,
> We feel the present DEITY, and taste
> The joy of GOD, to see a happy world.[1]

Nature poetry and meditative experience are already as closely
identified as they are to be for Wordsworth and Coleridge; and
in the lines that follow these in the 1730 version, Thomson's
language implies that response to nature is the human counterpart to the divine joy earlier displayed by the natural world:

> 'TIS HARMONY, that world-attuning power,
> By which all beings are adjusted, each
> To all around, impelling, and impell'd,
> In endless circulation, that inspires
> This universal smile. Thus the glad skies,
> The wide-rejoycing earth, the woods, the streams,
> With every LIFE they hold, down to the flower
> That paints the lowly vale, or insect-wing
> Wav'd o'er the shepherd's slumber, touch the mind
> To nature tun'd, with a light-flying hand,
> Invisible; quick-urging, thro' the nerves,
> The glittering spirits in a flood of day.[2]

As an attempt to analyse sense-perception, this may be confused;
but it is a confusion that usefully suggests how 'the mind/To
nature tun'd' becomes part of a 'universal smile'. The same
union of joyous natural world and responsive mind is to be
central to Wordsworth's philosophic poetry in the spring of

---

[1] 'Spring' (1730), ll. 859–65.   [2] Ibid., ll. 866–77.

1798; the Pedlar, in merging with the splendour of nature, becomes yet another expression of the divine mind that unifies all things—'His mind was a thanksgiving to the power/ That made him. It was blessedness & love.'[1] Like Wordsworth, Thomson is concerned not simply with nature, but with seeing it; not simply with a world attuned by the power of harmony, but with the human mind that recognizes it. Nature poetry is moving towards being about the imagination, and Wordsworth can take up where Thomson leaves off.

II. COWPER AND THE POETRY OF INTROSPECTION

In 1798, Coleridge was to call Cowper 'the best modern poet',[2] and in *Biographia Literaria* he writes of him as one of 'the first who combined natural thoughts with natural diction'.[3] He was undoubtedly the most important eighteenth-century influence on both the Conversation Poems and 'Tintern Abbey'. Where Thomson gave Wordsworth and Coleridge a poetry of claim, Cowper gave them a poetry of subtly evoked everyday experience. While *The Seasons* is held together by Thomson's imagination, *The Task* is held together by Cowper's tastes, views, and feelings. Nature gives way to the poet himself. Doctrinally, Cowper is directly opposed to Thomson, and Shaftesbury's place behind *The Seasons* is taken in *The Task* by the popular Methodist writer, James Hervey.[4] Hervey, although superficially full of Shaftesbury's enthusiasm for nature, insists that the natural world cannot be a substitute for God; divine revelation alone makes it fully significant:

the whole earth, and all that replenishes it, all that surrounds it, are full of his Presence . . . An habitual Belief of this Truth, gives Nature her *loveliest* Aspect, and lends her the most consummate Power to please. The Breath of Violets, and the Blush of Roses; the Music of the Woods, and the Meanders of the Stream; the aspiring Hill, the extended Plain, and all the Decorations of the Landschape; *then*

---

[1] 'The Ruined Cottage', MS. B: *PW* v. 382, ll. 140–1.

[2] See 'My First Acquaintance with Poets' (Howe, xvii. 120). It may well have been Lamb—for whom Cowper was an 'old favourite'—who initiated Coleridge's enthusiasm by his letters during 1796; see, for instance, Lucas, i. 73 and p. 73, below. For evidence that Lamb's influence was at its strongest in 1796, see George Whalley, 'Coleridge's Debt to Charles Lamb', *Essays and Studies* (1958), pp. 68–85.

[3] Shawcross, i. 16.

[4] See Roderick Huang, *William Cowper: Nature Poet* (London, 1957), pp. 17–35.

appear in their highest Attractives; *then* touch the Soul with the most refined Satisfaction; when GOD is seen—when GOD is heard—and GOD enjoyed in all.[1]

Cowper in turn writes 'His presence who made all so fair, perceived,/Makes all still fairer',[2] explicitly discarding Thomson's equation of responsiveness and communion with the divine mind:

> Acquaint thyself with God if thou would'st taste
> His works. Admitted once to his embrace,
> Thou shalt perceive that thou wast blind before;
> Thine eye shall be instructed, and thine heart
> Made pure, shall relish with divine delight
> 'Till then unfelt, what hands divine have wrought.[3]

For Cowper, 'Nature is but a name for an effect/Whose cause is God',[4] and his subject is no longer the life in nature but the life within. Yet although the emphasis has shifted from nature to man, Cowper's is the less sociable poem. As Coleridge put it, 'The love of nature seems to have led Thompson to a chearful religion; and a gloomy religion to have led Cowper to a love of nature. The one would carry his fellow-men along with him into nature; the other flies to nature from his fellow-men.'[5] Hazlitt was right when he said that Cowper viewed nature 'over his clipped hedges, and from his well-swept garden-walks';[6] but the landscape he explores is private as well as cultivated. The quiet pursuits of country life—'The Winter Morning Walk', 'The Winter Walk at Noon', 'The Winter Evening'—have moral importance, opposed as they are to the urban and social evils denounced elsewhere in the poem; but it is the retiredness of such a life, rather than its virtue, that *The Task* really celebrates.

Coleridge's famous phrase, 'divine Chit chat',[7] sums up both the charm and the limitations of Cowper's blank verse. Spun

---

[1] *Theron and Aspasio: or, a Series of Dialogues and Letters, upon the Most Important and Interesting Subjects* (3 vols., London, 1755), iii. 251.

[2] *The Task* (London, 1785), vi. 253–4.

[3] Ibid. v. 779–84.   [4] Ibid. vi. 223–4.

[5] Shawcross, i. 16n. For the distinction between Thomson's deism and Cowper's Evangelicalism, see also Norman Nicholson, *William Cowper* (London, 1951), pp. 92–6.

[6] *Lectures on the English Poets* (Howe, v. 91–2).

[7] To John Thelwall, December 1796 (Griggs, i. 279).

out of his daily life, coloured by his personal voice, it yet has none of the intensity of 'The Castaway' or 'Lines written during a period of insanity'. What Cowper gave Wordsworth and Coleridge was the ability to write about their feelings in a restrained and unpretentious way. Thomson had only very occasionally introduced himself into *The Seasons*—at the start of 'Winter', for instance, in a passage of retrospect that recalls the younger Wordsworth of 'Tintern Abbey' ('The sounding cataract/Haunted me like a passion . . . ', ll. 77–8):

> Pleas'd have I, in my chearful morn of life,
> When nurs'd by careless SOLITUDE I liv'd,
> And sung of Nature with unceasing joy,
> Pleas'd have I wander'd thro' your rough domain;
> Trod the pure virgin-snows, myself as pure;
> Heard the winds roar, and the big torrent burst . . .[1]

But the passage is Wordsworthian precisely in its sense of momentousness; it was Cowper's achievement to develop a sustained poetry of ordinariness. Unlike the Wordsworth of 1797, the Coleridge of the Conversation Poems had learned how to present his own experience within the domestic and subjective framework provided by *The Task*.[2] In particular, he had learned a kind of blank verse which, despite its jocular Miltonisms, offered a convincing literary approximation to the speaking voice. Cowper's musing discursiveness is aptly evoked by Hugh Blair's contemporary definition of the 'Writer of Simplicity':

A WRITER of Simplicity expresses himself in such a manner, that every one thinks he could have written in the same way . . . There are no marks of art in his expression; it seems the very language of nature; you see in the Style, not the writer and his labour, but the man, in his own natural character. . . . This is the great advantage of Simplicity of Style, that, like simplicity of manners, it shows us a man's sentiments and turn of mind laid open without disguise . . .

---

[1] 'Winter', ll. 7–12.

[2] There are many specific debts to *The Task*; cf. for instance 'Reflections on Entering into Active Life' and the vista of *The Task*, i. 163–76; 'The Nightingale' and 'This Lime-Tree Bower my Prison' and the bird-song passage, ibid. i. 200–9; 'Frost at Midnight' and the fireside reverie, ibid. iv. 286–332; and cf. also, at the same period, 'The Dungeon' and the released prisoner, ibid. i. 436–44. Before 1798, by contrast, Wordsworth had drawn on *The Task* only in the narrative context of 'The Ruined Cottage'; see pp. 165–7, below.

reading an author of Simplicity, is like conversing with a person of distinction at home, and with ease, where we find natural manners, and a marked character.[1]

'You see in the Style . . . the man', 'like conversing with a person of distinction at home': Blair describes our experience in reading *The Task*—experience not so much of style as of personality, the educated informality a means of self-revelation. As Cowper himself tells us, in a letter of 1782, such a style was by no means an effortless creation:

Every man conversant with verse-writing knows, and knows by painful experience, that the familiar style is of all styles the most difficult to succeed in. To make verse speak the language of prose, without being prosaic—to marshal the words of it in such an order as they might naturally take in falling from the lips of an extemporary speaker, yet without meanness, harmoniously, elegantly, and without seeming to displace a syllable for the sake of the rhyme, is one of the most arduous tasks a poet can undertake.[2]

Cowper's 'task' of making poetry out of a sofa—frivolously imposed and frivolously undertaken—turns into the no less difficult task of sustaining a one-sided conversation with the reader through 5,000 lines of blank verse. Wordsworth and Coleridge too had to learn to combine 'natural thoughts with natural diction' as Cowper had done. Coleridge's first attempts at a conversational style are uneasy, liable to lapse into the inflated Miltonics of his theological and political poetry, and it is only gradually that the Conversation Poem emerges as a sustained genre; Wordsworth was able to write 'Tintern Abbey' because he had Coleridge's experience behind him, and perhaps to some extent because he had developed a comparable idiom in his narrative poetry. Each transforms Cowper's 'divine Chit chat' into the voice of solitary meditation.

The Task can be merely cosy, or merely didactic; but at its best it offers a poetry of tranquillity, transcending its own ordinariness. Cowper's sensitive portrayal of the sights and sounds of nature amounts to portraying a state of mind. Take, for instance, his very beautiful lines describing the wind:

[1] *Lectures on Rhetoric and Belles Lettres*, i. 390–91.
[2] *The Correspondence of William Cowper*, ed. Thomas Wright (4 vols., London 1904), i. 429–30.

> Nor rural sights alone, but rural sounds
> Exhilarate the spirit, and restore
> The tone of languid Nature. Mighty winds
> That sweep the skirt of some far-spreading wood
> Of ancient growth, make music not unlike
> The dash of ocean on his winding shore,
> And lull the spirit while they fill the mind,
> Unnumber'd branches waving in the blast,
> And all their leaves fast flutt'ring, all at once.[1]

'And lull the spirit while they fill the mind' could almost have been written by Wordsworth, with its transference of sensation to inner life, its merging of natural and internal landscapes. Elsewhere, Cowper anticipates Wordsworth's ability to record sense-perception in a way that evokes the responding consciousness as much as the world to which it responds:

> THERE is in souls a sympathy with sounds,
> And as the mind is pitch'd the ear is pleas'd
> With melting airs or martial, brisk or grave.
> Some chord in unison with what we hear
> Is touched within us, and the heart replies.
> How soft the music of those village bells
> Falling at intervals upon the ear
> In cadence sweet! now dying all away,
> Now pealing loud again and louder still,
> Clear and sonorous as the gale comes on.[2]

'How soft the music of those village bells' has the intimacy and muted contentment of the voice that opens 'Frost at Midnight' or 'Tintern Abbey', where the reader is similarly allowed to overhear the poet's ruminative apprehension of his surroundings. Like the Tintern landscape, Cowper's church bells take one into the mind of the poet. The fluctuating sound has its answer ('the heart replies'), and the beautifully controlled movement of the verse in itself conveys the tranquil mood of the listener. Cowper's subject is sensibility—or, as he calls it, 'sympathy', the sympathy of hearer to sound, of mind to wind. Where Thomson sees the bond between man and nature as a shared activity, Cowper sees it as shared feeling:

---

[1] *The Task*, i. 181–9.

[2] Ibid. vi. 1–10. Cf. Wordsworth's first attempts during spring 1798 to describe similar experiences in fragmentary entries in the Alfoxden Notebook (*PW* v. 340–2).

> The heart is hard in nature, and unfit
> For human fellowship, as being void
> Of sympathy, and therefore dead alike
> To love and friendship both, that is not pleased
> With sight of animals enjoying life,
> Nor feels their happiness augment his own.[1]

Wordsworth's faith 'that every flower/Enjoys the air it breathes' ('Lines written in early spring', ll. 11–12) is the meeting point of Cowper's sensibility and Thomson's vision. Writing about the One Life, Wordsworth extends Cowper's 'sympathy' from animate to inanimate nature in a persuasive plea for a world of reciprocal feeling:

> Why is it we feel
> So little for each other but for this
> That we with nature have no sympathy,
> Or with such things as have no power to hold
> Articulate language
> _____
> And never for each other shall we feel
> As we may feel till we feel sympathy
> With nature in her forms inanimate,
> With objects such as have no power to hold
> Articulate language. In all forms of things
> There is a mind.[2]

What is subjective in Cowper's outlook becomes didactic here— 'In all forms of things/There is a mind'—but the appeal to feeling remains, providing as so often in Wordsworth's poetry the basis for one's acceptance of claims that are far-fetched in themselves. So long as seeing into the life of things remains an intuition personally felt and expressed, Wordsworth's creed presents few problems for the reader. Cowper's sensitivity and his concern with mood lie behind Wordsworth's ability to create great personal poetry out of his celebration of nature.

The Task at times anticipates Wordsworth so impressively that it is worth underlining what Cowper cannot do. To look at passages such as those which lie behind 'Frost at Midnight' or 'Tintern Abbey' is to discover that what seems to be a personal situation, in both poems, has a literary basis.[3] To look

---

[1] Ibid. vi. 321–6.   [2] DC MS. 14: *PW* v. 340. *II. ii.*
[3] See p. 119 and 105–9, below.

again is to be struck by the entirely new dimension which Wordsworth and Coleridge have given their inherited material. *The Task* is oddly muted, oddly limited in range for a poet who could elsewhere write with piercing anguish about solitude and madness. Cowper's evening by the fire remains simply a 'mood lethargic',[1] and his walk in the country culminates in a vista rather than a vision of harmony;[2] the meditative intensity of the Conversation Poem is not yet present. 'The Winter Walk at Noon' illustrates both Cowper's strengths and his limitations. Like the landscape at the start of 'Tintern Abbey', the distant sound of bells ('How soft the music of those village bells . . . ') introduces a passage of introspective recall:

> Wherever I have heard
> A kindred melody, the scene recurs,
> And with it all its pleasures and its pains.
> Such comprehensive views the spirit takes,
> That in a few short moments I retrace
> (As in a map the voyager his course)
> The windings of my way through many years.
> Short as in retrospect the journey seems,
> It seem'd not always short . . . [3]

These are the rhythms of thought—associative, exploratory, fluctuating in and out of the present—and Cowper's tone has all the nostalgic contentment of Wordsworth's:

> Again the harmony comes o'er the vale,
> And through the trees I view th'embattled tow'r
> Whence all the music. I again perceive
> The soothing influence of the wafted strains,
> And settle in soft musings as I tread
> The walk still verdant under oaks and elms,
> Whose outspread branches overarch the glade.[4]

The cadences are those of 'Tintern Abbey', with their lulling repetition ('Again . . . I again perceive . . . ') used to evoke a state of mind. The details of Cowper's setting ('th'embattled tow'r) have been fused with mood poetry; the effect is of someone in a landscape and yet at the same time set apart from it. The wafted strains soothe the listening poet into obliviousness

[1] *The Task*, iv. 299.
[2] See p. 75, below.
[3] *The Task*, vi. 12–20.
[4] Ibid. vi. 65–71.

as description at once suggests and gives way to inner life. We are apparently offered the world outside the poet, but it is introspective withdrawal which becomes his subject:

> No noise is here, or none that hinders thought.
> The red-breast warbles still, but is content
> With slender notes and more than half suppress'd.
> Pleased with his solitude, and flitting light
> From spray to spray, where'er he rests he shakes
> From many a twig the pendent drops of ice,
> That tinkle in the wither'd leaves below.
> Stillness accompanied with sounds so soft
> Charms more than silence. Meditation here
> May think down hours to moments.[1]

The small activities of birds and falling icicles become part of a calm that is as much internal as external. The tranquillity here, like that of Tintern, gives pleasure in its own right; but it is valued chiefly for what it leads to—'Meditation here/May think down hours to moments.' In Cowper's poetry, however, one finds nothing more. At the centre of this carefully evoked calm is a void—no revelation of feeling, no meditative insight. All Cowper can offer is the trite didacticism of 'Here the heart/May give an useful lesson to the head . . .'[2] *The Task* showed Coleridge and Wordsworth how to transform nature poetry into a poetry of introspection, but they themselves had to add the self-revelation and the meditative passion that is the greatness of 'Frost at Midnight' and 'Tintern Abbey'.

III. AKENSIDE AND THE POETRY OF MIND

'Perhaps', wrote Coleridge to Thelwall in 1796, 'you do not like Akenside—well—*but I do*—& so do a great many others—.'[3] By contrast with the vigorous animation of *The Seasons* or the sustained personal voice of *The Task*, *The Pleasures of Imagination* is all abstractions; as Johnson put it, 'attention deserts the mind and settles in the ear . . . as nothing is distinguished, nothing is remembered.'[4] Akenside's appeal must always have

[1] Ibid. vi. 76–85.
[2] Ibid. vi. 85–6. See also Humphry House, *Coleridge: The Clark Lectures 1951–52* (London, 1953), p. 73 for an excellent summary of the differences between Cowper's writing and the Coleridgean Conversation Poem.
[3] Griggs, i. 215.
[4] *Lives of the English Poets*, ed. G. B. Hill (3 vols., Oxford, 1905), iii. 417.

lain in his intellectuality. 'Those who have studied the meta-physics of mind,' wrote Mrs. Barbauld,

and who are accustomed to investigate abstract ideas, will read it with a lively pleasure; but those who seek mere amusement in a Poem, will find many far inferior ones better suited to their purpose. The judicious admirer of AKENSIDE will not call people from the fields and the highways to partake of his feast; he will wish none to read that are not capable of understanding him.[1]

If there was one person 'accustomed to investigate abstract ideas' it was Coleridge; and although Dorothy Wordsworth had been given Mrs. Barbauld's edition in the summer of 1795,[2] it is in his poetry that Akenside's influence is chiefly seen at this period. By late 1796, Akenside's '*head* and fancy' (as opposed to the '*heart* and fancy' of Bowles) are being singled out for admiration,[3] and besides borrowing the 1772 edition of Akenside from the Bristol Library over the Christmas of 1795–6,[4] Coleridge quotes at length from the three-book version of *The Pleasures of Imagination* in his *Moral and Political Lecture* of 1795.[5] Akenside's special significance lay in his linking of nature and the imagination—for him essentially comple-mentary, as his opening lines reveal:

> WITH what attractive charms this goodly frame
> Of nature touches the consenting hearts
> Of mortal men; and what the pleasing stores
> Which beauteous imitation thence derives
> To deck the poet's, or the painter's toil;
> My verse unfolds.[6]

[1] *The Pleasures of Imagination* (London, 1794), pp. 6–7.
[2] See *EY*, p. 151.   [3] See Griggs, i. 279.
[4] See George Whalley, 'The Bristol Library Borrowings of Southey and Cole-ridge, 1793–8', *Library*, 5th ser. iv (1949), 122. 'Religious Musings' came out in 1796 with a motto adapted from the 1772 version of *The Pleasures of the Imagination*, i. 49–59, published in *The Poems of Mark Akenside*, ed. Jeremiah Dyson (London, 1772).
[5] See *CCW* i: *Lectures 1795 On Politics and Religion*, ed. L. Patton and P. Mann, p. 13. The passages quoted correspond to Akenside's celebration of human potential in *The Pleasures of Imagination* (London, 1744), i. 151–69, and to his closing claim for response to the natural world as participation in the divine mind, ibid. iii. 615–29 (see pp. 54–5, below). Subsequent references are to the three-book version of 1744 unless specified.
[6] *The Pleasures of Imagination*, i. 1–6.

Nor is it simply a question of the natural world being mirrored by the artist. In Akenside's scheme, nature represents the meeting point of human and divine imagination; it is at once the focus for ordinary sense-perception (for him closely allied to creativity), and the supreme example of imaginative creation. 'The uncreated images of things' in the mind of God have been translated into actuality by the 'vital smile' and the 'breath' familiar from Thomson's *Seasons*:

> Hence the breath
> Of life informing each organic frame,
> Hence the green earth, and wild resounding waves;
> Hence light and shade alternate; warmth and cold;
> And clear autumnal skies and vernal show'rs,
> And all the fair variety of things.[1]

Our response to light and shade, heat and cold, the changing seasons and 'all the fair variety of things' gives us access to the world of God's imagination; in perceiving nature, we participate in the original act of creation itself. Such ideas were commonplace enough in themselves, but *The Pleasures of Imagination* presented them in a form that was peculiarly relevant to the Wordsworth of 1798. By this time he too was concerned with a transcendental significance at once perceived and created in nature by the imagination.

Akenside gives the most intellectual treatment to the studies of receptive calm found earlier in *The Seasons*. Using the famous image of Memnon's harp to describe and analyse sense-perception, he makes an implicit link between the responsive and the harmonious soul:

> As Memnon's marble harp, renown'd of old
> By fabling Nilus, to the quivering touch
> Of Titan's ray, with each repulsive string
> Consenting, sounded thro' the warbling air
> Unbidden strains; ev'n so did nature's hand
> To certain species of external things,
> Attune the finer organs of the mind:
> So the glad impulse of congenial pow'rs,
> Or of sweet sound, or fair-proportion'd form,
> The grace of motion, or the bloom of light,
> Thrills thro' imagination's tender frame,

[1] Ibid. i. 66, 72, 73–8.

> From nerve to nerve: all naked and alive
> They catch the spreading rays: till now the soul
> At length discloses every tuneful spring,
> To that harmonious movement from without,
> Responsive.[1]

This is perhaps the most ambitious attempt before Coleridge's 'Eolian Harp' to analyse the workings of a mind that is at once passive and active.[2] There is interaction as well as congruence between outer and inner, nature and imagination. 'Consenting' to 'congenial pow'rs', the soul becomes creative in its own right ('discloses every tuneful spring'). The harp metaphor suggests a mechanical miracle, but the language suggests an organic relationship; the mind, and the world it responds to, partake of the same shared harmony. For Akenside, as for Thomson, response to nature leads paradoxically to a suspension of sensory activity and to a heightened inner life—

> the passions gently sooth'd away,
> Sink to divine repose, and love and joy
> Alone are waking; love and joy, serene
> As airs that fan the summer.[3]

But Akenside is concerned with the processes of imaginative creation, not simply with contemplative reverie. The conclusion of the three-book *Pleasures of Imagination* of 1744 is a final claim for the resemblance between the responding mind and the activity of God: the mind

> appeals to nature, to the winds
> And rowling waves, the sun's unwearied course,
> The elements and seasons: all declare
> For what th'eternal maker has ordain'd
> The pow'rs of man: we feel within ourselves
> His energy divine: he tells the heart,

---

[1] *The Pleasures of Imagination,* i. 109–24.

[2] See pp. 70–1, below, and cf. also the resemblance between these lines and the lines added to 'The Eolian Harp' in the errata of *Sibylline Leaves* (1817):

> O! the one Life within us and abroad,
> Which meets all motion and becomes its soul,
> A light in sound, a sound-like power in light,
> Rhythm in all thought, and joyance every where . . .
>
> (*CPW* i. 101, ll. 26–9).

[3] *The Pleasures of Imagination,* i. 129–32.

He meant, he made us to behold and love
What he beholds and loves, the general orb
Of life and being; to be great like him,
Beneficent and active. Thus the men
Whom nature's works can charm, with GOD himself
Hold converse; grow familiar, day by day,
With his conceptions; act upon his plan;
And form to his, the relish of their souls.[1]

This must be among the most explicit statements about the
value of response to the natural world to be found in eighteenth-
century nature poetry. To respond is to 'feel within ourselves/
His energy divine', and—perhaps even more important for the
Wordsworth of the Yew-tree lines—to enter into relationship
('hold converse') with a divine mind whose beneficence and
activity is thereby communicated to 'the men/Whom nature's
works can charm'.

Both Akenside and Wordsworth represent their poet-seer as
the product of an ideal relationship between nature and the
imagination. The poet of *The Pleasures of Imagination* is as much a
man apart as Wordsworth's Pedlar; it is only to visionaries, as
distinct from philosophers or other seekers after truth and
knowledge, that creation is fully 'unveil'd':

On every part
They trace the bright impressions of his hand:
In earth or air, the meadow's purple stores,
The moon's mild radiance, or the virgin's form
Blooming with rosy smiles, they see portray'd
That uncreated beauty, which delights
The mind supreme. *They* also feel her charms;
Enamour'd, *they* partake th'eternal joy.[2]

Wordsworth at times follows Akenside in his account of the
Pedlar's education into perception of the One Life. Both trace
the stages of imaginative development through response to
fairy-tales and ghost-stories, and, later, through an awareness
of the laws of science as manifested in nature;[3] and both attach
special importance to the visionary's capacity to 'see' nature—
his receptivity to and retentiveness of the images presented by

[1] Ibid. iii. 620–33. [2] Ibid. i. 101–8.
[3] Cf. MS. B of 'The Ruined Cottage', *PW* v. 383, ll. 167–85; 384–5, ll. 226–35,
and *The Pleasures of Imagination*, i. 255–65; ii. 103–20.

the natural world. Akenside's concept of the imagination owes
something to Addison's extraordinarily passive definition in his
Spectator discussion of 'The Pleasures of the Imagination': 'It is
but opening the Eye, and the Scene enters. The Colours paint
themselves on the Fancy, with very little Attention of Thought
or Application of Mind in the Beholder.'[1] This concept of
imagination as 'painting' images on the inner eye is developed
by Akenside's metaphors of mirror and seal—metaphors for a
mind at once reflecting and imprinted by the natural world:

> For not th'expanse
> Of living lakes in summer's noontide calm,
> Reflects the bord'ring shade and sun-bright heav'ns
> With fairer semblance; not the sculptur'd gold
> More faithful keeps the graver's lively trace,
> Than he whose birth the sister-pow'rs of art
> Propitious view'd, and from his genial star
> Shed influence to the seeds of fancy kind;
> Than his attemper'd bosom must preserve
> The seal of nature. There alone unchang'd,
> Her form remains.[2]

The creative imagination not only mirrors, but makes permanent the changing forms of nature. To Wordsworth, similarly,
it is the Pedlar's capacity for mirroring nature that marks him
as a visionary—

> deep feelings had impressed
> Great objects on his mind, with portraiture
> And colour so distinct [that on his mind],

---

[1] *Spectator*, no. ccccxi (21 June 1712), ed. D. F. Bond (5 vols., Oxford, 1965),
iii. 538.

[2] *The Pleasures of Imagination*, iii. 358–68. In 1794 (see Reed, p. 152 and n.)
Wordsworth used Akenside's lake image to describe Dorothy's responsiveness in
one of the Windy Brow revisions to *An Evening Walk* (1793):

> Yes, thou art blest, my friend, with mind awake
> To Nature's impulse like this living lake,
> Whose mirrour makes the landscape's charms its own . . .
>   (DC MS. 9: *PW* i. 12 app. crit.)

The metaphor lingers on not only in Coleridge's 1795 reference to the 'Good and
Beauty' of nature, 'miniatured on the mind of the beholder, as a Landscape on a
Convex Mirror' (Griggs, i. 154), but in Wordsworth's description in the 1802
'Preface' of 'the mind of man as naturally the mirror of the fairest and most
interesting qualities of nature' (*Prose Works*, i, 140).

> They lay like substances, & almost seemed
> To haunt the bodily sense.[1]

—but 'deep feelings' have been added to the mechanical responsiveness of Addison and Akenside. The child is haunted, weighed down, by his imaginative experience; 'impressed' has taken on an affective sense beyond the figurative meaning of Akenside's seal image. Significantly, too, whereas in *The Pleasures of Imagination* it is nature that plays the active role of the engraving artist or impressing force, here it is the visionary himself. What had for Addison and Akenside been a passive receptivity becomes for Wordsworth an active power, as his own italics emphasize:

> He had received
> A precious gift, for as he grew in years
> With these impressions would he still compare
> All his ideal stores, his shapes, & forms,
> And being still unsatisfied with aught
> Of dimmer character, he thence attained
> An *active* power to fasten images
> Upon his brain, & on their pictured lines
> Intensely brooded, even till they acquired
> The liveliness of dreams.[2]

These lines have the expository air of Akenside's account of imaginative processes, but their allusive and unexpected meaning is entirely Wordsworthian. Although his starting-point is the 'impressions' received from the external world, Wordsworth's real concern is with an inner world—the 'ideal stores' of the Pedlar's mind. The brooding process, not the mere perceiving, is what matters now, and the images of nature acquire, not the life of actuality, but 'The liveliness of dreams'[3]—a life at

---

[1] 'The Ruined Cottage', MS. B: *PW* v. 381, ll. 81–5. The missing words are supplied from MS. D.

[2] Ibid.: *PW*: v. 381, ll. 85–94. Cf. Coleridge's famous objection to Newton in a letter of March 1801: '*Mind* in his system is always passive—a lazy Looker-on on an external world. If the mind be not *passive*, if it be indeed made in God's Image, & that too in the sublimest sense—the Image of the *Creator*—there is ground for suspicion, that any system built on the passiveness of the mind must be false, as a system' (Griggs, ii. 709).

[3] Cf. the 'addendum' to MS. B of 'The Ruined Cottage', where the Pedlar is one who had 'brooded' on his thoughts 'till Imagination's power/Condensed them to a passion' (*PW* v. 403, ll. 108–9).

once vivid and shadowy, at once more and less real, autonomous and dependent. Like Akenside, Wordsworth is theorizing,
and he is doing so on lines laid down by *The Pleasures of Imagination*; but his poetry allows for the transforming power of the
mind as Akenside's had not. Here too, his debt to an earlier
tradition has been the basis for an original development;
traditionalism and individuality work together to create a kind
of poetry that looks forward rather than back—away from
nature, and towards the final affirmation of *The Prelude* that

> the mind of man becomes
> A thousand times more beautiful than the earth
> On which he dwells . . . [1]

[1] *Prelude*, xiii. 446–8.

III 'The Whole One Self':
The Debt to Coleridge

THE Wordsworth of spring 1797 had been concerned with refutation: a year later he is concerned to affirm. Once again an immediate contemporary stands between him and his predecessors; as Godwin had given fresh relevance to the theme of perverted sensibility, so Coleridge gives a new dimension to the themes of nature, self, and imagination found in earlier nature poetry.[1] Coleridge's concern with what Mrs. Barbauld calls 'the metaphysics of mind'[2] is as much doctrinal as philosophic: 'Nature has her proper interest; & he will know what it is, who believes & feels, that every Thing has a Life of it's own, & that we are all *one Life*. A Poet's *Heart* & *Intellect* should be *combined*, *intimately* combined & *unified*, with the great appearances in Nature . . . '[3] This was written in 1802, but it is a passage that suggests what Coleridge brought to Wordsworth in the summer of 1797. Where Wordsworth in the Yew-tree lines had portrayed a fatal separation between head and heart, using 'the great appearances in Nature' only to externalize the conflict within, Coleridge offered a poetry of relationship. The problem which Wordsworth approached by way of moral and political philosophy was solved by Coleridge in ultimately Christian terms; instead of a failed system he had a flourishing faith. At the same time, the intimacy of the Conversation Poem allowed him to explore inner life as Wordsworth's fictions of guilt and alienation did not, combining self-revelation with doctrinal statement. Without Coleridge, Wordsworth could have written neither the visionary poetry of 'The Pedlar'[4] nor the confessional poetry of 'Tintern Abbey'. By 1798, he has

---

[1] The case for Coleridge's influence on the Wordsworth of 1797 is persuasively presented by Jonathan Wordsworth, *The Music of Humanity*, pp. 184–201.

[2] See p. 52, above.

[3] To William Sotheby, 10 September 1802 (Griggs, ii. 864).

[4] The title is used to distinguish the 250-odd lines of idealized biography, incorporated into MS. B of 'The Ruined Cottage' in 1798, from the original story of

emerged as the philosophic poet we know and admire, his blank verse at once massively serious and humanly forthcoming, the eccentricity of his earlier writing transcended for a meditative passion that is no less his own.

1. THE ONE LIFE

At the period when nature had been 'all in all' to the young Wordsworth, there had been

> no need of a remoter charm,
> By thought supplied, or any interest
> Unborrowed from the eye. ('Tintern Abbey', ll. 82–4)

An Evening Walk and *Descriptive Sketches* (1793) are largely picturesque in approach; at most, nature is sublime. Only in the important Windy Brow revisions to *An Evening Walk*, belonging to 1794,[1] is there any hint that nature could mean more than this. But although in some sense paving the way for Wordsworth's later belief in the One Life, the passages concerned seem to mirror the fashionable blend of science, sensibility, and Hartleianism found at the same period in Erasmus Darwin's *Botanic Garden* (1789–91)—a poem which we know to have influenced Wordsworth's couplet poetry elsewhere.[2] Just as Darwin had exclaimed

> 'But THOU! whose mind the well-attemper'd ray
> Of Taste and Virtue lights with purer day;
> Whose finer sense each soft vibration owns
> With sweet responsive sympathy of tones . . . '[3]

so Wordsworth celebrates

> A heart that vibrates evermore, awake
> To feeling for all forms that Life can take,
> That wider still its sympathy extends

Margaret; the two became separate poems in MS. D of 1799–1800. See Jonathan Wordsworth, *The Music of Humanity*, pp. 157–68.

[1] See Reed, pp. 22, 152.

[2] For Darwin's influence on Wordsworth's early narrative poetry, see pp. 137–8, below. The contemporary success of *The Botanic Garden* is described in *Biographia Literaria* (Shawcross, i. 11–12); Darwin's radical politics would have given him additional appeal to Wordsworth and Coleridge.

[3] *The Botanic Garden: A Poem, in Two Parts* (London, 1789–91), Pt. I: 'The Economy of Vegetation' (1791), i. 9–12. Cf. also the Hartleian terminology used by Samuel Rogers in *The Pleasures of Memory* (London, 1792), i. 169–84.

And sees not any line where being ends;
Sees sense, through Nature's rudest forms betrayed,
Tremble obscure in fountain, rock, and shade,
And while a secret power whose forms endears
Their social accents never vainly hears.[1]

The suggestion that Wordsworth was invoking the quasi-scientific ideas about animated matter current at the time is a plausible one;[2] certainly the terms he goes on to use imply that he had in mind the theories which underlie Darwin's fanciful presentation of the vegetable and mineral world. Addressing Dorothy—'Yes, thou art blest, my friend, with mind awake/To Nature's impulse . . . '[3]—Wordsworth moves on from her intuitive responsiveness, to the vision of

those to whom the harmonious doors
Of Science have unbarred celestial stores,
To whom a burning energy has given
That other eye which darts through earth and heaven,
Sees common forms prolong the endless chain
Of joy & grief, of pleasure and of pain,
Roams through all space and [   ] unconfined,
Explores the illimitable tracts of mind . . . [4]

'That other eye' is clearly doing something more specialized than seeing into the life of things, and the tracts of mind must be those of the human intellect rather than God.[5] The point is an important one: far from thinking in transcendental terms, Wordsworth is at this stage invoking the speculations of contemporary science. Moreover, there is nothing in his writing

[1] DC MS. 9: *PW* i. 10 app. crit.
[2] See Jonathan Wordsworth, *The Music of Humanity*, pp. 184–8, and, for the circles in which such ideas were current, see H. W. Piper, *The Active Universe* (London, 1962), pp. 16–28, 63–72.
[3] DC MS. 9: *PW* i. 12 app. crit.
[4] DC MS. 10: *PW* i. 13 app. crit. De Selincourt's text is a conflated one, but his conjectural order is plausible. The link between this passage and *The Botanic Garden* is also noticed by F. D. Klingender, apropos of the scientific movements of the 1790s, in *Art and the Industrial Revolution*, ed. and rev. Arthur Elton (London, 1968), pp. 40–1.
[5] Cf. the parallel phrase, 'the fields of thought', elsewhere in the Windy Brow revisions (DC MS. 9: *PW* i. 13 app. crit.), and the phrase used by Collins in 'The Manners. An Ode', ll. 1–2, where science and intellectual inquiry are abandoned for the arts and human observations with the words, 'FAREWELL, for clearer Ken design'd,/The dim-discover'd Tracts of Mind . . .': *Odes on Several Descriptive and Allegoric Subjects* (London, 1747), p. 41.

between 1794 and 1798 to suggest that science gave way to
pantheism as a means of making the natural world significant.
His interests are all with the human, the social, or the political;
a religious insight is conspicuously lacking.

Like Wordsworth, Coleridge would have been familiar with
a quasi-scientific concept of animated matter, and he too was
influenced by Darwin's view of the natural world.[1] But where
Wordsworth—in Coleridge's phrase—was 'at least a *Semi*-
atheist' when the two met fleetingly in 1796,[2] Coleridge had a
Christian basis for seeing no 'line where being ends'. As
Thomas Poole wrote of him in the summer of 1794, 'In religion
he is a Unitarian, if not a Deist; in politicks a Democrat, to the
utmost extent of the word.'[3] The juxtaposition here implies a
link: for the Coleridge of the mid-1790s, radicalism in religion
and radicalism in politics were inextricably intertwined. A
passage from his contribution to Southey's *Joan of Arc* (1796)—
later published as 'The Destiny of Nations'—shows how completely he identified Christianity and Liberty:

> For what is Freedom, but the unfetter'd use
> Of all the Powers which God for use had given?
> But chiefly this, with holiest habitude
> Of constant Faith, him First, him Last to view
> Thro' meaner powers and secondary things
> Effulgent, as thro' clouds that veil his blaze.
> For all that meets the bodily sense I deem
> Symbolical, one mighty alphabet
> For infant minds . . . [4]

'Religious Musings', at the same period, preaches a vision of
social change which is similarly Christian ('The present State
of Society. French Revolution. Millenium. Universal Redemp-

[1] See p. 65, below, for Darwin's influence on Coleridge's early Miltonics.
[2] To John Thelwall (Griggs, i. 216). For details of the links between Wordsworth
and Coleridge prior to 1797, see R. S. Woof, 'Wordsworth and Coleridge: Some
Early Matters', *Bicentenary Wordsworth Studies*, ed. Jonathan Wordsworth, pp.
76–91.
[3] Mrs. Henry Sandford, *Thomas Poole and his Friends* (2 vols., London, 1888),
. 97.
[4] *Joan of Arc, An Epic Poem* (Bristol, 1796), ii. 13–21 (*CPW* i. 132, ll. 13–20).
'The Destiny of Nations' was first published in its entirety in *Sibylline Leaves* (1817).
For an account of the collaboration on *Joan of Arc*, see George Whalley, 'Coleridge,
Southey and "Joan of Arc"', *N & Q* N.S. i (1954), 67–9.

tion').[1] The political element in Coleridge's early Miltonics was to be of less lasting importance than their insistence on communion. Preoccupied as he is with self-transcendence and fulfilment, Coleridge gives a central place to ideas of perceived relationship—relationship, that is, with God as manifested through the intermediary of nature. As he put it in the first of his 'Lectures on Revealed Religion' in 1795, paraphrasing Akenside,

The Omnipotent has unfolded to us the Volume of the World, that there we may read the Transcript of himself. In Earth or Air the meadow's purple stores, the Moons mild radiance, or the Virgins form Blooming with rosy smiles, we see pourtrayed the bright Impressions of the eternal Mind.[2]

The idea of nature implied here is a traditional one, but it is also one that Coleridge's theological reading had tended to reinforce. Looking back, he himself described his beliefs at this period as 'a compound of Philosophy & Christianity'.[3] He was influenced in turn by a succession of thinkers (in Southey's words, 'Hartley was ousted by Berkeley, Berkeley by Spinoza, and Spinoza by Plato. . . . The truth is that he plays with systems'[4]) whom he attempted to combine and reconcile. The philosopher adopted at any given moment has his part to play in the on-going process of Coleridge's attempts to define the relationship between the individual mind and the mind of God. In formulating his definitions, Coleridge feels equally free to call on materialist and idealist traditions. It would be rash to set up any single influence to the exclusion of others; but it is possible to identify central elements in his thinking about nature as derived from two representatives of these apparently opposed traditions—from the Unitarian Priestley on the one

---

[1] Argument to 'Religious Musings' in *Poems on Various Subjects* (1796), p. [137] (*CPW* i. 108). For the relationship of 'Religious Musings' to contemporary political and religious thought, and especially to Gilbert Wakefield's pamphlet *The Spirit of Christianity, compared with the Spirit of the Times* (1794), see H. W. Piper, pp. 47–50. This aspect of Coleridge's poem is also explored by J. A. Appleyard, *Coleridge's Philosophy of Literature* (Cambridge, Mass., 1965), pp. 38–42.

[2] *CCW* i: *Lectures 1795 On Politics and Religion*, ed. L. Patton and P. Mann, p. 94 (the passage approximates to *The Pleasures of Imagination*, i. 99–108).

[3] To Sir George and Lady Beaumont, 1 October 1803 (Griggs, ii. 999).

[4] To William Taylor, 11 July 1808; J. W. Robberds, *A Memoir of the Life and Writings of the late William Taylor of Norwich* (2 vols., London, 1843), ii. 216.

hand, and from Berkeley on the other. Each can be seen as providing a doctrinal basis for the transcendental landscapes, at once God-infused and God-veiling, that recur in Coleridge's poetry during the 1790s and reappear in Wordsworth's during 1798.

Joseph Priestley (enthroned in 'Religious Musings'—'Lo! Priestley there, Patriot, and Saint, and Sage'[1]) was not only the chief spokesman for the radical religion adopted by Coleridge, but one of the foremost European scientists of the period and the editor of Hartley. Coleridge was later to be embarrassed by the beliefs emphatically announced in *Joan of Arc* —

> 'Glory to thee, FATHER of Earth and Heaven!
> 'All-conscious PRESENCE of the Universe!
> 'Nature's vast ever-acting ENERGY!
> 'In will, in deed, IMPULSE of All to all . . . ' [2]

—alluding, in a punning note, to the Unitarian doctrine of the humanity of Christ: 'I was at that time one of the *Mongrels*, the *Josephidites* . . . '[3] Along with his Unitarian doctrines, Coleridge had taken over Priestley's quasi-scientific theory of God as energy: 'the Divine Being, and his energy, are absolutely necessary to that of every other being. His power is the very *life and soul* of every thing that exists . . . '[4] The logical extension of this position was to deny the distinction between material and spiritual worlds—'If they say that, on my hypothesis, there is no such thing as matter, and that every thing is spirit, I have no objection . . . ';[5] as Coleridge wrote later, in *Biographia Literaria*, Priestley 'stript matter of all its material properties; substituted spiritual powers . . . '[6] In *Joan of Arc*, accordingly, the dead Newtonian universe, with its 'subtle fluids, impacts, essences . . .

---

[1] *Poems on Various Subjects* (1796), l. 395; (*CPW* i. 123 app. crit.). Cf. also Coleridge's sonnet on Priestley in the *Morning Chronicle* for 11 December 1794 (*CPW* i. 81–2).

[2] *Joan of Arc*, ii. 442–5 (*CPW* i. 146–7, ll. 459–62).

[3] *CPW* i. 147n; i.e. one of the followers of Joseph Priestley, who believed that Joseph had been Christ's father.

[4] *Disquisitions Relating to Matter and Spirit* (2nd edn., 2 vols., Birmingham, 1782), . 42.

[5] *Disquisitions Relating to Matter and Spirit* (London, 1777), p. 353.

[6] Shawcross, i. 91.

Untenanting Creation of its God',[1] is replaced by a Priestleian system of informing, omnipresent Mind. Though tentatively introduced ('Here we pause humbly'), this is clearly the theory of the natural world adopted by Coleridge himself:

> as one body is the aggregate
> Of atoms numberless, each organiz'd;
> So by a strange and dim similitude,
> Infinite myriads of self-conscious minds
> Form one all-conscious Spirit, who directs
> With absolute ubiquity of thought
> All his component monads, that yet seem
> With various province and apt agency
> Each to pursue its own self-centering end.
> Some nurse the infant diamond in the mine;
> Some roll the genial juices thro' the oak;
> Some drive the mutinous clouds to clash in air . . . [2]

In its attempt to define, Coleridge's language spans science, theology, and the Rosicrucian fancifulness of Darwin's *Botanic Garden*.[3] Though seeming to us incongruous, his monads clearly lie behind the motion and spirit that 'rolls through all things' in 'Tintern Abbey'—as do the 'plastic' powers of 'Religious Musings',

> that interfus'd
> Roll thro' the grosser and material mass
> In organizing surge![4]

This quasi-scientific belief in an active universe, expressed with such excitement in Coleridge's Miltonics—

> There is one Mind, one omnipresent Mind,
> Omnific. His most holy name is LOVE.[5]

—underlies the Conversation Poems and in 1798 becomes the One Life of Wordsworth's doctrinal blank verse.

Priestley stressed an immanent, ever-present God in nature; Berkeley's view was of a God perceived through, yet veiled by,

---

[1] *Joan of Arc*, ii. 34, 37 (*CPW* i. 132, ll. 32, 35). 'Sir Isaac Newton's Deity seems to be alternately operose and indolent . . .' (*Joan of Arc*, p. 42n.)

[2] Ibid. ii. 41–52 (*CPW* i. 133, ll. 40–52 and app. crit.).

[3] For Coleridge's debt to Darwin, see H. W. Piper, pp. 40–1.

[4] ll. 432–4 (*CPW* i. 124, ll. 405–7).

[5] Ibid., ll. 119–20 (*CPW* i. 113, ll. 105–6).

the natural world. Priestley saw the divine presence as a question of faith rather than perception by the senses, but he was prepared to support his position by citing the symbolic manifestations recorded in the Bible:

the idea which the scriptures give us of the divine nature is that of a Being, properly speaking, *every where present*, constantly supporting, and at pleasure controling the laws of nature, but not the object of any of our senses; and that, out of condescension, as it were, to the weakness of human apprehension, he chose, in the early ages of the world, to signify his peculiar presence by some *visible symbol*, as that of a supernatural bright cloud, or some other appearance, which could not but impress their minds with the idea of a real local presence.[1]

For Berkeley, the natural world provides a continuous symbolic revelation of the divine mind:

As in reading other Books, a wise Man will choose to fix his Thoughts on the Sense and apply it to use, rather than lay them out in Grammatical Remarks on the Language; so in perusing the Volume of Nature, it seems beneath the Dignity of the Mind to affect an Exactness in reducing each particular *Phænomenon* to general Rules, or shewing how it follows from them. We should propose to our selves nobler Views, such as to recreate and exalt the Mind, with a prospect of the Beauty, Order, Extent, and Variety of natural Things: Hence, by proper Inferences, to enlarge our Notions of the Grandeur, Wisdom, and Beneficence of the CREATOR . . .[2]

A Priestleian theory of animated matter can exist in *Joan of Arc* alongside a Berkeleian definition of Christian fulfilment—

> him First, him Last to view
> Thro' meaner powers and secondary things
> Effulgent, as thro' clouds that veil his blaze.
> For all that meets the bodily sense I deem
> Symbolical, one mighty alphabet
> For infant minds . . .[3]

In 'Religious Musings', too, the organizing 'Monads of the infinite mind' exist side by side with a Berkeleian belief that 'Life is a vision shadowy of Truth':

---

[1] *Disquisitions Relating to Matter and Spirit*, p. 113.
[2] *A Treatise Concerning the Principles of Human Knowledge* (London, 1734), pp. 128–9, I. cix.
[3] *Joan of Arc*, ii. 16–21 (*CPW* i. 132, ll. 15–20).

> The veiling clouds retire,
> And lo! the Throne of the redeeming God
> Forth flashing unimaginable day
> Wraps in one blaze earth, heaven, and deepest hell.[1]

'This paragraph is intelligible to those, who, like the Author, believe and feel the sublime system of Berkley [*sic*]', noted Coleridge in the 1797 edition. Coleridge's allegiance had been divided in the Miltonics of the mid-1790s, but Berkeley was in the ascendancy by December 1796—'I am a Berkleian', he claimed boldly in a letter to Thelwall, denying that he was a materialist,[2] and when he sent 'This Lime-Tree Bower my Prison' to Southey in a letter of July 1797, he explained its transcendental landscape with the words: 'You remember, I am a *Berkleian*.'[3] In 'Frost at Midnight', the following year, it is a Berkeleian lesson that nature once more offers to Coleridge's child:

> so shalt thou see and hear
> The lovely shapes and sounds intelligible
> Of that eternal language, which thy God
> Utters, who from eternity doth teach
> Himself in all, and all things in himself.
> Great universal Teacher! . . . [4]

Coleridge has it both ways: nature both is God and speaks of him, both manifests and symbolizes the divine mind.

What is important for Coleridge the poet is that his theological reading provides him with potent metaphors of communion and revelation. Whether as light or language, God is always present in nature. It is this knowledge that, in Coleridge's words, 'fraternizes man':

> 'Tis the sublime of man,
> Our noontide Majesty, to know ourselves
> Parts and proportions of one wond'rous whole:
> This fraternizes man . . . [5]

Brotherhood is the traditional Christian answer to the struggle of man against man; but Coleridge goes further than this. For

---

[1] ll. 423, 425–8 (*CPW* i. 124, ll. 396, 398–401). [2] Griggs, i. 278.
[3] Ibid. i. 335.
[4] *Fears in Solitude . . . To which are added, France, an Ode; and Frost at Midnight* (London, 1798), p. 22 (*CPW* i. 242, ll. 58–63).
[5] 'Religious Musings', ll. 141–4 (*CPW* i. 113–14, ll. 126–8).

him the individual's consciousness is profoundly altered by the knowledge of being part of something greater than himself. Wordsworth's answer to crippling self-absorption had been a slenderly defined benevolence: Coleridge's was the One Life:

> A sordid solitary thing,
> Mid countless brethren with a lonely heart
> Thro' courts and cities the smooth Savage roams
> Feeling himself, his own low Self the whole,
> When he by sacred sympathy might make
> The whole ONE SELF! SELF, that no alien knows!
> SELF, far diffus'd as Fancy's wing can travel!
> SELF, spreading still! Oblivious of it's own,
> Yet all of all possessing![1]

Despite their clumsy rhetoric, these lines triumphantly proclaim the possibility of liberation from the burden of self. The individual's solitude and his capacity to enter into relationship are to be the recurrent subject of Coleridge's poetry. 'Religious Musings' and the *Joan of Arc* passages had been largely theoretical; speculative and proselytizing in manner, they offer little scope for exploring inner experience. But side by side with his Miltonics, Coleridge had begun to evolve a genre which allowed him to write in openly personal terms about the states of mind and the problems that concerned him most deeply. In the preface to *Poems* (1796) he had felt the need to defend himself against the charge of 'querulous egotism', insisting that private feelings can have general interest: 'What is the PUBLIC but a term for a number of scattered individuals of whom as many will be interested in these sorrows as have experienced the same or similar?'[2] But the Conversation Poem needs no such defence; as Hazlitt wrote later, 'Mr. Coleridge talks of himself, without being an egotist, for in him the individual is always merged with the abstract and general.'[3] The abstract theology of his earlier Miltonics is translated into the language of subjective experience; and it was this that made it possible for Wordsworth to write not only 'The Pedlar', but his own Conversation Poem, 'Tintern Abbey'.

---

[1] 'Religious Musings', ll. 169–77 (*CPW* i. 114–15, ll. 149–57). Cf. ' "he who is absorbed in self will be vicious—whatever may be his speculative opinions" '; to John Thelwall, 22 June 1796 (Griggs, i. 221).

[2] *Poems on Various Subjects* (1796), pp. [v], vii (*CPW* ii. 1135–6).

[3] *The Spirit of the Age* (Howe, xi. 31).

II. THE CONVERSATION POEM

From the start, Coleridge's chief problem in the Conversation Poem was to reconcile mood poetry with the expression of ideas.[1] In 'The Eolian Harp' of 1795 one can see the genre coming into being, but as yet not fully integrated. There is no reason to think that when he began to write 'Effusion XXXV', dated 'Clevedon, August 20th, 1795', Coleridge had in mind anything more ambitious than the other 'effusions' of sentiment published in *Poems* (1796). As it stands in the 'Rugby' MS., the first draft of 'The Eolian Harp' describes an amorous domestic idyll. Its idiom is at once prosaic and fanciful—Thomson's already poetic breeze that 'blows from yon extended field/Of blossom'd beans'[2] has become 'What snatches of perfume/ The noiseless gale from yonder bean-field wafts!'[3] The tone is that of a lover's compliment ('the star of eve/Serenely brilliant, like thy polish'd Sense'),[4] and the central values—'Innocence and Love'—are emblematically represented by the flowers that overgrow Coleridge's Clevedon cottage. At this stage, the harp of the poem's later title stands chiefly for Sara ('half willing to be woo'd'), whose upbraidings at Coleridge's caresses 'Tempt to repeat the wrong!'[5] The origins of Coleridge's image are still literary rather than philosophic—Thomson's 'Ode on Aeolus's Harp' rather than Boehme, Cudworth, or Priestley:

> Those tender notes, how kindly they upbraid
> With what soft woe they thrill the lover's heart?
> Sure from the hand of some unhappy maid
> Who dy'd of love, these sweet complainings part.[6]

---

[1] For two general studies of the genre, see R. H. Fogle, 'Coleridge's Conversation Poems', *Tulane Studies in English*, v (1955), 103–10, and Albert Gérard, 'The Systolic Rhythm: The Structure of Coleridge's Conversation Poems', *EC* x (1960), 307–19.

[2] 'Spring', ll. 458–9.

[3] 1st draft: *CPW* ii. 1021, ll. 9–10. Cf. the 2nd draft, 'How exquisite the Scents/ Snatch'd from yon Bean-field!' (*CPW* ii. 1022, ll. 9–10).

[4] Ibid.: *CPW* ii. 1021, ll. 7–8.   [5] Ibid.: *CPW* ii. 1021, ll. 15, 17.

[6] *A Collection of Poems*, ed. Robert Dodsley, iii (2nd edn., London, 1748), 211. See p. 71 n., below, for the philosophic origins of the image. Coleridge is also drawing on the sub-Shakespearian mood poetry of his time—cf., for instance, 'Moon-Light', in the *Gentleman's Magazine*, lix (May 1789), 448: 'HERE on this bank, while shine the stars so clear,/Come, Lucy, let us sit . . .'; but his chief literary source apart from the *Ode* would have been the description of Aeolus' harp in Thomson's *Castle of Indolence* (London, 1748), sts. xi–xli.

So far, this is an 'effusion' of mood rather than thought. If the progression of the second, extended draft is anything to go by, it became a philosophic poem almost by accident. The harp image—an important metaphor for interaction and reciprocal response—clearly offered too many possibilities to be left as it stood, and Coleridge went on to analyse the undercurrent of mysterious activity present even in the most tranquil of moods:

> And now it's strings
> Boldlier swept, the long sequacious notes
> Over delicious Surges sink and rise
> In aëry voyage, Music such as erst
> Round rosy bowers (so Legendaries tell)
> To sleeping Maids came floating witchingly
> By wand'ring West winds stoln from Faery land . . . [1]

Although this is moving away from the pastoral idyll of the opening lines, it is not noticeably more philosophic. But for all their fanciful exoticism, the lines introduce a new and important idea—that the mind in a state of relaxation may somehow be in contact with a world beyond reality. Like the winds that come from the fields of sleep in the 'Immortality Ode', the 'wand'ring West winds stoln from Faery land' speak of the mystery latent in ordinary experience.

The significant change in direction occurs when Coleridge transforms the Eolian harp into an explicit metaphor for the processes of the mind. It is here, for the first time, that one finds writing charcteristic of the Conversation Poem at its best—the subtle analysis of an inner state, the attempt to define mental activity that takes place without conscious volition:

> And thus, my Love! as on the midway Slope
> Of yonder Hill I stretch my limbs at noon
> And tranquil muse upon Tranquillity.
> Full many a Thought uncall'd and undetain'd
> And many idle flitting Phantasies
> Traverse my indolent and passive Mind
> As wild, as various, as the random Gales
> That swell or flutter on this subject Lute.[2]

What fascinates Coleridge is the coexistence of action and passivity. Ostensibly the mind is focused on itself, reflexive and reflective: 'And tranquil muse upon Tranquillity'. Yet,

[1] 2nd draft: CPW ii. 1022, ll. 17–23.   [2] Ibid.: CPW ii. 1022, ll. 28–35.

like 'this *subject* Lute', it is also an instrument played on by external forces, 'traversed' by thoughts that are as much beyond its control as the wind. Its power, in fact, is not so much indwelling as inbreathed. Coleridge brings a philosophical approach to bear on the paradox. In *Joan of Arc* he had written:

> Infinite myriads of self-conscious minds
> Form one all-conscious Spirit, who directs
> With absolute ubiquity of thought
> All his component monads . . . [1]

Using language no less speculative, he extends the harp image until it too defines the sense in which the individual's consciousness is both autonomous and dependent, both distinct from the mind of God and derived from it:

> And what if All of animated Life
> Be but as Instruments diversly fram'd
> That tremble into thought, while thro' them breathes
> One infinite and intellectual Breeze,
> And all in diff'rent Heights so aptly hung,
> That Murmurs indistinct and Bursts sublime,
> Shrill Discords and most soothing Melodies,
> Harmonious from Creation's vast concent—
> Thus *God* would be the universal Soul,
> Mechaniz'd matter as th'organic harps
> And each one's Tunes be that, which each calls I. [2]

The meeting of Coleridge the poet and Coleridge the thinker has at last taken place—even if what one notices most, at this

---

[1] *Joan of Arc*, ii. 44–7 (*CPW* i. 133, ll. 43–7 and app. crit.); see p. 65, above. Cf. Priestley's *Disquisitions Relating to Matter and Spirit* (2nd edn.), i. 42: 'Nor, indeed, is making the deity to *be*, as well as to *do* every thing, *in this sense*, any thing like the opinion of Spinoza; because I suppose a source of infinite power, and superior intelligence, from which all inferior beings are derived; that every inferior intelligent being has a consciousness distinct from that of the supreme intelligence.'

[2] 2nd draft: *CPW* ii. 1022–3, ll. 36–46. A number of philosophic sources for the harp metaphor have been suggested; see N.P. Stallknecht, *Strange Seas of Thought* (Durham, N.C., 1945), pp. 106–7 for Boehme; C. G. Martin, 'Coleridge and Cudworth: A Source for "The Eolian Harp"', *N & Q* N.S. xiii (1966), 173–6; and, for Priestley, H. W. Piper, ' "The Eolian Harp" Again', *N & Q* N.S. xv (1968), 23–5. Poetic uses of the image that Coleridge would also have known include Darwin's *Botanic Garden*, I. i. 183–6, and Akenside's *Pleasures of Imagination*, i. 109–24—later echoed in the famous passage about the One Life ('O! the one Life, within us and abroad') which first appears in 'The Eolian Harp' with the errata to *Sibylline Leaves* (1817).

stage, is the failure of the two to cohere. 'Mechaniz'd matter' jostles uneasily with the exquisite scents of the bean-field, 'One infinite and intellectual Breeze' with 'wand'ring West winds stoln from Faery land', while the sentimental lute and the organic harp coexist unhappily. The clash of idioms draws attention to a change in seriousness, and Coleridge does his best to pull the poem together by dramatizing the unexpected break with its opening. Sara checks his intellectual daring, and the entire passage—pared down to a mere five lines in the published version—is sloughed off as

> Shapings of the unregen'rate Soul,
> Bubbles, that glitter as they rise and break
> On vain Philosophy's aye-babbling Spring . . . [1]

Coleridge has evolved the philosophic centre of the Conversation Poem, but he is not yet able to handle it.

'Reflections on Entering Active Life' (later retitled 'Reflections on Having Left a Place of Retirement') concerns the tension between the meditative and the active, the private and the political. Published in the *Monthly Magazine* for October 1796, it bore the significant sub-title 'A Poem, which affects not to be POETRY';[2] the Conversation Poem has emerged as a distinct genre in its own right, attempting to capture the quality of internal experience through the unobtrusiveness of its blank verse. As early as 1794, writing to Southey, Coleridge had been uneasy about the cumbrous intellectuality of his poetry: 'I cannot write without a *body* of *thought*—hence my *Poetry* is crowded and sweats beneath a heavy burthen of Ideas and Imagery!'[3] His unease was backed up by criticism from Lamb during 1796. Lamb had been brow-beaten into reading 'Religious Musings' with 'uninterrupted feelings of profound admiration', but he complained guardedly that, although 'noble', it was 'elaborate', and had something 'approachᵍ to tumidity';[4] by late 1796, he was urging openly:

Cultivate simplicity, Coleridge, or rather, I should say, banish elaborateness; for simplicity springs spontaneous from the heart,

---

[1] 2nd draft: *CPW* ii. 1023, ll. 50–2.

[2] '*Sermoni propriora*' in *Poems* (2nd edn., 1797). The label 'Conversation Poem' first appears in *Lyrical Ballads* as the sub-title of 'The Nightingale'.

[3] Griggs, i. 137.   [4] Lucas, i. 10,1,8.

and carries into daylight its own modest buds and genuine, sweet, and clear flowers of expression. I allow no hot-beds in the gardens of Parnassus.[1]

It is Cowper whom Lamb sets up as his model, in contrast to Coleridge's much-admired Bowles: 'I am jealous of your fraternising with Bowles, when I think you relish him more than Burns or my old favourite, Cowper',[2] he wrote, and by the end of 1796 he could rely on Coleridge's agreement: 'I have been reading the "Task" with fresh delight. I am glad you love Cowper. I could forgive a man for not enjoying Milton, but I would not call that man my friend, who should be offended with the "divine chit-chat of Cowper".'[3] Coleridge was not yet calling Cowper 'the best modern poet' as he was by 1798,[4] but it must have been about this time that he began to see *The Task* as relevant to his own poetry. He was rewarded by Lamb's praise: 'The Eolian Harp' had been 'charming', 'most exquisite', but 'Reflections on Entering into Active Life' provoked the comment: 'write thus . . . and I shall never quarrel with you about simplicity'.[5] The poem opens by re-creating the idyll at the start of 'The Eolian Harp'—this time handled with reflective unpretentiousness:

> LOW was our pretty cot: our tallest rose
> Peep'd at the chamber-window. We could hear
> (At silent noon, and eve, and early morn)
> The sea's faint murmur: in the open air
> Our myrtles blossom'd, and across the porch
> Thick jasmines twin'd . . . [6]

Myrtles can blossom and jasmines twine without being 'Meet emblems . . . of Innocence and Love!'[7] Sentimentality is distanced in the Bristol merchant's envy of 'a spot, which you might aptly call/The VALLEY of SECLUSION' ('he paus'd, and look'd . . . And said, *it was a blessed little place*!').[8] Subdued and intimate, Coleridge's writing has a new fidelity to atmosphere; 'The sea's faint murmur' and 'the viewless sky-lark's note' replace

---

[1] Ibid. i. 55–6. For Lamb's criticisms, cf. also George Whalley, *Essays and Studies* (1958), pp. 68–85.
[2] Ibid. i. 73.   [3] Ibid. i. 66.   [4] See Howe, xvii. 120.   [5] Lucas, i. 10, 59.
[6] *Monthly Magazine*, ii (October 1796), 732 (*CPW* i. 106, ll. 1–6).
[7] 'The Eolian Harp', 1st draft: *CPW* ii. 1021, l. 5.
[8] *Monthly Magazine*, ii. 732 (*CPW* i. 106, ll. 8–9, 14–17 and app. crit.)

the fanciful Eolian harp of the earlier 'effusion'. The lark's
song is still a self-conscious metaphor for domestic happiness—

> 'Such, sweet girl!
> Th'inobtrusive song of happiness:
> Unearthly minstrelsy! then only heard
> When the soul seeks to hear: when all is hush'd,
> And the heart listens!'[1]

—but this snatch of dialogue does more than reinforce the
'conversational' frame of reference. As the pastoral exoticism of
'The Eolian Harp' had not, the sense-transference here (' "when
all is hush'd,/And the heart listens!" ') takes one into a world
of inner calm—the 'retirement' that is the poem's theme.

What Coleridge has learned from the deepening and unfolding
movement of his earlier poem is the ability to relate the
particular to the general, the domestic to the metaphysical.
'Reflections on Entering into Active Life' presents this relationship via landscape. The song of happiness, associated with 'The
Valley of Seclusion', gives way to the sense of 'Omnipresence'
aroused by an unlimited vista. Coleridge is working within a
descriptive tradition inherited from Thomson and Cowper. But
the impressive vistas which in *The Seasons* and *The Task* come as
the climax to a reflective, nature-loving walk take on new
meaning: they translate the abstract claims of *Joan of Arc* and
'Religious Musings' into apprehensible reality. Thomson's
'bursting Prospect', with its representative fields and villages
and spiry towns, leads to the horizon not to infinity—

> Meantime you gain the Height, from whose fair Brow
> The bursting Prospect spreads immense around;
> And snatch'd o'er Hill and Dale, and Wood and Lawn,
> And verdant Field, and darkening Heath between,
> And Villages embosom'd soft in Trees,
> And spiry Towns by dusky Columns mark'd
> Of rising Smoak, your Eye excursive roams:
> Wide-stretching from the *Hall*, in whose kind Haunt
> The *Hospitable Genius* harbours still,
> To Where the broken Landskip, by Degrees,
> Ascending, roughens into ridgy Hills;
> O'er which the *Cambrian* Mountains, like far Clouds
> That skirt the blue Horizon, doubtful, rise.[2]

[1] *Monthly Magazine*, ii. 732 (*CPW* i. 107, ll. 22–6).
[2] 'Spring' (1744), ll. 946–58.

—while Cowper's landscape, with its distant ploughman, its winding river and 'fav'rite elms', ends in bathos ('Scenes must be beautiful which daily view'd/Please daily'):

> Here Ouse, slow winding through a level plain
> Of spacious meads with cattle sprinkled o'er,
> Conducts the eye along his sinuous course
> Delighted. There, fast rooted in his bank
> Stand, never overlook'd, our fav'rite elms
> That screen the herdsman's solitary hut;
> While far beyond and overthwart the stream
> That as with molten glass inlays the vale,
> The sloping land recedes into the clouds;
> Displaying on its varied side, the grace
> Of hedge-row beauties numberless, square tow'r,
> Tall spire, from which the sound of chearful bells
> Just undulates upon the list'ning ear;
> Groves, heaths, and smoking villages remote.[1]

At first Coleridge's vista seems just another in this tradition; but landscape has been infused, not simply with the onlooker's feelings, but with transcendental implications entirely lacking in the earlier passages:

> O what a goodly scene! *Here* the bleak mount,
> The bare bleak mountain speckl'd thin with sheep;
> Grey clouds, that shadowing spot the sunny fields;
> And river, now with bushy rocks o'erbrow'd,
> Now winding bright and full with naked banks;
> And seats, and lawns, the abbey, and the wood,
> And cots and hamlets, and faint city-spire:
> The channel *there*, the islands, and white sails,
> Dim coast, and cloudlike hills, and shoreless ocean!
> It seem'd like Omnipresence! God, methought,
> Had built him there a temple! the whole world
> Was *imag'd* in its vast circumference.
> No wish profan'd my overwhelmed heart:
> Blest hour! it was a luxury—*to be*![2]

Like Thomson and Cowper, Coleridge starts with detail and goes on to suggest distance by generalizing: unlike them, he builds into his description religious implications which allow landscape to be expressive of, and finally usurped by, the sense

---

[1] *The Task*, i. 177–8, 154–6. See also p. 109, below.
[2] *Monthly Magazine*, ii. 732 (*CPW* i. 107, ll. 29–42 and app. crit.)

of God. The transcendentalism emerges without strain because description has become a means of evoking response; one reads 'It *seem'd* like Omnipresence!' or 'God, *methought*,/Had built him there a temple!' not as qualifications, but as a reminder of the personal emotion which gives the passage its excitement: 'Blest hour! it was a luxury—*to be*!' The clumsy rhetoric of Coleridge's Miltonics has been translated into the language of subjective experience.

'Reflections of Entering into Active Life' celebrates withdrawal; the secluded idyll of the opening lines gives way only to the greater privacy of communion with God. But—as in 'The Eolian Harp'—Coleridge is forced to discard what he has evoked so well. Having convinced us of their value, he undermines both domestic tranquillity and meditative excitement as the self-indulgence of a visionary. In doing so, he was following William Crowe's 'local' poem, *Lewesdon Hill* (1788). Like 'Frost at Midnight' and 'Tintern Abbey', 'Reflections on Entering into Active Life' uses a literary source to shape a personal problem. Crowe's poem describes a similar mood of 'peaceful contemplation' on the summit of Lewesdon Hill, only to reject retirement as an inadequate response to the urgency of political struggle:

> But conscience, which still censures on our acts,
> That awful voice within us, and the sense
> Of an hereafter, wake and rouse us up
> From such unshaped retirement; which were else
> A blest condition . . .
>
> .   .   .   .
>
> . . . to remove, according to our power,
> The wants and evils of our brother's state,
> 'Tis meet we justle with the world . . . [1]

It was a sentiment which Coleridge's own political views would have made him share. 'Th'inobtrusive song of happiness' is interrupted by the voice of conscience:

> Was it right,
> While my unnumber'd brethren toil'd and bled,

---

[1] *Lewesdon Hill* (Oxford, 1788), pp. 5–6. See also C. G. Martin, 'Coleridge and William Crowe's "Lewesdon Hill"', *MLR* lxii (1967), 400–6. For the similar dependence on literary sources in 'Frost at Midnight' and 'Tintern Abbey', see p. 119 and p. 105–9, below.

> That I should dream away the trusted hours
> On rose-leaf beds, pamp'ring the coward heart
> With feelings all too delicate for use?[1]

Coleridge's public commitment produces a less subtle poetry than the private musing that has gone before, and the poem is divided against itself, denying meditative experience its value. The interplay between public and private results only in the uneasy, regretful compromise of the coda:

> Yet oft when after honourable toil
> Rests the tir'd mind, and waking loves to dream,
> My spirit shall revisit thee, dear cot![2]

Once more, Coleridge has evolved a central feature of the Conversation Poem without being able to use it.

'The Eolian Harp' fails to accommodate its own philosophic statement, 'Reflections on Entering into Active Life' fails to reconcile public and private worlds. But 'This Lime-Tree Bower my Prison' perfectly demonstrates Coleridge's control over his genre. Sent to Southey in a letter of July 1797, it must in some sense have been written for Wordsworth's benefit: its central figure, 'Lam'd by the scathe of fire' and mentally crippled by self-pity, is clearly the Coleridgean equivalent to the brooding recluse of the Yew-tree lines. Coleridge's poem concerns the power of the mind to blight or enrich experience— to make a prison of a lime-tree bower (as the recluse had made his surroundings an emblem of his own sterility), or to transcend self and join in a harmonious natural world. At first we share the 'querulous egotism' of the poet, left behind with his scalded foot while Charles Lamb and the Wordsworths walk on the hills above Stowey:

> Well—they are gone: and here must I remain,
> Lam'd by the scathe of fire, lonely & faint,
> This lime-tree bower my prison. They, meantime,
> My friends, whom I may never meet again,
> On springy heath, along the hill-top edge,
> Wander delighted . . . [3]

Where Wordsworth's poem had outlined only a theoretical remedy for this state of mind, Coleridge enacts it in the change

[1] *Monthly Magazine*, ii. 732 (*CPW* i. 107, ll. 44–8 and app. crit.)
[2] Ibid. ii. 732 (*CPW* i. 108, ll. 63–5).
[3] Griggs, i. 334–5 (*CPW* i. 178–9, ll. 1–8 and app. crit.)

of mood he portrays. As in 'The Ancient Mariner', a moment of imaginative participation in another's joy brings about this change. Like the landscape in 'Reflections on Entering into Active Life', the scene here plays a key part in relating the individual to the spiritual world. This time, however, the transcendental experience is attributed to someone else—to Charles Lamb, an appropriate *alter ego* as the Wordsworth of 1797 was not. Like Coleridge himself, he has 'hunger'd after Nature many a year/In the great City pent': unlike Coleridge, he has suffered 'evil & pain/And strange calamity' without losing his Christian resignation; his soul remains 'sad yet bowed'.[1] Moreover, he too is a Unitarian. The reminiscence of *Joan of Arc*, where God—'Heaven's eternal Sun'—is 'Effulgent, as thro' clouds that veil his blaze',[2] reveals the excitement of Lamb's experience to be doctrinal in origin ('You remember, I am a *Berkleian*'):

> Ah slowly sink
> Behind the western ridge; thou glorious Sun!
> Shine in the slant beams of the sinking orb,
> Ye purple Heath-flowers! Richlier burn, ye Clouds!
> Live in the yellow Light, ye distant Groves!
> And kindle, thou blue Ocean! So my friend
> Struck with joy's deepest calm, and gazing round
> On the wide view, may gaze till all doth seem
> Less gross than bodily, a living Thing
> That acts upon the mind, and with such hues
> As cloathe the Almighty Spirit, when he makes
> Spirits perceive His presence![3]

The opening lines of description are crudely impressive, their function not so much to describe as to suggest the underlying significance of the landscape: 'So my friend/Struck with joy's deepest calm . . . ' To the recluse of the Yew-tree lines, landscape contained only beauty; however responsive, the gazing onlooker remained isolated. But for Lamb, gazing discloses 'a living Thing/That acts upon the mind'. What he experiences is a moment of communion, of interaction between God and

---

[1] Griggs, i. 335 (*CPW* i. 179, ll. 29–32 and app. crit.). The reference is to Lamb's private tragedy—Mary Lamb's insanity and manslaughter of her mother in 1796
[2] *Joan of Arc*, ii. 28, 18 (*CPW* i. 132, ll. 26 and app. crit., 17).
[3] Griggs, i. 335 (*CPW* i. 179–80, ll. 32–43 and app. crit.)

the self: 'The whole ONE SELF! SELF, that no alien knows!'[1]

The vision which Coleridge was able to offer Wordsworth is subtly implied in the perceiving consciousness of the poem. Within the dramatic framework of 'This Lime-Tree Bower my Prison', Lamb's experience has meant for the alienated poet a moment of self-forgetful response:

> A Delight
> Comes sudden on my heart, and I am glad
> As I myself were there![2]

Earlier, closely-observed natural description had been associated with Lamb and the Wordsworths on their walk, looking down (in Coleridge's imagination) on the 'rifted Dell . . . Whose plumy ferns for ever nod and drip/Spray'd by the waterfall'.[3] Now Coleridge for the first time 'sees' his own lime-tree bower—no longer a prison—and the description very beautifully authenticates his renewed sense of harmony:

> Nor in this bower
> Want I sweet sounds or pleasing shapes. I watch'd
> The sunshine of each broad transparent Leaf
> Broke by the shadows of the Leaf or Stem,
> Which hung above it: and that Wall-nut Tree
> Was richly ting'd: and a deep radiance lay
> Full on the ancient ivy which usurps
> Those fronting elms . . . [4]

The glory of Lamb's sunset is reflected in Coleridge's bower. The changing light and the lovingly traced details of leaf and stem convince, as nothing else could, that the poem's development of mood is organic rather than imposed. Not that it is without explicit didacticism. On the contrary, Coleridge is at pains to state his moral: 'Henceforth I shall know/That nature ne'er deserts the wise & pure.' ' 'Tis well', he adds,

> to be bereav'd of promis'd good
> That we may lift the soul, & contemplate
> With lively joy the joys, we cannot share.[5]

[1] 'Religious Musings', l. 174 (*CPW* i. 115, l. 154).
[2] Griggs, i. 335 (*CPW* i. 180, ll. 43–5).
[3] Ibid. i. 335 (*CPW* i. 179, ll. 9–16, 178 app. crit.)
[4] Ibid. i. 335 (*CPW* i. 180, ll. 45–54 and app. crit.)
[5] Ibid. i. 336 (*CPW* i. 181, ll. 59–60, 65–7).

Nature becomes a potentially moral force in its own right, and the negative exhortation of the Yew-tree lines is transformed into a positive claim for the value of emotional identification. The closing lines skilfully blend dramatic and symbolic elements with Coleridge's underlying moral purpose:

> My Sister & my Friends! when the last Rook
> Beat it's straight path along the dusky air
> Homewards, I bless'd it; deeming, it's black wing
> Cross'd, like a speck, the blaze of setting day,
> While ye stood gazing; or when all was still,
> Flew creaking o'er your heads, & had a charm
> For you, my Sister & my Friends! to whom
> No sound is dissonant, which tells of Life![1]

The affirmation is that of 'The Ancient Mariner'. Like the water-snakes, the creaking rook is grotesque; its beauty comes from the onlooker's sense of its participation in a harmonious universe—the universe to which he too belongs. In blessing it, Coleridge makes himself one with the shared joy from which he had felt excluded at the start of the poem. The final line—'No sound is dissonant, which tells of Life!'—is triumphantly inclusive.

This, then, is what Coleridge could offer Wordsworth in the summer of 1797. His work on the incomplete *Osorio*[2]—like Wordsworth's play, concerned with guilt and isolation—would have emphasized the doctrinal lesson; two excerpts later included in *Lyrical Ballads* as 'The Dungeon' and 'The Foster-Mother's Tale', and presumably written during the summer, show Coleridge going out of his way to preach a religion of nature. Like 'This Lime-Tree Bower my Prison', 'The Dungeon' treats the subject of an earlier poem by Wordsworth from a Coleridgean standpoint. In 'The Convict' of 1796, Wordsworth had attacked the penal system and advocated transportation as an alternative to prison ('My care, if the arm of the mighty were mine,/Would plant thee where yet thou might'st

[1] Griggs, i. 336 (*CPW* i. 181, ll. 68–76 and app. crit.)

[2] Two and a half acts of *Osorio* had been read to Wordsworth in June 1797 (see *EY*, p. 189). Coleridge was at work on it during August, and in September he took it 'finished to the middle of the 5th act' to Bowles (see Griggs, i. 344–5 and *EY*, p. 192). For some of the issues it deals with, see A. B. Fox, 'Political and Biographical Background of Coleridge's *Osorio*', *JEGP* lxi (1962), 258–67.

blossom again').[1] Coleridge begins by restating Wordsworth's lurid account of the convict's condition, but the solution he then offers is his own—not Botany Bay, but nature:

> With other ministrations thou, O nature!
> Healest thy wandering and distempered child:
> Thou pourest on him thy soft influences,
> Thy sunny hues, fair forms, and breathing sweets,
> Thy melodies of woods, and winds, and waters,
> Till he relent, and can no more endure
> To be a jarring and a dissonant thing,
> Amid this general dance and minstrelsy . . .   (ll. 20–7)[2]

The beautiful, and very Wordsworthian line, 'Thy melodies of woods, and winds, and waters', implies once more the metaphor of musical harmony; and like the poet in 'This Lime-Tree Bower my Prison', the convict 'wins back his way,/His angry spirit healed and harmonized' (ll. 28–9) through the ministry of nature. *Osorio* concerns in part the revolt of a Moorish minority against an inquisitorial Catholic church, and the theme of religious oppression is developed in 'The Foster-Mother's Tale' —the story of a changeling child who comes from nature and finally returns to it. He grows up 'most unteachable',

> And never learnt a prayer, nor told a bead,
> But knew the names of birds, and mocked their notes,
> And whistled, as he were a bird himself . . .   (ll. 30–2)

'Though he prayed,' we are told, 'he never loved to pray/With holy men, nor in a holy place' (ll. 45–6). His unorthodoxy leads to persecution, and the tale ends with his flight into a life of primitive freedom in the New World. Like the Moors, whose beliefs are represented as a kind of nature worship,[3] and like

---

[1] DC MS. 2: *PW* i. 314, ll. 51–2. The MS. reads 'army' for 'arm'. 'The Convict' was published in the *Morning Post* for 14 December 1797, presumably to help fulfil Coleridge's arrangement with Stuart (see Griggs, i. 359–60n.).

[2] Cf. Cowper's prisoner, released to nature from 'some unwholesome dungeon' ('He walks, he leaps, he runs—is wing'd with joy,/And riots in the sweets of ev'ry breeze', *The Task*, i. 443–4), and Young's 'peevish, dissonant, rebellious String,/Which jars in the grand Chorus', *The Complaint: Or, Night-Thoughts on Life, Death, & Immortality*, 'The Consolation [Night the Ninth]' (London, 1745), p. 19.

[3] Cf. the virtuous Moor, duped by the villain, who 'worships Nature in the hill and valley,/Not knowing what he loves, but loves it all!' (*Osorio*, i. 245–6: *CPW* ii. 529).

the hero of the play, who hears 'The voice of that Almighty One, who lov'd us,/In every gale that breath'd',[1] the changeling is the product of Coleridge's own Christian-based nature religion. It was this religion to which Wordsworth—hitherto 'at least a *Semi*-atheist'[2]—became a convert between 1797 and 1798.

[1] *Osorio*, i. 291–2: *CPW* ii. 577.
[2] Griggs, i. 216.

IV *The Lyric Voice of Spring 1798*

WRITING to his brother George in March 1798, Coleridge quotes not his own poetry—as he had done in a similar context the previous October—but his friend's. It is his own thinking, however, that the lines reflect. Wordsworth has now accepted fully the Coleridgean solution to the problem explored nine months before in the Yew-tree lines:

I love fields & woods & mounta[ins] with almost a visionary fondness —and because I have found benevolence & quietness growing within me as that fondness [has] increased, therefore I should wish to be the means of implanting it in others—& to destroy the bad passions not by combating them, but by keeping them in inaction.

> Not useless do I deem
> These shadowy Sympathies with things that hold
> An inarticulate Language: for the Man
> Once taught to love such objects, as excite
> No morbid passions, no disquietude,
> No vengeance & no hatred, needs must feel
> The Joy of that pure principle of Love
> So deeply, that, unsatisfied with aught
> Less pure & exquisite, he cannot chuse
> But seek for objects of a kindred Love
> In fellow natures, & a kindred Joy.
> Accordingly, he by degrees perceives
> His feelings of aversion softened down,
> A holy tenderness pervade his frame!
> His sanity of reason not impair'd,
> Say rather that his thoughts now flowing clear
> From a clear fountain flowing, he looks round—
> He seeks for Good & finds the Good he seeks.
> Wordsworth.—[1]

Not, perhaps, great poetry—but a measure of the thoroughness with which Wordsworth has absorbed Coleridge's ideas. He is

---

[1] Griggs, i. 397–8. The passage corresponds to the 'Addendum' to MS. B of 'The Ruined Cottage' (*PW* v. 400–1, ll. 1–18).

now a moralist and visionary with a need to preach that equals Coleridge's. The passage here forms the draft conclusion to 'The Ruined Cottage'—by this stage comprising not only the story of Margaret, but an idealized biography describing the Pedlar's education by nature. Wordsworth's own new-found belief in the One Life is attributed to his narrator. A central feature of this doctrinal blank verse is its certainty; that a feeling for the natural world must change and improve the individual is asserted as inexorable logic. The lyric poetry of spring 1798, and, later, 'Tintern Abbey', grow out of such writing. The difference is that Wordsworth's certainty has been qualified by a personal, even domestic, context. Still fervent, still basically didactic, Wordsworth gives subjective colouring to the doctrine which he elsewhere states with the absoluteness of a recent convert. In the process, he discovers the personal voice which is to be central to his poetry. The lyrics are as doctrinal as the blank verse that lies behind them; but they express, not so much Wordsworth's beliefs, as the mood in which he felt 'The Joy of that pure principle of Love/So deeply . . . '

I. THE LYRIC BACKGROUND

Wordsworth's discovery of a personal voice in the lyrics of spring 1798—a voice at once earnest and playful, thoughtful and uncalculated—is accentuated by contrast with his earlier lyric writing. 'Lines written near Richmond, upon the Thames, at Evening', copied into Cottle's manuscript book in March 1797[1] and included in *Lyrical Ballads* alongside the lyrics of 1798, could hardly be more different. Anonymous and polished, the lines depend for their effect on the reader's recognition of source and allusion. They go back to Wordsworth's undergraduate years, originating in a sonnet draft written under the influence of Bowles's *Fourteen Sonnets* (1789), to which Wordsworth had responded with the same enthusiasm as the schoolboy Coleridge ('My earliest acquaintances will not have forgotten the undisciplined eagerness and impetuous zeal, with which I laboured to make proselytes').[2] In retrospect, Bowles's influence on the

[1] See G. H. Healey, *The Cornell Wordsworth Collection* (Ithaca, N.Y., 1957), facing p. 400.
[2] Shawcross, i. 9. Wordsworth had bought Bowles's sonnets during the Christmas vacation of 1789–90; see *Recollections of the Table-Talk of Samuel Rogers*, ed.

1790s seemed disproportionate even to Coleridge,[1] but he transformed late-eighteenth-century sensibility, with its taste for picturesque landscape, into a vein of plaintive, moralized elegy which had a special appeal to his contemporaries.[2] Coleridge was later to link him with Cowper as the poet of natural feeling—'the first who combined natural thoughts with natural diction; the first who reconciled the heart with the head';[3] but it must have been chiefly his sadness that made him popular: 'MY heart has thank'd thee, BOWLES! for those soft strains/Whose sadness soothes me,'[4] wrote Coleridge in the mid-1790s, and when he thought of dedicating his next volume of poems to Bowles, Lamb gently satirized the impulse:

Genius of the sacred fountain of tears, it was he who led you gently by the hand through all this valley of weeping, showed you the dark green yew trees and the willow shades where, by the fall of waters, you might indulge an uncomplaining melancholy, a delicious regret for the past, or weave fine visions of that awful future,

> When all the vanities of life's brief day
> Oblivion's hurrying hand hath swept away . . . [5]

Byron was later to call Bowles 'The maudlin Prince of mournful sonneteers'.[6] In 1796, when Coleridge compiled a selection of his favourite sonnets to be bound with Bowles's, he singled out their most affecting traits:

Alexander Dyce (London, 1856), p. 258n., and Mary Moorman, *William Words-worth: A Biography*, pp. 124–5. Other poems showing Bowles's influence are 'Written in very early Youth', 'When slow from pensive twilight's latest gleams', and 'Sweet was the walk along the narrow lane' (see Reed, pp. 305–6).

[1] Ibid. i. 15. For Bowles's influence on Coleridge, see Lucyle Werkmeister, 'Coleridge, Bowles, and "Feelings of the Heart"' ', *Anglia*, lxxviii (1960), 55–73.

[2] See G. S. Fayen, 'The Pencil and the Harp of William Lisle Bowles', *MLQ* xxi (1960), 301–14 for an interesting discussion of the basis of Bowles's contemporary success.

[3] Shawcross, i. 16. In a letter of 1796, Coleridge also calls Bowles 'the most tender, and, with the exception of Burns, the only *always-natural* poet in our Language' (Griggs, i. 278).

[4] 'Effusion I', *Poems on Various Subjects* (1796), p. 45 (*CPW* i. 85, ll. 1–2). This is a later version of the sonnet originally published in the *Morning Post* for 26 December 1794.

[5] 14 November 1796 (Lucas, i. 56–7). The quotation approximates to some lines from Bowles's *Verses to John Howard, F.R.S. on his State of Prisons and Lazarettos* (1789).

[6] *English Bards and Scotch Reviewers* (London, 1809), l. 214.

those Sonnets appear to me the most exquisite, in which moral Sentiments, Affections, or Feelings, are deduced from, and associated with, the scenery of Nature. Such compositions . . . create a sweet and indissoluble union between the intellectual and the material world. . . . Hence, the Sonnets of BOWLES derive their marked superiority over all other Sonnets; hence they domesticate with the heart, and become, as it were, a part of our identity.[1]

The distinctiveness of Bowles's sonnets lay not only in their accessibility ('they domesticate with the heart'), or their power to arouse sympathetic identification ('become, as it were, a part of our identity'), but in their characteristic use of *paysage moralisé*.

By 1802, Coleridge had become impatient with this

perpetual trick of *moralizing* every thing—which is very well, occasionally—but never to see or describe any interesting appearance in nature, without connecting it by dim analogies with the moral world, proves faintness of Impression. . . . A Poet's *Heart* & *Intellect* should be *combined*, *intimately* combined & *unified*, with the great appearances in Nature—& not merely held in solution & loose mixture with them, in the shape of formal Similies—[2]

'Bowles has indeed the *sensibility* of a poet; but he has not the *Passion* of a great Poet,' he concluded, implicitly contrasting him with Wordsworth. In the early 1790s, however, Bowles's meditative-descriptive technique had been imitated by Wordsworth himself. The early draft for 'Lines written near Richmond' recasts the picturesque descriptions of *An Evening Walk* in the manner of *Fourteen Sonnets*:

> How rich in front with twilight's tinge impressed
> Between the dim-brown forms impending high
> Of shadowy forests slowly sweeping by

---

[1] Preface to Coleridge's untitled selection of sonnets, bound up with Bowles's *Sonnets, and Other Poems* (4th edn., Bath, 1796), p. [1]; Dyce Collection, Victoria and Albert Museum (*CPW* ii. 1139).

[2] To William Sotheby, 10 September 1802; Griggs, ii. 864. See the discussion of Bowles's sonnet formula and Coleridge's changing views by M. H. Abrams, 'Wordsworth and Coleridge on Diction and Figures', *English Institute Essays: 1952* (New York, 1954), pp. 193–6, and again in 'Structure and Style in the Greater Romantic Lyric', *From Sensibility to Romanticism*, pp. 539–44, as well as W. K. Wimsatt in 'The Structure of Romantic Nature Imagery', *The Verbal Icon* (Lexington, Ky., 1954), pp. 105–10. Cf. also Coleridge's parody ('for, ah! how soon/Eve darkens into night') in the first of his 'Nehemiah Higginbottom' sonnets in the *Monthly Magazine* for November 1797 (*CPW* i. 210, ll. 3–4).

Glows the still wave, while facing the red west
The silent boat her magic path pursues,
Nor heeds how dark the backward wave the while
Some dreaming loiterer with perfidious smile
Alluring onward: such the fairy views
In [   ] colouring clad that smile before
The poet thoughtless of the following shad[es]
Witness that Son of grief who in these glades
Mourned his dead friend—suspend the dashing oar[1]

The Fenwick Note tells us that the sonnet was based on first-
hand observation—'It was during a solitary walk on the banks
of the Cam that I was first struck with this appearance, &
applied it to my own feelings . . .'[2] But the application was
second-hand. The characteristic shift from landscape to sententiousness (from the darkening scene to life, from boatman to
poet) betrays Bowles's influence. The same use of picturesque
description—this time as a simile for illusory hope—occurs in
Fourteen Sonnets:

EVENING, as slow thy placid shades descend,
    Veiling with gentlest hush the landscape still,
    The lonely battlement, and farthest hill
And wood; I think of those that have no friend;
    Who now perhaps, by melancholy led,
From the broad blaze of day, where pleasure flaunts,
Retiring, wander 'mid thy lonely haunts
    Unseen; and mark the tints that o'er thy bed
Hang lovely, oft to musing fancy's eye
    Presenting fairy vales, where the tir'd mind
    Might rest, beyond the murmurs of mankind,
Nor hear the hourly moans of misery.
    Ah! beauteous views, that hope's fair gleams the while,
    Should smile like you, and perish as they smile![3]

The sonnet depends on a trick: pensiveness is evoked through
description, then transferred from landscape to the human
scene; responding to the picturesque, we find ourselves responding to a generalization about life. Self-regarding suffering
is disguised in the sententiousness of the final couplet. This
'perpetual trick of *moralizing* every thing' is precisely what

---

[1] DC MS. 11.   [2] *PW* i. 324.
[3] 'Sonnet VI', *Fourteen Sonnets, Elegiac and Descriptive* (Bath, 1789), p. 15.

Wordsworth's draft picks up, relying on the reader's recognition not so much of a shared emotion as of a fashionable mannerism.[1]

When Wordsworth came to rewrite his sonnet draft in the mid-1790s, he made it more literary, not less. The closing lines ('Witness that Son of grief who in these glades/Mourned his dead friend—suspend the dashing oar') had already referred to Collins's *Ode Occasion'd by the Death of Mr. Thomson*:

> REMEMBRANCE oft shall haunt the Shore
>   When THAMES in Summer-wreaths is drest,
> And oft suspend the dashing Oar
>   To bid his gentle Spirit rest[2]

Collins is one of the many poets echoed in *An Evening Walk*, and it is not surprising that Wordsworth should have invoked him at this stage; what is surprising is that as late as 1796 or 1797 he should choose to rewrite his sonnet almost entirely in terms of his earlier allusion. The poem's new title invokes the 'Advertisement' to Collins's *Ode* ('THE Scene of the following STANZAS is suppos'd to lie on the *Thames* near *Richmond*'),[3] and the poet

> Who, pouring here a *later* ditty,
>   Could find no refuge from distress,
> But in the milder grief of pity.   (ll. 30–2)

is identified in a footnote as Collins, lamenting Thomson. Wordsworth's evasion of his own poetic identity is total. But at least Collins provides a worth-while model:

> IN yonder Grave a DRUID lies
>   Where slowly winds the stealing Wave!
> The *Year*'s best Sweets shall duteous rise
>   To deck *it's* POET's sylvan Grave!
>
> In yon deep Bed of whisp'ring Reeds
>   His airy Harp shall now be laid,
> That He, whose Heart in Sorrow bleeds
>   May love thro' Life the soothing Shade.[4]

---

[1] Wordsworth's first published poem, 'Sonnet, on Seeing Miss Helen Maria Williams Weep at a Tale of Distress', in the *European Magazine*, xi (March 1787), 202, shows a similar reliance on its association with a fashionable contemporary; Helen Maria Williams is celebrated by crudely exaggerating the terms of her own poetry.

[2] ll. 13–16, *Ode Occasion'd by the Death of Mr. Thomson* (London, 1749), p. 6.

[3] Ibid., p. [4].

[4] ll. 1–8, ibid., p. 5.

The setting of Thomson's grave—its stealing wave and whispering reeds—becomes emblematic; Thomson, nature's own poet-priest, is surrounded in death by the symbols and the subject of his poetry.[1] The literary allusion preserves an elegiac freshness in the midst of its classicism. Wordsworth's response to the *Ode* is implied by his rejection of Bowles's cloying self-pity. Collins becomes the type of poet mourning for poet (rather than himself), and instead of lamenting the poet's illusions Wordsworth is now prepared to celebrate them:

> —And let him nurse his fond deceit,
> And what if he must die in sorrow!
> Who would not cherish dreams so sweet,
> Though grief and pain may come tomorrow?
>
> (ll. 13–16)

The later version is affirmative as well as elegiac, and the lacerated soul of Bowles's poet-self gives way to an image of calm and permanence:

> Oh glide, fair stream! for ever so;
> Thy quiet soul on all bestowing,
> 'Till all our minds for ever flow
> As thy deep waters now are flowing.
>
> Vain thought! yet be as now thou art,
> That in thy waters may be seen
> The image of a poet's heart,
> How bright, how solemn, how serene!   (ll. 21–8)[2]

Wordsworth is saying more than he had done in the original draft, and saying it more effectively; yet for all its accomplishment, one senses a void at the heart of the poem. By choosing to invoke the grief of an earlier poet, he has once more side-stepped his individual situation:

---

[1] The reeds invoke the Aeolian harp of *The Castle of Indolence*, the sweets of the changing year, *The Seasons*. For Thomson's significance as poet–priest ('druid'), see J. M. S. Tompkins, 'In Yonder Grave a Druid Lies', *RES* xxii (1946), 1–16.

[2] Wordsworth has increased the allusiveness by recollecting the famous lines from Denham's *Coopers Hill* (new edn., London, 1655), p. 10, where the Thames is similarly invoked: 'O could I flow like thee, and make thy streame/My great example, as it is my theme . . .'; see *Lyrical Ballads 1798*, ed. W. J. B. Owen (London, 1967), addenda.

> Remembrance! as we glide along,
> For him suspend the dashing oar,
> And pray that never child of Song
> May know his freezing sorrows more.   (ll. 33–6)

Whether under the influence of Bowles or Collins, Wordsworth had projected himself as a poet, and a poet within a tradition. By 1798, he has come to think of himself as 'a man speaking to men'. Instead of invoking his forerunners, Wordsworth dramatizes his own feelings, in his own voice. But as Coleridge reveals when he calls Bowles and Cowper 'the first who combined natural thoughts with natural diction', the poet of the 1790s had to be shown how to write naturally. If Cowper is the most important influence on the blank verse of the Conversation Poem and 'Tintern Abbey', Burns must be the most important influence on Wordsworth's lyric writing. What he provided was not so much specific source-material as an approach to poetry. His stance in the preface to the Kilmarnock edition is a fashionable one—

THE following trifles are not the production of the Poet, who, with all the advantages of learned art, and perhaps amid the elegancies and idlenesses of upper life, looks down for a rural theme, with an eye to Theocrites or Virgil. . . . Unacquainted with the necessary requisites for commencing Poet by rule, he sings the sentiments and manners, he felt and saw in himself and his rustic compeers around him, in his and their native language.[1]

—but the freshness, energy, and lack of condescension in the poetry itself justify his claims. Though not in any genuine sense a ploughman poet, he is (or becomes) a man speaking to men. Wordsworth himself writes perceptively about the irrelevance of biographical fact to Burns:

Neither the subjects of his poems, nor his manner of handling them, allow us long to forget their author. On the basis of his human character he has reared a poetic one, which with more or less distinctness presents itself to view in almost every part of his earlier, and, in my estimation, his most valuable verses. This poetic fabric, dug out of the quarry of genuine humanity, is airy and spiritual:— and though the materials, in some parts, are coarse, and the disposition is often fantastic and irregular, yet the whole is agreeable and

---

[1] *Poems, Chiefly in the Scottish Dialect* (Kilmarnock, 1786), p. iii.

strikingly attractive. Plague, then, upon your remorseless hunters after matter of fact . . . [1]

This belongs to 1816; but Wordsworth's awareness that a poetic self had to be created rather than revealed must go back to 1798, when the Pedlar, 'His eye/Flashing poetic fire', repeats the songs of Burns,[2] and when 'The Ruined Cottage' takes its epigraph from Burns's 'Epistle to J. L. *****k, An Old Scotch Bard':

> Gie me ae spark o'Nature's fire,
> That's a' the learning I desire;
> Then tho' I drudge thro' dub an' mire
>   At pleugh or cart,
> My Muse, tho' hamely in attire,
>   May touch the heart.[3]

With its lack of self-consciousness and its emphasis on ordinary feeling, the epistle states Burns's aims far more persuasively than the Kilmarnock preface:

> I am nae *Poet*, in a sense,
> But just a *Rhymer* like by chance,
> An' hae to Learning nae pretence,
>   Yet, what the matter?
> Whene'er my Muse does on me glance,
>   I jingle at her.[4]

Poetry like this derives its energy from the rhythms and tones of colloquial speech. As Wordsworth was to do in 1798, Burns arrived at his poetic self by rejecting a literary idiom for a spoken one. He was helped, where Wordsworth was not, by dialect; but in his poetry the voice is never merely local.

Burns uses a lyric context to assert his central value—humanity. Wordsworth goes much further; his lyric writing is essentially doctrinal, and in this it owes something to the hymns of an evangelical period. The same hymn-writing

---

[1] *A Letter to a Friend of Robert Burns*, 1816 (*Prose Works*, iii. 123).

[2] 'The Ruined Cottage', MS. B: *PW* v. 387–8, ll. 266–8. Cf. also the allusion to the 'trottin burn' of 'To W. S****n, Ochiltree', *PW* v. 395, l. 550.

[3] ll. 73–8, *Poems, Chiefly in the Scottish Dialect*, p. 199 (see *PW* v. 379). By this time Burns had taken his place beside Cowper in Coleridge's estimation; see R. S. Woof, 'Coleridge and Thomasina Dennis', *UTQ* xxxii (1962–3), 39. Cf. also Wordsworth's later tribute to Burns and Cowper (*PW* iii. 442).

[4] ll. 49–54, ibid., p. 198.

tradition which Blake transformed in *Songs of Innocence* and *Songs of Experience* (1789 and 1794)[1] emerges—with less emphasis on the gap between religion and reality, but still with a bias towards parody—in Wordsworth's lyric writing of spring 1798. Watts's *Divine Songs, Attempted in Easy Language for the Use of Children* (1715) had been so often reprinted and anthologized during the eighteenth century as to become part of a common heritage, and for all their threatening morality they played an important part in creating a popular devotional idiom. The impulse towards the vernacular is explicit in Watts's versions of the *Psalms of David* (1719), where the alien rituals and obscure allusions of Jewish poetry become accessible to the ordinary worshipper:

if it should appear that I have aimed at the *Sublime*, yet I have generally kept within the Reach of an unlearned Reader: I never thought the Art of sublime Writing consisted in flying out of Sight; nor am I of the Mind of the *Italian*, who said, *Obscurity begets Greatness*. I have always avoided the Language of the Poets where it did not suit the Language of the Gospel.

IN many of these Composures I have just permitted my Verse to rise above a Flat and indolent Style; yet I hope it is every where supported above the just Contempt of the Criticks; tho' I am sensible that I have often subdu'd it below their Esteem; because I would neither indulge any bold Metaphors, nor admit of hard Words, nor tempt an ignorant Worshipper to sing without his Understanding.[2]

With this insistence on popular worship goes Watts's attempt to recapture the original impulse of the psalms—spontaneous devotional enthusiasm: 'Let us remember that the very Power of *Singing* was given to human Nature chiefly for this purpose, that our warmest Affections of Soul might break out into natural or divine Melody, and the Tongue of the Worshipper express his own Heart.'[3] Watts's child sings of divine power in terms of the world he knows, his praise rooted in his own experience:

---

[1] See John Holloway, *Blake: The Lyric Poetry*, Studies in English Literature, No. 34 (London, 1968), pp. 37–52.

[2] *The Psalms of David Imitated in the Language of the New Testament* (London, 1719), pp. xxv–vi.

[3] Ibid., p. xii.

I Sing th'Almighty Power of God,
    That made the Mountains rise,
  That spread the flowing Seas abroad,
    And built the lofty Skies.

.   .   .   .

Lord, how thy Wonders are display'd
    Where'er I turn mine Eye,
If I survey the Ground I tread,
    Or gaze upon the Sky.

There's not a Plant or Flower below
    But makes thy Glories known . . . [1]

Wordsworth's celebration of nature relies on the same heartfelt simplicity, but Watts's evangelical fervour has been replaced by doctrine of a more personal and subtly imagined kind. What both poets share is their concern to make belief accessible —to carry it out of the church or the book and into the heart.

II. THE LYRICS OF SPRING 1798

Wordsworth's lyric writing of spring 1798 reflects the doctrines of his philosophic blank verse. The difference lies in the quality of belief. 'The Pedlar' lacks human interest, above all. Its central figure exists to make a theoretical point, and he is deliberately isolated from the ordinary world in order to accentuate his experience of nature—at times terrifying, grand, impersonal; at times animated by the ebb and flow of the creative imagination; at times benign, transformed, harmonious. Wordsworth is concerned, not so much with the Pedlar himself, as with the momentousness of his vision, through which he makes his claims for the One Life. Structurally, 'The Pedlar' focuses on two climactic passages—ecstatic encounters with landscape which have behind them the vistas of 'Reflections on Entering into Active Life' and 'This Lime-Tree Bower my Prison'. The first of these describes, quite unequivocally, a moment of mystical communion:

                      He looked,
            The Ocean and the earth beneath him lay
            In gladness and deep joy. The clouds were touched

[1] 'Praise for Creation and Providence', *Divine Songs Attempted in Easy Language for the Use of Children* (London, 1715), pp. 2–3.

> And in their silent faces did he read
> Unutterable love. Sound needed none
> Nor any voice of joy: his spirit drank
> The spectacle. Sensation, soul and form
> All melted into him. They swallowed up
> His animal being. In them did he live
> And by them did he live. They were his life.
> *In such access of mind*, in such high hour
> Of visitation from the living God
> He did not feel the God: he felt his works.
> Thought was not. In enjoyment it expired.
> Such hour by prayer or praise was unprofaned,
> He neither prayed, nor offered thanks or praise,
> His mind was a thanksgiving to the power
> That made him. It was blessedness & love.[1]

The experience is at once reciprocal and subsumed into the Pedlar's unified and unifying consciousness. On one hand 'his spirit drank/The spectacle'; on the other, response ('sensation'), the responding spirit ('soul'), and landscape ('form'), all fuse. The spirit drinks but 'they' swallow him up. We are specifically told that 'Thought was not', that the hour, though a 'visitation from the living God', is 'unprofaned' by prayer or praise; for all its rhetorical excitement the passage is carefully argued— Wordsworth is describing the apotheosis of response, a moment in which the mind *is* what it communes with, and therefore has no need of communion as such. Syntax and language work towards defining an experienced unity in ocean and earth, sky and onlooker, with Christian associations ('the living God', 'blessedness & love') deployed so as to transform sensation into religious experience. Such writing has to be called mystical, but the perceived world is in no way obliterated or transcended. On the contrary, it is triumphantly omnipresent. One expects Wordsworth to exclaim as Coleridge had done in 'Reflections on Entering into Active Life': 'Blest hour! it was a luxury—*to be*!'

The second great climax of 'The Pedlar' contains Words-worth's most explicitly liturgical statement of belief:

---

[1] MS. B: *PW* v. 382, ll. 124–41. See also the valuable discussion of this passage by John Jones in *The Egotistical Sublime*, pp. 81–3, and for an extended discussion of 'The Pedlar' as a whole, Jonathan Wordsworth, *The Music of Humanity*, pp. 233–41.

with bliss ineffable
He felt the sentiment of being, spread
O'er all that moves, & all that seemeth still,
O'er all, which lost beyond the reach of thought,
And human knowledge, to the human eye
Invisible, yet liveth to the heart;
O'er all that leaps, & runs, & shouts, & sings,
Or beats the gladsome air, o'er all that glides
Beneath the wave, yea in the wave itself
And mighty depth of waters. Wonder not
If such his transports were; for in all things
He saw one life, & felt that it was joy.
One song they sang . . . [1]

Subjectively presented, the intuition derives its authority from psalmic rhythms and phrasing. But Wordsworth's rhetoric is subtle as well as powerful. The opposition between 'all that moves' and 'all that seemeth still' is a false one; Wordsworth has slipped in the suggestion that nothing is still ('seemeth'), that all things live. He goes on to support it by appealing not to the mind or the eye, but to the heart; and the tension syntactically prolonged between 'O'er all, which . . . liveth to the heart' evokes an insight at once deep and simple, far-seeing and obvious. By the time we reach the incantatory line, 'O'er all that leaps, & runs, & shouts, & sings', we are no longer questioning; and the emphatic repetitions of 'Beneath the wave, yea in the wave itself/And mighty depth of waters' act as a metaphor for belief (so deep, so all-embracing), not just an allusion to fish. The lines celebrate the Pedlar's individual insight—'in all things/He saw one life, & felt that it was joy'— in a way that makes it impossible for the reader to remain detached. The proselytizing impulse behind 'The Pedlar' inevitably limits its appeal, and to some extent its lasting relevance; although Wordsworth himself was never to reject it, the One Life plays a smaller and smaller part in his poetry. But his insistent, highly wrought claims are a remarkable achievement in their own right, and their fervour underlies the lyrics of the following months.

For all that it is rooted in one man's response and intuition, the Pedlar's visionary experience remains oddly impersonal.

---

[1] Ibid.: *PW* v. 385, ll. 241–53.

The lyrics are both more subdued and more immediate, their tone not simply intimate but domestic too—'Lines written at a small distance from my House' are 'sent by my little Boy' to 'my sister', and the family eats breakfast, does housework, puts on outdoor clothes like any other. Wordsworth's theme is the flouting of domestic routine by an impulsive response to the season:

> It is the first mild day of March:
> Each minute sweeter than before,
> The red-breast sings from the tall larch
> That stands beside our door.
>
> There is a blessing in the air,
> Which seems a sense of joy to yield
> To the bare trees, and mountains bare,
> And grass in the green field.
>
> My Sister! ('tis a wish of mine)
> Now that our morning meal is done,
> Make haste, your morning task resign;
> Come forth and feel the sun.
>
> Edward will come with you, and pray,
> Put on with speed your woodland dress,
> And bring no book, for this one day
> We'll give to idleness.   (ll. 1–16)

Charm and freshness are new qualities in Wordsworth's writing. These opening stanzas, with their urgency and ordinariness, colour the claims that follow. The generalized landscapes of 'The Pedlar' (ocean, cloud, sun) have become particular; the Pedlar, one feels, would have been blinded by the One Life to the individual qualities of a red-breast by his door or the grass in the fields. Doctrinal statement, too, has been replaced by something more openly subjective:

> Love, now an universal birth,
> From heart to heart is stealing,
> From earth to man, from man to earth,
> —It is the hour of feeling.   (ll. 21–4)

A surprising claim, taken literally (as it has to be), but justified by the logic of feeling, the mood in which the poet can regulate his year with a 'living Calendar' of his own ('We from today, my friend, will date/The opening of the year' ll. 19–20). The language of 'Tintern Abbey' is offered in a playful context:

> And from the blessed power that rolls
> About, below, above;
> We'll frame the measure of our souls,
> They shall be tuned to love.   (ll. 33–6)

The poetry is delicately poised between gaiety and solemnity— the gaiety of song or dance in the unobtrusive musical metaphor, and the expansive solemnity with which the blessed power manifests itself. The harmony and communion celebrated so overwhelmingly in 'The Pedlar' are humanized by the lyric idiom, and Wordsworth ends by reminding us that this is simply a day off: 'Then come, my sister! come, I pray,/With speed put on your woodland dress . . . ' (ll. 37–8). The all-pervading 'sentiment of being' is a joyous interruption, transforming the everyday rather than ignoring it.

'Lines written at a small distance from my House' celebrates the mood in which the philosophic poetry of the previous weeks had been written; 'Lines written in early spring', a month later, admits that the world may not be one of harmony and love after all. The poem centres on a clash between the optimism of Wordsworth's creed and his awareness that the One Life leaves the problems of ordinary life unsolved.[1] On the face of it, this is the lyric that contains some of Wordsworth's most astonishing assertions: 'And 'tis my faith that every flower/Enjoys the air it breathes' (ll. 11–12). But such claims are made in a context of uncertainty. 'And 'tis my faith', 'And I must think, do all I can', 'If such be of my creed the plan'—the expressions of optimism are increasingly qualified by a tone of puzzled, pained doubt, just as in 'Tintern Abbey' the 'chearful faith that all which we behold/Is full of blessings' (ll. 134–5) is undercut by consciousness of a dreary reality. Wordworth's mood is complex, precarious, yet precisely evoked:

> I heard a thousand blended notes,
> While in a grove I sate reclined,

---

[1] The invasion of Switzerland had taken place in late January 1798; for its effect on Wordsworth's changing political views, see J. C. Maxwell, 'Wordsworth and the Subjugation of Switzerland', *MLR* lxv (1970), 16–18.

> In that sweet mood when pleasant thoughts
> Bring sad thoughts to the mind.

> To her fair works did nature link
> The human soul that through me ran;
> And much it griev'd my heart to think
> What man has made of man.   (ll. 1–8)

The tone is both pleased and sad: 'In that sweet mood . . . '
The mingling of certainty and doubt is intensely Wordsworthian. Recognition of joyous well-being in the natural
world—the trailing periwinkle, the hopping birds and budding
twigs—coexists with the awareness that man destroys the joy in
himself. Wordsworth's lament echoes Young ('Man hard of
Heart to man!', 'Man is to Man the sorest, surest Ill'),[1] or
Burns's dirge, 'Man was made to mourn', playing off a traditional, hard-learned knowledge against the poem's own
whimsical subjectivity. An intuition of harmony can never be
reconciled with the actuality of suffering and discord:

> If I these thoughts may not prevent,
> If such be of my creed the plan,
> Have I not reason to lament
> What man has made of man?   (ll. 21–4)

'Lines written in early spring' faces this irreconcilability; it
concedes that although 'Nature never did betray/The heart
that loved her' ('Tintern Abbey', ll. 123–4), the human heart
constantly betrays Nature.

To bring the One Life into daily experience is to be forced to
qualify it. 'Lines written in early spring' becomes a poem not so
much of belief as of the wish to believe; hence its poignancy. It
was only when forced to defend his beliefs, or at least to argue
them anew, that Wordsworth returned to the certainty of his
philosophic blank verse. 'Expostulation and Reply' and 'The
Tables turned', we are told, 'arose out of conversation with a
friend who was somewhat unreasonably attached to modern
books of moral philosophy';[2] their yoking of high spirits and
seriousness is the result. Wordsworth marshals all the arguments
of his draft conclusion to 'The Ruined Cottage'—his most
sustained attack on a barren and divisive rationalism:

---

[1] *The Complaint: Or, Night-Thoughts on Life, Death, & Immortality*, 'Night the
Third. Narcissa' (London, 1742), p. 17.
[2] 1798 'Advertisement' (*Prose Works*, i. 117); the friend was Hazlitt.

> was it meant
> That we should pore & dwindle as we pore,
> For ever dimly pore on things minute,
> On solitary objects, still beheld
> In disconnection dead & spiritless,
> And still dividing & dividing still
> Break down all grandeur, still unsatisfied
> With our unnatural toil, while littleness
> May yet become more little: waging thus
> An impious warfare with the very life
> Of our own souls. Or was it ever meant
> That this majestic imagery, the clouds
> The ocean & the firmament of heaven
> Should lie a barren picture on the mind.[1]

There is more zeal than tact in this; yet Wordsworth's insistence ('pore & dwindle as we pore,/For ever dimly pore', 'still dividing & dividing still', 'while littleness/May yet become more little') makes his point stylistically—such reductiveness can only breed sameness. The majestic imagery of nature, in altering our perspective (from the small to the great), also reminds us that there is another way of looking. The barren picture lying on the mind implies the alternative—interpenetration, interaction, fruitful absorption as opposed to fruitless poring:

> Thus deeply drinking in the soul of things
> We shall be wise perforce & we shall move
> From strict necessity along the path
> Of order & of good. Whate'er we see
> Whate'er we feel by agency direct
> Or indirect shall tend to feed & nurse
> Our faculties & raise to loftier heights
> Our intellectual soul.[2]

For Wordsworth himself, such conclusions had been 'Condensed . . . to a passion' by the power of imagination;[3] but for us they have an air of over-simplification. Wordsworth seems too sure that 'strict necessity' will operate, and the organic metaphors of feeding and nursing never come to life. He puts it better else-

---

[1] MS. B: *PW* v. 402, ll. 58–71.   [2] Ibid.: *PW* v. 402–3, ll. 92–9.
[3] Ibid.: *PW* v. 403, l. 109.

where, in a fragment from the Alfoxden Notebook which shares the same theme as 'Expostulation and Reply':

> There is a holy indolence
> Compared to which our best activity
> Is ofttimes deadly bane.
> They rest upon their oars,
> Float down the mighty stream of tendency
> In the calm mood of holy indolence,
> A most wise passiveness in which the heart
> Lies open and is well content to feel
> As nature feels, and to receive her shapes
> As she has made them.[1]

'This one day/We'll give to idleness' ('Lines written at a small distance from my House', ll. 15–16) was not such a frivolous suggestion as it seemed.

The dreaming poet figures elsewhere during the spring of 1798, in Coleridge's 'Nightingale' ('he had better far have stretch'd his limbs/Beside a brook in mossy forest-dell . . . ', ll. 25–6). Wordsworth gives the same answer to his busy friend; receptive being is better than blinkered doing. His counter-admonition has the air of a *jeu d'esprit*, on the lines of verse 'expostulations' in contemporary magazines, in which love is attacked and defended, nostalgia indulged and rejected.[2] Wordsworth's jocularity masks his earnestness; his lesson of idleness may be diametrically opposed to Watts's 'How doth the little busy bee', but it is put forward with no less seriousness. At first the school-masterish tone belongs to his friend—

> 'Where are your books? that light bequeath'd
> 'To beings else forlorn and blind!
> 'Up! Up! and drink the spirit breath'd
> 'From dead men to their kind.'
> ('Expostulation and Reply', ll. 5–8)

—but Wordsworth's reply has its own quiet zeal:

> Books! 'tis a dull and endless strife,
> Come, hear the woodland linnet,

---

[1] DC MS. 14: *Prelude*, p. 566. These lines must shortly precede the concluding 'Addendum' to 'The Ruined Cottage' (see Reed, pp. 321, 339).

[2] See Robert Mayo, *PMLA* lxix (1954), 515.

How sweet his music; on my life
There's more of wisdom in it.
　　　　('The Tables turned', ll. 9–12)

This is a poetry of statement rather than exploration, witty,
definitive, almost epigrammatic ('We murder to dissect', 'The
Tables turned', l. 28). Doctrine is at its most succinct—yet
each line lingers thoughtfully:

> 'Nor less I deem that there are powers,
> 'Which of themselves our minds impress,
> 'That we can feed this mind of ours,
> 'In a wise passiveness.
>
> 'Think you, mid all this mighty sum
> 'Of things for ever speaking,
> 'That nothing of itself will come,
> 'But we must still be seeking?'
> 　　　　('Expostulation and Reply', ll. 21–8)[1]

'This mighty sum'—the wealth of wholeness as opposed to the
poverty of disconnection—counters in a single phrase the restless
seeking of 'was it meant/That we should pore . . . ' Drifting
down the stream of tendency had seemed more exploratory in
blank verse, but for all their compression, these quatrains have
the same meditative seriousness.

　　The debate between intuitive and rational thought is at its
most persuasive when Wordsworth himself becomes the butt.
'We are seven' and 'Anecdote for Fathers, shewing how the
art of lying may be taught' are jokes at his own expense, guying
his didacticism and cutting him down to size as a teacher. Both
poems concern the tussle between a benign but officious adult
and a child obstinately true to its own logic; and both under-
mine the complacent and bullying morality offered to eighteenth-century children by those who wanted to improve them.
Watts had made them sing:

> O 'Tis a lovely thing for Youth
> To walk betimes in Wisdom's way:

---

[1] Wordsworth may be recollecting Cowper's

> 　　　　　　　Here the heart
> May give an useful lesson to the head,
> And learning wiser grow without his books.
> 　　　　　　(*The Task*, vi. 85–7)

> To fear a Lye, to speak the Truth,
> That we may trust to all they say.
>
> But Lyars we can never trust,
> Tho' they should speak the thing that's true,
> And he that does one fault at first,
> And lyes to hide it, makes it two.
>
> .   .   .   .
>
> Then let me always watch my Lips,
> Lest I be struck to Death and Hell,
> Since God a Book of Reckoning keeps
> For every Lye that Children tell.[1]

Wordsworth sets out to show how the education administered by adults may misfire—'the art of lying may be taught'; while the child of 'We are seven' is wise and happy precisely because she lacks the 'Solemn Thoughts of God and Death' which Watts's hymns try to instil—

> There is an Hour when I must die,
> Nor do I know how soon 'twill come;
> A thousand Children young as I
> Are call'd by Death to hear their Doom.[2]

At once whimsical and suggestive, Wordsworth's poems offer a covert generalization about the nature and value of a child's own intuitions.

These Wordsworthian children are seen in idealized terms: 'Her eyes were fair, and very fair,/—Her beauty made me glad' ('We are seven', ll. 11–12), 'I have a boy of five years old,/His face is fair and fresh to see' ('Anecdote for Fathers', ll. 1–2). But each goes on to reveal an inspired obstinacy at odds with adult preconceptions. The adult of 'Anecdote for Fathers', idle and happy, comes up with his inconsequential question—

> 'My little boy, which like you more,'
> I said and took him by the arm—
> 'Our home by Kilve's delightful shore,
> 'Or here at Liswyn farm?'   (ll. 25–8)

—and the child gives his equally unthinking reply (' "At Kilve I'd rather be/Than here at Liswyn farm" ', ll. 35–6). His reward is a verbal shaking designed to elicit a rational reply:

---

[1] 'Against Lying', *Divine Songs Attempted in Easy Language for Children*, pp. 22–3.
[2] 'Solemn Thoughts of God and Death', ibid., p. 15.

'Now, little Edward, say why so;
'My little Edward, tell me why;'
'I cannot tell, I do not know.'
'Why this is strange,' said I.   (ll. 37–40)

The adult's insistence on reason-giving ('And five times did I
say to him,/"Why? Edward, tell me why?" ', ll. 47–8) is
matched in 'We are seven' by his lesson in counting. Again, the
tussle springs from a random, benign enquiry (' "Sisters and
brothers, little maid,/How many may you be?" ', ll. 13–14):

'Seven are we,
'And two of us at Conway dwell,
'And two are gone to sea.

'Two of us in the church-yard lie,
'My sister and my brother,
'And in the church-yard cottage, I
'Dwell near them with my mother.'

'You say that two at Conway dwell,
'And two are gone to sea,
'Yet you are seven . . . '   (ll. 18–27)

Adult and child reckon the facts of their existence in a different
way, and inevitably they arrive at different answers. For one
the living child runs about and the dead does not; for the other,
the child beneath the ground is no less a brother or sister. The
matter-of-factness of the child's remark—' "I sit and sing to
them" ' (l. 44)—beautifully suggests the peaceful continuity
which for her exists between life and death, in contrast to the
adult's consciousness of division and finality. 'We are seven'
ends with a humorous exasperation that is deliberately incon-
clusive, 'Anecdote for Fathers' with the little boy's desperate
parody of rational processes—' "At Kilve there was no weather-
cock,/And that's the reason why" ' (ll. 55–6). Despite Wordsworth's earnestness ('Could I but teach the hundredth part/Of
what from thee I learn', ll. 59–60), the encounters have been
too acutely told for the lesson to lie heavy, and these wry,
quirky accounts of his own misplaced didacticism tell one as
much as the witty self-justification of 'Expostulation and Reply'
and 'The Tables turned'. The Wordsworth of spring 1798 was
bound to be a preacher; but his poetry teaches most when least
assertive, most fully alive to the interplay of feeling and belief.

V 'Tintern Abbey' and the Renewal of Tradition

MORE than any other, 'Tintern Abbey' is the poem for which Wordsworth's predecessors had smoothed the way. But it is here, where he is most uncritically indebted to the past, that his uniqueness is most strongly felt. His fruitful merging of eighteenth-century genres is matched by his renewal of tradition. The culminating landscape-poem, 'Tintern Abbey' is also the poem which completes the shift from nature to the individual; the poet's attitude to an unchanging landscape becomes a way of measuring the change that has taken place within. On the face of it, Wordsworth's subject is meditative retreat—an attempt to lighten 'the heavy and the weary weight/Of all this unintelligible world' (ll. 40–1) by withdrawing from it; certainly its subdued admission of change and loss makes 'Tintern Abbey' among his greatest elegies. But it is also a poem of rededication, infused with the doctrinal fervour of 'The Pedlar'. In 1800, Wordsworth noted: 'I have not ventured to call this Poem an Ode; but it was written with a hope that in the transitions, and the impassioned music of the versification, would be found the principal requisites of that species of composition.'[1] This ode-like orchestration, a building up and falling away of rhythmic power, is central to its quiet passion. Self-exploratory and self-communing, 'Tintern Abbey' proffers a statement of belief; individual consciousness finds its fullest expression in the consciousness of something beyond the self—'A motion and a spirit' which rolls through all things. Memory allows the poet to experience the essential continuity of the changing self: belief allows him to experience another dimension of relationship altogether, that of the One Life. Landscape serves as the point of reference for Wordsworth's greatest theme, the growth of a poet's mind.

[1] PW ii. 517.

I. LANDSCAPE AND THE POET

'Not a line of it was altered, and not any part of it written down till I reached Bristol',[1] Wordsworth recalled of 'Tintern Abbey' in 1843, and there is no reason to doubt him. Established traditions of landscape poetry made it possible to compose a poem as complex as 'Tintern Abbey' during a tour of only a few days.[2] To start with, there were the topographical episodes which occupy key positions in the poetry of Thomson, Cowper, and Akenside. All three play a part in shaping 'Tintern Abbey', and all three make the link between landscape and the poetic imagination which is central to Wordsworth's exploration of changing identity. Lyttelton's walk through Hagley Park, added to 'Spring' in 1744, allows Thomson to celebrate man— as represented by his patron and friend—at the centre of the natural world. Cowper's 'walk in the country', near the start of *The Task*, establishes the controlling consciousness and central values of his poem. Akenside's passage of elegiac retrospect in Book IV of the 1772 edition of *The Pleasures of the Imagination* re-creates the poetic landscape that has shaped his own imaginative growth.[3] Coming as it does at the point where Thomson moves from the natural world to man himself— 'STILL let my Song a nobler Note assume,/And sing th'infusive Force of Spring on Man . . .'[4]—Lyttelton's walk forms a suitable climax to 'Spring'. Thomson displays his patron as the perfect human being: poet, philosopher, and benefactor. He is the pensive solitary of pre-Romantic poetry, a lover of nature, and a man who sees into the life of things:

> Pure Serenity apace
> , Induces Thought, and Contemplation still.
> By swift degrees the Love of Nature works,
> And warms the Bosom; till at last sublim'd
> To Rapture, and enthusiastic Heat,
> We feel the present DEITY, and taste

---

[1] I.F. note (*PW* ii. 517).

[2] For Wordsworth's movements on his second Wye tour, see J. B. McNulty, 'Wordsworth's Tour of the Wye: 1798', *MLN* lx (1945), 291–5.

[3] The existence of these condensed topographical episodes makes it less likely that Wordsworth owes a direct debt to the full-length topographical poems surveyed in R. A. Aubin's *Topographical Poetry in XVIII-Century England* (New York, 1936).

[4] 'Spring' (1744), ll. 864–5.

> The Joy of GOD to see a happy World.
>   THESE are the Sacred Feelings of thy Heart,
> Thy Heart inform'd by Reason's purest Ray,
> O LYTTLETON, the Friend![1]

Cowper's presentation of himself at the start of *The Task* has equal relevance to the Wordsworth of 'Tintern Abbey'. The frivolous chronicle of the sofa gives way with a comically improvised transition ('but gouty limb/Though on a SOFA, may I never feel . . .')[2] to Cowper's real subject—his tastes, opinions, way of life, and, in particular, his feeling for nature. Mock-pomposity modulates into the introspective writing that is *The Task*'s most important legacy to Wordsworth:

> For I have loved the rural walk through lanes
> Of grassy swarth close cropt by nibbling sheep,
> And skirted thick with intertexture firm
> Of thorny boughs: have loved the rural walk
> O'er hills, through valleys, and by rivers brink,
> E'er since a truant boy I pass'd my bounds
> T'enjoy a ramble on the banks of Thames.
> And still remember, nor without regret
> Of hours that sorrow since has much endear'd,
> How oft, my slice of pocket store consumed,
> Still hung'ring pennyless and far from home.
> I fed on scarlet hips and stoney haws . . . [3]

'For I have loved . . . have loved . . . And still remember . . . How oft . . .': tone and phrasing look forward to 'Tintern Abbey'. Both poets evoke the past in order to colour the present with nostalgia ('And still remember, nor without regret'), and the 'truant boy' rambling beside the Thames provides a muted anticipation of the younger Wordsworth who had bounded like a roe over mountains, by rivers and streams. Both, despite their sense of change, reaffirm an enduring response to landscape, and Wordsworth's 'Therefore am I still/A lover of the meadows and the woods' (ll. 103–4) had been anticipated by Cowper's

> scenes that sooth'd
> Or charm'd me young, no longer young, I find
> Still soothing and of power to charm me still.[4]

---

[1] 'Spring' (1744), ll. 893–902.   [2] *The Task*, i. 107–8.   [3] Ibid. i. 109–20.
[4] Ibid. i. 141–3.

Infused as it is with personal feeling, 'Tintern Abbey' mirrors patterns of celebration and reaffirmation established in earlier poetry.

The bond with nature is matched by the bond with another human being. *The Seasons* and *The Task* reveal that Dorothy's presence in 'Tintern Abbey' ('My dearest Friend,/My dear, dear Friend . . . My dear, dear Sister!') owes as much to literature as to life. Like the joyous natural world, Lyttelton has paired:

> Perhaps thy lov'd LUCINDA shares thy Walk,
> With Soul to thine attun'd. Then Nature all
> Wears to the Lover's Eye a Look of Love;
> And all the Tumult of a guilty World,
> Tost by ungenerous Passions, sinks away.
> The tender Heart is animated Peace;
> And as it pours it's copious Treasures forth,
> In vary'd Converse, softening every Theme,
> You, frequent-pausing, turn, and from her Eyes,
> Where meeken'd Sense, and amiable Grace,
> And lively Sweetness dwell, enraptur'd, drink
> That nameless Spirit of etherial Joy,
> Inimitable Happiness! which Love,
> Alone, bestows, and on a favour'd Few.[1]

The experience ('The tender Heart is animated Peace') is almost that of 'Tintern Abbey', with its eye made quiet and its living soul. Wordsworth could have found such an evocation of mood elsewhere, but behind his fervent address to Dorothy lies the same imagined communion; Thomson's 'and from her Eyes . . . enraptur'd, drink/That nameless Spirit of etherial Joy' becomes Wordsworth's

> and read
> My former pleasures in the shooting lights
> Of thy wild eyes. (ll. 118–20)

But where Lyttelton's Lucinda simply completes a definition of the good life, Dorothy offers a link with the past: 'Oh! yet a while/May I behold in thee what I was once . . .' (ll. 120–1). 'Tintern Abbey' is about a saddened self searching for renewal, not just about a shared pleasure in picturesque scenery, and

[1] 'Spring' (1744), ll. 932–45.

Dorothy—like nature—serves as a talisman for permanence.
Her counterpart in *The Task* is Cowper's soberly affectionate
tribute to Mrs. Unwin:

> And witness, dear companion of my walks,
> Whose arm this twentieth winter I perceive
> Fast lock'd in mine, with pleasure such as love
> Confirm'd by long experience of thy worth
> And well-tried virtues could alone inspire—
> Witness a joy that thou hast doubled long.
> Thou know'st my praise of nature most sincere,
> And that my raptures are not conjured up
> To serve occasions of poetic pomp,
> But genuine, and art partner of them all.[1]

The presence of a loved companion endorses the poet's own
presence in a well-loved landscape, and the stability of the
relationship is transferred to the poet's feeling for nature.
Cowper's quiet sincerity becomes Wordsworth's more earnest
plea for Dorothy to remember that he—

> so long
> A worshipper of Nature, hither came,
> Unwearied in that service: rather say
> With warmer love, oh! with far deeper zeal
> Of holier love.   (ll. 152–6)

—and his own closing tribute overflows with emotion:

> Nor wilt thou then forget,
> That after many wanderings, many years
> Of absence, these steep woods and lofty cliffs,
> And this green pastoral landscape, were to me
> More dear, both for themselves, and for thy sake.   (ll. 156–60)

Dorothy's presence allows Wordsworth to affirm a central
element in the poem's chastened vision: his humanity. The
Tintern landscape is more dear not only because he now has a
doctrinal reason for valuing it, but because it is intertwined
with his love for another person. The younger self of the first
Wye tour had been fugitive and solitary: the self of five years
later brings relationship with him.

Wordsworth begins his poem where Thomson and Cowper

---

[1] *The Task*, i. 144–53.

leave off. The climaxes of these earlier topographical episodes are the vistas that reappear, infused with new transcendental significance, in the Coleridgean Conversation Poem. As Thomson describes Lyttelton's kingdom, the eye is 'snatch'd' from Hagley Hall at its centre to the boundaries of his domain, taking in a representative landscape of hill and dale, town and village. There is no merging of man and nature; nature is rather the setting for a human ideal. The scene is impressive—'The bursting Prospect spreads immense around'[1]—but does not go beyond its anthropocentric implications. Cowper is more subjective, with his lingering, Wordsworthian opening:

> How oft upon yon eminence, our pace
> Has slacken'd to a pause, and we have borne
> The ruffling wind scarce conscious that it blew . . . [2]

But although he dwells lovingly on the landscape before him, picking out familiar landmarks ('our fav'rite elms') and catching 'the sound of chearful bells', the painstaking detail does not take one into his mind. Church spire and 'smoking villages remote' are distant only in the physical sense; nature is reassuringly normalized, and leads inevitably to renewed appreciation: 'Scenes must be beautiful which daily view'd/Please daily. . . .'[3] Wordsworth's opening description of the Wye valley builds on these earlier passages. But now landscape evokes inner life, and imaginative re-creation has taken over from the faithful cataloguing of detail in *The Seasons* and *The Task*. It is not so much the scene that stands out as the poet's presence in it:

> Five years have passed; five summers, with the length
> Of five long winters! and again I hear
> These waters, rolling from their mountain-springs
> With a sweet inland murmur.—Once again
> Do I behold these steep and lofty cliffs,
> Which on a wild secluded scene impress
> Thoughts of more deep seclusion; and connect
> The landscape with the quiet of the sky.

---

[1] 'Spring' (1744), l. 947. The entire passage is quoted on p. 74, above.
[2] *The Task*, i. 154–6.
[3] Ibid. i. 177–8. See also p. 75, above. The difference between Cowper's passage and 'Tintern Abbey' is also explored by Myrddin Jones, 'Wordsworth and Cowper: the Eye made Quiet', *EC* xxi (1971), 236–47.

> The day is come when I again repose
> Here, under this dark sycamore, and view
> These plots of cottage-ground, these orchard-tufts,
> Which, at this season, with their unripe fruits,
> Among the woods and copses lose themselves,
> Nor, with their green and simple hue, disturb
> The wild green landscape. Once again I see
> These hedge-rows, hardly hedge-rows, little lines
> Of sportive wood run wild; these pastoral farms
> Green to the very door; and wreathes of smoke
> Sent up, in silence, from among the trees,
> With some uncertain notice, as might seem,
> Of vagrant dwellers in the houseless woods,
> Or of some hermit's cave, where by his fire
> The hermit sits alone.   (ll. 1–23)

The incantatory rhetoric signals Wordsworth's concern with what is apprehended rather than seen: 'Five years have passed . . . again I hear . . . Once again/Do I behold . . . I again repose/Here . . .' The mingling of description and abstraction— cliffs and seclusion, sky and quiet—is aimed at the inner eye, while the repetition of 'green' ('green and simple hue . . . The wild green landscape . . . Green to the very door') merges detail into unity, absorbing cottages, hedgerows, and farms into the calm of nature. The imaginary hermit and the 'vagrant dwellers in the houseless woods'—the charcoal-burners whose very existence is called in doubt ('as might seem')—suggest how far we have moved from reality.[1] This peaceful fusion of pastoral and imagined worlds, outer and inner, enacts the poet's own withdrawal into the seclusion he describes. The last word of the passage ('alone') crystallizes its mood of self-communing solitude.

The Tintern landscape is as much a landscape of memory as it is the picturesque scene described by the topographical writers whose influence shows itself in the imaginary hermit.[2]

---

[1] See also James Benziger, 'Tintern Abbey Revisited', PMLA lxv (1950), 154–62, on the 'paysage moralisé' created by the opening description.

[2] Cf. Gilpin's remark that 'Every thing around breathes an air so calm, and tranquil; so sequestered from the commerce of life, that it is easy to conceive, a man of warm imagination, in monkish times, might have been allured by such a scene to become an inhabitant of it'; Observations on the River Wye, and several Parts of South Wales, &c. relative chiefly to Picturesque Beauty (London, 1782), p. 32. Mary

Its seclusion helps to set the poet off on his private journey into the past. In Book IV of *The Pleasures of the Imagination*, Akenside similarly returns to the past in an attempt to explore the development of the creative imagination:

> A different task remains; the secret paths
> Of early genius to explore: to trace
> Those haunts where Fancy her predestin'd sons,
> Like to the Demigods of old, doth nurse
> Remote from eyes profane.[1]

'The secret paths' through which the young poet wanders are his by tradition—

> Yet not the more
> Cease I to wander where the Muses haunt
> Cleer Spring, or shadie Grove, or Sunnie Hill,
> Smit with the love of sacred Song . . . [2]

—and the Miltonic setting reappears, still symbolic but now naturalized, in a remembered landscape that must surely be among Akenside's most beautiful passages of blank verse:

> Ye happy souls
> Who now her [Fancy's] tender discipline obey,
> Where dwell ye? What wild river's brink at eve
> Imprint your steps? What solemn groves at noon
> Use ye to visit, often breaking forth
> In rapture 'mid your dilatory walk,
> Or musing, as in slumber, on the green?
> —Would i again were with you!—O ye dales
> Of Tyne, and ye most ancient woodlands; where
> Oft as the giant flood obliquely strides,
> And his banks open, and his lawns extend,
> Stops short the pleased traveller to view
> Presiding o'er the scene some rustic tower
> Founded by Norman or by Saxon hands:
> O ye Northumbrian shades, which overlook
> The rocky pavement and the mossy falls

Moorman, *William Wordsworth*, p. 402n., notes the debt to Gilpin's charcoal-burners; for other topographical writers whose account of the Wye valley may have influenced Wordsworth, see also my note, ' "Tintern Abbey" and Topographical Prose', *N & Q* N.S. xviii (1971), 366–9.

[1] *The Pleasures of the Imagination* (1772), iv. 20–4; see the posthumous *Poems of Mark Akenside* (London, 1772) for the four-book version.

[2] *Paradise Lost*, iii. 26–9.

> Of solitary Wensbeck's limpid stream;
> How gladly i recall your well-known seats
> Belov'd of old, and that delightful time
> When all alone, for many a summer's day,
> I wander'd through your calm recesses, led
> In silence by some powerful hand unseen.[1]

With 'Would i again were with you', Akenside's personal involvement surfaces, transforming imaginative participation into elegy. The neo-classical invocations ('O ye dales/Of Tyne . . .', 'O ye Northumbrian shades . . .') introduce a past as vividly recollected as Wordsworth's—'that delightful time/ When all alone, for many a summer's day . . .' Behind the Wye lies the Wansbeck, established as a poet's river; and the Wordsworth who had 'bounded . . . Wherever nature led' (ll. 69–71) is descended from the poet who had wandered in a Northumbrian valley, 'led/In silence by some powerful hand unseen'. Akenside is led by a nature muse, Wordsworth by nature itself; but the difference is largely one of terminology. So too with Akenside's closing affirmation:

> Nor will i e'er forget you. nor shall e'er
> The graver tasks of manhood, or the advice
> Of vulgar wisdom, move me to disclaim
> Those studies which possess'd me in the dawn
> Of life, and fix'd the color of my mind
> For every future year . . . [2]

The sober certainty is that of Wordsworth's own tribute to the Wye valley. Both poets celebrate landscape as a shaping power in their imaginative growth—a permanently formative influence on 'the color of [the] mind'. For Wordsworth, there is too a source of regeneration ('life and food/For future years', ll. 65–6).

The undercurrent of elegy in both Akenside and Wordsworth is ultimately a Miltonic legacy. Behind the nostalgia of one, and the more searching exploration of loss and change in

---

[1] *The Pleasures of the Imagination* (1772), iv. 24–45. The general resemblance of this passage to Wordsworth's blank verse was long ago pointed out by D. N. Smith in *The Oxford Book of Eighteenth Century Verse* (Oxford, 1926), p. x.

[2] Ibid. iv. 46–51.

the other, is Milton's powerful lament for his blindness.[1] His stance of endurance in the face of adversity—

> I Sing with mortal voice, unchang'd
> To hoarse or mute, though fall'n on evil dayes,
> On evil dayes though fall'n, and evil tongues . . . [2]

—reappears in 'Tintern Abbey' as Wordsworth's startlingly misanthropic account of 'The dreary intercourse of daily life' ('evil tongues', 'rash judgements', 'the sneers of selfish men', 'greetings where no kindness is', ll. 129–32). Both represent themselves not only as visionaries, but as suffering individuals. The distinction of 'Tintern Abbey' lies partly in recapturing the authenticity of Miltonic elegy, weakened as it had been by the indiscriminate melancholy of the eighteenth century. But it is also the fullest expression of a specifically eighteenth-century genre. Wordsworth's potent intertwining of elegy and land-scape could not have occurred without the topographical elegy, or 'revisit' poem—the most popular elegiac vehicle of the period, combining as it did Gilpin's feeling for the picturesque with Akenside's pre-Romantic sensibility. Where Goldsmith's *Deserted Village* (1770) had lamented a changing place, the topographical elegy mourns personal loss.[3] Place becomes a way of contrasting past and present selves. Wordsworth's title ('Lines written . . . on Revisiting the Banks of the Wye') and his opening ('Five years have passed . . .') announce his choice of genre. Given the circumstances of the poem's composition, his choice was unsurprising; but long before 1798 he had contemplated a poem on these lines. Behind the opening of 'Tintern Abbey' lies a blank verse fragment, probably belonging to the previous year, which already uses the 'revisit' formula to suggest the interplay of inner and outer worlds:

> Yet once again do I behold the forms
> Of these huge mountains and yet once again
> Standing beneath these elms I hear thy voice

---

[1] Coleridge draws attention to the opening of *Paradise Lost*, Book III, in the revised defence of 'Egotism' that prefaces *Poems* (1797).

[2] *Paradise Lost*, vii. 24–6.

[3] Samuel Rogers in *The Pleasures of Memory* (1792) and Robert Southey in 'The Retrospect', included in his and Lovell's *Poems* (1795), both draw on Goldsmith's method to lament change within themselves rather than a village.

> Beloved Derwent, that peculiar voice
> Heard in the stillness of the evening air,
> Half-heard and half created.[1]

Behind this fragment, in turn, lies a sonnet draft that goes back to the mid-1790s and the period of Bowles's influence:

> Derwent again I hear thy evening call
> Blend with the whispers of these elms that meet
> Round this dear lodge nor as the moon I greet
> That seems to rock [?] rock their summits tall
> And think how I have watched [?][2]

The title Wordsworth gave to his draft ('On returning to a Cottage, a favourite residence of the author, after a long absence') implies the genre popularized by the eighteenth-century sonneteers who influenced his early lyric writing.

The special usefulness of the 'revisit' poem lies in providing Wordsworth with a means of asserting continuity as well as change—the continuity of the poet's developing consciousness. The formula which reappears in 'Tintern Abbey', profoundly modified by Wordsworthian sensibility, can be seen at its simplest in Warton's widely imitated sonnet, 'To the River Lodon':

> AH! what a weary race my feet have run,
> Since first I trod thy banks with alders crown'd,
> And thought my way was all through fairy ground,
> Beneath thy azure sky, and golden sun:
> Where first my muse to lisp her notes begun!
> While pensive memory traces back the round,
> Which fills the varied interval between;
> Much pleasure, more of sorrow, marks the scene.
> Sweet native stream! those skies and suns so pure
> No more return, to chear my evening road!
> Yet still one joy remains, that not obscure,
> Nor useless, all my vacant days have flow'd,
> From youth's gay dawn to manhood's prime mature;
> Nor with the Muse's laurel unbestow'd.[3]

[1] Pierpoint Morgan Library: *PW* v. 340. I. The sheet originally formed part of the early notebook now reconstituted as DC MS. 13; for the date, see Reed, p. 346.

[2] DC MS. 2. Cf. the description of the moon, rocked to and fro by the wind in the branches of an ash, *Prelude* iv. 77-83. For the date of the draft, see Reed, pp. 16 154.

[3] *Poems. A New Edition* (1777), p. 83.

'AH! what a weary race my feet have run,/Since first I trod thy banks . . .': 'Though changed, no doubt, from what I was, when first/I came among these hills . . .' (Tintern Abbey', ll. 67–8)— Wordsworth's hours of weariness were hours that he was bound to have endured when he chose this genre, and his intertwining of recollection and renewal in 'Tintern Abbey' was an inherited motif. The impetus towards his early sonnet would have come from Bowles—imitated also by Coleridge in his own sonnet of the mid-1790s, 'To the River Otter' ('DEAR native Brook! wild Streamlet of the West!/How many various-fated Years have past . . .').[1] Bowles's 'To the River Itchin, near Winton', had given Warton's formula a characteristic intimacy of tone:

> ITCHIN, when I behold thy banks again,
>> Thy crumbling margin, and thy silver breast,
>> On which the self-same tints still seem to rest,
> Why feels my heart the shiv'ring sense of pain?
>> Is it, that many a summer's day has past
> Since, in life's morn, I carol'd on thy side?
> Is it, that oft, since then, my heart has sigh'd,
>> As Youth, and Hope's delusive gleams, flew fast?
> Is it that those, who circled on thy shore,
> Companions of my youth, now meet no more?
>> What'er the cause, upon thy banks I bend
> Sorrowing, yet feel such solace at my heart,
>> As at the meeting of some long-lost friend,
>> From whom, in happier hours, we wept to part.[2]

Bowles takes for granted the reader's recognition of his theme (Warton's explicit 'AH! what a weary race my feet have run . . .'); the plaintive 'Is it . . .?', 'Is it . . .?', 'Is it . . .?' needs no answer ('Whate'er the cause . . .'). His evasion of the central elegiac commonplace creates a new sensibility. The hesitancy goes with a refusal to name any emotion more definite than a 'shiv'ring sense of pain', and where Warton parades his feelings before the reader, Bowles takes him into his confidence. Appropriately, his consolation is not the Muse's laurel,

---

[1] Coleridge's untitled collection of sonnets, p. 5 (*CPW* i. 48). See also W. K. Wimsatt in *The Verbal Icon*, pp. 105–10, for the parallel between Coleridge's sonnet and Bowles's.

[2] *Fourteen Sonnets, Elegiac and Descriptive*, p. 9.

but relationship—the comfort of friendship renewed ('As at the meeting of some long-lost friend'). The difference is central to Bowles's appeal; in Coleridge's phrase, his sonnets 'domesticate with the heart'.[1]

From Bowles's 'To the River Itchin' to Wordsworth's exploration of the same themes in 'Tintern Abbey' is a big step. Bowles himself provides a stepping-stone with his long topographical elegy, *Monody, written at Matlock* (1791)—like 'Tintern Abbey', an attempt to suggest the on-going processes of loss and growth. Behind Bowles's poem lies the elegiac landscape from Book IV of *The Pleasures of the Imagination*; the *Monody* too casts back to the young poet, and its opening lines greet not just a place, but a muse:

> MATLOCK, amid thy hoary-hanging views,
> Thy glens that smile sequester'd, and thy nooks
> Which yon forsaken cragg all dark o'erlooks,
> Once more I meet the long-neglected Muse,
> As erst when by the mossy brink, and falls
> Of solitary WENSBECK, or the side
> Of CLYDSDALE's cliffs, where first her voice she tried,
> We wander'd in our youth—Since then the thralls
> That wait life's upland road, have chill'd her breast,
> And much, as much they might, her wing deprest—
> Wan Indolence resign'd, her dead'ning hand
> Laid on her heart, and Fancy her cold wand
> Dropt at the frown of Fortune; yet once more
> I call her, and once more her converse sweet,
> 'Mid the still limits of this lone retreat
> I wooe; if yet delightful as of yore
> My heart she may revisit, nor deny
> The soothing aid of some sweet melody![2]

—another reminder that Wordsworth's Wye is in origin a poet's river, and that its cliffs have behind them the poetry-inspiring cliffs of Clydesdale and Matlock. More important, landscape is already being used to suggest the potential continuity of imaginative experience; past and present converge as the poet re-encounters the original source of his inspiration. The difference between 'Tintern Abbey' and the *Monody* is that Words-

---

[1] *CPW* ii. 1139 (see p. 86, above).
[2] *Monody, written at Matlock, October 1791* (Salisbury, 1791), pp. 1–2.

worth is able to write openly about himself. Lacking a vocabu-
lary of introspection, Bowles has to fall back on clumsy per-
sonification and the moralized landscape which is his speciality.
An earlier self becomes 'Hope, a golden-tressed boy';[1] saddening experience is reflected in the slowly darkening scene;
the possibilities of permanence and endurance are represented
by Matlock's 'lofty craggs', and those of tranquillity by the
quietly flowing river:

> Like Peace, a hermit in some craggy dell
> Retir'd, and bidding the loud throng farewel,
> I see thee still thy peaceful course pursue,
> Making such gentle music as might cheer
> The weary passenger that journeys near.[2]

In 'Tintern Abbey', by contrast, there is a beautiful understatement of similar associations—between the river, with its
'sweet inland murmur' (1.4), and retirement; between the
hermit and peace.[3]

For both Wordsworth and Bowles, the landscape of permanence and calm becomes a source of future restoration in the
face of change and uncertainty within themselves. Wordsworth's
acknowledgement of enduring influence ('I have owed to
them,/In hours of weariness, sensations sweet . . .', ll. 27–8) is
anticipated by the phrasing of Bowles's entreaty:

> Nor may I, sweet stream,
> From thy lone banks and limits wild depart,
> (Where now I meditate my pensive theme)
> Without some mild improvement on my heart
> Pour'd sad, yet pleasing: so may I forget
> The crosses and the cares that sometimes fret
> Life's smoothest channel, and each wish prevent
> That marrs the silent current of Content![4]

Even the characteristically Wordsworthian transition is there
('Nor less, I trust,/To them I may have owed another gift . . .',
ll. 36–7). What is lacking is the authenticating struggle to

---

[1] Ibid., p. 3.   [2] Ibid., p. 7.
[3] Bowles's counterpart to the hermit is 'Some weary Bard', who has retreated to
a 'reed-roof'd hermitage' at Matlock to meditate on experience that has been at
once saddening and humanizing (see *Monody*, pp. 9–10).
[4] Ibid., p. 8.

define, and the resonance of underlying emotion, always present in 'Tintern Abbey'. One is left unmoved by Bowles's gloomy musings about the human state and his muted optimism, while the 'reconciled' conclusion seems as contrived as the sun-illuminated landscape which is his closing metaphor ('Bright bursts the sun upon the shaggy scene . . .'):[1]

> Tho' brief the time, and short our course to run,
> Awhile, O DERWENT, on thy winding side,
> (Ere yet the parting paths of life divide)
> Let us rejoice, seeking what may be won
> From the laborious day, or Fortune's frown:
> Here may we ere the sun of life goes down,
> Erewhile regardless of the morrow dwell;
> Then to our destin'd roads, and speed us well![2]

The echo of 'Lycidas' has to work over-time. Where Bowles relies on literary association, Wordsworth in 'Tintern Abbey'—a poem at least as dependent on its predecessors—seems to shape his experience without help from the past. The inherited pattern of elegy and reconciliation takes on new life, allowing him to explore, as if it had never been done before, the change which absence and experience have wrought in his younger self.

II. IDENTITY AND BELIEF

For all that 'Tintern Abbey' owes to the past, its most important debt is to the poetry written by Wordsworth and Coleridge themselves during the first half of 1798. 'The Pedlar' provided the impulse towards a statement of belief, 'Frost at Midnight' provided an impressive model for the kind of poetry which Bowles had failed to write, and which Wordsworth himself had never previously attempted—the poetry of inner life. In 'Frost at Midnight' the familiar themes of loss and renewal are subsumed into a new concern with the power of the mind to link past, present, and future in organic relationship. Like Bowles's *Monody*, Coleridge's poem is an elegy for a past self; but another principle of organization is now at work—not the meditative-descriptive parallel, but imagination. Where earlier Conversation Poems had centred on moments of trans-

[1] *Monody*, p. 12.   [2] Ibid., p. 13.

cendental experience or insight, 'Frost at Midnight' centres on
a Wordsworthian 'spot of time', a vivid recollection of childhood experience which looks forward to Part I of the 1799
Prelude.[1] Both poems invite entry into the poet's consciousness,
and both use the processes of self-realization—their recognition
of becoming as well as of changing—to demonstrate the essential continuity of inner life. Coleridge's source, the fireside
reverie from Book IV of Cowper's *Task* ('The Winter Evening'),[2] is a similar attempt to capture the quality, if not the
drama, of individual consciousness. For Cowper, the wintry
scene outside exists chiefly to heighten the cosiness indoors—

> How calm is my recess, and how the frost
> Raging abroad, and the rough wind, endear
> The silence and the warmth enjoy'd within.[3]

—but already there is the basis for Coleridge's muting of the
outer world to intensify activity within the mind; and, although Cowper does no more than suggest its magic, the
mysteriously transformed landscape is to reappear as the central symbol of 'Frost at Midnight':

> To-morrow brings a change, a total change!
> Which even now, though silently perform'd,
> And slowly, and by most unfelt, the face
> Of universal nature undergoes.[4]

In Coleridge's poem, the 'secret ministry of frost' becomes an
analogue both for the silent, inner workings of thought, and for
the transforming power of the imagination. As the natural
world is transfigured, the world of the individual changes its
face from one of solitude and self-imprisonment to one of
relationship and freedom.

Coleridge's opening, like the start of 'Tintern Abbey',

---

[1] For the basis of *The Prelude*—Wordsworth's exploration of childhood experience in the 'spots of time' written during the winter of 1798–9—see Jonathan
Wordsworth, 'The Growth of a Poet's Mind', *Cornell Library Journal*, No. 11 (1970),
3–24.

[2] See Humphry House, *Coleridge: The Clark Lectures 1951–2*, pp. 78–9, for a
valuable comparison of 'Frost at Midnight' and its source, and, more recently,
Norman Fruman in *Coleridge, The Damaged Archangel* (London, 1972), pp. 305–
310.

[3] *The Task*, iv. 308–10.   [4] Ibid. iv. 322–5.

suggests a mind turned inward; the external world is merged into the calm of thought:

> THE Frost performs it's secret ministry,
> Unhelp'd by any wind. The owlet's cry
> Came loud—and hark, again! loud as before.
> The inmates of my cottage, all at rest,
> Have left me to that solitude, which suits
> Abstruser musings: save that at my side
> My cradled infant slumbers peacefully.
> 'Tis calm indeed! so calm, that it disturbs
> And vexes meditation with it's strange
> And extreme silentness. Sea, hill, and wood,
> This populous village! Sea, and hill, and wood,
> With all the numberless goings on of life
> Inaudible as dreams![1]

'Sea, hill, and wood . . . Sea, and hill, and wood'—the repetition is lulling, but not sleepy. Coleridge's surroundings are 'Inaudible as dreams', but his younger self achieves the vividness of a present reality; 'the numberless goings on of life' have been displaced by memory. At the start of 'Tintern Abbey', evidence of human activity ('These plots of cottage-ground, these orchard-tufts', l. 11) is similarly merged into a 'wild green landscape' whose inhabitants are visible only in 'smoke/Sent up, in silence, from among the trees' (ll. 18–19). The silence that 'disturbs/And vexes meditation' in 'Frost at Midnight' suggests both the heightened awareness of midnight solitude, and the way in which silence has itself become the most important sign of mental life. In Hazlitt's phrase, it is a 'busy solitude'.[2] In 'Frost at Midnight', the suppressed paradox—a disquieting quiet—signals the suspension of ordinary sense-perception. In 'Tintern Abbey', Wordsworth's unexpected yet persuasive abstracts translate the Wye landscape into an internal one:

> Once again
> Do I behold these steep and lofty cliffs,
> Which on a wild secluded scene impress
> Thoughts of more deep seclusion . . .   (ll. 4–7)

---

[1] *Fears in Solitude . . . To which are added, France, an Ode; and Frost at Midnight*, p. 19 (*CPW* i. 240, ll. 1–13).

[2] Howe, xix. 11.

Coleridge's 'Inaudible as dreams' is paralleled by Wordsworth's 'forms of beauty' that 'have not been to [him],/As is a landscape to a blind man's eye' (ll. 24–5). Both poets transfer the language and associations of ordinary perception to an unfamiliar context in order to evoke another kind of perception altogether—that of the mind's eye. The conventions of descriptive poetry are subtly disrupted to create the mental landscapes which are the real subjects of both 'Frost at Midnight' and 'Tintern Abbey'.[1]

The major achievement of the Conversation Poem is its fusion of subjective experience and philosophic statement. Feeling and meaning interpenetrate, and the discursiveness of *The Task* gives way to a kind of poetry that is both more economical and more profound. In 'Frost at Midnight', the random reflections of Cowper's fire-gazing become the basis for a poem about the power of the imagination to bring mind and nature into creative relationship. The point of reference for its movement to and fro in time is the 'stranger', the sooty film on the grate—described by Cowper with the mock-seriousness which allows him to comprehend the ordinary within his Miltonic idiom:

> Nor less amused have I quiescent watch'd
> The sooty films that play upon the bars
> Pendulous, and foreboding in the view
> Of superstition prophesying still
> Though still deceived, some strangers near approach.[2]

To Coleridge, the restless play of the film becomes a metaphor for the mind's unceasing activity. But the projection of his own life onto other things has troubling implications. Is adult consciousness self-reflecting, self-imprisoned, no longer a means of effecting entry into either the world of the imagination or the world beyond the self?

> Only that film, which flutter'd on the grate,
> Still flutters there, the sole unquiet thing,
> Methinks, it's motion in this hush of nature
> Gives it dim sympathies with me, who live,
> Making it a companionable form,

---

[1] See C. C. Clarke, *Romantic Paradox: An Essay on the Poetry of Wordsworth* (London, 1962), pp. 44–53, for an interesting discussion of this merging of inner and outer worlds.

[2] *The Task*, iv. 291–5.

> With which I can hold commune. Idle thought!
> But still the living spirit in our frame,
> That loves not to behold a lifeless thing,
> Transfuses into all it's own delights,
> It's own volition, sometimes with deep faith,
> And sometimes with fantastic playfulness.
> Ah me! amus'd by no such curious toys
> Of the self-watching subtilizing mind,
> How often in my early school-boy days,
> With most believing superstitious wish
> Presageful have I gaz'd upon the bars,
> To watch the *stranger* there! and oft belike,
> With unclos'd lids, already had I dreamt
> Of my sweet birthplace, and the old church-tower,
> Whose bells, the poor man's only music, rang
> From morn to evening, all the hot fair-day,
> So sweetly . . .[1]

The recollection of 'the hot fair-day' releases Coleridge's imagination into the free flow of memory. The vivid 'spot of time' experienced by the child is in contrast to the adult's mental processes ('the self-watching subtilizing mind'), and his daydream paradoxically brings a fuller encounter with reality. The adult's mind experiences itself: the child's imagination relives the whole stretch of the fair-day ('From morn to evening . . .').

Wordsworth's poem is similarly concerned with the function of memory as a means of regeneration for the imprisoned self ('in lonely rooms, and mid the din/Of town and cities', ll. 26–7) and as a means of enrichment for the depleted imagination. Landscape replaces hearth as the focal point for the fluctuations of consciousness and oblivion, analysis and reverie, on which the larger rhythms of 'Tintern Abbey' depend. It is a focal point constituted not so much by the scene before Wordsworth as by the 'picture of the mind' within:

> Though absent long,
> These forms of beauty have not been to me,
> As is a landscape to a blind man's eye . . .

.   .   .   .

[1] *Fears in Solitude* etc., pp. 20–1 (*CPW* i. 241–2, ll. 15–31 and app. crit.).

And now, with gleams of half-extinguish'd thought,
With many recognitions dim and faint,
And somewhat of a sad perplexity,
The picture of the mind revives again . . .   (ll. 23–5, 59–62)

The Tintern landscape, Wordsworth implies, lives most fully
and most permanently in the mind's eye; and it is this hinterland—the area lying between experience and recall, past and
present—that his poem explores. Nature becomes a catalyst
for the continuities of memory, and Wordsworth's present
serves, like Coleridge's, as a means of plumbing the past. Both
poets confront the gulf between adult self-consciousness and
a younger, more vitally absorbed self, and both lament the
passing of uncomplicated response. Just as Coleridge has lost the
child's mental freedom—his independence of the actual—so
Wordsworth has lost a feeling for nature 'That had no need of a
remoter charm,/By thought supplied' (ll. 82–3). 'Frost at
Midnight' and 'Tintern Abbey' are alike in mourning that loss
of participation which is to be the subject of a later, and greater,
pair of elegies—the Immortality Ode and 'Dejection'.

Like these later elegies, both poems hold out possibilities for
imaginative renewal. In 'Frost at Midnight', the sleeping
child provides an assurance of future contact with the natural
world. Coleridge's London school-days are to be relived in the
Berkeleian landscape which at once teaches, and is, the divine
imagination:

> I was rear'd
> In the great city, pent mid cloisters dim,
> And saw nought lovely but the sky and stars.
> But *thou*, my babe! Shalt wander, like a breeze,
> By lakes and sandy shores, beneath the crags
> Of ancient mountain, and beneath the clouds,
> Which image in their bulk both lakes and shores
> And mountain crags: so shalt thou see and hear
> The lovely shapes and sounds intelligible
> Of that eternal language, which thy God
> Utters, who from eternity doth teach
> Himself in all, and all things in himself.[1]

This is not only a powerful image of communion, but an image
of freedom and unconstraint; the adult is liberated in the

[1] Ibid., p. 22 (*CPW* i. 242, ll. 51–62); see p. 66, above.

breeze-like, inspirational wanderings of his child. In 'Tintern Abbey', it is Dorothy who gives access to experience from which the poet himself is now debarred; if Hartley offers freedom, she offers intensity:

> in thy voice I catch
> The language of my former heart, and read
> My former pleasures in the shooting lights
> Of thy wild eyes. Oh! yet a little while
> May I behold in thee what I was once,
> My dear, dear Sister! . . . (ll. 117–22)

Through these younger selves, 'Frost at Midnight' and 'Tintern Abbey' affirm a new bond—not only between past and present, but between present and future, and, indirectly, with nature itself. Coleridge's closing lines of benediction are among the most tenderly evocative he ever wrote:

> Therefore all seasons shall be sweet to thee
> Whether the summer clothe the general earth
> With greenness, or the redbreasts sit and sing
> Betwixt the tufts of snow on the bare branch
> Of mossy apple-tree while all the thatch
> Smokes in the sun-thaw: whether the eave-drops fall
> Heard only in the trances of the blast,
> Or whether the secret ministry of cold
> Shall hang them up in silent icicles,
> Quietly shining to the quiet moon,
> Like those, my babe! which ere tomorrow's warmth
> Have capp'd their sharp keen points with pendulous drops,
> Will catch thine eye, and with their novelty
> Suspend thy little soul; then make thee shout,
> And stretch and flutter from thy mother's arms
> As thou would'st fly for very eagerness.[1]

The quietness of the icicles accentuates an implied responsiveness; and as they shine *to* the noon, the child, bird-like, flutters towards the icicles—his untrammelled movement restoring contact with the natural world. The word 'flutter', used earlier of the sooty film moving on the grate, is a reminder that the activity which previously mirrored only the mind's restlessness ('sole unquiet thing') now signifies an imagination vividly

[1] *Fears in Solitude* etc., pp. 22–3 (*CPW* i. 242–3, ll. 65–74 and app. crit.).

in touch with something other than itself. In 'Tintern Abbey', the communion envisaged is a peculiarly Wordsworthian one—

> Therefore let the moon
> Shine on thee in thy solitary walk;
> And let the misty mountain winds be free
> To blow against thee . . .   (ll. 135–8)

—but Dorothy's struggle with the elements, like the Old Cumberland Beggar's, suggests harmony; hers is to be a mysterious and un-self-conscious sharing in the forces of nature.[1] Where the younger Wordsworth of five years before had been 'haunted' by the sounding cataract, his sister, like Lucy, is offered the possibility of fusion: 'And beauty born of murmuring sound/Shall pass into her face' ('Three years she grew', ll. 29–30). Coleridge's child has been freed by nature: Dorothy is absorbed into its very life.

But Dorothy's presence in the closing movement of 'Tintern Abbey' also allows Wordsworth to pick up a motif that has been present throughout: 'The still, sad music of humanity'. Where 'The Pedlar' had refused to admit problems, 'Tintern Abbey' evokes the painful perplexities of human existence, and hence the need for consolations—the 'Abundant recompense' of the One Life and the humanized imagination. Wordsworth's record of the changing significance which nature held for him has behind it his account of the Pedlar's visionary education. But the account has been modified to fit its new context. The young Pedlar had been overwhelmed by the intensity of his inner life. His world was at once solid and ghostly, made up of the visionary imagery—mountain, sky, and water—which Wordsworth uses throughout his poetry to express 'the presence

---

[1] Cf. a jotting in the Alfoxden Notebook:

> and beneath the star
> Of evening let the steep and lonely path
> The steep path of the rocky mountain side
> Among the stillness of the mountains hear
> The panting of thy breath.
> (DC MS. 14: *PW* v. 341. *II. vi*)

It has been suggested that these lines are linked with the composition of 'Tintern Abbey'; but they may equally represent work on 'The Old Cumberland Beggar', along with other draft fragments in the Alfoxden Notebook (see *Lyrical Ballads 1798*, ed. W. J. B. Owen, pp. 149–50 and n.).

& the power/Of greatness'.[1] The universal mind is perceived with unique and ambiguous intensity:

> many an hour in caves forlorn
> And in the hollow depths of naked crags
> He sate, and even in their fixed lineaments
> Or from the power of a peculiar eye
> Or by creative feeling overborne
> Or by predominance of thought oppressed
> Even in their fixed and steady lineaments
> He traced an ebbing and a flowing mind . . . [2]

Perhaps deliberately, perhaps because he was in the last resort unclear himself, Wordsworth begs the question of whether the divine mind is actually manifested in nature. What emerges, however, is not so much an uncertainty about whether the One Life is perceived or created, as the power and weight ('overborne', 'oppressed') of the child's experience. Such experience can have no place in 'Tintern Abbey', a poem that celebrates the attainment of vision at the expense of participation. Rather, Wordsworth draws on the Pedlar's adolescent restlessness ('many a time he wish'd the winds might rage/When they were silent')[3] and his response to those aspects of nature which reflect his own disquietude:

> I have heard him say
> That at this time he scann'd the laws of light
> With a strange pleasure of disquietude
> Amid the din of torrents . . . [4]

In 'Tintern Abbey', the fevered Pedlar reappears as a figure both fleeing and searching, finding in nature the fulfilment of an urgent but undefined need. But his turbulence is located firmly in the past,

> when like a roe
> I bounded o'er the mountains, by the sides
> Of the deep rivers, and the lonely streams,
> Wherever nature led; more like a man
> Flying from something that he dreads, than one
> Who sought the thing he loved. For nature then

---

[1] 'The Ruined Cottage', MS. B: *PW* v. 381, ll. 80–1.
[2] Ibid.: *PW* v. 381–2, ll. 100–7.   [3] Ibid.: *PW* v. 384, ll. 225–6.
[4] Ibid.: *PW* v. 385, ll. 229–32.

(The coarser pleasures of my boyish days,
And their glad animal movements all gone by,)
To me was all in all.—I cannot paint
What then I was. The sounding cataract
Haunted me like a passion: the tall rock
The mountain, and the deep and gloomy wood,
Their colours and their forms, were then to me
An appetite: a feeling and a love,
That had no need of a remoter charm,
By thought supplied, or any interest
Unborrowed from the eye.   (ll. 68–84)

The tone is that of a changed and chastened man reviewing his experience—at times at a loss to evoke it ('I cannot paint/ What then I was'), but thereby enabled to be more effectively categorical: 'nature then . . . To me was all in all.' Belief comes as a substitute for passion, the intensity of the past is played off against a present sobriety. Growth in 'The Pedlar' had been growth towards completion and balance: growth in 'Tintern Abbey' is also a movement away from emotions of the highest importance, now only to be recaptured through the intermediary of memory, or with the help of another and younger self.

'Tintern Abbey' represents an attempt to integrate Wordsworth's beliefs into the world in which he himself actually lived. Where nature shapes the Pedlar into a seer, 'sublime' and 'comprehensive',[1] the Wordsworth of 'Tintern Abbey' finds it a source of restoration in the face of loneliness and distress. Compared to the passages in 'The Pedlar' from which they derive, the central affirmations of 'Tintern Abbey' are tentatively made.[2] Wordsworth's earlier conviction gives way to an expressive verbal groping which suggests a mind in the act of formulating the beliefs that had actually been asserted months before. His writing embodies that struggle to define which, as he wrote apropos of 'The Thorn', accompanies most attempts 'to communicate impassioned feelings'.[3] At times he seems to be giving himself time to think, elaborating 'sensations sweet' as 'feelings too/Of unremembered pleasure'; side-tracking

---

[1] Ibid.: *PW* v. 383, l. 157.
[2] The passages are quoted on pp. 93–5 above.
[3] 1800 note to 'The Thorn' (*PW* ii. 513).

again with 'such, perhaps,/As may have had no trivial influence . . .' (ll. 32–3), and only embarking on his central claims with an unassuming negative transition:

> Nor less, I trust,
> To them I may have owed another gift,
> Of aspect more sublime; that blessed mood,
> In which the burthen of the mystery,
> In which the heavy and the weary weight
> Of all this unintelligible world
> Is lighten'd:—that serene and blessed mood,
> In which the affections gently lead us on,
> Until, the breath of this corporeal frame,
> And even the motion of our human blood
> Almost suspended, we are laid asleep
> In body, and become a living soul:
> While with an eye made quiet by the power
> Of harmony, and the deep power of joy,
> We see into the life of things.   (ll. 36–50)

Even when he is well under way, Wordsworth continues to explain ('that blessed mood . . . that serene and blessed mood'); but by now his repetitions have become a means of both mirroring and holding in check an underlying emotion. When painstaking definition is transcended by the steady excitement of seeing into the life of things, his achievement outdoes the triumph of the sun-touched landscape in 'The Pedlar'. God-given revelation is replaced by a more arduous intuition; in 'Tintern Abbey' there is a burthen of mystery to be lightened, an unintelligible world to be understood. Ecstatic participation ('Thought was not. In enjoyment it expired')[1] gives way to a carefully authenticated process, a recognizable state of mind and body. Breath, blood, sleep—the familiar terms make the shift from physical to mental activity accessible, as the earlier 'visitation from the living God'[2] is not. The eye made quiet by harmony and joy seems as much a shared experience as sleep.

It is characteristic of 'Tintern Abbey's' ebb and flow that the confidence of its first meditative climax should give way to misgiving ('If this/Be but a vain belief', ll. 50–1); characteris-

---

[1] 'The Ruined Cottage', MS. B: *PW* v. 382, l. 137.
[2] Ibid.: *PW* v. 382, l. 135.

tic, too, that Wordsworth's confident declaration about the past ('Not for this/Faint I, nor mourn nor murmur,' ll. 86–7) should be undercut by its elegiac tone. This is the context for Wordsworth's most successful poetic statement of his belief in the One Life. 'The Pedlar' had side-stepped the question of subjectivity ('He had a world about him—'twas his own'):[1] in 'Tintern Abbey', the more subjective poem, belief is more completely endorsed. Like Wordsworth himself, the reader is disturbed by 'the joy/Of elevated thoughts', discovering them unexpectedly in the midst of uncertainty. Again the moment of insight is casually introduced—with 'And', this time, instead of 'Nor':

> And I have felt
> A presence that disturbs me with the joy
> Of elevated thoughts; a sense sublime
> Of something far more deeply interfused,
> Whose dwelling is the light of setting suns,
> And the round ocean, and the living air,
> And the blue sky, and in the mind of man,
> A motion and a spirit, that impels
> All thinking things, all objects of all thought,
> And rolls through all things. (ll. 94–103)

Beside its counterpart in 'The Pedlar' ('in all things/He saw one life . . .'),[2] the passage is deliberately uncategorical. 'The sentiment of being'[3] becomes 'a sense sublime/Of something far more deeply interfused'—something elusive as well as impressive. The earlier momentousness had been unqualified, but now Wordsworth is 'disturbed', the One Life is perceived with an effort ('far more deeply interfused'). This is more subtle writing than that of 'The Pedlar', and when Wordsworth chooses to use the earlier antiphonal rhetoric it is correspondingly more effective. Vigorous archetypal life ('all that leaps, & runs, & shouts . . .')[4] is replaced by a new concept of being, shared by sea, sky, air, and the human mind. It is only now that Wordsworth introduces the assertive language of power, the motion that rolls through all things. Most of the work is done by the verse itself, with its assured rhythms and the inclusive

---

[1] Ibid.: *PW* v. 388, l. 283.
[2] Ibid.: *PW* v. 385, ll. 251–2 (see p. 95, above).
[3] Ibid.: *PW* v. 385, l. 242.   [4] Ibid.: *PW* v. 385, l. 247.

repetition of 'all'. But Wordsworth's rhetoric contains an added dimension of meaning. The crudely animal life of 'The Pedlar' has been transformed by adjectives that suggest the perceived qualities of the world, of sun, ocean, air, and sky—'setting', 'round', 'living', 'blue'—and, in doing so, suggest also the all-embracing presence and ever-present vitality of the human mind itself; 'and in the mind of man'. 'All thinking things, all objects of all thought' reaches out to suggest not simply the existence of mind in all things, but the irradiation of all things by the mind.

The central impulse of 'Tintern Abbey' is that of *The Prelude*—an attempt to make permanent the vision that is threatened by the processes of change and growth recorded in the poem:

> I see by glimpses now; when age comes on,
> May scarcely see at all, and I would give,
> While yet we may, as far as words can give,
> A substance and a life to what I feel:
> I would enshrine the spirit of the past
> For future restoration.[1]

Already by the end of 'Tintern Abbey' Wordsworth has projected himself and Dorothy forward to a time when separation, experience, and mortality turn the present into the past. His anchoring of identity to landscape enshrines the source of 'future restoration'—that vision, at once philosophic and humanized, transcendent and accessible, which is central to his greatest poetry.

[1] *Prelude*, xi. 338–43.

PART II

'THE MOVING ACCIDENT IS NOT MY TRADE'

('Hart-Leap Well')

VI 'The Tragic Super-Tragic' and Salisbury Plain

WORDSWORTH'S earliest attempts to portray suffering are clumsy and overstated, 'The tragic super-tragic', in contrast to the effective understatement of his later narrative poetry:

> Then common death was none, common mishap,
> But matter for this humour everywhere,
> The tragic super-tragic, else left short.
> Then, if a Widow, staggering with the blow
> Of her distress, was known to have made her way
> To the cold grave in which her Husband slept,
> One night, or haply more than one, through pain
> Or half-insensate impotence of mind
> The fact was caught at greedily, and there
> She was a Visitant the whole year through,
> Wetting the turf with never-ending tears,
> And all the storms of Heaven must beat on her.[1]

Long before he wrote these lines, he had adopted a technique of moving restraint. With 'The Ruined Cottage', the drama of distress sketched in *The Prelude* becomes a tragedy of disrupted relationships, humane in its assumptions yet transfigured by the Wordsworthian imagination. His starting-point, while still at school in the late 1780s, had been 'The notions and the images of books'[2]—notions and images like those of Joseph Warton's 'Ode to Fancy':

> Let us with silent footsteps go
> To charnels and the house of woe,
> To Gothic churches, vaults, and tombs,
> Where each sad night some virgin comes,
> With throbbing breast, and faded cheek,
> Her promis'd bridegroom's urn to seek;
> Or to some Abby's mould'ring tow'rs,
> Where, to avoid cold wint'ry show'rs,

[1] *Prelude*, viii. 530–41.　　　　　　[2] Ibid. viii. 517.

> The naked beggar shivering lies,
> While whistling tempests round her rise,
> And trembles lest the tottering wall
> Should on her sleeping infants fall.[1]

The stock figures of grief and destitution, with their landscape of distress—ruins and inclement weather—reappear in Wordsworth's early poetry as he too pays lip-service to contemporary sensibility or exploits suffering for the purposes of humanitarian protest. Out of such writing comes his first major narrative poem. *Salisbury Plain*,[2] originally based on the story of the Female Vagrant, attempts to recast these pathetic episodes as a sustained attack on the conditions of the dispossessed, the victims of war, and the social outlaw. Not yet as profound or as meditative as 'The Ruined Cottage', *Salisbury Plain* nonetheless marks Wordsworth's commitment to the realities of human suffering.

I. PATHOS AND PROTEST POETRY

Wordsworth's self-parody in *The Prelude* goes on to allude specifically to his earliest surviving study of suffering, the episode of the female beggar incorporated into *An Evening 'Walk*. What he laughs at is the 'wild obliquity' by which a drooping foxglove can conjure up a spectacle of distress—a kind of pathetic fallacy in reverse:

> behold!
> If such a sight were seen, would Fancy bring
> Some Vagrant thither with her Babes, and seat her
> Upon the turf beneath the stately Flower
> Drooping in sympathy, and making so
> A melancholy Crest above the head
> Of the lorn Creature, while her Little-Ones,
> All unconcerned with her unhappy plight,
> Were sporting with the purple cups that lay
> Scatter'd upon the ground.[3]

---

[1] *A Collection of Poems*, ed. Robert Dodsley, iii (1748), 81. See Carol Landon's valuable essay, 'Some Sidelights on *The Prelude*', *Bicentenary Wordsworth Studies*, p. 373.

[2] *Salisbury Plain*—as distinct from the version published in 1842 as *Guilt and Sorrow*—properly comprises the two early poems referred to as 'A Night on Salisbury Plain' (MS. 1) and 'Adventures on Salisbury Plain' (MS. 2).

[3] *Prelude*, viii. 550–9.

In *An Evening Walk*, the female beggar is introduced by way of contrast with a female swan, and (as *The Prelude* implies) she is there to satisfy contemporary sensibility rather than the demands of the poem itself:

> Fair swan! by all a mother's joys caress'd,
> Haply some wretch has ey'd, and call'd thee bless'd;
> Who faint, and beat by summer's breathless ray,
> Hath dragg'd her babes along this weary way . . . [1]

Wordsworth's self-parody recollects in particular the beggar's pathetic attempts to amuse her children—

> Pleas'd thro' the dusk their breaking smiles to view,
> Oft has she taught them on her lap to play
> Delighted, with the glow-worm's harmless ray
> Toss'd light from hand to hand; while on the ground
> Small circles of green radiance gleam around.[2]

—a passage that is significantly found in rough drafts going back to 1788, there coloured by the pathos of the pseudo-antiquarian ballad, *Hardyknute*:

> Much she wish'd to lay
> Her cheek to its cold cheek
> But wet and chill the tears that from her eyes
> Flow'd like a stream.
>
> Unconscious of her woes another babe
> Sat by, and smiled, delighted—for it held
> A glow worm in its little hand,
> At which it looked
> Delighted: while it toss'd it to and fro
> It gazed the stars that on the brow of night
> Dim twinkl'd
>
> I could a tale unfold
> Of that unhappy family, more sad,
> More piteous in its circumstance
>
> When the storm howl'd and beat the rain of night
> And Hardyknute beheld his castle wall

---

[1] *An Evening Walk* (London, 1793), ll. 241–4.   [2] Ibid., ll. 274–8.

> Gloomy and dark; nor knew the woeful woe
> Of his unhappy daughter Fairly Fair—[1]

As it happens, the draft offers us not a piteous tale, but a poignant detail—the contrast between the mother's grief and the child's impervious gaiety—of a kind that will surface a decade later in 'The Mad Mother'. For the next few years, however, Wordsworth's portrayal of suffering is more often dictated by the conventions of the time, whether pathetic, sensational, or humanitarian. Not until *Salisbury Plain* is there any real insight into the nature of destitution and unbalance.

Prelude Book VIII and Warton's 'Ode to Fancy' invoke the two chief stereotypes of the poetry of suffering—on the one hand, the 'Widow, staggering with the blow/Of her distress', and on the other, the destitute or outcast mother. The widow, and the virgin visiting her promised bridegroom's urn, suffer mentally, their unbalance implied in the obsessive rituals of mourning. The vagrant and the naked beggar, their plight mirrored by flower or ruin, suffer physically in their exposure to the elements. At first Wordsworth accepts this compartmentalized view; only much later, in the storm-beaten thorn or the ruined cottage, does he achieve the transfer of physical suffering to the insentient world which allows him to deal fully with inner states. *An Evening Walk* presents the female beggar in terms of grotesquely exaggerated torment—first burning, then freezing, first assailed by 'arrowy fire', then by 'bitter showers'. The howling storm of the earlier draft is rewritten as a lurid melodrama of Tempest and Light'ning, Fear and Death:

> Oh! when the bitter showers her path assail,
> And roars between the hills the torrent gale,
> —No more her breath can thaw their fingers cold,
> Their frozen arms her neck no more can fold;
> Scarce heard, their chattering lips her shoulder chill,

---

[1] DC MS. 2; there is another draft in DC MS. 6. For the date of both, see Reed, pp. 307–10. Wordsworth's reference is to the 'fragmentary' final stanza of Lady Wardlaw's *Hardyknute* (Edinburgh, 1719), p. 12:

> Loud and chill blew westlin Wind,
> Sair beat the heavy Shower,
> Mirk grew the Night ere Hardyknute
> Wan near his stately Tower . . .

And her cold back their colder bosoms thrill;
All blind she wilders o'er the lightless heath,
Led by Fear's cold wet hand, and dogg'd by Death;
Death, as she turns her neck the kiss to seek,
Breaks off the dreadful kiss with angry shriek.
Snatch'd from her shoulder with despairing moan,
She clasps them at that dim-seen roofless stone.—
'Now ruthless Tempest launch thy deadliest dart!
Fall fires—but let us perish heart to heart.'
Weak roof a cow'ring form two babes to shield,
And faint the fire a dying heart can yield;
Press the sad kiss, fond mother! vainly fears
Thy flooded cheek to wet them with its tears;
Soon shall the Light'ning hold before thy head
His torch, and shew them slumbering in their bed,
No tears can chill them, and no bosom warms,
Thy breast their death-bed, coffin'd in thine arms.[1]

The snatch of dialogue, later to be used with such poignant
restraint in Wordsworth's narrative poetry, at this stage reveals only his distance from his subject. A reference in 1842 to
'the mischievous influence of Darwin's dazzling manner'[2]
points to the model for his early sensationalist treatment of
suffering. It is disquieting to put the death of the female beggar
beside the fanciful tragedy of Tremella, a frozen fungus, in
The Botanic Garden. Darwin's note inadvertently undercuts
the cliché by which suffering and exposure are equated in late
eighteenth-century poetry: 'I have frequently observed fun-
gusses of this Genus on old rails and on the ground to become
a transparent jelly, after they had been frozen in autumnal
mornings . . .':[3]

> Round the dark craggs the murmuring whirlwinds blow,
> Woods groan above, and waters roar below;
> As o'er the steeps with pausing foot she moves,
> The pitying Dryads shriek amid their groves;
> She flys,—she stops,—she pants—she looks behind,
> And hears a demon howl in every wind.

[1] *An Evening Walk*, ll. 279–300.
[2] *PW* iii. 442 (MS. note of 1842). Cf. Coleridge's *Biographia Literaria* reference to
the ephemeral popularity of *The Botanic Garden* (Shawcross, i. 11–12), and Jonathan Wordsworth, *The Music of Humanity*, pp. 50–1.
[3] *The Botanic Garden*, II (1789), p. 36n.

> —As the bleak blast unfurls her fluttering vest,
> Cold beats the snow upon her shuddering breast;
> Through her numb'd limbs the chill sensations dart,
> And the keen ice-bolt trembles at her heart.
> 'I sink, I fall! oh, help me, help!' she cries,
> Her stiffening tongue the unfinish'd sound denies;
> Tear after tear adown her cheek succeeds,
> And pearls of ice bestrew the glistering meads;
> Congealing snows her lingering feet surround,
> Arrest her flight, and root her to the ground;
> With suppliant arms she pours the silent prayer,
> Her suppliant arms hang crystal in the air;
> Pellucid films her shivering neck o'erspread,
> Seal her mute lips, and silver o'er her head,
> Veil her pale bosom, glaze her lifted hands,
> And shrined in ice the beauteous statue stands.[1]

Darwin has evoked our pity only to suggest how much more decorative Tremella is after her icy metamorphosis. He can get away with manipulating the reader's feelings because we recognize his basic frivolity; Wordsworth is in a different position. When the shrieking dryads and howling demons of *The Botanic Garden* reappear as Death, breaking off 'the dreadful kiss with angry shriek', or 'the keen ice-bolt' becomes the 'deadliest dart' of a 'ruthless Tempest', or Tremella herself becomes a real woman frozen to death, his human sympathy is inevitably called in question.

Wordsworth's next attempt at narrative exchanged some of Darwin's glitter for Thomson's realism. The description of the snow-mazed farmer in 'Winter' is the major eighteenth-century precursor of these later deaths by cold. Darwin and Wordsworth both personify the horrors of exposure ('And hears a demon howl in every wind', 'Led by Fear's cold wet hand, and dogg'd by Death'); Thomson, by contrast, makes even such perils as pits, bogs, and precipices the product of the imagination. For the farmer, lost in his own unrecognizable

---

[1] *The Botanic Garden*, II. i. 387–408. The couplet draft in DC MS. 7 where the original blank verse draft reaches virtually its final form in *An Evening Walk*, ll. 279–300, dates from roughly the same period as the publication of the second part of *The Botanic Garden* in 1789. Reed groups this draft with the earlier ones in DC MSS. 2 and 6 as belonging to 1788 (see Reed, pp. 309 and n., 310), but there is no reason why it should not date from the following year and thus reflect the immediate impact of Darwin on the young Wordsworth.

fields, the real dangers are exhaustion and despair. The reality is at once more prosaic and more frightening than anything in *The Botanic Garden* or *An Evening Walk*:

> down he sinks
> Beneath the shelter of the shapeless drift,
> Thinking o'er all the bitterness of death,
> Mixt with the tender anguish nature shoots
> Thro' the wrung bosom of the dying man,
> His wife, his children, and his friends unseen.
> In vain for him th'officious wife prepares
> The fire fair-blazing, and the vestment warm;
> In vain his little children, peeping out
> Into the mingling rack, demand their sire,
> With tears of artless innocence. Alas!
> Nor wife, nor children more shall he behold,
> Nor friends, nor sacred home. On every nerve,
> The deadly winter seizes; shuts up sense;
> And, o'er his stronger vitals creeping cold,
> Lays him along the snows, a stiffen'd corpse,
> Unstretch'd, and bleaching in the northern blast.[1]

The farmer's lethargy tells one more about dying of exposure than all Tremella's frozen tears, and his dying thoughts of family and friends permit him to be human rather than heroic. In *Descriptive Sketches*, farmer becomes chamois-hunter, his setting the Alps. Wordsworth's showy idiom continues to reflect Darwin's influence ('The Demon of the snow with angry roar / Descending . . .'),[2] but the end of the hunter's audacious, doomed climb goes back to Thomson:

> Then with despair's whole weight his spirits sink,
> No bread to feed him, and the snow his drink,
> While ere his eyes can close upon the day,
> The eagle of the Alps o'ershades his prey.
> —Meanwhile his wife and child with cruel hope
> All night the door at every moment ope;
> Haply that child in fearful doubt may gaze,
> Passing his father's bones in future days,
> Start at the reliques of that very thigh,
> On which so oft he prattled when a boy.[3]

---

[1] 'Winter', ll. 379–95.   [2] *Descriptive Sketches* (London, 1793), ll. 400–1.
[3] Ibid., ll. 404–13. For another episode by Wordsworth which may date from this period, and which seems to have formed the basis for Coleridge's 'Old Man of

Wordsworth is still intrigued by the macabre ('the reliques of that very thigh,/On which so oft he prattled . . .'), but he has made a new attempt to convey the despair and anxiety involved in such a death. He goes still further in revising the episode of the female beggar, during his 1794 work on *An Evening Walk*. Her fate is shifted onto another, anonymous woman, and a note added to authenticate the manner of her death ('These verses relate the catastrophe of a poor woman who was found dead on Stanemoor two winters ago with her two children whom she had in vain attempted to protect from the storm in the manner here described'):

> —Ah then, to baffle the relentless Storm,
> She tries each fond device Despair can form,
> Beneath her stiffened coats to shield them strives,
> With love whose providence in death survives.
> When morning breaks I see the [   ] swain,
> Sole moving shape in all that boundless plain,
> Start at her stedfast form by horror deck'd,
> Dead, and as if in act to move, erect.—[1]

Once again the episode ends on a distinctly macabre note: but Wordsworth has replaced the earlier woman's heroic challenge to the elements with a credible gesture of protection. Horror, now externalized in the reaction of the swain who discovers the frozen tableau, is no longer taken for granted. Wordsworth is at last beginning to look critically at his earlier approach to the poetry of suffering.

But the major change which took place in Wordsworth's narrative writing during the 1790s was not so much a shift from sensationalism to realism, as a preparedness to see suffering in terms of unbalance as well as physical privation. As he grew more concerned with—perhaps simply more aware of—human feeling, the drama of exposure to the elements gave way to the drama within. The *Prelude* allusion to 'The tragic super-tragic' has behind it a tradition scarcely less lugubrious than Wordsworth's self-parody. The bereaved virgin of Warton's 'Ode' figures in Blair's *Grave* of 1743:

---

the Alps' (published in the *Morning Post* for 8 March 1798), see J. W. Smyser, *PMLA* lxv (1960), 422; R. S. Woof, *SB* xv (1962), 167–9; and Reed, p. 23 and n.

[1] DC MS. 9: *PW* i. 28–9 app. crit. and 29n. For the factual basis claimed by Wordsworth's note, see Jonathan Wordsworth, *The Music of Humanity*, p. 52n.

> The new-made *Widow* too, I've sometimes spy'd,
> Sad Sight! slow moving o'er the prostrate Dead:
> Listless, she crawls along in doleful Black,
> Whilst Bursts of Sorrow gush from either Eye,
> Fast-falling down her now untasted Cheek.
> Prone on the lowly Grave of the Dear Man
> She drops; whilst busy-meddling Memory,
> In barbarous Succession, musters up
> The past Endearments of their softer Hours,
> Tenacious of its Theme. Still, still she thinks
> She sees him, and indulging the fond Thought,
> Clings yet more closely to the senseless Turf,
> Nor heeds the Passenger who looks that Way.[1]

Blair, however, is interested in the imagination as well as in tears—'Still, still she thinks/She sees him'. The widow's state is as much morbid as pathetic. Wordsworth himself clearly draws on *The Grave* for his own study of obsessive bereavement in *The Borderers*. Blair's widow has become 'A maid, who fell a prey to the Lord Clifford', and his sentimental gloom is displaced by the gothic colouring of Wordsworth's play:

>   alas!
> What she had seen and suffered—the poor wretch,
> It turned her brain—and now she lives alone
> Nor moves her hands to any needful work.
> She eats the food which every day the peasants
> Bring to her hut, and so the wretch has lived
> Ten years; and no one ever heard her voice
> But every night at the first stroke of twelve
> She quits her house, and in the neighbouring church-yard
> Upon the self-same spot, in rain or storm,
> She paces out the hour 'twixt twelve and one,
> She paces round and round, still round and round
> And in the church-yard sod her feet have worn
> A hollow ring; they say it is knee-deep—[2]

Like Martha in 'The Thorn', the woman is seen from a distance, characterized only by the compulsiveness of her grief and surrounded by a fog of hearsay ('they say it is knee-deep'). Later, Wordsworth provides an eye-witness account that takes up

---

[1] *The Grave* (London, 1743), ll. 72–84.
[2] MS. B: *PW* i. 143, ll. 381–95 and app. crit.

Blair's stress on the widow's oblivious absorption ('Nor heeds the Passenger who looks that Way'):

> 'Twas a calm night as I remember well
> The moon shone clear; the air was still—so still,
> The trees were silent as the graves beneath them;
> The church-clock from within the steeple tower
> Tick'd audibly—a full half hour did I
> Prolong my watch; I saw her pacing round
> Upon the self same spot, still round and round
> Her lips for ever moving.[1]

Here the woman's setting both complements and expresses her silent preoccupation. Calm night, still air, and silent trees focus our attention on the inner life revealed by her moving lips. Compulsiveness has become introspection, and the furrowed ring of turf gives way to a realization of the woman's mental state; spectacle is replaced by insight. Wordsworth is on the way to creating a poetry of suffering—whether understated as the mere lack of will to survive, in 'The Ruined Cottage', or released in a single, haunting cry (' "O misery!" ') in 'The Thorn'.

Wordsworth's concern with unbalance is matched by his growing concern with social victims. Like many of his contemporaries, he turned to narrative poetry to express his indignation at the plight of the poor, the dispossessed, and the casualties of war. In his 'Letter to the Bishop of Llandaff', written in early 1793, Wordsworth alludes in passing to the legal enforcement of inadequate wages and the consequent gulf between rich and poor—

Even from the astonishing amount of the sums raised for the support of one description of the poor may be concluded the extent and greatness of that oppression, whose effects have rendered it possible for the few to afford so much, and have shewn us that such a multitude of our brothers exist in even helpless indigence.[2]

—and he goes on to attack 'an infatuation which is now giving up to the sword so large a portion of the poor, and consigning the rest to the more slow and more painful consumption of want'.[3] It is anti-war protest, as well as the more general

[1] MS. B: *PW* i. 150, ll. 573–9 and app. crit.
[2] DC MS. 8: *Prose Works*, i. 43.   [3] Ibid.: *Prose Works*, i. 49.

humanitarian protest of the period, that provides the chief impulse behind *Salisbury Plain*. Already in *An Evening Walk* Wordsworth had adapted the pathetic episode to topical ends. The female beggar is a soldier's widow—along with her orphan children, the central figure in anti-war protest of the 1790s:

> —With backward gaze, lock'd joints, and step of pain,
> Her seat scarce left, she strives, alas! in vain,
> To teach their limbs along the burning road
> A few short steps to totter with their load,
> Shakes her numb arm that slumbers with its weight,
> And eyes through tears the mountain's shadeless height;
> And bids her soldier come her woes to share,
> Asleep on Minden's charnel plain afar;
> For hope's deserted well why wistful look?
> Chok'd is the pathway, and the pitcher broke.[1]

Unexpectedly, the passage provides one of the underlying symbols of 'The Ruined Cottage'—'The useless fragment of a wooden bowl' which the Pedlar finds beside Margaret's overgrown well;[2] the metaphor of hopelessness, used with such restraint in the later poem, is characteristically explicit here. Understatement is not to be the method of the protest poetry of the 1790s. Southey and Coleridge, in *Joan of Arc* and *Religious Musings*, both rely on the war-widow to come forward 'with damning eloquence' and 'Against the mighty plead!',[3] and both use her anguish for propagandist purposes. Even the passage which most closely anticipates the plight of Margaret in 'The Ruined Cottage', from Southey's *Joan of Arc*, uses mental torment primarily as a weapon to turn against the oppressor:

> At her cottage door,
> The wretched one shall sit, and with dim eye
> Gaze o'er the plain, where on his parting steps
> Her last look hung. Nor ever shall she know
> Her husband dead, but tortur'd with vain hope,
> Gaze on—then heart-sick turn to her poor babe,
> And weep it fatherless![4]

[1] *An Evening Walk*, ll. 247–56.
[2] MS. B: *PW* v. 389, l. 341.
[3] *Joan of Arc*, iii. 445–6. Cf. *Religious Musings*, ll. 316–20 (*CPW* i. 120, ll. 296–300), and, for yet another war-widow, Fawcett's *Art of War* (London, 1795), pp. 16–17.
[4] Ibid. vii. 325–31. Cf. also the passage describing a war-widow in the revised

Salisbury Plain is the first poem to make the destitute war-widow significant in her own right rather than a symbol of oppression.

In *An Evening Walk*, Wordsworth had of course been referring to earlier wars. He was clearly recollecting Langhorne's 'Apology for Vagrants' from *The Country Justice* (1774–7):

> Perhaps on some inhospitable Shore
> The houseless Wretch a widow'd Parent bore;
> Who, then, no more by golden Prospects led,
> Of the poor Indian begg'd a Leafy bed.
> Cold on Canadian Hills, or Minden's Plain,
> Perhaps that Parent mourn'd her Soldier slain;
> Bent o'er her Babe, her Eye dissolv'd in Dew,
> The big Drops mingling with the Milk He drew,
> Gave the sad Presage of his future Years,
> The Child of Misery, baptiz'd in Tears![1]

Langhorne's influence on the early Wordsworth can be gauged from his much later tribute to *The Country Justice* in a letter of 1837: 'As far as I know, it is the first Poem, unless perhaps Shenstone's Schoolmistress be excepted, that fairly brought the Muse into the Company of common life, to which it comes nearer than Goldsmith, and upon which it looks with a tender and enlightened humanity . . .'[2] It is difficult to think of Langhorne as in any real sense the poet of 'common life'; though enlightened and conscientious, his stance is scarcely one of identification. But his humanitarian emphasis made him a powerful counterbalance to writers like Darwin, and his concern with social victims underlies Wordsworth's much more far-reaching protest in *Salisbury Plain*. Langhorne's is essentially

---

Book I of Southey's poem—*Joan of Arc* (2nd edn., 2 vols., Bristol, 1798), i. 110–12—which may in turn owe something to Wordsworth's 'Ruined Cottage'; the revisions took place during the autumn of 1797 (see Curry, i. 153), and it is possible that Southey saw or knew of Wordsworth's poem.

[1] *The Country Justice* (London, 1774–7), i (1774), pp. 17–18. It was evidently Wordsworth's anxiety to avoid a direct echo of Langhorne that led him to change 'Asleep on Minden's charnel plain afar' to 'Asleep on Bunker's charnel hill afar' in the 'Errata' of *An Evening Walk*. For a brief discussion of Wordsworth's debt to *The Country Justice*, see also Roger Sharrock, 'Wordsworth and John Langhorne's "The Country Justice" ', *N & Q* N.S. i (1954), 302–4. The passage quoted here was sufficiently well known to have been illustrated by Joseph Wright of Derby in his picture, 'The Dead Soldier' of 1789; see Benedict Nicolson, *Joseph Wright of Derby* (2 vols., London, 1968), i. 65–6, 153–4; ii, Plate 281.

[2] *LY* ii. 829.

a poetry of indignation, aiming to shock the reader out of his assumptions by confronting him with glaring miscarriages of justice or shortcomings in poor-law administration. One episode, perhaps the best-known, has special relevance to the kind of problem which Wordsworth sets his readers in *Salisbury Plain*. A thief on the run stumbles on a dead woman who has just given birth to a child on a desolate heath:

> The pitying Robber, conscious that, pursued,
> He had no Time to waste, yet stood and view'd;
> To the next Cot the trembling Infant bore,
> And gave a Part of what He stole before;
> Nor known to Him the Wretches were, nor dear,
> He felt as Man, and dropp'd a human Tear.
>   Far other Treatment She who breathless lay,
> Found from a viler Animal of Prey.
>   Worn with long Toil on many a painful Road,
> That Toil increas'd by Nature's growing Load,
> When Evening brought the friendly Hour of Rest,
> And all the Mother throng'd about her Breast,
> The Ruffian Officer oppos'd her Stay,
> And, cruel, bore her in her Pangs away,
> So far beyond the Town's last Limits drove,
> That to return were hopeless, had She strove.
> Abandon'd there—with Famine, Pain and Cold,
> And Anguish, She expir'd—the rest I've told.
>   'Now *let* Me swear—For, by my Soul's last Sigh,
> 'That Thief shall live, that Overseer shall die.'
>   Too late!—His Life the generous Robber paid,
> Lost by that Pity which his Steps delay'd![1]

Wordsworth's method in *Salisbury Plain* is to consist of a series of encounters—with the Female Vagrant, with a quarrelling family, with a dying woman—each providing the same step-by-step illustration of the poem's message; like Langhorne, Wordsworth suggests that the only refuge of the poor lies in mutual compassion. Wordsworth, however, goes much further. There is no moral conflict in siding with Langhorne's robber against the parish officer, but Wordsworth's sailor is a murderer. The artificially clear-cut issues of protest poetry have come

---

[1] *The Country Justice*, ii (1775), pp. 25–6. The link between this episode and the sailor's story in *Salisbury Plain* is suggested by Roger Sharrock, *N & Q* N.S. i. 302–4.

close to the painful conflict of tragedy. Langhorne aims to provoke his reader (' "Now *let* Me swear . . ." '): Wordsworth aims to take him beyond indignation to an appalled identification with the victims of hardship and oppression in an unjust society.

The other major influence on protest writers of the late eighteenth century would have been Goldsmith—mentioned alongside Langhorne in Wordsworth's tribute. To this period, *The Deserted Village* was the greatest of all laments for dispossession:

> Sweet smiling village, loveliest of the lawn,
> Thy sports are fled, and all thy charms withdrawn;
> Amidst thy bowers the tyrant's hand is seen,
> And desolation saddens all thy green:
> One only master grasps the whole domain . . . [1]

But none of Goldsmith's successors recaptures his nostalgia; *The Country Justice* offers us tears of outrage—

> Harmless to you his Towers, his Forests rise,
> That swell with Anguish my indignant Eyes;
> While in those Towers raz'd Villages I see,
> And Tears of Orphans watering every Tree.[2]

—and Wordsworth in 'The Female Vagrant' bleakly records a process which the smallholder is powerless to resist:

> Then rose a mansion proud our woods among,
> And cottage after cottage owned its sway,
> No joy to see a neighbouring house, or stray
> Through pastures not his own, the master took . . . (ll. 39–42)

But Wordsworth differs from his predecessors in using the theme of dispossession to explore the emotions of the dispossessed themselves. Like Goldsmith, he mourns a lost idyll, yet it is not the passing of the idyll for its own sake that matters most to him. His subject is human—not a village, not a place, but individual men and women. In *The Deserted Village* Goldsmith had expressed the disruption of an entire community by exhibiting a single family:

---

[1] *The Deserted Village* (London, 1770), ll. 35–9.
[2] *The Country Justice*, iii (1777), p. 12.

> Good Heaven! what sorrows gloom'd that parting day,
> That called them from their native walks away;
> When the poor exiles, every pleasure past,
> Hung round their bowers, and fondly looked their last,
> And took a long farewell, and wished in vain
> For seats like these beyond the western main;
> And shuddering still to face the distant deep,
> Returned and wept, and still returned to weep.
> The good old sire, the first prepared to go
> To new found worlds, and wept for others woe.
> But for himself, in conscious virtue brave,
> He only wished for worlds beyond the grave.
> His lovely daughter, lovelier in her tears,
> The fond companion of his helpless years,
> Silent went next, neglectful of her charms,
> And left a lover's for her father's arms.[1]

Both poets are concerned with uprooted families, but where Goldsmith depicts a tableau, Wordsworth takes one inside the minds of the Female Vagrant and her father as they leave their home after ruin and eviction:

> Can I forget that miserable hour,
> When from the last hill-top, my sire surveyed,
> Peering above the trees, the steeple tower,
> That on his marriage-day sweet music made?
> Till then he hoped his bones might there be laid,
> Close by my mother in their native bowers:
> Bidding me trust in God, he stood and prayed,—
> I could not pray:—through tears that fell in showers,
> Glimmer'd our dear-loved home, alas! no longer ours!
>
> (ll. 55–63)

Goldsmith's figures are deliberately generalized; the 'widowed' solitary thing/That feebly bends beside the plashy spring, exists to tell us about Auburn—'The sad historian of the pensive plain'.[2] In 'The Female Vagrant', however, protest goes with an interest in the workings of human feeling—in the old man's affection for the church where he was married and his wife lies buried, in his daughter's despairing inability to pray. Wordsworth is not only moving away from the static episode or tableau; he is moving away from the social victim, dwarfed

<hr>

[1] *The Deserted Village*, ll. 363–78.   [2] Ibid., ll. 129–30, 136.

by the injustice he exists to expose, towards the human being
and his individual capacity for suffering.

II. 'SALISBURY PLAIN'

The most impressive protest poem of its time was undoubtedly
Salisbury Plain.[1] How much it mattered to Wordsworth himself
can be gauged from its development during the mid-1790s.
Focused at first on the story of the Female Vagrant, it became
in effect a new poem when the complementary story of the
sailor was added in 1795. Still intended for publication in
1798, it underwent further revision in 1799.[2] The basis of 'A
Night on Salisbury Plain' (as Wordsworth wanted to call the
earliest surviving version)[3] probably goes back to a period even
before 1793. The story of the Female Vagrant begins as little
more than a reworking of the stock humanitarian themes,
couched in a Spenserian stanza probably inspired by Shenstone
or, more recently, by Beattie's *Minstrel*.[4] Introduced as a fading
village maiden ('Might Beauty charm the canker worm of
pain/The rose on her sweet cheek had ne'er declined'),[5] the
Female Vagrant is presented in terms of a shattered idyll—lost
beauty, lost love, lost well-being, Like Goldsmith, Wordsworth
describes a way of life in order to make its disruption the more
painful, but as yet Goldsmith's method is used to very limited
effect. We are shown the regular alternations of work and play
in the Female Vagrant's past, but the equation of employment
and happiness is never made as it is to be in 'The Ruined
Cottage', and when we are told that 'The loom stood still'[6]
there are none of the tragic overtones of the later poem. Dispossession first, then the ravages of war, precipitate her into

[1] For an excellent account of *Salisbury Plain*, see S. C. Gill, ' "Adventures on
Salisbury Plain" and Wordsworth's Poetry of Protest 1795-7', *SR* xi (1972), 48–65.

[2] See Griggs, i. 400, 411–12; *EY*, p. 256; and Reed, pp. 333–6.

[3] See *EY*, p. 136. For a brief account of this version and for a complete text, see
S. C. Gill, 'The Original *Salisbury Plain*: Introduction and Text', *Bicentenary
Wordsworth Studies*, ed. Jonathan Wordsworth, pp. 142–79. Both versions are discussed more fully by P. D. Sheats in *The Making of Wordsworth's Poetry, 1785–1798*,
pp. 84–94, 108–18.

[4] Shenstone's *Schoolmistress* (1737 and 1742) and Thomson's *Castle of Indolence*
(1748) had revived the Spenserian stanza earlier in the eighteenth century, but it
may have been *The Minstrel* (1771–4) which served as Wordsworth's more immediate model; Beattie's 'Advertisement' had enumerated the advantages of the
Spenserian stanza for a long poem.

[5] MS. 1: *PW* i. 105 app. crit., ll. 47–8.   [6] Ibid.: *PW* i. 110, l. 269.

dependence on a precarious family happiness, and finally into the unrelieved despair with which the second part of the poem is largely concerned. With this second part, 'A Night on Salisbury Plain' emerges as a forerunner—however crude— of Wordsworth's mature studies of suffering. The narrative sweeps relentlessly towards, not disaster, but its aftermath, alienation:

> 'All perished, all in one remorseless year
> Husband and children one by one by sword
> And scourge of fiery fever: every tear
> Dried up, despairing, desolate, on board
> A British ship I waked as from a trance restored.'[1]

Released from a nightmare world of carnage, famine, and death by the calm of her homeward voyage, the Female Vagrant wakes to another kind of dream. Unlike the sailors on the man-of-war, she has no 'pleasant thoughts of home,' no capacity for tears:

> 'Some mighty gulf of separation passed
> I seemed transported to another world;
> A dream resigned with pain when from the mast
> The impatient mariner the sail unfurled
> And whistling called the wind that hardly curled
> The silent seas. The pleasant thoughts of home
> With tears his weather-beaten cheek impearled.
> For me, farthest from earthly port to roam
> Was best, my only wish to shun where man might come.'[2]

The 'mighty gulf of separation' is more than the gulf between war and peace; it is the gulf between living and no longer having a reason to live:

> 'And oft robbed of my perfect mind I thought
> At last my feet a resting-place had found.
> Here will I weep in peace so Fancy wrought,
> Roaming the illimitable waters round,
> Here gaze of every friend but Death disowned,
> All day my ready tomb the ocean flood.
> To break my dream the vessel reached its bound
> And homeless near a thousand homes I stood
> And near a thousand tables pined and wanted food.'[3]

---

[1] Ibid.: *PW* i. 111, ll. 302–6 and app. crit.
[2] Ibid.: *PW* i. 114, ll. 352–60 and app. crit.
[3] Ibid.: *PW* i. 114, ll. 361–9 and app. crit.

This is the peace of despair, a withdrawal from human bonds ('of every friend but Death disowned') which is tragic in its implications. Like Margaret in 'The Ruined Cottage', the Female Vagrant loses her humanity through losing those she loves; set ashore, she can only become a wanderer, for without human ties there can be 'no house in prospect but the tomb'.[1] Her rootlessness reflects a deeper deprivation.

The story of the Female Vagrant is framed by poetry of a quite different kind. Wordsworth's hallucinatory experiences as he crossed Salisbury Plain in the summer of 1793[2] are combined with a mood of bitter social protest to produce writing of dramatic oddity and violence. On one level, at least, 'A Night on Salisbury Plain' is a record of private desolation that looks forward to the *Prelude* accounts of guilt, fear, and 'visionary dreariness'. The benighted traveller who later encounters the Female Vagrant and listens to her story crosses the plain in a state which cannot be explained by his weariness, hunger, and thirst. These are part of a larger desolation—lack of human contact in a landscape whose 'wastes of corn' bring none of the familiar, reassuring associations: 'where the sower dwelt was nowhere to be found'.[3] The emptiness is dreamlike, and with dreamlike panic and ineffectuality the traveller hails a far-off, unhearing shepherd—

> No sound replies but winds that whistling near
> Sweep the thin grass and passing, wildly plain;
> Or desert lark that pours on high a wasted strain.[4]

Later on in the poem, the Female Vagrant describes her encounter with a figure who symbolizes the plain's obscure hostility to human life:

> The woman told that through a hollow deep
> As on she journeyed far from spring or bower,
> An old man beckoning from the naked steep
> Came tottering sidelong down to ask the hour;
> There never clock was heard from steeple tower.
> From the wide corn the plundering crows to scare
> He held a rusty gun. In sun and shower,

---

[1] MS. 1: *PW* i. 118, l. 447 and app. crit. [2] See *Prelude*, xii. 312–53.
[3] MS. 1: *PW* i. 96, l. 27 and app. crit.
[4] Ibid.: *PW* i. 96, ll. 34–6 and app. crit.

Old as he was, alone he lingered there,
His hungry meal too scant for dog that meal to share.[1]

Everything in this land-locked solitude suggests a relentless whittling away of humanity. The clock is too far, the meal too small for a dog to share; the old man totters, and his gun is rusty. Yet he still pointlessly asks the time in a timeless landscape, clinging to human habits in a setting where they have no relevance. Only the plundering crows can triumph over their environment. For the traveller, there is menace as well as hopelessness; like the crows, the very elements seem predatory—'He stood the only creature in the wild/On whom the elements their rage could wreak . . .'[2] The hallucinations of druid rites which follow enact his state of mind. 'Mocked as by a hideous dream', he is urged to

'Fly ere the fiends their prey unwares devour;
'Or grinning, on thy endless tortures scowl
'Till very madness seem a mercy to thy soul.'[3]

Despite the luridness of the writing, the traveller's flight 'as if his terror dogged his road' is entirely convincing. Later, Wordsworth tries to play down the traveller's vision, reinterpreting it in the light of local superstition; he and the Female Vagrant meet nothing more supernatural than each other at the lonely 'spital' in which they take shelter. But the neurotic, disturbing power of Wordsworth's writing can no more be disowned than it can be integrated into the poem as a whole.

'A Night on Salisbury Plain' contains a powerful imaginative expression of Wordsworth's own horror and rejection of social institutions. This was the period of his worst relationship with society—unemployed, disapproved of by his family, separated from Annette and his child in France. It was a melodramatic way of putting it, but he too must have looked with resentment at 'those, who on the couch of Affluence rest/By laughing Fortune's sparkling cup elate'.[4] His problems, however, were

---

[1] Ibid.: *PW* i. 103–4 app. crit., ll. 6–14.
[2] Ibid.: *PW* i. 99, ll. 102–3 and app. crit.
[3] Ibid.: *PW* i. 100 app. crit. For a similarly horrific use of druidic associations ('dying babes in wicker prisons', 'Fiends triumphant'), see *The Botanic Garden*, II. iii. 101–8.
[4] Ibid.: *PW* i. 335.

not merely personal; like other radicals of the period he was profoundly alienated from the policies of the Government, now committed to war against France; and he had just come from watching the British fleet arming off Portsmouth.[1] The traveller's hallucinations represent the persecutions and terrors of contemporary society. The Female Vagrant is no better off than the savage who once lived his precarious existence on the plain; druids no longer offer human sacrifice, but the light of reason serves only to illuminate the appalling sacrifices offered up in the name of civilization:

> Though from huge wickers paled with circling fire
> No longer horrid shrieks and dying cries
> To ears of Demon-Gods in peals aspire,
> To Demon-Gods a human sacrifice;
> Though Treachery her sword no longer dyes
> In the cold blood of Truce, still, reason's ray
> What does it more than while the tempests rise,
> With starless glooms and sounds of loud dismay
> Reveal with still-born glimpse the terrors of our way?[2]

Consolations are few in such a world. As in 'The Ruined Cottage', the imperviousness and continuity of nature in the face of human distress offer an obscure comfort, and with the end of the Female Vagrant's story and the coming of dawn the mood changes. But as the wanderers look down on a peopled and welcoming valley in the light of morning, Wordsworth underlines his cheerless moral:

> think that life is like this desart broad,
> Where all the happiest find is but a shed
> And a green spot 'mid wastes interminably spread.[3]

Clumsy as it is, Wordsworth's metaphor endorses the more effective symbolism of the desolate plain, with its fleeing, cowering figures overwhelmed by storm and night. The druidic

[1] See Reed, pp. 144-5. The predicament of radical intellectuals at this period is well described by E. P. Thompson, 'Disenchantment or Default? A Lay Sermon', *Power and Consciousness*, ed. C. C. O'Brien and W. D. Vanech (London, 1969), pp. 149-81.
[2] MS. 1: *PW* i. 339, st. 48. Wordsworth's use of the druids to reinforce social criticism is interestingly paralleled by Thomas Love Peacock; see A. L. Owen, *The Famous Druids* (Oxford, 1962), pp. 158-9.
[3] Ibid.: *PW* i. 339, st. 47.

imagery has been sufficiently powerful to license the violence of his closing exhortation:

> Heroes of Truth, pursue your march, uptear
> Th'Oppressor's dungeon from its deepest base;
> High o'er the towers of Pride undaunted rear
> Resistless in your might the herculean mace
> Of Reason; let foul Error's monster race
> Dragged from their dens start at the light with pain
> And die; pursue your toils, till not a trace
> Be left on earth of Superstition's reign,
> Save that eternal pile which frowns on Sarum's plain.[1]

Wordsworth lacks an appropriate language of protest, and his Godwinian invocation to Reason is supremely mismatched with the archaism of *The Faerie Queene*. Yet the contorted rhetoric and Spenserian associations ('Error's monster race') graphically convey Wordsworth's vision, both of a monstrous world and of the wished-for millennium.

The highly-wrought writing which surrounds the story of the Female Vagrant accentuated its slightness. Wordsworth himself seems to have seen that 'A Night on Salisbury Plain' could not hold together, and the expanded poem of 1795–6— 'Adventures on Salisbury Plain'—is radically altered in focus. Transformed into a sailor on the run after committing a murder, the traveller himself becomes the new centre of interest, adding another theme of protest to the original anti-war message of 1793. 'It's object', wrote Wordsworth of the revised poem in autumn 1795, 'is partly to expose the vices of the penal law and the calamities of war as they affect individuals.'[2] Wordsworth's position is that of Godwin in *Political Justice*, where crime is represented as the result of intolerable social oppression: 'A numerous class of mankind are held down in a state of abject penury, and are continually prompted by disappointment and distress to commit violence upon their more fortunate neighbours.'[3] The sailor has been press-ganged, then cheated by a corrupt bureaucracy of the earnings he had hoped to bring back to his family. In a mood of desperation, he robs and kills a traveller near his home, and flees. Wordsworth's interest

---

[1] Ibid.: *PW* i. 340–1; cf. Charles Lloyd in 'Oswald' (quoted p. 18, above).
[2] *EY*, p. 159.   [3] *Political Justice*, i. 9.

in such moments of isolated and desperate violence is emphasized by an episode later on in the poem. As they cross the plain together, sailor and Female Vagrant come on a man striking down his playful child in sudden, uncontrolled anger. The child on the ground appears to the sailor as an image of the man he has murdered, and he expostulates with the father, who repents and kisses his son. But repentance cannot save the sailor himself, for 'justice' is implacably concerned not with his better nature but with retribution. Once more, Wordsworth's position is Godwinian:

It cannot be just that we should inflict suffering on any man, except so far as it tends to good. Hence it follows that the strict acceptation of the word punishment by no means accords with any sound principles of reasoning. . . . To punish [a man] upon any hypothesis for what is past and irrecoverable . . . must be ranked among the wildest conceptions of untutored barbarism.[1]

The symbol of this 'untutored barbarism' in 'Adventures on Salisbury Plain' is the gibbet with its chained corpse, a cautionary sight familiar to eighteenth-century travellers. At the start of the poem, it overwhelms the sailor with terror and inspires his previously unmotivated flight across the plain—a landscape now suggestive not simply of a harsh and desolate world, but of the isolation brought about by one man's crime against another. At the end of the poem, the gibbet recurs, this time bearing the chained corpse of the sailor himself:

> They left him hung on high in iron case,
> And dissolute men, unthinking & untaught,
> Planted their festive [?booths] beneath his face;
> And to that spot which idle thousands sought,
> Women & children were by fathers brought;
> And now some kindred sufferer driven, perchance
> That way when into storm the sky is wrought,
> Upon his swinging corpse his eye may glance
> And drop as he once dropp'd in miserable trance.[2]

---

[1] *Political Justice*, ii. 693–4.

[2] MS. 2: *PW* i. 127, ll. 658–66 and app. crit. By 1842 Wordsworth no longer had the courage to offer his readers 'the intolerable thought' with which the earlier poem had ended:

> His fate was pitied. Him in iron case
> (Reader, forgive the intolerable thought)
> They hung not . . .
> (*Guilt and Sorrow*, ll. 658–60)

The cycle of suffering can only be perpetuated ('And now some kindred sufferer . . .') in a society that is at once vengeful and uncaring.

'Adventures on Salisbury Plain' shows not only an appalled awareness of society's indifference to the criminals it has created, but remarkable insight into the psychology of guilt. Wordsworth's source for the sailor's story had been crudely sensational—the confession of Jarvis Matchan, a sailor who murdered a drummer-boy in 1780 and six years later confessed to his companion as they tramped across Salisbury Plain in a storm. Widely reported at the time,[1] Matchan's confession was supposed to have been prompted by supernatural manifestations of divine wrath. In Wordsworth's poem (as in *Peter Bell*) it is not the supernatural that accuses him, but his own conscience. Contact with his kind—with the Female Vagrant, with the quarrelling family, and finally with his own wife—makes his crime increasingly insupportable. It is the accidental meeting with his wife, now destitute and dying, that brings him at last to give himself up. Wordsworth's handling of the sailor's remorse shows the humanity of his vision in *Salisbury Plain*. Ostensibly, he draws on a passage from Fawcett's *Art of War* (1795) describing the murderer's conscience-stricken torment:

> He starts, when nothing stirr'd;—'Who speaks?'—he asks,
> When no one spoke; and mutters things unheard
> With nimble-moving lips that send no sound.
> Disturb'd e'en in the stillest room he lies;
> Kept by no noise awake, no sleep he finds,
> Or no oblivion finds it.[2]

But Wordsworth's purpose is very different. The guilt of Fawcett's assassin exists to expose, by contrast, society's acceptance of mass murder in war. The sailor's torment, however, suggests his fundamental redeemability and his value as a human being.

[1] See, for instance, reports under 'Principal Occurrences' in the *New Annual Register for 1786* (1787), pp. 27–8, and *Gentleman's Magazine*, lvi (June 1786), 521. The entire story is quoted from a lost pamphlet, *A Narrative of the Life, Confession, and Dying Speech of Jarvis Matchan*, in R. H. Barham's *Ingoldsby Legends; or Mirth and Marvels*, ed. R. H. Dalton Barham (2 vols., London, 1870), ii. 253–5. I owe this information to Stephen Gill's unpublished thesis, 'Wordsworth's Salisbury Plain: An Edition of the Three Texts with an Essay on their Place in the Development of his Poetry' (Edinburgh, 1968), Appendix III.

[2] *The Art of War*, p. 44.

What breaks him is the knowledge of the irreparable harm he has done to his wife:

> For him alternate throbbed his pulse & stopp'd;
> And when at table placed the bread he took
> To break it, from his faltering hands it dropp'd,
> While on those hands he cast a rueful look.
> His ears were never silent, sleep forsook
> His nerveless eyelids stiffen'd even as lead;
> All through the night the floor beneath him shook
> And chamber trembled to his shuddering bed;
> And oft he groan'd aloud, 'Oh God that I were dead!'[1]

The sailor is unmanned by his essential goodness. When he gives himself up, his death comes as a travesty of justice; but it is also a mercy:

> Blest be for once the stroke which ends, tho' late
> The pangs which from thy halls of terror came,
> Thou who of Justice bear'st the violated name.[2]

The echo of *Lear* is a reminder that, like the story of the Female Vagrant, his has been a tragedy of waste.

Beside the psychological insight and unflinching intention of the sailor's story, that of the Female Vagrant was bound to seem lightweight. The version excerpted for *Lyrical Ballads* in 1798 was at some stage expanded and revised in an attempt to give it new stature.[3] As well as an increased element of protest (additional stanzas on the theme of dispossession and the horrors of war), Wordsworth achieves a considerable gain in narrative subtlety. In 'A Night on Salisbury Plain', little had been made of the stoppage of work with the outbreak of war—'The loom

---

[1] MS. 2: *PW* i. 125, ll. 631–9 and app. crit. For Fawcett's influence on Wordsworth, see also Arthur Beatty, 'Joseph Fawcett: The Art of War', *University of Wisconsin Studies in Language and Literature*, ii (Madison, 1918), 224–69.

[2] Ibid.: *PW* i. 126, ll. 655–7 and app. crit. Again, there is a marked change of attitude in the 1842 text:

> 'O welcome sentence which will end though late,'
> He said, 'the pangs that to my conscience came
> Out of that deed. My trust, Saviour! is in thy name!'
> (*Guilt and Sorrow*, ll. 655–7)

[3] By early 1799, Wordsworth had decided to 'invent a new story for the woman', but he regarded 24 stanzas as 'the utmost tether allowed to the poor Lady' (*EY*, pp. 256–7).

stood still: unwatched the idle gale/Wooed in deserted shrouds the unregarding sail'[1]—but in the final version, the link is made, as it is to be in 'The Ruined Cottage', between work and well-being, idleness and deracination: 'The empty loom, cold hearth, and silent wheel,/And tears that flowed for ills which patience could not heal' (ll. 89–90). Again, the stiff personifications of the earlier version ('How changed at once! for Labour's chearful hum/Silence and Tears and Misery's weeping train . . .')[2] are transformed into a subdued and realistic statement of hardship: ''Twas a hard change, an evil time was come;/We had no hope, and no relief could gain' (ll. 91–2). But the major development is the new weight given to the Female Vagrant's state of mind after her return. Wordsworth makes it clear that she starves not only because society fails to feed her, but because she fails to feed herself. She is 'By grief enfeebled' (l. 181), not just by hunger—like Margaret, deprived of the will to survive. Hers is the inertia of despair:

> Ill was I then for toil or service fit:
> With tears whose course no effort could confine,
> By high-way side forgetful would I sit
> Whole hours, my idle arms in moping sorrow knit.
>
> I lived upon the mercy of the fields,
> And oft of cruelty the sky accused . . .   (ll. 249–54)

Her state of mind is revealed not so much by tears as by a stance ('my idle arms in moping sorrow knit'), and by her unbalanced vision of a hostile world ('And oft of cruelty the sky accused'). Significantly, the Female Vagrant's final lament—'But, what afflicts my peace with keenest ruth/Is, that I have my inner self abused . . .' (ll. 258–9)—is echoed later by Margaret, in 'The Ruined Cottage': ' "I am changed,/And to myself", said she, "have done much wrong . . ." '[3] The two women have wronged themselves as Tess has done when Angel Clare finds her in Sandbourne: 'his original Tess had spiritually ceased to recognize the body before him as hers—allowing it to drift, like

---

[1] MS. 1: *PW* i. 110, ll. 269–70.
[2] Ibid.: *PW* i. 110, ll. 271–2 and app. crit.
[3] MS. B: *PW* v. 396, ll. 602–3. It is hard to see Margaret as a prostitute, but as Meyer suggests (*Wordsworth's Formative Years*, p. 132), this would be an appropriate culmination of the Female Vagrant's exploitation by society.

a corpse upon the current, in a direction dissociated from its living will.'[1] Hardy's insight, paralleled in 'The Ruined Cottage', is already anticipated in 'The Female Vagrant'; and the two writers have in common their painful vision of a world in which the oppressed can only strike back at the oppressor by sealing their own doom as victims. Like *Tess of the d'Urbervilles*, *Salisbury Plain* extenuates neither suffering nor injustice, and its final note is one of tragic protest rather than consolation.

[1] *Tess of the d'Urbervilles* (Wessex edn., London, 1912), p. 484.

VII 'Tales of Silent Suffering' and the Wordsworthian Solitary

MARGARET'S story in 'The Ruined Cottage' prompted Wordsworth to define the narrative method which he had evolved since writing *Salisbury Plain*:

> 'Tis a common tale
> By moving accidents uncharactered,
> A tale of silent suffering, hardly clothed
> In bodily form, & to the grosser sense
> But ill adapted, scarcely palpable
> To him who does not think.[1]

It is the meditativeness that is new ('scarcely palpable/To him who does not think'). *Salisbury Plain* had asked its readers to think, but its message was clearly stated. In 'The Ruined Cottage' Wordsworth's meaning is less easily grasped; social injustice has given way to the silent suffering explored by his greatest narrative poetry and most eloquently expressed in the figure of the Wordsworthian solitary. Nothing happens to Margaret except desertion; nothing happens to the beggar of 'Old Man Travelling' except old age. Wordsworth is now concerned with states of being rather than the state of society, and the significance attached to suffering is imaginative and philosophic rather than simply humanitarian. It is not that he has become a less humane poet, but that his vision is directed beyond topical issues to the permanent themes of loss, change, and mortality. The poetry that results is as much reflective as narrative; its events are whittled away to leave a genre closer to meditation than to story-telling, its technique deliberately self-effacing. For all its reticence, such poetry is a powerful vehicle for Wordsworth's own vision. Less openly than the 'experimental' ballads of 1798, it implies the same assumptions about narrative—not simply that 'the feeling therein developed

[1] MS. B: *PW* v. 393, ll. 486–91.

gives importance to the action and situation and not the action and situation to the feeling',[1] but that, in Coleridge's words, the most ordinary aspects of life become significant 'where there is a meditative and feeling mind to seek after them'.[2]

I. PLAIN AND SIMPLE TALES

In Wordsworth's narrative poetry of 1797–8, the obtrusive rhetoric of his earlier writing has been replaced by a blank verse approximating to the sober and involved voice of the poet himself, as he confronts the subject of his poetry. The technique is almost that of contemporary prose reporting—by the 1790s a fashionable genre in its own right, combining as it did authenticity, pathos, and an interest in the unvarnished reality of ordinary people's lives. Dr. Burney's complaint, when he reviewed *Lyrical Ballads* in 1799, constitutes an indirect tribute:

When we confess that our author has had the art of pleasing and interesting in no common way by his natural delineation of human passions, human characters, and human incidents, we must add that these effects were not produced by the *poetry*:—we have been as much affected by pictures of misery and unmerited distress, in *prose*.[3]

The kind of material Dr. Burney had in mind could be found in any contemporary magazine—in the *Weekly Entertainer*, for instance, which Wordsworth read and contributed to during the mid-1790s.[4] Under the title 'Interesting Trials for Murder' appears an account of infanticide which could well have become the basis for a ballad by Wordsworth or Southey:

On Friday March 11, 1796, this poor creature, who is the wife of a labouring man, was about to heat her oven, and being short of wood, had broken down a rail or two from the fencing round the plantation of a gentleman in the neighbourhood; some of her neighbours threatened her with a prosecution, and told her she would be transported for it. This so much alarmed her mind, and the idea of being separated from her child, whom she had always appeared remarkably fond of, so wrought on her imagination, that she formed the horrible design of putting her to death, in order, that, by surrendering herself into the hands of justice she might be executed for the murder; and so be for ever reunited in Heaven to that babe whom she had loved more than life: As soon, therefore, as her

---

[1] 1800 'Preface' (*Prose Works*, i. 128). [2] Shawcross, ii. 5.
[3] *Monthly Review*, xxix (June 1799), 203.
[4] See J. R. MacGillivray, *RES* N.S. v (1954), 62–6.

husband was gone out to his labour, she proceeded to put this diabolical design in execution; she filled a large tub with water, and, taking the child in her arms, was about to plunge it in the water, when the babe, smiling in its mother's face, disarmed her for the moment, and she found herself unable to commit the horrid act; she then lulled the babe to sleep at her breast, and wrapping a cloth round it, plunged it into the tub, and held it under water till life became extinct; then took it out of the tub, and laid it on the bed, and, taking her hat and cloak, locked her street door, and left her key at a neighbour's for her husband when he should return from his labour; she then proceeded to walk eight or nine miles to a Magistrate, and, requesting admission to him, told him the whole story, concluding with an earnest desire immediately to be executed.[1]

Prosaic detail, matter-of-factness, and the absence of any explicit comment on the woman's state of mind—let alone any expression of sympathy—are central to the poignancy of effect. What guidance there is ('this diabolical design', 'the horrid act') becomes counter-productive, and the reader has to construe the bare facts of the woman's desperation for himself. The implications go far beyond what we are actually told, subsuming pity and horror into an understanding of the power of love and fear when the two combine in a simple mind.

The anecdotes printed in contemporary magazines were aimed at a public educated for the past generation by Henry Mackenzie. His central assumption—'I love myself (and am apt therefore, from a common sort of weakness, to imagine that other people love) to read nature in her smallest character'[2]—inspires his confident yet casual glimpses of human nature. *The Man of Feeling* is represented as an arbitrary but authentic 'bundle of little episodes, put together without art, and of no importance on the whole, with something of nature, and little else in them'.[3] The 'something of nature, and little else' may entail an apparent rejection of artifice, but it aims to

[1] *Weekly Entertainer*, xxvii (28 March 1796), 253. Cf. the anecdote recorded in *Southey's Common-Place Book*, ed. J. W. Warter (4 vols., London, 1849–51), iv. 198—'This will balladize'—which became the basis for Southey's infanticide poem, 'The Mad Woman', published anonymously in *The Annual Anthology* (2 vols., Bristol, 1799–1800), ii (1800), 70–3; for the attribution, see Kenneth Curry, 'The Contributors to *The Annual Anthology*', *Papers of the Bibliographical Society of America*, xlii (1948), 60.

[2] *Julia de Roubigné* (2 vols., London, 1777), i. x–xi.

[3] *The Man of Feeling*, p. viii.

involve the reader in Harley's experiences in a peculiarly direct way. One episode, Harley's encounter with an old soldier, provides an obvious parallel for Wordsworth's narrative method in 'The Discharged Soldier' of early 1798.[1] Mackenzie's soldier derives his significance entirely from the onlooker's consciousness. The leisurely narrative allows us to enter into the encounter as it takes place:

The sun was now in his decline, and the evening remarkably serene, when [Harley] entered a hollow part of the road, which winded between the surrounding banks, and seamed the sward in different lines, as the choice of travellers had directed them to tread it. It seemed to be little frequented now, for some of those had partly recovered their former verdure. The scene was such as induced Harley to stand and enjoy it; when, turning round, his notice was attracted by an object, which the fixture of his eye on the spot he walked had before prevented him from observing.

An old man, who from his dress seemed to have been a soldier, lay fast asleep on the ground; a knapsack rested on a stone at his right hand, while his staff and brass-hilted sword were crossed at his left.

Harley looked on him with the most earnest attention. He was one of those figures which Salvator would have drawn; nor was the surrounding scenery unlike the wildness of that painter's backgrounds. The banks on each side were covered with fantastic shrubwood, and at a little distance, on the top of one of them, stood a finger-post, to mark the directions of two roads which diverged from the point where it was placed. A rock, with some dangling wild flowers, jutted out above where the soldier lay; on which grew the stump of a large tree, white with age, and a single twisted branch shaded his face as he slept. His face had the marks of manly comeliness impaired by time; his forehead was not altogether bald, but its hairs might have been numbered; while a few white locks behind crossed the brown of his neck with a contrast the most venerable to a mind like Harley's. 'Thou art old, said he to himself, but age has not brought thee rest for its infirmities: I fear those silver hairs have not found shelter from thy country, though that neck has been bronzed in its service.' The stranger waked. He looked at Harley with the appearance of some confusion: it was a pain the latter knew too well to think of causing in another; he turned and went on. The old man readjusted his knapsack, and followed in one of the tracks on the opposite side of the road.

---

[1] See Reed, pp. 321, 323, 327; and Beth Darlington, 'Two Early Texts: *A Night-Piece* and *The Discharged Soldier*', *Bicentenary Wordsworth Studies*, pp. 425–48.

When Harley heard the tread of his feet behind him, he could not help stealing back a glance at his fellow traveller. He seemed to bend under the weight of his knapsack; he halted on his walk, and one of his arms was supported by a sling, and lay motionless across his breast. He had that steady look of sorrow, which indicates that its owner has gazed upon his griefs till he has forgotten to lament them; yet not without those streaks of complacency, which a good mind will sometimes throw into the countenance, through all the incumbent load of its depression.[1]

Despite the painstaking detail, there is a sense of heightened reality; the figure of the soldier in his rugged setting appears to us through the medium of Salvator Rosa's painting. The care of Mackenzie's description suggests realism, but the transforming vision suggests a writer well-versed in the picturesque. In 'The Discharged Soldier', Wordsworth too sees the figure on the road before him in terms of his own state of mind:

> in his very dress appear'd
> A desolation, a simplicity
> That appertained to solitude.[2]

The spectacle is one to which he responds imaginatively rather than humanely, and like Mackenzie he has to re-encounter the soldier as a man; each rejects the picture, the abstraction, for awareness of a suffering individual. Yet something of the former strangeness remains. In motion, the two figures have an impressiveness which suggests that their hardship has obscurely dignified them. As Wordsworth is later to do, Mackenzie transforms the encounter into a way of exploring the imaginative significance of suffering; and like Wordsworth's, his technique is as much meditative as narrative.

Distracted women as well as distressed soldiers formed part of Mackenzie's stock-in-trade. His own treatment has a modish Shakespearian poignancy; Harley's encounter with an inmate of Bedlam exploits the pretty distraction and pathetic song of Ophelia, while censoring the bawdiness which could make her madness genuinely disturbing:

'My Billy is no more! said she, do you weep for my Billy? Blessings on your tears! I would weep too, but my brain is dry; and it burns,

---

[1] *The Man of Feeling*, pp. 176–80.
[2] DC MS. 16: *Prelude*, iv. 417–19 and p. 538.

it burns, it burns!'—She drew nearer to Harley.—'Be comforted, young lady, said he, your Billy is in heaven.' 'Is he, indeed? and shall we meet again? . . . when I can, I pray; and sometimes I sing; when I am saddest, I sing:—You shall hear me, hush!

> 'Light be the earth on Billy's breast,
> 'And green the sod that wraps his grave!'[1]

Wordsworth too has his Ophelia, in a blank verse fragment dating from the late 1780s; here madness is signified by

> A blade of Grass with which she talk'd and smiled
> And kissed and dew'd it with her tears—
> It grew upon her dead love's grave . . . [2]

But his most effective use of Mackenzie's mode is in a prose fragment, probably belonging to his undergraduate days. Its quality can be gauged by putting it beside another prose description, 'The Unfortunate Eleonora. A Scrap', again from the *Weekly Entertainer*:

YOU have seen this miserable being—every person who has frequented Islington, or Canonbury, or Highbury, or places adjacent, and many persons in London, are acquainted with her person.—A dull, dreadful melancholy has long since seized her, and her mental faculties are gone—the once gay Eleonora . . . is now become the outcast of society, a solitary wanderer, clothed with filthy rags, and supported by precarious charity—a total stranger to a bed, reposing at night in a barn, or a hovel, or under a hay-rick, and not unfrequently, in damp and cold weather, obliged to take up her abode in the public streets![3]

As her name suggests, Eleonora is seen through literary spectacles; the parade of realism—actual London districts, her sleeping-places in barn, hovel, rick, or street—goes with a covert appeal to the reader's emotions. What is lacking is any real interest in the woman's state of mind; instead, we are invited to dwell on the fact that she was once as respectable as ourselves. Wordsworth, by contrast, shows Mackenzie's method

[1] *The Man of Feeling*, pp. 63–4.

[2] DC MS. 2. See Carol Landon, *Bicentenary Wordsworth Studies*, p. 372, for a conjectural dating of 1787 or 1788, and for the stanzaic version also preserved in DC MS. 2.

[3] *Weekly Entertainer*, xxviii (12 September 1796), 214–15.

at its best. Called simply 'A Tale', the prose fragment describes an encounter with a figure as striking in her way as the old soldier, but with something of the Bedlam Ophelia's exaltation:

Her dress, if you except a black hat (which bore no other marks than that of being drench'd in rain) tied by a dark green ribband which knotted under chin, was not much more warm or becoming than that of such of those numerous wretches, the poor, the lame, and the blind, who have no fire but the light of a Window seen at a distance, and whose candle is the little [?glow-worm]. Her eyes were large and blue; and from the wrinkles of her face (which, from their fineness, seemed rather the wrinkles of Sorrow than of Years) it was easy to see they had been acquainted with weeping; yet had not perpetual tears been able to extinguish a certain wild brightness which, at the first view, might have been mistaken for the wildness of great Joy. But it was far different—it too plainly indicated she was not in her true and perfect mind.[1]

Wordsworth has not only seen the incongruous and ineffectual hat—he has also imagined what it is to be homeless ('no fire but the light of a Window seen at a distance'). A state of mind comprising both grief and elation is subtly authenticated by the finely wrinkled face and the large, wild eyes. The woman he describes is not another Eleonora; she is the first, and not least memorable, of Wordsworth's solitaries, transformed by suffering and the onlooker's imagination.

The restraint and apparent fidelity of these prose studies are to be seen also in Cowper's 'Crazy Kate', one of the most important forerunners of 'The Ruined Cottage', and frequently excerpted from *The Task* as an independent poem. Where Ophelia provides a model for the pretty pathos of Mackenzie's mad girl, Desdemona's 'willow' speech (moving for what it implies but does not say) underlies the reticence of Cowper's writing:

> My mother had a maid call'd Barbary,
> She was in love, and he she lov'd prov'd mad,
> And did forsake her; she had a song of 'willow',
> An old thing 'twas, but it express'd her fortune,
> And she died singing it . . . [2]

---

[1] DC MS. 2: *Prose Works*, i. 8. Owen and Smyser omit the interlined phrase, 'such of those numerous wretches'. For the date, see Reed, pp. 313–14.

[2] *Othello*, IV. iii. 26–30.

In 'Crazy Kate', prose reporting fuses with this inherited simplicity and pathos to create the basic idiom of Wordsworth's poetry of suffering:

> There often wanders one, whom better days
> Saw better clad, in cloak of sattin trimm'd
> With lace, and hat with splendid ribband bound.
> A serving maid was she, and fell in love
> With one who left her, went to sea and died.
> Her fancy followed him through foaming waves
> To distant shores, and she would sit and weep
> At what a sailor suffers; fancy too
> Delusive most where warmest wishes are,
> Would oft anticipate his glad return,
> And dream of transports she was not to know.
> She heard the doleful tidings of his death,
> And never smil'd again. And now she roams
> The dreary waste; there spends the livelong day,
> And there, unless when charity forbids,
> The livelong night. A tatter'd apron hides,
> Worn as a cloak, and hardly hides a gown
> More tatter'd still; and both but ill conceal
> A bosom heaved with never-ceasing sighs.
> She begs an idle pin of all she meets,
> And hoards them in her sleeve; but needful food,
> Though press'd with hunger oft, or comelier cloaths,
> Though pinch'd with cold, asks never.—Kate is craz'd.[1]

'A serving maid was she, and fell in love . . .': 'She was in love, and he she lov'd prov'd mad . . .' Cowper establishes the shift of emphasis from story to state of mind, from event to feeling, which is to be the hall-mark of Wordsworth's narrative method. Shakespeare's implied emotion ('she had a song of "willow"') becomes in Cowper the indirect presentation of feeling characteristic of 'The Ruined Cottage' and 'Michael'. The reader is asked to infer Crazy Kate's state of mind from her tatters and hoarded pins, her aimless roaming and inconsequential

---

[1] *The Task*, i. 534–56. Lamb, praising Southey's *Joan of Arc* for its 'anecdotes', writes: 'I am delighted with the very many passages of simple pathos abounding throughout the poem—passages which the author of "Crazy Kate" might have written' (Lucas, i. 14–15). 'Crazy Kate' is also discussed by Charles Ryskamp, 'Wordsworth's *Lyrical Ballads* in Their Time', *From Sensibility to Romanticism*, pp. 363–4, and by Jonathan Wordsworth, *The Music of Humanity*, pp. 61–2.

begging, just as Margaret's decline is read in the neglect of her garden. Kate's bosom 'heaved with never-ceasing sighs' is slipped in unobtrusively, almost as if it has been noticed by the reader himself; Wordsworth achieves the same effect in 'The Ruined Cottage', when Margaret's sighs come on the Pedlar's ear, he 'knew not how, and hardly whence they came'.[1] In both cases, the reader detects feeling, and the act of detection draws him into relationship with the sufferer.

These studies, whether verse or prose, have in common their concern with ordinary people, and it is not surprising that the same period should have seen a redefinition of pastoral— the genre traditionally concerned with the simplicities of rural life. Pope's definition, 'an imitation of the action of a shepherd', had carried with it an explicit rejection of realism ('We must . . . use some illusion to render a Pastoral delightful; and this consists in exposing the best side only of a shepherd's life, and in concealing its miseries').[2] Johnson reacted with his closely argued attack on the neo-classical conventions of 'golden age' pastoral; and it is his Virgilian definition—' "a poem in which any action or passion is represented by its effects upon a country life" '[3]—that paves the way for Hugh Blair's demand in the 1780s, 'why may not Pastoral Poetry take a wider range?':

Human nature, and human passions, are much the same in every rank of life; and wherever these passions operate on objects that are within the rural sphere, there may be a proper subject for Pastoral. . . . The various adventures which give occasion to those engaged in country life to display their disposition and temper; the scenes of domestic felicity or disquiet; the attachment of friends and of brothers; the rivalship and competitions of lovers; the unexpected successes or misfortunes of families, might give occasion to many a pleasing and tender incident; and were more of the narrative and sentimental intermixed with the descriptive in this kind of Poetry, it would become much more interesting than it now generally is, to the bulk of readers.[4]

---

[1] MS. B: *PW* v. 397, l. 637.

[2] 'A Discourse on Pastoral Poetry', *The Poems of Alexander Pope*, ed. John Butt (11 vols., London and New Haven, Conn., 1961–9), i. 27.

[3] *Rambler*, No. 37 (24 July 1750), *The Yale Edition of the Works of Samuel Johnson* (8 vols., London and New Haven, Conn., 1958–68), iii. 201.

[4] *Lectures on Rhetoric and Belles Lettres*, ii. 346–7. The developing pastoral tradition is discussed more fully by S. M. Parrish, *The Art of the Lyrical Ballads*, pp. 162–73.

Blair cited Gessner's idylls as his model for a less restricted version of pastoral—perhaps swayed by the attitude to simple people implied in the preface to Gessner's *Rural Poems* of 1762 ('Their hearts, as yet inaccessible to corruption, preserve their primitive integrity').[1] Had he written a little later, it would surely have been Burns, in 'The Cotter's Saturday Night', who provided the best example of a genre adapted to portraying country life with realism and feeling. At much the same moment in the 1780s Burns was writing

> it may be some entertainment to a curious observer of human na-
> ture to see how a plough-man thinks, and feels, under the pressure
> of Love, Ambition, Anxiety, Grief with the like cares and passions,
> which, however diversified by the Modes, and Manners of life,
> operate pretty much alike I believe, in all the Species—[2]

Redefined in this way, pastoral took on new life. More impor-
tant still, the pastoral eclogue—a dramatic or semi-dramatic presentation of the themes outlined by Blair—became a means of transforming the verse episode into a free-standing narrative genre. In the 1790s Robert Southey (as often, an index to contemporary taste) turned to the eclogue as a vehicle for topical themes. His 'Botany Bay Eclogues' parallel *Salisbury Plain* in their attempt to explore the feelings and psychology of the social victim,[3] and in the late 1790s his 'English Eclogues' focus on subjects drawn from rural life. Indirectly, this renewal of the pastoral eclogue informs Wordsworth's developing concept of narrative, prompting his adoption of the more econo-
mical and subtly dramatized mode seen in 'The Ruined Cottage' and, later, 'The Brothers'.

Southey's 'Botany Bay Eclogues' use the form to give new force to familiar tales of misfortune and distress. Through dramatic monologue or dialogue, they vividly recreate the plight of social outcasts—prostitutes, felons, and the casualties of war. In 'Edward and Susan', the Australian setting reflects not simply exile, but the convict's unreconciled state of mind:

[1] *Rural Poems* (London, 1762), p. xvii.
[2] *Robert Burns's Commonplace Book 1783–1785*, ed. J. C. Ewing and Davidson Cook (Glasgow, 1938), p. 1.
[3] Apparently in existence by mid-1794 (see Curry, i. 58), Southey's 'Botany Bay Eclogues' were not published until *Poems* (1797); one appeared separately in the *Monthly Magazine* for January 1798 (see below).

> Ah, Susan! humble is indeed this cot,
> And well it suits the outcast's wretched lot;
> Well suits the horror of this barren scene,
> A mind as drear as comfortless within.
> 'Tis just that I should tread the joyless shore,
> List to the wintry tempest's sullen roar,
> Plough up the stubborn and ungrateful soil,
> Earn the scant pittance of a felon's toil,
> And sleep scarce shelter'd from the nightly dew,
> Where howls around the dismal Kangaroo.
> This I have merited, but then to know
> Susan partakes her barbarous husband's woe,
> Unchang'd by insult, cruelty, and hate,
> Partakes an outcast's bed, a felon's fate,
> To see her fondly strive to give relief,
> Forget his crimes, and only share his grief—
> And then on all my actions past to dwell,
> My crimes, my cruelties—'tis worse than hell.[1]

There is nothing especially distinguished about such writing, but powerfully-stated remorse has taken over from the simplified emotions of pastoral tradition. Having seen the eclogue as a means of dramatizing protest, Southey went on to see that it offered a way to focus interest on the incidents of ordinary life. His models were the German 'idylls' to which he was introduced by the translator William Taylor of Norwich, during a visit in the early summer of 1798:

> FROM what William Taylor has told me of the Idylls of Gessner and Voss, and the translation he has shown me of one of Goethe, I am tempted to introduce them here. Surely I also can seize the fit objects of common life, and place them in the right point of view.[2]

This was the project that became 'English Eclogues', published in 1799 as an innovation with specifically German origins.[3]

---

[1] *Monthly Magazine*, v (January 1798), 42. Southey's ideas about the kangaroo are confused; cf. his mention of 'the kangaroo's sad note/Deepening in distance' in another 'Botany Bay Eclogue', 'Elinor', published in *Poems* (1797).

[2] *Southey's Common-Place Book*, iv. 95; for Southey's visit to Taylor, see Curry, i. 165. The translation which Southey had been shown was 'The Wanderer'; see Southey's letter to Taylor, J. W. Robberds, *A Memoir of the Life and Writings of the Late William Taylor of Norwich*, i. 213. 'The Wanderer, An Idyll' was published in the *Monthly Magazine*, vi (August 1798), 120–1. Cf. also Jonathan Wordsworth, *The Music of Humanity*, Appendix I, pp. 261–8.

[3] See *Poems* (1799), ii. 183.

Southey sets out to naturalize the 'idyll', creating a genre which is primarily sociological and humanitarian in emphasis. 'The Witch', for instance, uses its dialogue between modern curate and old-fashioned parishioners to portray rustic superstition from a self-consciously enlightened point of view:

CURATE   Good day Farmer!
                  Nathaniel what art nailing to the threshold?
NATHANIEL   A horse-shoe Sir, 'tis good to keep off witchcraft,
                  And we're afraid of Margery.
CURATE   Poor old woman!
                  What can you fear from her?
FATHER   What can we fear?
                  Who lamed the Miller's boy? who rais'd the wind
                  That blew my old barn's roof down? who d'ye think
                  Rides my poor horse a'nights? . . .

          .   .   .   .

NATHANIEL   What makes her sit there moping by herself,
                  With no soul near her but that great black cat?
                  And do but look at her!
CURATE   Poor wretch! half blind
                  And crooked with her years, without a child
                  Or friend in her old age, 'tis hard indeed
                  To have her very miseries made her crimes![1]

Southey preaches to the converted rather than to the meditatively-inclined. For him the eclogue gives dramatic focus to clear-cut issues and topical themes, seldom aiming to create the reflective awareness of suffering and old age, mortality and change, which is to be Wordsworth's special achievement.

But it is 'Hannah'—the earliest and most poignant of Southey's 'English Eclogues'—which provides the closest forerunner of Wordsworth's poetry of suffering. Published in the *Monthly Magazine* for October 1797, it was apparently written before Southey's visit to Taylor and seems to belong to almost exactly the same period as the earliest drafts of 'The Ruined

---

[1] *Poems* (1799), ii. 220–1. There is an obvious link here with Wordsworth's 'Goody Blake, and Harry Gill'; see my article, 'Southey's Debt to *Lyrical Ballads* (1798)', *RES* N.S. xxii (1971), 20–36. Southey had criticized Wordsworth's ballad for a tendency to encourage superstition (see *Critical Review*, xxiv. 200).

Cottage'.[1] The poem was originally sub-titled 'A Plain Tale', but 'Plain' was changed to 'Plaintive' by the printer,[2] the two epithets suggesting how well defined the genre had become.[3] The bare outlines of Hannah's story are sloughed off in a few lines:

> She bore, unhusbanded, a mother's name,
> And he who should have cherish'd her, far off
> Sail'd on the seas . . . [4]

Like Crazy Kate ('A serving maid was she, and fell in love/ With one who left her, went to sea and died'),[5] Hannah is interesting not for what has happened to her, but for its aftermath. Her significance lies in her decline and death. With the narrator, we come on the funeral in a country lane, forget her story, and then recall it in the cool of evening:

> it was eve
> When homewardly I went, and in the air
> Was that cool freshness, that discolouring shade
> That makes the eye turn inward.[6]

Hannah's 'plain and simple tale,' like Margaret's, can find room only in the meditative mind. The difference is that Southey has a limited ability to portray suffering; pathos too easily becomes vacuousness ('So she pin'd, and pin'd away,/And for herself and baby toil'd and toil'd . . .'),[7] and the culminating snatch of dialogue—used so effectively by Wordsworth—labours the point rather than allowing it to emerge:

---

[1] 'Hannah' was sent to Coleridge before his letter of mid-September 1797 (see Griggs, i. 345–6); Southey was later to plagiarize 'The Ruined Cottage' in his own poem of the same name, but the absence of verbal echoes in 'Hannah' suggests that it was an independent response to the same literary fashion. See also the discussion of 'Hannah' by Jonathan Wordsworth, *The Music of Humanity*, pp. 63–4 and n.

[2] See J. W. Robberds, *A Memoir of the Life and Writings of the Late William Taylor*, i. 238.

[3] The plain and plaintive tale had earned itself a parody by 1799, in 'Joseph. An attempt at Simplicity', published in the *Monthly Mirror*, vii (March 1799), 175. Cf. also the third of Coleridge's 'Nehemiah Higginbottom' sonnets in the *Monthly Magazine* for 1797 (*CPW* i. 211).

[4] *Monthly Magazine*, iv (October 1797), 287.

[5] *The Task*, i. 537–8. Southey also had a factual source; see Curry, i. 153 and *Poems* (1799), ii. 202n.

[6] *Monthly Magazine*, iv. 287.   [7] Ibid. iv. 287.

> 'Poor girl!' her mother said,
> 'Thou has suffer'd much!'—'Aye, mother; there is none
> 'Can tell what I have suffer'd!' she reply'd . . . [1]

More authentic is Southey's portrayal of the breakdown of Hannah's relationship with her child—her inability to express affection matched by its indifference. Like Robert and Margaret, Hannah requires well-being in order to sustain human bonds; she dies, as Margaret does, because the disruption of one relationship undermines all others. In its restrained and thoughtful presentation and its insight into the psychology of desertion, 'Hannah' marks the transition between the pathetic episodes of the eighteenth century and Wordsworth's poetry of suffering.

II. THE POETRY OF SUFFERING

The period between *Salisbury Plain* and 'The Ruined Cottage' shows Wordsworth working towards a narrative poetry whose insight and scope are entirely new. Surviving fragments from 1796–7 suggest that he was again toying with the idea of a story about a woman's suffering and decline, and at least beginning to think in terms of the blank verse idiom of the following year. Two passages probably composed at the same time in mid-1796 use as their starting-point the Dorset heath that later reappears in 'The Ruined Cottage'. The first, in which Wordsworth has identified himself so completely with his speaker that it comes as a shock to discover her to be a woman, describes yet another benighted and storm-beaten traveller:

> The sun was sunk
> And, fresh-indented, the white road proclaimed
> The self-provided waggoner gone by.
> Me from the public way the [common] hope
> Of shorter path seduced, and led me on
> Where smooth-green sheep-tracks thridded the sharp furze
> And kept the choice suspended having chosen.
> The time exacted haste and steps secure
> From such perplexity, so to regain
> The road now more than a long mile remote
> My course I slanted, when at once winds rose
> And from the rainy east a bellying cloud

[1] *Monthly Magazine*, iv. 287.

> Met the first star & hurried on the night.
> Now fast against my face and whistling ears
> My loose wet hair and tattered bonnet flapped
> With thought-perplexing noise . . . [1]

The meticulous, authenticating detail recalls Mackenzie's technique in *The Man of Feeling*.[2] We are inside the speaker, seeing the wheel-marks she sees on the road before her, hearing the noises of wet hair and flapping bonnet, sharing her envy of 'the self-provided waggoner' as the storm comes on. In the second fragment, Wordsworth reverts to a debased Spenserian stanza, and a further woman is introduced, who begins to tell a story not unlike that of the Female Vagrant. Her faded beauty, lost idyll, and plaintive song ('So plaintive-sad, the tones might well agree/With one who sang from very grief of soul')[3] are balanced by a realistic portrayal of deracination:

> Strait to the door a ragged woman came,
> Who with arms linked and huddling elbows press'd
> By either hand a tattered jacket drew
> With modest care across her hollow breast
> That showed a skin of sickly yellow hue.
> 'With travel spent' she cried 'you needs must be
> If from the heath arrived; come in and rest with me.'[4]

The woman's huddling gesture reveals a state of mind as well as body. Wordsworth is evoking inner life, as he evokes Margaret's, through everyday actions—through the contrast between the woman's constrained stance and her unexpectedly forthcoming words, or the 'fruitless look of fondness' with which she feeds her child:

> Then from a mat of straw a boy she raised
> Who seemed though weak in growth three winters old,
> And with a fruitless look of fondness gazed
> On his pale face and held him at her breast . . . [5]

---

[1] DC MS. 2: *PW* i. 292–3, ll. 6–21. The missing word is supplied from a draft. For the dates of these two fragments, see Reed, pp. 344–5, and for their relationship to 'The Ruined Cottage', see ibid., p. 337. Robert Woof suggests that Wordsworth may have had in mind the Spenserian and Shakespearian versions of a fragment called 'The Heath', on which he had also drawn in *Salisbury Plain*, by another Lake District poet, J. B. Farish; see T. W. Thompson, *Wordsworth's Hawkshead*, Appendix I (b).

[2] See pp. 162–3, above.

[3] DC MS. 2: *PW* i. 294, ll. 71–2.

[4] Ibid.: *PW* i. 294, ll. 78–84.

[5] Ibid.: *PW* i. 294, ll. 98–101.

In offering shelter to the traveller, nourishment to her child, the woman reveals the actual poverty of her resources; all she has to offer is feeling. Her tears—'The o'erflow of inmost weakness'[1]—confirm the identification of physical privation and mental suffering.

A later blank verse fragment, probably belonging to the spring of 1797, goes on to develop this equation of poverty and deracination more fully. Wordsworth's first fully articulated study of neurosis, it is also among his most deeply felt. His indignant identification takes the form of an anguished account addressed to the woman he describes:

> I have seen the Baker's horse
> As he had been accustomed at your door
> Stop with the loaded wain, when o'er his head
> Smack went the whip and you were left as if
> You were not born to live, or there had been
> No bread in all the land.[2]

The writing has the emotional force of outrage, yet the method is far more restrained than it would once have been. The woman's poverty is suggested by a single detail—the horse that stops 'As he had been accustomed', the smack of the whip that sends him on. At the heart of this study is the woman's response to the passing waggon:

> she saw what way my eyes
> Were turn'd and in a low and fearful voice
> She said—that waggon does not care for us.
> The words were simple but her look and voice
> Made up their meaning, and bespoke a mind
> Which being long neglected and denied
> The common food of hope was now become
> Sick and extravagant,—by strong access
> Of momentary pangs driv'n to that state
> In which all past experience melts away
> And the rebellious heart to its own will
> Fashions the laws of nature.[3]

---

[1] DC MS. 2: *PW* i. 295, l. 115.

[2] DC MS. 13: *PW* i. 315–16, ll. 39–44. De Selincourt prints the fragment as part of 'Incipient Madness'. For the date, see Reed, p. 346, and for the relationship of the Baker's Cart lines to 'The Ruined Cottage', see ibid., p. 337, and Jonathan Wordsworth, *The Music of Humanity*, pp. 5–7.

[3] Ibid.: *PW* i. 316, ll. 52–3, 56–65.

Wordsworth for the first time uses dialogue as it is to be used in 'The Ruined Cottage', and he does so with a full awareness of his own method. What the woman says is little enough, but it takes its meaning from 'her look and voice', and reveals the state that she herself could never articulate ('bespoke a mind ... become/Sick and extravagant'). A draft in the margin stresses the morbidity behind her words, reflecting as they do a mind

> by misery and rumination deep
> Tied to dead things and seeking sympathy
> In sticks and stones . . . [1]

Wordsworth's treatment of privation contains a new and important psychological insight. There is nothing symbolic about the woman's need for bread, but its metaphoric associations are used to suggest the intertwining of physical and mental well-being. Unable to buy bread, the woman is also 'denied/ The common food of hope'; starving, she is also attacked by 'strong access/Of momentary pangs'—pangs in which despair and hunger are mingled. It is this equation of everyday and emotional needs which is to be central to 'The Ruined Cottage', where Robert's desertion of his family is bound up with unemployment, and Margaret's failure to keep up her cottage and garden, with the breakdown of the vital relationship.

As first conceived in spring 1797, 'The Ruined Cottage' had been an unrelieved tragedy; lacking the elaborate dramatic structure of 1798, it also lacked its reconciling vision.[2] Margaret's desertion and death, always at the core of the poem, at this stage provided its dominant mood. Wordsworth later noted that the closing section of her story had been written first; whether or not this was so, it survives in a transcript sent by Coleridge to Estlin during June 1797.[3] In describing Margaret's final decline and the dereliction of her cottage, the passage suggests the central method of the poem—the dual functioning of description as elegy. Wordsworth seems to have found

---

[1] Ibid.: *PW* i. 316, ll. 54–5. De Selincourt incorporates these lines into his text.
[2] For the development of 'The Ruined Cottage', see Jonathan Wordsworth, *The Music of Humanity*, pp. 9–22, and, for the dramatic framework in particular, pp. 87–101.
[3] See Griggs, i. 327–8, and the I.F. note to *The Excursion* (*PW* v. 373).

a clue for his presentation of Margaret's anguish in the disquietude and suspense of Southey's war-widow—

> Nor ever shall she know
> Her husband dead, but tortur'd with vain hope,
> Gaze on . . . [1]

'The Ruined Cottage' turns on the paradox of Margaret's despairing apathy and her heightened inner life. Ever seeing and failing to see her returning husband, her eye is 'busy in the distance, shaping things/That made her heart beat quick';[2] her pathetic questioning of each passer-by reveals her consuming hope while accentuating its futility. As Margaret herself grows weaker, her feelings seem to intensify, and the closing lines transform Southey's 'tortur'd with vain hope' into a statement, not so much of hope's vainness, as of its tenacity:

> Yet still
> She loved this wretched spot, nor would for worlds
> Have parted hence: and still, that length of road,
> And this rude bench one torturing hope endeared,
> Fast rooted at her heart; and, Stranger, here
> In sickness she remained, and here she died,
> Last human tenant of these ruined walls—[3]

The implications of Margaret's passive suffering go beyond anything endured by her predecessors. She suffers realistically, humanly, yet at the same time she is transfigured by Wordsworthian elegy. We see her not only in terms of her relationship to husband and child, but in terms of her relationship to nature itself—and hence in a generalized context of change and permanence. Another early draft contains a desolate lament for her usurped humanity and her over-run cottage. The living woman and the dead one are brutally juxtaposed, and the domestic well-being of the past contrasts with the encroaching natural life by which it is at once parodied and desecrated:

---

[1] *Joan of Arc*, vii. 328–30 (see p. 143, above).
[2] Griggs, i. 327: *PW* v. 399, ll. 706–7.
[3] Ibid. i. 328: *PW* v. 399, ll. 736–42 and app. crit. The metaphor of 'Fast rooted' is picked up in later versions of the poem by the apple-tree which Margaret fears will be 'dead & gone/Ere Robert come again' (MS. B: *PW* v. 398, ll. 675–6), revealing at once her inability to survive and her enduring hope.

> Many a passenger
> Has blest poor Margaret for her gentle looks
> When she upheld the cool refreshment drawn
> From that forsaken well, and no one came
> But he was welcome, no one went away
> But that it seemed she loved him—She is dead
> And nettles rot and adders sun themselves
> Upon the floor where I have seen [her] sit
> And rock her baby in its cradle. She
> Is dead and in her grave—And this poor hut
> Stripp'd of its outward garb of household flower[s]
> Of rose and jasmine offer[s] to the wind
> A cold bare wall whose top you see is trick[ed]
> With weeds and the rank spear grass . . . [1]

The suffering of a single, ordinary woman is invested with the tragic significance of mortality itself. The symbolic method by which the decay of the cottage is identified with Margaret's own decline serves as a general metaphor for human transience. It is this aspect of the poem that especially concerned Wordsworth when he returned to it in 1798. Now, the death of the individual and all that dies with him is reconciled by invoking the permanence of nature.

Wordsworth's transforming vision allows Margaret to lose the torment of consciousness in death: 'She sleeps in the calm earth, & peace is here',[2] the Pedlar tells the poet. Figures like the Discharged Soldier, the Old Cumberland Beggar, the Leech-Gatherer, the blind London beggar of *Prelude* Book VII, achieve their calm through suffering itself. It is in this that Wordsworth's solitaries differ from the pathetic ex-soldiers and beggars of the contemporary magazines.[3] Sickness, old age, privation, blindness free them from the urgency of human existence as well as making them objects of compassion. They exist in a hinterland between the human and the animal, the

---

[1] MS. A: *PW* v. 389–90, ll. 348–61 and app. crit.

[2] 'Addendum' to MS. B: *PW* v. 403, l. 122.

[3] Cf., for instance, Thomas Moss's well-known 'Beggar's Petition', *Gentleman's Magazine*, lxi (September 1791), 852; 'On Seeing an Old Man', ibid. lvi (January 1786), 65; or the excerpt quoted in the *English Review*, xviii (1792), 18. Even the best of the many contemporary analogues, Robert Anderson's 'The Soldier, A Fragment', from *Poems on Various Subjects* (Carlisle, 1798), seems closer to Mackenzie's writing (see pp. 162–3, above) than to Wordsworth's.

distressed and the prophetic, the transient and the permanent.[1] Like other Wordsworthian solitaries, the old man of 'Old Man Travelling' and 'The Old Cumberland Beggar' is in some sense a projection of Wordsworth's state of mind. Description merges unobtrusively into vision. It is clear from the study in which both poems originate, the 'Description of a Beggar' of spring or early summer 1797, that Wordsworth began by attempting to define the exact nature of the old man's bow-bent, oblivious existence:

> Bow-bent, his eyes for ever on the ground
> He plies his weary journey, seeing still
> And never knowing that he sees some straw,
> Some scattered leaf or mark which in one track
> The nails of cart or chariot wheel have left
> Impressed on the white road, in the same line
> At distance still the same.[2]

We see the road through the old man's eyes, sharing the visual confines of his world. At the same time, we are told that he never knows what he sees—that his gaze is entirely mechanical, no more conscious of the road than the cart-wheels whose track he follows:

> On the ground
> His eyes are turned and as he moves along
> They move along the ground . . . [3]

Wordsworth at once shows us the old man's world and insists that he is unaware of it, at once encourages us to identify with him and denies the basis of the identification. Half-absorbed into the natural landscape through which he passes, the old man is less alive than the flitting birds which he neither notices nor disturbs. Even his motion seems less than human, almost less than living: 'his slow foot-steps scarce/Disturb the summer dust', 'the miller's dog/Is tired of barking at him', 'Him even

---

[1] For an illuminating discussion of Wordsworth's solitaries as 'borderers', see Jonathan Wordsworth, 'William Wordsworth 1770–1969', *Proceedings of the British Academy*, lv (1970), 211–28.

[2] The MS. of 'Description of a Beggar', in the Pierpoint Morgan Library, forms part of the dismantled early notebook (DC MS. 13) that also contained MS. A of 'The Ruined Cottage' and the Baker's Cart lines; see Reed, p. 346. These lines become ll. 52–8 of 'The Old Cumberland Beggar'.

[3] [DC MS. 13] ('The Old Cumberland Beggar', ll. 45–7).

the slow-paced waggon leaves behind.'[1] But for Wordsworth, what the old man *is* does not comprise his total meaning. Just as the Discharged Soldier has his 'stately air of mild indifference' as well as his debilitation, or the Leech-Gatherer his other-worldly, admonitory resignation as well as his prosaic trade, so the old beggar possesses an enviable calm as the complement of his insensibility. This second aspect is developed to form the basis of 'Old Man Travelling'.

'Old Man Travelling' focuses on the suppressed paradox of its sub-title: 'Animal Tranquillity and Decay'.[2] Earlier, we were told that the old man existed without consciousness: now he seems to express thought in every movement, his existence no longer animal but transfigured by calm. The careful, conscientious description gives way to abstract definition:

> The little hedge-row birds,
> That peck along the road, regard him not.
> He travels on, and in his face, his step,
> His gait, is one expression; every limb,
> His look and bending figure, all bespeak
> A man who does not move with pain, but moves
> With thought—He is insensibly subdued
> To settled quiet: he is one by whom
> All effort seems forgotten, one to whom
> Long patience has such mild composure given,
> That patience now doth seem a thing, of which
> He hath no need. He is by nature led
> To peace so perfect, that the young behold
> With envy, what the old man hardly feels.   (ll. 1–14)

The hesitant rhythms, and the listing ('in his face, his step,/His gait . . .', 'every limb,/His look and bending figure . . .'), suggest painstaking observation; but the central definition uses quite different terms: 'A man who does not move with pain, but moves/With thought.' This shift from physical to abstract should be disconcerting—yet it occurs almost without one noticing it, disguised by Wordsworth's reflective tone. The

---

[1] Ibid. ('The Old Cumberland Beggar', ll. 59–66).

[2] Described by Wordsworth as 'an overflowing' from 'The Old Cumberland Beggar' (see *PW* iv. 447), the poem is more properly an overflowing from 'Description of a Beggar', in the form of draft material which was then entered as fair copy at much the same time elsewhere in the same notebook.

casual substitution of 'thought' for 'pain' suggests a new way of seeing the old man. 'He is insensibly subdued/To settled quiet' mingles acknowledgement of his obliviousness with a persuasively evoked calm; then—again casually—Wordsworth introduces his most questionable yet suggestive definition of the old man's state; he is

> one to whom
> Long patience has such mild composure given,
> That patience now doth seem a thing, of which
> He hath no need.   (ll. 9–12)

The old beggar's quiet may be animal, his patience a quality imposed rather than self-originating, but both quiet and patience retain an absolute value—a 'peace so perfect, that the young behold/With envy, what the old man hardly feels' (ll. 13–14). 'Hardly', here, softens the denial of the old man's capacity for feeling, but it also leaves the options open.[1] His is either a very special state, one we crave for ourselves, or a very ordinary one; but we are never forced to choose between them. The equivocation points not so much to a sleight of hand on Wordsworth's part, as to a longing that it might be so—that by a partial loss of his humanity the old man should also have earned a reprieve from the urgent and troubling pressures to which humans are subject. It is incongruous, therefore, that in the version of the poem published in *Lyrical Ballads* he should emerge from his animal tranquillity to tell a human story:

> —I asked him whither he was bound, and what
> The object of his journey; he replied
> 'Sir! I am going many miles to take
> 'A last leave of my son, a mariner,
> 'Whom from a sea-fight has been brought to Falmouth,
> 'And there is dying in an hospital.'   (ll. 15–20)[2]

As John Jones has pointed out, the added lines 'do violence to the nature of the old man': 'Just as Wordsworth is admonished

---

[1] Cf. Wordsworth's similarly equivocal use of 'hardly' and 'almost' in 'The Idiot Boy'—of the pony, 'You hardly can perceive his joy' (l. 406), or 'The grass you almost hear it growing' (l. 295).

[2] The appearance of the MS. suggests that these lines were added at a later date, perhaps when Wordsworth was gathering material for *Lyrical Ballads*. Cf. Southey's use of the old man's reply for anti-war protest in his 'English Eclogue', 'The Sailor's Mother', *Poems* (1799), ii. 207.

by "the whole body" of the Leech-Gatherer, of which his stream-like voice is one constituent, even so does the total aspect of the old man perfectly "bespeak" his condition. He does not need to do or say anything—he is.'[1] One might go further and say that Wordsworth's old man, as first conceived, *could* not have spoken. The man whose peace is that of the impervious natural world is given precisely those articulate human involvements from which he should be exempt.

In 'The Old Cumberland Beggar' of spring 1798, Wordsworth went on to explore the old man's 'vital anxiousness'— the residual humanity which the work-house would extinguish.[2] We first see him scanning his scraps of food 'with a fix'd and serious look /Of idle computation' that may parody human activity, but also touchingly reveals the tenacity of the one interest left to him. It is an interest he shares with the birds around him, yet at the same time he is distinguished by it:

> from a bag
> All white with flour, the dole of village dames,
> He drew his scraps and fragments, one by one,
> And scann'd them with a fix'd and serious look
> Of idle computation. In the sun,
> Upon the second step of that small pile,
> Surrounded by those wild unpeopled hills,
> He sate, and eat his food in solitude;
> And ever, scatter'd from his palsied hand,
> That still attempting to prevent the waste,
> Was baffled still, the crumbs in little showers
> Fell on the ground, and the small mountain birds,
> Not venturing yet to peck their destin'd meal,
> Approached within the length of half his staff. (ll. 8–21)[3]

The 'little hedge-row birds' of 'Old Man Travelling' had ignored the passing beggar: these birds recognize him as human, a competitor in the struggle for survival. His idle computation, and his ineffectual attempt not to waste crumbs, at once affirm his distinctness and reveal the narrowing-down of his world to

[1] *The Egotistical Sublime*, p. 63.
[2] For the composition of 'The Old Cumberland Beggar', see Reed, p. 342.
[3] Cf. the mendicant in Michael Bruce's 'Lochleven', 'Bowbent with age, that on the old gray stone,/Sole sitting, suns him in the public way', *Poems on Several Occasions* (Edinburgh, 1770), p. 89.

the most fundamental need of all. As 'Old Man Travelling' does not, 'The Old Cumberland Beggar' asks us for pity—but pity of a socially cohesive rather than divisive or condescending kind. It is an argument for the uses of compassion that sets out to beat the utilitarians at their own game.[1] The old man's role in society is to enlarge our sensibilities, to arouse 'The first mild touch of sympathy and thought' (l. 106), and at the same time to heighten our awareness of our own state—to jog the passing horseman into reflection; to remind 'the robust and young,/The prosperous and unthinking' (ll. 111–12) of their own well-being; to provide the pleasure of giving to the woman who 'from her chest of meal/Takes one unsparing handful' (ll. 150–1).[2] Wordsworth's version of political economy is an imaginative one, and characteristically generous in its definitions. It is easy to denounce his final plea for the old man's liberty as self-indulgent—the mere fulfilment of idiosyncratic theories about harmony between man and nature, without thought to the person concerned;[3] but the poem's attack on institutionalization implies an essentially humane respect for the individual:

> Then let him pass, a blessing on his head!
> And, long as he can wander, let him breathe
> The freshness of the vallies, let his blood
> Struggle with frosty air and winter snows,
> And let the charter'd wind that sweeps the heath
> Beat his grey locks against his wither'd face.
> Reverence the hope whose vital anxiousness
> Gives the last human interest to his heart.
>
> . . . .
>
> Let him be free of mountain solitudes,
> And have around him, whether heard or not,
> The pleasant melody of woodland birds.
>
> . . . .

[1] See Stephen Gill, 'Wordsworth's Breeches Pocket: Attitudes to the Didactic Poet', *EC* xix (1969), 385–401.

[2] Cf. Samuel Rogers on the pleasures of giving in *The Pleasures of Memory* (London, 1792), ll. 123–32, and the comparison of this passage with Wordsworth's poem by H. O. Brogan, 'The Old Beggar in Wordsworth and Rogers', *N & Q* N.S. xv (1968), 329–30.

[3] See, for instance, Cleanth Brooks, 'Wordsworth and Human Suffering: Notes on Two Early Poems', *From Sensibility to Romanticism*, pp. 373–87.

And let him, *where* and *when* he will, sit down
Beneath the trees, or by the grassy bank
Of high-way side, and with the little birds
Share his chance-gather'd meal, and, finally,
As in the eye of Nature he has liv'd,
So in the eye of Nature let him die.
(ll. 164–71, 176–8, 184–92)

Unlike the chartered streets of Blake's London, the wind here
has a genuine liberty; and it is this freedom—rather than the
charitable imprisonment of the workhouse—that Wordsworth
wishes on the old beggar. There is no sense that he is being
sacrificed to doctrine. One is struck instead by the imaginative-
ness of Wordsworth's benediction. Lamb puts it well: 'Here the
mind knowingly passes a fiction upon herself, first substituting
her own feelings for the Beggar's, and, in the same breath
detecting the fallacy, will not part with the wish.'[1] The work-
house merely offers the old man food and shelter: Wordsworth
endows him with a human identity, a heart as well as a body.
These studies of human extremity may equivocate with suffering, but they also reverence the vital anxiousness of life itself.

[1] To William Wordsworth, January 1801 (Lucas, i. 239).

VIII 'Magazine Poetry' and the Poetry of Passion

'THE term *Magazine-poetry* has usually been considered as synonymous with the most trivial and imperfect attempts at writing verse', commented the *Monthly Magazine* in 1796.[1] Planning a periodical of his own, two years before, Wordsworth himself had complained of 'the trash which infests the magazines';[2] yet *Lyrical Ballads* uses many of the themes and genres most popular in the poetry-sections. The children and deserted mothers, the insane, the destitute, and the aged who recur in the 'complaints' and 'anecdotes' and 'pathetic tales' of the 1790s all have their counterparts in Wordsworth's writing.[3] The difference, however, is not merely qualitative; it is one of kind. 'The Reader cannot be too often reminded that Poetry is passion: it is the history or science of feelings,' Wordsworth wrote in 1800;[4] and the definition embraces both his purpose of portraying 'the great and simple affections of our nature', and his adoption of 'the real language of men'.[5] Wordsworth's attempt to impersonate elemental passion may have an inherent artificiality; but in 1802 he justified it on the grounds of the poet's capacity for dramatic identification: 'it will be the wish of the Poet to bring his feelings near to those of the persons whose feelings he describes, nay, for short spaces of time perhaps, to let himself slip into an entire delusion, and even confound and identify his own feelings with theirs . . .'[6] It is this identification which magazine poetry rejects, and it does so partly through its use of language. Even at its most pitying, it sustains a literary idiom at odds with the distress it

Godwin

---

[1] 'Preface', *Monthly Magazine*, i (February 1796), iv.

[2] 8 June 1794; *EY*, p. 126. Cf. Coleridge's condemnation of some of his own lines as 'most miserably magazinish' in 1794 (Griggs, i. 141).

[3] See Robert Mayo, *PMLA* lxix (1954), 486–522.

[4] 1800 note to 'The Thorn' (*PW* ii. 513).

[5] 1800 'Preface' (*Prose Works*, i. 126, 118).

[6] 1802 'Preface' (*Prose Works*, i. 138).

portrays. Wordsworth's assault on 'the gaudiness and inane phraseology of many modern writers'[1] constitutes an assault on their lack of engagement; his own writing, by contrast, attempts to bridge the gap between literature and life, asserting a community of feeling between sophisticated and simple, literate and illiterate.

I. 'THE REAL LANGUAGE OF MEN'

Wordsworth's earlier preparedness to work within the conventions of magazine poetry can be seen in poems like 'The Convict', 'The Hour Bell Sounds', and 'Address to the Ocean'—all belonging to 1796, and all published in newspapers or magazines.[2] Although in some sense forerunners of the later studies of extremity and distress, these show Wordsworth using the minor genres of his time simply to express his views or display his expertise. 'The Convict', for instance, voices the same outrage against the penal system as *Salisbury Plain*; but both its anapaestic rhythm and its protest were fashionable in the magazines.[3] Satiric contrast and exaggeration accentuate the plight of the convict in his gothic dungeon:

> The thick-ribbed walls that o'ershadow the gate
> Resound—and the dungeon unfolds;
> I pause—my sight clears—and at length through the grate
> That outcast of Pity behold.[4]

In the unpublished version, Wordsworth sets the prisoner's despair against an ironic account of the war-crimes that are not only tolerated, but endorsed, by society:

> From the mighty destroyers, the plagues of their kind
> What corner of earth is at rest;
> While Fame with great joy blows her trumpet behind
> And the work by Religion is blest.[5]

---

[1] 1798 'Advertisement' (*Prose Works*, i. 116).

[2] 'The Convict' and 'The Hour Bell Sounds' appeared in the *Morning Post* for 14 December 1797 and 10 May 1798 respectively, 'Address to the Ocean' in the *Weekly Entertainer*, xxviii (21 November 1796), 419. For the dates of all three poems, see Reed, pp. 344–5.

[3] For the metre, cf., for instance, the translation of Bürger's satiric 'Menagerie of the Gods', in the *Monthly Magazine*, i (May 1796), 313; M. G. Lewis's famous ballad, 'Alonzo the Brave and Fair Imogine', in *The Monk* (1796) also inspired many anapaestic imitations.

[4] DC MS. 2: *PW* i. 313, ll. 9–12 and app. crit.

[5] Ibid.: *PW* i. 313 app. crit. De Selincourt prints 'the mind' for 'their kind'.

Basically a poem about political injustice, 'The Convict' forces its readers to question their own consciences ('is there one . . . who self-questioned can inly reply/That he is more worthy of being than thou?'),[1] and its denunciation of the prison system echoes Godwin in *Caleb Williams*: 'Alas, he that has observed the secrets of a prison, well knows that there is infinitely more torture in the lingering existence of a criminal, in the silent, intolerable minutes that he spends, than in the tangible misery of whips and racks.'[2] Significantly, the version published in the *Morning Post* was censored to leave only a philanthropic plea for transportation: 'My care, if the arm of the mighty were mine,/Would plant thee where yet thou might'st blossom again.'[3] Analogues for the tamer version abound. 'A Prison', for instance, in the *Gentleman's Magazine* for 1798, dwells as Wordsworth had done on the prisoner's torment ('Strange unknown fears possess his anxious breast,/When midnight spreads her darksome gloom . . .'); and another 'Convict', from the *Gentleman's Magazine* for 1785, offers a complacent picture of British justice commuting the death-sentence for theft to transportation ('And now far distant from the scenes of wealth,/This poor man's lightest toil there gives him bread . . .').[4] With its radicalism suppressed, Wordsworth's 'Convict' seems little different.

Where 'The Convict' merely intensifies a topical theme, 'The Hour Bell Sounds' and 'Address to the Ocean' demonstrate Wordsworth's technical facility. 'The Hour Bell Sounds'— translated from some verses in Helen Maria Williams's *Letters Containing a Sketch of the Politics of France* (1795)[5]—recreates the

---

[1] DC MS. 2: *PW* i. 314 app. crit.

[2] *Caleb Williams*, ii. 212; cf. Wordsworth's 'While he numbers the slow-pacing minutes, intent/On the fetters that link him to death' (DC MS. 2: *PW* i. 313, ll. 15–16 and app. crit.).

[3] *Morning Post*, 14 December 1797 (*PW* i. 314, ll. 51–2).

[4] *Gentleman's Magazine*, lxviii (September 1798), 795; lv (April 1785), 306. Cf. also Bowles's influential *Verses to John Howard, F.R.S. on his State of Prisons and Lazarettos* (1789) for a gothic dungeon, wasted prisoner, and philanthropic visitor like Wordsworth's.

[5] See Carol Landon, 'Wordsworth's Racedown Period: Some Uncertainties Resolved', *Bulletin of the New York Public Library*, lxviii (1964), 105–9. Helen Maria Williams had supplied her own 'imitation' of the original; see *Letters Containing a Sketch of the Politics of France* (2 vols., London, 1795), ii. 41.

plaintiveness of its French original, taking Helen Maria Williams's own studies of claustrophobic emotion as its model:

> THE hour-bell sounds, and I must go:
>> Death waits!—again I hear him calling.
> No cowardly desires have I,
>> Nor will I shun his face appalling.
> I die in faith and honours rich,
>> But, ah! I leave behind my treasure
> In widowhood and lonely pain—
>> To live were surely then a pleasure![1]

Poignant by virtue of its historical context ('The two following Verses from the French . . . were written by a French Prisoner, as he was preparing to go to the Guillotine'),[2] Wordsworth's translation looks forward to the mingled regret and stoicism in 'The Complaint of a forsaken Indian Woman'; the later poem, however, has an idiom that communicates the conflict with far greater urgency. This contrast between the literariness of 1796 and the directness of 1798 is still clearer in 'Address to the Ocean'. The opening lines (' "HOW long will ye round me be roaring" ') allude to Coleridge's recently published 'Complaint of Nina-thoma'—

> HOW long will ye round me be swelling,
>> O ye blue-tumbling waves of the Sea?
> Not always in Caves was my dwelling,
>> Nor beneath the cold blast of the Tree.[3]

—which is itself an Ossianic adaptation of Gay's famous ballad from *The What D'Ye Call It* (1715):

> 'TWAS when the Seas were roaring
>> With hollow Blasts of Wind;
> A Damsel lay deploring,
>> All on a Rock reclin'd.[4]

[1] *Morning Post*, 10 May 1798 (drafts and fair copy survive in DC MS. 2). Cf. Helen Maria Williams's 'Queen Mary's Complaint': 'But, oh, pale moon! what ray of thine/Can sooth a misery like mine!'; *Poems* (1786), ii. 183.

[2] Ibid., 10 May 1798.

[3] *Poems on Various Subjects* (1796), p. 86 (*CPW* i. 39, ll. 1–4). Wordsworth acknowledges the allusion in a footnote; J. R. MacGillivray, *RES* N.S. v (1954), 64, suggests that he was deliberately inviting comparison between his own and Coleridge's poem.

[4] *The What D'Ye Call It* (London, 1715), p. 32. See C. B. Teske, 'Gay's " 'Twas when the seas were roaring" and the Rise of Pathetic Balladry', *Anglia*, lxxxi

Wordsworth's version outdoes the pathetic ballad on its own terms, exploiting a fashionable metre and adding a heightened drama of his own:

> 'HOW long will ye round me be roaring,'
>   Once terrible waves of the sea?
> While I at my door sit deploring
>   The treasure ye ravish'd from me.
> When shipwreck the white surf is strewing,
>   This spray-beaten thatch will ye spare?
> Come—let me exult in the ruin
>   Your smiles are put on to prepare.[1]

'Address to the Ocean' remains an exercise within a convention, remarkable partly for its assurance and intensity, but chiefly for its refusal to transcend a literary view of emotion.

Wordsworth in poems such as these might well have been described as a magazine poet. His contrasting fidelity to the real language and feelings of men in *Lyrical Ballads* has behind it an entirely different view of poetry. As early as 1763, in his *Critical Dissertation on the Poems of Ossian*, Hugh Blair had written that 'ancient poems' present to us 'The history of human imagination and passion';[2] and his *Lectures on Rhetoric and Belles Lettres*, delivered in Edinburgh for over twenty years before their publication in 1783, provided the basis for Wordsworth's later definition: 'THE most just and comprehensive definition which, I think, can be given of Poetry, is, "That it is the language of passion, or of enlivened imagination, formed, most commonly, into regular numbers." '[3] Blair's mistrust of artificial, 'literary' composition would have reinforced Wordsworth's criticism of his contemporaries for their 'gaudiness and inane phraseology':

when Poetry became a regular art, studied for reputation and for gain, Authors began to affect what they did not feel. Composing

---

(1965), 411–25, for the transformation of Gay's near-parody into a pathetic ballad when excerpted from its dramatic context.

[1] *Weekly Entertainer*, xxviii (21 November 1796), 419.

[2] *A Critical Dissertation on the Poems of Ossian* (London, 1763), p. 1. This account of Ossian was incorporated in many subsequent editions of Macpherson's poetry and would have constituted the standard view of its importance.

[3] *Lectures on Rhetoric and Belles Lettres*, ii. 312. See also M. H. Abrams, *The Mirror and the Lamp* (New York, 1953), pp. 95–6, for Blair's contribution to Wordsworth's critical views.

coolly in their closets, they endeavoured to imitate passion, rather than to express it; they tried to force their imagination into raptures, or to supply the defect of native warmth, by those artificial ornaments which might give Composition a splendid appearance.[1]

According to Blair, the true origins of poetry were primitive; it was in 'the age of hunters and of shepherds' and among 'the simplest form of manners among mankind' that poetry was at its purest and most affecting:

in its ancient original condition, [poetry] was perhaps more vigorous than it is in its modern state. It included then, the whole burst of the human mind; the whole exertion of its imaginative faculties. It spoke then the language of passion, and no other; for to passion, it owed its birth. Prompted and inspired by objects, which to him seemed great, by events which interested his country or his friends, the early Bard arose and sung. He sung indeed in wild and disorderly strains; but they were the native effusions of his heart; they were the ardent conceptions of admiration or resentment, of sorrow or friendship, which he poured forth. It is no wonder, therefore, that in the rude and artless strain of the first Poetry of all nations, we should often find somewhat that captivates and transports the mind.[2]

Red Indian poetry—later known to Wordsworth from his reading of travel-writers like Hearne and Bartram—could be cited as a contemporary instance of this impassioned primitivism:

It is chiefly in America, that we have had the opportunity of being made acquainted with men in their savage state. We learn from the particular and concurring accounts of Travellers, that, among all the nations of that vast continent, especially among the Northern Tribes, with whom we have had most intercourse, music and song are, at all their meetings, carried on with an incredible degree of enthusiasm; that the Chiefs of the Tribe are those who signalize themselves most on such occasions; that it is in Songs they celebrate their religious rites; that, by these they lament their public and private calamities, the death of friends, or the loss of warriors; express their joy on their victories; celebrate the great actions of their nation, and their heroes; excite each other to perform brave exploits in war, or to suffer death and torments with unshaken constancy.[3]

[1] Ibid. ii. 323.   [2] Ibid. ii. 314, 322–3.   [3] Ibid. ii. 314–15.

Wordsworth's experiment is an attempt to re-create the urgency and passion of a poetry springing directly from human experience—looking not only to a primitive context, but to the everyday.[1]

Coleridge had the relevant volume of Blair's *Lectures* on loan from the Bristol Library during the early months of 1798,[2] and Wordsworth's description of the Pedlar provides clear evidence that his theories had been discussed and assimilated:

> much had he seen of men,
> Their manners, their enjoyments & pursuits,
> Their passions & their feelings, chiefly those
> Essential and eternal in the heart
> Which mid the simpler forms of rural life
> Exist more simple in their elements
> And speak a plainer language.[3]

For Blair, as for Wordsworth, the 'refinements of society' served to 'disguise the manners of mankind'—whereas in primitive societies,

Their passions have nothing to restrain them: their imagination has nothing to check it. They display themselves to one another without disguise; and converse and act in the uncovered simplicity of nature. As their feelings are strong, so their language, of itself, assumes a poetical turn. Prone to exaggerate, they describe every thing in the strongest colours; which of course renders their speech picturesque and figurative.[4]

In the famous passage from the 1800 'Preface', Wordsworth makes an identical claim for the enduring simplicities of rural life in his own day and country:

Low and rustic life was generally chosen because in that situation the essential passions of the heart find a better soil in which they can attain their maturity, are less under restraint, and speak a plainer and more emphatic language; because in that situation our elementary feelings exist in a state of greater simplicity and consequently may be more accurately contemplated and more forcibly communicated . . . [5]

---

[1] For some implications of Wordsworth's choice, see also Roger Sharrock, 'Wordsworth's Revolt against Literature', *EC* iii (1953), 396–412.

[2] See George Whalley, *Library*, 5th ser. iv (1949–50), 125.

[3] 'The Ruined Cottage', MS. B: *PW* v. 380–1, ll. 60–6.

[4] *A Critical Dissertation on the Poems of Ossian*, p. 2.

[5] *Prose Works*, i. 124.

Wordsworth was not alone, either in his primitivism or in his search for an alternative idiom. What set him apart was his extension of Blair's theory of poetry to the world immediately round him—his belief that ordinary people, as well as Red Indians, expressed themselves undisguisedly and forcefully in a language which poetry could use.

Wordsworth's adoption of 'the language of conversation' had behind it a century of primitive pastiche—whether Celtic, Norse, Oriental, or Turkish.[1] Blair's claims for Ossian suggest the release from Augustan verse conventions offered by Macpherson:

if to feel strongly, and to describe naturally, be the two chief ingredients in poetical genius, Ossian must ... be held to possess that genius in a high degree ... has he the spirit, the fire, the inspiration of a poet? Does he utter the voice of nature? Does he elevate by his sentiments? Does he interest by his descriptions? Does he paint to the heart as well as to the fancy? Does he make his readers glow, and tremble, and weep? These are the great characteristicks of true poetry.[2]

In 1815 Wordsworth complained of the very mannerisms which had seemed so authentic to Blair ('every thing ... is ... defined, insulated, dislocated, deadened,—yet nothing distinct. It will always be so when words are substituted for things').[3] But the passage he quotes from *Temora* (1763) in support of his criticism reveals why Macpherson had appealed so strongly to his time:

THE blue waves of Ullin roll in light. The green hills are covered with day. Trees shake their dusky heads in the breeze. Grey torrents pour their noisy streams.—Two green hills, with aged oaks, surround a narrow plain. The blue course of a stream is there; on its banks stood Cairbar of Atha.—His spear supports the king: the red eyes of his fear are sad. Cormac rises in his soul, with all his ghastly wounds.[4]

[1] Cf. Coleridge's 1798 revamping of Wordsworth's schoolboy verses, 'Beauty and Moonlight', as 'Lewti; or, the Circassian's Love Chant'; see J. W. Smyser, *PMLA* lxv (1950), 421–2, and R. S. Woof, *SB* xv (1962), 170.

[2] *A Critical Dissertation on the Poems of Ossian*, p. 74.

[3] 'Essay, Supplementary to the Preface', 1815 (*Prose Works*, iii. 77).

[4] *Temora, an Ancient Epic Poem* (London, 1763), pp. 3–4. 'Precious memorandums from the pocket-book of the blind Ossian!' comments Wordsworth derisively (*Prose Works*, iii. 77).

Incantatory, cumulative, emotional, this is a style calculated to make its readers 'glow, and tremble, and weep'. Collins, in the preface to his *Persian Eclogues* of 1742, had suggested the usefulness of orientalism for a poet wishing to extend his range, and it is easy to see how his 'Argument of their being Original' could shade into Macpherson's fabrication of Ossian:

> There is an Elegancy and Wildness of Thought which recommends all their Compositions; and our Genius's are as much too cold for the Entertainment of such Sentiments, as our Climate is for their Fruits and Spices. If any of these Beauties are to be found in the following Eclogues, I hope my Reader will consider them as an Argument of their being Original. I received them at the Hands of a Merchant . . . [1]

What is at issue is literary, rather than literal, authenticity; Macpherson and Collins rely on rhythm and syntax, with a sprinkling of exotic names, to create the illusion of a Celtic past or far-off Persia. The exclamations and the compulsive refrain by which Wordsworth suggests the foreignness of his forsaken Indian woman follow the pattern set by Collins's 'Hassan; or, the Camel-driver' half a century earlier:

> *Sad was the Hour, and luckless was the Day,*
> *When first from* Schiraz' *Walls I bent my Way.*

> Ah! little thought I of the blasting Wind,
> The Thirst or pinching Hunger that I find!
> Bethink thee, Hassan, where shall Thirst assuage,
> When fails this Cruise, his unrelenting Rage?
> Soon shall this Scrip its precious Load resign,
> Then what but Tears and Hunger shall be thine?[2]

Collins's orientalism does more than assert the camel-driver's alienness—it accentuates his anguish. The unfamiliar predicament serves to underline a recognizable humanity, just as the Indian woman, left to die by a savage custom, voices in a peculiarly arresting way feelings that are common to all civilizations ('the last struggles of a human being at the approach of death').[3] Exoticism becomes a means of making us respond freshly to the familiar—a means both of emphasis and renewal.

---

[1] *Persian Eclogues. Written originally for the Entertainment of the Ladies of Tauris* (London, 1742), p. [iii].

[2] ll. 13–20, ibid., p. 11.　　　　　　　　[3] 1800 'Preface' (*Prose Works*, i. 126).

'An American chief, at this day, harangues at the head of his tribe, in a more bold metaphorical style, than a modern European would adventure to use in an Epic poem',[1] wrote Blair. It is this assumption that Wordsworth relies on in 'The Complaint of a forsaken Indian Woman'. Behind him lay a thriving tradition of 'Indian' poetry—often, used simply as a means of revitalizing pastoral,[2] but at times showing alien customs strikingly superimposed on a common humanity. Warton's 'Dying Indian', for instance, exploits the gap between reader and speaker to make us wonder the more at the bond they share:

> THE dart of Izdabel prevails! 'twas dipt
> In double poison—I shall soon arrive
> At the blest island, where no tigers spring
> On heedless hunters; where anana's bloom
> Thrice in each moon; where rivers smoothly glide,
> Nor thundering torrents whirl the light canoe
> Down to the sea; where my forefathers feast
> Daily on hearts of Spaniards!—[3]

The mingling of celebration and savagery may be strange, but the concept of an afterlife is not. Humanity is viewed in a new light, but it remains human. The same ferocity dominates the famous 'Death-Song of a Cherokee Indian', and here again the speaker's defiance implies a fortitude which we are used to admiring in a different context:

> The sun sets in night, and the stars shun the day,
> But glory remains when their lights fade away:
> Begin, ye tormenters, your threats are in vain,
> For the son of Alknomook will never complain.
>
> Remember the arrows he shot from his bow;
> Remember your chiefs by his hatchet laid low;
> Why so slow?—Do you think I will shrink from the pain?
> No:—The son of Alknomook will never complain.

[1] *A Critical Dissertation on the Poems of Ossian*, p. 2.
[2] See, for instance, Joseph Warton's 'American Love Ode', included in Thomas Warton, Sen.'s *Poems on Several Occasions* (1748), and Bowles's 'American Indian's Song', in *Sonnets, with Other Poems* (3rd edn., 1794).
[3] *A Collection of Poems*, ed. Robert Dodsley, iv (1755), 209–10.

> Remember the wood where in ambush we lay,
> And the scalps which we bore from your nation away.
> Now the flame rises fast,—you exult in my pain;
> But the son of Alknomook can never complain.
>
> I go to the land where my father is gone;
> His ghost shall rejoice in the fame of his son.
> Death comes like a friend, he relieves me from pain:
> And thy son, o Alknomook, has scorn'd to complain.[1]

The exultant, taunting chant is outlandish, yet the heroic values are entirely comprehensible. Wordsworth offers a subtler, more domestic insight into death, but the forsaken Indian woman's 'Before I see another day,/Oh let my body die away!' (ll. 9–10) has the same directness as 'Death comes like a friend, he relieves me from pain', and the two death-songs are alike in moving us because we share the emotions of their savage speakers.

The exotic was one aspect of eighteenth-century primitivism, the homely another. When Wordsworth turned to 'the real language of men', he had behind him a well-established tradition of dialect poetry. Like primitive poetry, the traditional Scots ballad had seemed to offer a direct insight into the human heart; here too, as Pinkerton wrote in 1781, was an apparently uncalculated appeal to and from the heart.

the dialect in which the Scottish Ballads are written gives them a great advantage in point of touching the passions. Their language is rough and unpolished, and seems to flow immediately from the heart. We meet with no concettos or far-fetched thoughts in them. They possess the pathetic power in the highest degree, because they do not affect it; and are striking, because they do not meditate to strike.[2]

But it was Burns who made the fullest and most influential use of dialect—not only to project himself, but to portray the situations and feelings of rustic life. In 'The Vision', it is specifically a Scots muse who teaches him his 'manners-painting strains,/

[1] The death-song appears in a note to Joseph Ritson's 'Historical Essay on the Origin and Progress of National Song', in *A Select Collection of English Songs* (3 vols., London, 1783), i. iin. See also F. E. Farley, 'The Dying Indian', *Anniversary Papers by Colleagues and Pupils of George Lyman Kittredge* (Boston, Mass., and London, 1913), pp. 251–60, for other poems in this genre.

[2] 'Dissertation II', *Scottish Tragic Ballads*, ed. John Pinkerton (London, 1781), p. xxxv.

The *loves*, the *ways* of simple swains',[1] and dialect at once creates and licenses the appeal of poems like 'The death and dying words of Poor Mailie, the Author's only pet Yowe, an unco mournfu' Tale', or 'The auld Farmer's new-year-morning Salutation to his auld Mare, Maggie, on giving her the accustomed ripp of Corn to hansel in the new-year'. As their titles suggest, these poems are partly light-hearted; but their humour coexists with tenderness. Because 'Their language is rough and unpolished, and seems to flow immediately from the heart', we are touched by the farmer's affectionate remarks to the horse he has grown old with—

> *A Guid New-year* I wish you Maggie!
> Hae, there's a ripp to thy auld baggie:
> Tho' thou's howe-backet, now, an' knaggie,
>   I've seen the day,
> Thou could hae gaen like only staggie
>   Out owre the lay.[2]

—or charmed by the ovine respectability of Mailie's advice to her yew-lamb:

> O, may thou ne'er foregather up,
> Wi' onie blastet, moorlan *toop*;
> But ay keep mind to moop an' mell,
> Wi' sheep o' credit like thysel![3]

Comical though it is, Mailie's maternal solicitude has its own dignity; and her invective ('onie blastet, moorlan *toop*'), like the farmer's disrespect to his mare ('thy auld baggie'), is as much an indirect revelation of feeling as Betty's scolding of her idiot boy. Burns in his preface had claimed to sing 'the sentiments and manners, he felt and saw in himself and his rustic compeers around him, in his and their native language';[4] by using a language without literary associations, he has extended the range of our sympathies to include even the feelings of a sheep. Wordsworth flaunts 'the language of conversation' more provocatively, and his extension of our sympathies is announced in a more doctrinaire way, but his aim is essentially the same— to create poetry that at once disarms and involves us in the simple feelings it depicts.

[1] ll. 241–2, *Poems, Chiefly in the Scottish Dialect*, p. 97.
[2] ll. 1–6, ibid., p. 118.   [3] ll. 53–6, ibid., p. 65.   [4] Ibid., p. iii.

II. THE POETRY OF PASSION

The pieces written specifically for *Lyrical Ballads* in the early summer of 1798 reflect Wordsworth's conscious commitment to poetry of passion. Despite superficial resemblances, they have little but their themes in common with the poetry of the magazines,[1] drawing instead on a more substantial tradition of humane and identified writing. The closest analogues to 'The Complaint of a forsaken Indian Woman', 'The last of the Flock', and 'The Mad Mother' are to be found respectively in the poetry of Cowper and Burns and in the traditional ballad. To put 'Lady Bothwell's Lament' beside 'The Mad Mother' reveals the Scots ballad as the obvious forerunner of Wordsworth's poignant naturalism:

> BALOW, my babe, ly still and sleipe!
> It grieves me sair to see thee weipe:
> If thoust be silent, Ise be glad,
> Thy maining maks my heart ful sad.
> Balow, my boy, thy mithers joy,
> Thy father breides me great annoy.
> > Balow, my babe, ly stil and sleipe,
> > It grieves me sair to see [thee] weipe.[2]

Naïve and expressive, this lullaby seems to be uttered by a real woman, overheard in real grief. It also offers a genuine insight into the psychology of desertion. The child takes its father's place, as in 'The Mad Mother', becoming a lover without the power to hurt or desert:

> Bairne, sin thy cruel father is gane,
> Thy winsome smiles maun eis my paine;
> My babe and I'll together live,
> He'll comfort me whan cares doe greive:
> My babe and I right saft will ly,
> And quite forgeit man's cruelty.
> > Balow, &c.[3]

---

[1] Cf., for instance, Miss Holcroft's 'Penitent Mother', *Monthly Magazine*, iii (February 1797), 142; or 'Elegy, occasioned by the present frequent and pernicious custom of monopolizing Farms', ibid. ii (December 1796), 890.

[2] *Reliques of Ancient English Poetry*, ed. Thomas Percy (3 vols., London, 1765), ii. 194–5. Cf. also the expanded literary version in *The Ancient and Modern Scots Songs*, ed. David Herd (Edinburgh, 1769), pp. 30–2.

[3] Ibid. ii. 196.

At the heart of her lament lies the mother's awareness of betrayal—ironically, a betrayal that the baby, a boy-child, seems
bound by the terms of the poem to repeat:

> Ly stil, my darling, sleipe a while,
> And whan thou wakest, sweitly smile:
> But smile nat, as thy father did,
> To cozen maids: nay God forbid!
> Bot yett I feire, thou wilt gae neire
> Thy fatheris hart, and face to beire.
> Balow, &c.[1]

The intimate, soliloquizing tone powerfully suggests both the
mother's isolation and the increased vulnerability of her dependence on a single relationship; her retreat from male cruelty
leaves her yet more pitifully exposed. Wordsworth too stresses
the mad mother's precarious allegiance to a fantasy world
created to protect her against the reality of desertion, and the
same naïve idiom implies her inability to cope with the experience. In both cases, there is a pathetic inadequacy in the language, a fatal simplicity in the internal rhymes at the close of
each stanza:

> If thoust be silent, Ise be glad,
> Thy maining maks my heart ful sad.[2]

> If thou art mad, my pretty lad,
> Then I must be for ever sad.   (ll. 89–90)

We not only read poetry like this, we read through it, to
emotions it barely articulates.

Wordsworth's lament concerns madness as well as grief. It is
a madness close to gaiety, like that of the woman in his earlier
'Tale' ('Her eyes . . . had been acquainted with weeping; yet
had not perpetual tears been able to extinguish a certain wild
brightness which, at the first view, might have been mistaken
for the wildness of great Joy'):[3]

> 'Sweet babe! they say that I am mad,
> But nay, my heart is far too glad;
> And I am happy when I sing
> Full many a sad and doleful thing . . .'   (ll. 11–14)

[1] Ibid. ii. 195.   [2] Ibid. ii. 194.
[3] DC MS. 2: *Prose Works*, i. 8 (see p. 165, above).

Unbalance isolates the mad mother from an ordinary world, identifying her with the wild, free existence of the American forests described by Bartram and Hearne:

> Her eyes are wild, her head is bare,
> The sun has burnt her coal-black hair,
> Her eye-brows have a rusty stain,
> And she came far from over the main.
> She has a baby on her arm,
> Or else she were alone;
> And underneath the hay-stack warm,
> And on the green-wood stone,
> She talked and sung the woods among;
> And it was in the English tongue.   (ll. 1–10)[1]

The final line comes as a shock after this alien, sun-burned gaiety. Like the 'Youth from Georgia's shore', in 'Ruth', the mad mother retains an essential wildness; hers is an Indian resourcefulness and fearlessness among snows and rivers which transmute a familiar English landscape into the richer, private world of the imagination:

> 'Then do not fear, my boy! for thee
> Bold as a lion I will be;
> And I will always be thy guide,
> Through hollow snows and rivers wide.
> I'll build an Indian bower; I know
> The leaves that make the softest bed:
> And if from me thou wilt not go,
> But still be true 'till I am dead,
> My pretty thing! then thou shalt sing,
> As merry as the birds in spring.'   (ll. 51–60)

The child is not only wooed by his mother as once she was wooed, he is offered the male protection that has been denied her. Wordsworth suggests the complexity of mutual need when he reveals that while the mother protects her child, the child in turn saves his mother:

---

[1] Cf. also 'The Mother's Lullaby', in Joseph Ritson's *Ancient Songs, from the Time of King Henry the Third, to the Revolution* (London, 1792), p. 198:

> Thy father, sweete Infant, from mother ys gone,
>   Sing Lully Lully Lully,
> And she in the woodes heere w^t thee lefte alone . . .
>   (ll. 10–13)

'Suck, little babe, oh suck again!
It cools my blood; it cools my brain . . .' (ll. 31–2)

'Oh! love me, love me, little boy!
Thou art thy mother's only joy . . .' (ll. 41–2)

'The babe I carry on my arm,
He saves for me my precious soul . . .' (ll. 47–8)

The precariousness of this new dependency is revealed by a sudden glimpse in the penultimate stanza:

'—Where art thou gone my own dear child?
What wicked looks are those I see?
Alas! alas! that look so wild,
It never, never came from me:
If thou art mad, my pretty lad,
Then I must be for ever sad.' (ll. 85–90)[1]

If the child proves to be merely a reflection of its mother, the salvation it offers will be illusory. Hauntingly, inconclusively, Wordsworth leaves her with her fantasy: ' "Now laugh and be gay, to the woods away!" ' (l. 99).

'The Mad Mother' gives new life to an inherited theme through its imaginative portrayal of unbalance. The familiar becomes similarly strange in 'The Complaint of a forsaken Indian Woman', another poem about solitude—this time, the solitude of death. Wordsworth's source is Hearne's account of an Indian custom, abandoning the sick who are unable to keep up with the tribe on their journey. Hearne had seen the custom chiefly in terms of its conflict with instinctive human feelings; the relatives of the sick, he tells us, 'walk away crying', and the woman he sees abandoned in this way comes up with his party three times before 'At length, poor creature! she dropt behind'.[2] Wordsworth's poem focuses on the state of mind of the dying woman, 'cleaving in solitude to life and society'.[3] Cowper's

---

[1] Wordsworth seems to be recalling a passage from MS. A of *The Borderers*, in which a mother describes her crazed, solitary wanderings with a child who, seeing no other face but hers, mimics her expression of madness (see *PW* i. 354, ll. 48–59).

[2] *A Journey from Prince of Wales's Fort in Hudson's Bay, to the Northern Ocean* (London, 1795), pp. 202–3. Wordsworth would have been familiar with similar material in Bartram; cf., for instance, the old chief's speech to his tribe, *Travels through North and South Carolina* (London, 1792), p. 498.

[3] 1800 'Preface' (*Prose Works*, i. 126).

'Verses, supposed to be written by Alexander Selkirk, during his solitary Abode in the Island of Juan Fernandez' had already used the castaway's plight to emphasize the torment of solitude. Despite its religious slant, Cowper's poem is basically concerned with human consolations—not Christian belief so much as the 'sound of the church going bell', with all its associations is communal worship. The castaway's yearning for his kind of poignantly evoked:

> Ye winds that have made me your sport,
>   Convey to this desolate shore,
> Some cordial endearing report
>   Of a land I shall visit no more.
> My friends do they now and then send
>   A wish or a thought after me?
> O tell me I yet have a friend,
>   Though a friend I am never to see.
>
> How fleet is a glance of the mind!
>   Compar'd with the speed of its flight,
> The tempest itself lags behind,
>   And the swift winged arrows of light.
> When I think of my own native land,
>   In a moment I seem to be there;
> But alas! recollection at hand
>   Soon hurries me back to despair.[1]

The unsophisticated rhythms and stilted language constrain the speaker's emotion without stifling it. The effect is that of an ordinary man compelled to voice his loneliness by extraordinary circumstances; like the forsaken Indian woman, he is one singled out from many by his plight. Both castaways are defined through their need for relationship, and the same alternation between imagined contact and actual isolation makes Wordsworth's poem too a lament about solitude, as much as approaching death:

> Oh wind that o'er my head art flying,
> The way my friends their course did bend,
> I should not feel the pain of dying,
> Could I with thee a message send.
> Too soon, my friends, you went away;
> For I had many things to say.   (ll. 45–50)

---

[1] Poems (1782–5), i (1782), 307–8.

Like Cowper, Wordsworth implies that the impulse to communicate fails only with life itself.

In 1802, Wordsworth invoked the stanza beginning 'Ye winds that have made me your sport . . .' to illustrate his theory of poetic diction: 'it would be equally good whether in prose or verse, except that the Reader has an exquisite pleasure in seeing such natural language so naturally connected with metre.'[1] It would be truer to say that the combination of a spoken idiom with an intrusive metre and an artificial word-order ('My friends do they now and then send . . .') accentuates the 'naturalness' of the feeling. Wordsworth captures this quality in 'The Complaint of a forsaken Indian Woman'—a chant animated by the same loneliness and longing, but made subtly alien by end-stopped lines and unfamiliar turns of phrase:

> Before I see another day,
> Oh let my body die away!
> In sleep I heard the northern gleams;
> The stars they were among my dreams;
> In sleep did I behold the skies,
> I saw the crackling flashes drive;
> And yet they are upon my eyes,
> And yet I am alive.
> Before I see another day,
> Oh let my body die away!   (ll. 1–10)

Each statement is complete in itself, but it is the cumulative effect that gives the poem its meaning. Returning again and again to the fixed point of her approaching death, the Indian woman voices the contradiction between her stoicism and her longing for child and friends, between fatalism and rebellion—contradictions which must persist while she remains alive:

> Then here contented will I lie;
> Alone I cannot fear to die.
>
> Alas! you might have dragged me on
> Another day, a single one!   (ll. 19–22)[2]

The fluctuating movement and compulsive refrain evoke the ebb and flow of her strength, the last flickering of consciousness:

---

[1] 'Appendix', 1802 'Preface' (*Prose Works*, i. 164).
[2] Cf. also the additional stanzas exploring the conflict, in Dorothy's *Journal* for 1800 (see *PW* ii. 475–6).

> My fire is dead: it knew no pain;
> Yet is it dead, and I remain.
> All stiff with ice the ashes lie;
> And they are dead, and I will die.   (ll. 11–14)

With the dead fire beside her and the contrasting brilliance of the northern lights above, the Indian woman reproaches herself as if she has betrayed her own will to live: 'Too soon my heartless spirit failed' (l. 24). Life drains away as we listen, and the entreaty of the opening stanza becomes statement in the closing lines: 'I feel my body die away,/I shall not see another day' (ll. 69–70).

'The last of the Flock' confronts, not death, but destitution— the plight of the labouring poor. Burns's 'Man was made to mourn. A Dirge' was clearly in Wordsworth's mind during the spring of 1798,[1] and its lament for the human condition shapes his poem. In a letter of 1788, Burns expressed his indignant identification with the lot of the working class:

Man is by no means a happy creature.—I do not speak of the Selected Few, favored by partial Heaven; whose souls are tuned to Gladness amid Riches, & Honors, & Prudence, & Wisdom.—I speak of the neglected Many, whose nerves, whose sinews, whose days, whose thoughts, whose independance, whose peace, nay, whose very gratifications & enjoyments, the instinctive gift of Nature, are sacrificed & sold to those few bloated Minions of Heaven!—

If I thought you had never seen it, I would transcribe for you a stanza of an old Scots Ballad, 'The life & age of Man;' beginning thus—

> ' 'Twas in the sixteen hundredth year
>   Of God & fifty-three
> Frae Christ was born that brought us dear,
>   As Writings testifie'—

I had an old Grand uncle, with whom my Mother lived a while in her girlish years; the good old man, for such he was, was long blind ere he died, during which time, his most voluptuous enjoyment was to sit down & cry, while my Mother would sing the simple old song of, The Life & Age of Man.—

---

[1] See, for instance, the echo of Burns's refrain in 'Lines written in early spring' ('Have I not reason to lament/What man has made of man?', ll. 23–4) and 'Simon Lee' ('Alas! the gratitude of men/Has oftner left me mourning', ll. 103–4).

It is this way of thinking, it is these melancholey truths, that make Religion so precious to the poor miserable Children of men.—[1]

The same consciousness of a 'neglected Many' and an unjust social order underlies 'Man was made to mourn'. Burns uses the traditional encounter of the *chanson d'aventure* but reverses the expectations of spring, youth, and love, to present a figure of anonymous, timeless suffering:

> WHEN chill November's surly blast
>   Made fields and forests bare,
> One ev'ning, as I wand'red forth,
>   Along the banks of AIRE,
> I spy'd a man, whose aged step
>   Seem'd weary, worn with care,
> His face was furrow'd o'er with years,
>   And hoary was his hair.[2]

In this unaccommodating world, injustice and inequality, waste and age, 'Regret, Remorse, and Shame' make death the only recompense. But this is not just a poem about the human condition; Burns's target is the special bitterness of poverty and oppression:

> See, yonder poor, o'erlabour'd wight,
>   So abject, mean and vile,
> Who begs a brother of the earth
>   To give him leave to toil;
> And see his lordly *fellow-worm*,
>   The poor petition spurn,
> Unmindful, tho' a weeping wife,
>   And helpless offspring mourn.
>
> If I'm design'd yon lordling's slave,
>   By Nature's law design'd,
> Why was an independent wish
>   E'er planted in my mind?
> If not, why am I subject to
>   His cruelty, or scorn?
> Or why has Man the will and pow'r
>   To make his fellow mourn?[3]

---

[1] *The Letters of Robert Burns*, ed. J. De L. Ferguson (2 vols., Oxford, 1931), i. 246.
[2] ll. 1–8, *Poems, Chiefly in the Scottish Dialect*, p. 160.
[3] ll. 57–72, ibid., pp. 163–4.

When Burns calls the labourer 'abject, mean and vile', he is not only being ironic; like Wordsworth in 'Lines written in early spring', he is lamenting 'What man has made of man'.

'The last of the Flock' similarly goes beyond protest to elegy. Apparently based on an actual encounter,[1] it confronts us with a figure of homely pathos:

> In distant countries I have been,
> And yet I have not often seen
> A healthy man, a man full grown,
> Weep in the public roads alone. (ll. 1–4)

With tears on his cheeks and a lamb in his arms, Wordsworth's shepherd is an individual and touching case of the social hardship denounced by Burns. The central irony is that of a poor-law whose charity comes too late; the shepherd must sell the flock he has built up over the years before the parish can help him to feed his children (' "Do this; how can we give to you," /They cried, "what to the poor is due?" ', ll. 49–50). The glib language of bureaucracy contrasts with the shepherd's despairing tally of his dwindling flock:

> 'To see it melt like snow away!
> For me it was a woeful day.'
>
> 'They dwindled one by one away;
> For me it was a woeful day.'
>
> 'And every week, and every day,
> My flock, it seemed to melt away.'
> (ll. 59–60, 69–70, 89–90)

Where the old man of Burns's dirge had spoken with the authority of universal suffering, the shepherd utters his despair in the language of everyday, personal bitterness:

> 'I sold a sheep as they had said,
> And bought my little children bread,
> And they were healthy with their food;
> For me it never did me good.'
>
> 'And I may say that many a time
> I wished they all were gone . . .'
>
> 'And now I care not if we die,
> And perish all of poverty.' (ll. 51–4, 67–8, 39–40)

---

[1] See I.F. note to 'The last of the Flock' (*PW* ii. 476).

This is the state of mind which in 'The Ruined Cottage' culminates in Robert's desertion of his family. What work means to Robert, his flock means to the shepherd—a way of life on which happiness depends. Stripped of one, he is stripped of the other, alienated, suspicious, and disorientated:

> 'And every man I chanc'd to see,
> I thought he knew some ill of me.
> No peace, no comfort could I find,
> No ease, within doors or without,
> And crazily, and wearily,
> I went my work about.'   (ll. 73–8)

Worse still, his growing children seem not only to devour the flock, but, with it, his capacity for love:

> 'Alas! it was an evil time;
> God cursed me in my sore distress,
> I prayed, yet every day I thought
> I loved my children less;
> And every week, and every day,
> My flock, it seemed to melt away.'   (ll. 85–90)

' "God cursed me in my sore distress" ' goes one further than Burns; even religion fails to alleviate the lot of the working man. Poetry like this not only exposes a social problem, the limitations of institutionalized charity as a means of dealing with poverty—it lays bare the psychological experience of the victim. 'If the author be a wealthy man, he ought not to have suffered this poor peasant to part with *the last of the flock*', wrote Dr. Burney in his review of *Lyrical Ballads*.[1] Naïvely, he suggests Wordsworth's success in making us respond to the poetry of passion as if to passion itself.

'Simon Lee, the Old Huntsman, with an incident in which he was concerned' shows the poet, as Dr. Burney would have wished, helping another victim of circumstances. Its method extends the implications of a poetry of passion to narrative ('the feeling therein developed gives importance to the action and situation . . .'); Wordsworth's experiment with language has merged with his ballad experiment. The 'incident' of the poem's title concerns the old man's pathetic gratitude when the poet effortlessly severs a rotten stump at which Simon himself had laboured ineffectually:

---

[1] *Monthly Review*, xxix (June 1799), 207.

> The tears into his eyes were brought,
> And thanks and praises seemed to run
> So fast out of his heart, I thought
> They never would have done.
> —I've heard of hearts unkind, kind deeds
> With coldness still returning.
> Alas! the gratitude of men
> Has oftner left me mourning.   (ll. 97–104)[1]

That Simon should be grateful for so little, when life has deprived him of so much, crystallizes the poem's underlying theme: the pathos and incongruity of old age. The jaunty ballad idiom conflicts with elegy. Simon's present—his shrunken body and enfeebled gardening—contrasts poignantly with the lost ballad world to which he belongs:

> No man like him the horn could sound,
> And no man was so full of glee;
> To say the least, four counties round
> Had heard of Simon Lee;
> His master's dead, and no one now
> Dwells in the hall of Ivor;
> Men, dogs, and horses, all are dead;
> He is the sole survivor.   (ll. 17–24)

The careless vitality of the opening lines is displaced by desolation and finality ('Men, dogs, and horses, all are dead'), and celebration becomes lament: 'no one now/Dwells in the hall of Ivor'. From the comic double rhyme (Ivor/survivor) emerges Simon's tragedy; the 'survivor', he is also a casualty of time, his blue huntsman's coat at odds with his need to scrape a living from the soil. The sound of the hunting-pack may stir him as strongly as ever, but age forces him into a new role. Wordsworth's insistence on Simon's swollen ankles is not tiresomely prosaic; it is a reminder of the tactlessness of old age itself.

The long catalogue of privation and diminished faculties which takes up most of 'Simon Lee' is interrupted when Wordsworth turns to his reader, challenging the expectations which he himself has aroused by his use of a ballad idiom:

---

[1] See also the interesting discussion of this closing stanza in J. F. Danby's *The Simple Wordsworth* (London, 1960), pp. 46–7.

My gentle reader, I perceive
How patiently you've waited,
And I'm afraid that you expect
Some tale will be related.

O reader! had you in your mind
Such stores as silent thought can bring,
O gentle reader! you would find
A tale in every thing.   (ll. 69–76)

'Gentle reader' does more than invoke the broken contract
between poet and audience; it appeals for the compassionate
involvement which alone gives meaning to the 'incident' in
Simon's garden. 'It is the honourable characteristic of Poetry
that its materials are to be found in every subject which can
interest the human mind', begins the 'Advertisement' of 1798.[1]
'Simon Lee' aims to extend our sympathies—much as the
literature of sensibility had done—by revealing that the hum-
blest episodes of everyday life have a bearing on the human
condition. Compare, for instance, the man mourning his dead
ass in Sterne's *Sentimental Journey* (1768): 'He then took his
crust of bread out of his wallet again, as if to eat it; held it some
time in his hand—then laid it upon the bit of his ass's bridle—
looked wistfully at the little arrangement he had made—and
then gave a sigh.'[2] Yorick's comment on this vignette is
paralleled by Wordsworth's upsurge of emotion at the end of
'Simon Lee'—'Shame on the world! said I to myself—Did we
love each other, as this poor soul but loved his ass—'twould be
something.'[3] Wordsworthian sensibility ('Alas! the gratitude
of men/Has oftner left me mourning', ll. 103–4) is similarly
educative; the difference is that we have to think as well as
feel, and from the struggle to understand the elusive meaning
of the poem's last lines comes a new involvement. The impatient
reader is forced to discover in himself the reflective values—
'Such stores as silent thought can bring'—which vindicate
Wordsworth's method. Like the other laments of 1798, 'Simon

[1] *Prose Works*, i. 116.
[2] *A Sentimental Journey through France and Italy* (2 vols., London, 1768), i. 124.
[3] Ibid. i. 128. Cf. also the overflow of emotion at the end of 'Anecdote for Fathers'
('O dearest, dearest boy! my heart/For better lore would seldom yearn . . .'
ll. 57–8).

Lee' embodies the central impulse of the Lyrical Ballads experiment—Wordsworth's attempt to provide a more significant literary experience than his readers were used to finding in the overworked themes and genres of their time.

IX *The Ballad Revival and the 1790s*

'It is supposed, that by the act of writing in verse an Author makes a formal engagement that he will gratify certain known habits of association', wrote Wordsworth in the 1800 'Preface' to *Lyrical Ballads*.[1] The challenge of the 1798 volume lay in its refusal to fulfil audience expectations—in particular, expectations about the ballad. His readers were not only required to find 'A tale in every thing' ('Simon Lee', l. 76), but forced to look critically at the fashion for supernatural and pseudo-antiquarian balladry which had reached its peak during the mid-1790s. Along with many of their contemporaries, Wordsworth and Coleridge tried their hand at this by-product of the ballad revival. Both were influenced by the German poet, Gottfried Bürger, whose ballads appeared in translation during the 1790s and offered a striking model for their own up-dating of traditional themes and techniques. But where Coleridge accepted the supernatural, Wordsworth reacted against it. Although Bürger undoubtedly attracted him for a time, the uncongenial values of the supernatural ballad led him to create a new kind of ballad emphasizing the importance of the everyday, of feeling rather than situation. The questions Wordsworth asks—what is a story? What makes an adventure? What part does the mind play in creating both?—culminate in the open anti-supernaturalism of *Peter Bell*. Rooted as it is in an ephemeral fashion, the ballad experiment offers the most illuminating example of Wordsworth's self-defining relation to his literary context. Nowhere is his contemporaneity more marked, and nowhere is his divergence more individual.

---

[1] *Prose Works*, i. 122.

I. THE LITERARY BALLAD

Wordsworth's famous claim for Percy's *Reliques*—that English poetry 'has been absolutely redeemed by it'—goes with a generous acknowledgement of his own debt:

I do not think that there is an able writer in verse of the present day who would not be proud to acknowledge his obligations to the Reliques; I know that it is so with my friends; and, for myself, I am happy in this occasion to make a public avowal of my own.[1]

Behind this 'public avowal' lies the full weight of the ballad revival. In 1800, when he invoked 'The Babes in the Wood' in support of his own poetic theories, Wordsworth still felt the need to caution the reader against 'a mode of false criticism which has been applied to Poetry in which the language closely resembles that of life and nature'.[2] But he could rely on his reader knowing Addison's defence of the ballad, a hundred years before. However apologetically, the *Spectator* papers had made a case for 'The Babes in the Wood' which might almost have been made by Blair or Wordsworth himself:

This Song is a plain simple Copy of Nature, destitute of all the Helps and Ornaments of Art. The Tale of it is a pretty Tragical Story, and pleases for no other Reason, but because it is a Copy of Nature. There is even a despicable Simplicity in the Verse; and yet, because the Sentiments appear genuine and unaffected, they are able to move the Mind of the most polite Reader with inward Meltings of Humanity and Compassion.[3]

Percy too bases his claims for the ballad on qualities bound up with its lack of sophistication:

In a polished age, like the present, I am sensible that many of these reliques of antiquity will require great allowances to be made for them. Yet have they, for the most part, a pleasing simplicity, and many artless graces, which in the opinion of no mean critics have been thought to compensate for the want of higher beauties, and if they do not dazzle the imagination, are frequently found to interest the heart.[4]

[1] 'Essay, Supplementary to the Preface', 1815 (*Prose Works*, iii. 78).
[2] 1800 'Preface' (*Prose Works*, i. 152).
[3] *Spectator*, No. lxxxv (7 June 1711), ed. D. F. Bond, i. 362–3.
[4] *Reliques of Ancient English Poetry*, i. x.

Increasingly, to say that the traditional ballad 'interests the heart' is to say that it expresses all that is most lasting and important in human feeling. The ballad collections which follow Percy are prefaced in terms that grow less defensive as they gain in critical sophistication. Pinkerton, for instance, in the introduction to his *Scottish Tragic Ballads* of 1781, shares Blair's assumptions about the origins of poetry ('the original language of men in an infant state of society'), and again the ballad-makers' power to move is linked directly with their lack of literary pretension: 'Their mode of expression was simple and genuine. They of consequence touched the passions truly and effectively.'[1] Like Blair's primitive bards, they appealed with special directness to 'the passions and the ear', and because 'The passions of men have been and will be the same through all ages',[2] their writing is held to have the same timeless validity as that of Homer, Shakespeare, and Ossian. With these credentials, the ballad was bound to have important connotations for Wordsworth in 1798.

Yet the traditional ballad seems to have had little direct influence on Wordsworth's experiment. Of all the poems written during spring 1798, only 'The Mad Mother' (and, less certainly, 'The Thorn') owes anything to a traditional source.[3] Wordsworth's purchase of the *Reliques* did not take place until his arrival in Germany later the same year,[4] and it is tempting to think that he returned to Percy by way of imitators like Bürger; certainly 'Lucy Gray', composed during his Goslar stay,[5] owes more to the style of the 'justly admired' stanza of 'The Babes in the Wood' later cited in the 1800 'Preface' ('These pretty Babes with hand in hand/Went wandering up and down . . .')[6] than do any of the ballads of 1798:

> The storm came on before its time,
> She wander'd up and down,
> And many a hill did Lucy climb
> But never reached the Town.   (ll. 29–32)

The colloquial vigour and flamboyance of Wordsworth's ballad experiment has no real counterpart in the traditional

---

[1] 'Dissertation I', *Scottish Tragic Ballads*, pp. x, xvii.
[2] Ibid., p. xvii.
[3] See pp. 196–7, above, and 242, below.
[4] See *DWJ* i. 31.
[5] See Reed, p. 256 and n.
[6] *Prose Works*, i. 154.

ballad. Nor does it help to invoke the popular broadside. All one has to go on are the later references to street ballads in *The Prelude*—the 'English Ballad-singer' and 'files of ballads' in the London streets[1]—and a pious hope expressed to Wrangham ten years after the event:

I have so much felt the influence of these straggling papers, that I have many a time wished that I had talents to produce songs, poems, and little histories, that might circulate among other good things in this way, supplanting partly the bad; flowers and useful herbs to take place of weeds. Indeed some of the Poems which I have published were composed not without a hope that at some time or other they might answer this purpose.[2]

Wordsworth had been anticipated in his hope by the missionary efforts of Hannah More; but unlike hers, the ballads of 1798 can never have been seriously intended for an unsophisticated audience. Only 'Goody Blake, and Harry Gill' ('one of the rudest of this collection')[3] is at all reminiscent of broadside—and even here Wordsworth is far closer to Hannah More's imitations in the *Cheap Repository* series than to the genuine broadside.[4] His originality lay in approaching the imitation ballad from a startlingly anti-literary direction. The effect is quite distinct from the literary ballads of his contemporaries, but the impulse—revitalizing, sophisticated, and self-conscious —is the same.

Scott's 1830 'Essay on Imitations of the Ancient Ballad' pays tribute to the literary ballad as a recognizable genre in its own right—'a new species of poetry', in Scott's words,

which in some cases endeavoured to pass itself as the production of genuine antiquity, and in others, honestly avowed an attempt to emulate the merits and avoid the errors with which the old ballad was encumbered; and in the effort to accomplish this, a species of composition was discovered, which is capable of being subjected to peculiar rules of criticism, and of exhibiting excellencies of its own.[5]

'The Ancient Mariner', with its gothic encrustations, provides a lasting monument to this new genre. Wordsworth's interest

---

[1] See *Prelude*, vii. 195–6, 209.   [2] 5 June 1808; *MY* i. 248.
[3] 1800 'Preface' (*Prose Works*, i. 150).   [4] See pp. 237–9, below.
[5] *The Poetical Works of Sir Walter Scott, Bart.*, ed. J. G. Lockhart (11 vols., Edinburgh, 1833–4), iv. 14–15.

in pseudo-antiquarianism goes back to an earlier stage. Apart from his reference to Lady Wardlaw's *Hardyknute* (one of the famous eighteenth-century ballad imitations),[1] 1788 saw Wordsworth copying Chatterton, the most remarkable, as well as the most controversial of pseudo-antiquarian writers. Chatterton's 'Bristowe Tragedie: or the Dethe of Syr Charles Bawdin' is one of the few imitations to recapture the fatalism of the traditional ballad, but the best known of Chatterton's poems was undoubtedly the gothic 'Minstrelles Songe' from his play, *Ælla: A Tragycal Enterlude*:

> Harke! the ravenne flappes hys wynge,
> In the briered delle belowe;
> Harke! the dethe-owle loude dothe synge,
> To the nyghte-mares as heie goe;
>> Mie love ys dedde,
>> Gonne to hys deathe-bedde,
>> Al under the wyllowe tree.[2]

The first version of Wordsworth's 'Dirge.—Sung by a Minstrel', probably belonging to early 1788, openly alludes to Chatterton's 'Songe':

> List! the bell-Sprite stuns my ears
>> Slowly calling for a maid
> List!—each worm with trembling hears
>> And stops for joy his dreadful trade.

> For nine times the death-bell's Sprite
>> Sullen for the Virgin cried
> And they say at dead of night
>> Before its time the taper died.
>> Mie love ys dedde
>> Gone to her deathbedde
>> Al und[er the willowe] tree.[3]

---

[1] See pp. 135–6 and n., above.

[2] *Ælla*, ll. 865–71, *Poems, Supposed to have been written at Bristol by Thomas Rowley, and Others* (London, 1777).

[3] DC MS. 2: *PW* i. 267, ll. 1–11. The second version of the 'Dirge'—for a boy rather than a maid, and reflecting the pseudo-Shakespearianism of Collins's 'Song' from *Cymbeline* rather than Chatterton's 'Songe'—belongs to almost the same time, or very shortly after. Reed, p. 78 and n., assumes a reverse order of composition; but it is unlikely that Wordsworth would have drafted the opening stanzas of the version for a maid in DC MS. 2 after entering the same stanzas in fair copy as part of the version for a boy. I am grateful to Paul Betz for drawing this to my attention.

Ten years later, Wordsworth was equally alert to a fashionable gothicism; but by then he was prepared to experiment rather than imitate.

Both Chatterton and the young Wordsworth had used antiquarianism to revive the sentimental ballad—a genre, Scott remarked, 'as unlike to a minstrel ballad, as a lady assuming the dress of a Shepherdess for a masquerade, is different from the actual Sisly of Salisbury Plain'.[1] John Aikin, in his *Essays on Song-Writing* (1772), offers the best description of its attempt to combine pastoral simplicity with contemporary sensibility:

the genius of the age has chiefly been characterized by the correct, elegant, and tender; and a real or affected taste for beautiful simplicity has almost universally prevailed. This has produced several imitations of the antient ballad as a serious composition, turned however in its general subject from the story of martial adventure to the pathetic tale of the peaceful village. It is a just taste, founded upon real observation of nature, which enjoins simplicity of expression in every attempt to engage the sympathetic emotions . . . [2]

Aikin has in mind the innumerable pathetic ballads of the eighteenth century—tales of jilted maidens and haunted lovers like Mallet's 'William and Margaret' or Tickell's 'Lucy and Colin'. Chatterton's 'Songe' and Wordsworth's 'Dirge' both rework the gothic portents of Tickell's ballad—

> Three Times, all in the dead of Night,
>   A Bell was heard to ring,
> And at her Window, shrieking thrice,
>   The Raven flapp'd his Wing . . . [3]

—and Wordsworth's 'Ballad' of 1787 is simply an adaptation of the tales of broken vows told by Mallet and Tickell (' "And will you leave me thus alone/And dare you break your vow . . ." ').[4] A much-needed antidote to 'the pathetic tale of the peaceful village' was provided by the ballad of horror and the supernatural. Scott describes the 1790s as 'A period when

---

[1] 'Essay on Imitations of the Ancient Ballad' (Lockhart, iv. 27).

[2] *Essays on Song-Writing: with a Collection of . . . English Songs* (London, 1772), p. 29.

[3] *Lucy and Colin* (Dublin, 1725), st. 3.

[4] DC MS. 2: *PW* i. 265, ll. 1–2.

this particular taste . . . was in the most extravagant degree of fashion',[1] and M. G. Lewis's *Tales of Wonder* (1801) is the representative anthology. In 1798, Lewis wrote to Scott, 'The Plan, which I propose to myself, is to collect all the *marvellous* Ballads, that I can lay my hands upon, and publish them under the title of "Tales of Terror".'[2] From the start, there was an element of light-heartedness about the plan. Lewis goes on to say that 'a Ghost or a Witch is a sine-qua-non ingredient in all the dishes, of which I mean to compose my hobgoblin repast';[3] by 1801, when *Tales of Wonder* finally appeared, parody had become a central ingredient, with Lewis's 'Giles Jollup the Grave, and Brown Sally Green' travestying his own 'Alonzo the Brave, and Fair Imogine'—the ballad which had done so much to boost the fashion when it appeared in *The Monk* in 1796. The second edition of *Tales of Wonder* had a companion volume, *Tales of Terror* (1801), put out by the same publisher in the same format, and given over entirely to parody. Whether or not Lewis and his collaborators were responsible,[4] it is a reminder that the fashion was short-lived. By 1801, 'the passion for ballads and ballad-mongers [had] been for some time on the wane', Scott remembers,[5] and the 'Introductory Dialogue' to *Tales of Terror* asserts that the avid ballad-reader was surfeited: 'WHAT, scribble tales? Oh! cease to play the fool!/Christmas is past, and children gone to school . . .'[6]

But things had been very different in 1796. Scott, for instance, 'finding Lewis in possession of so much reputation', was encouraged 'to attempt the style of poetry by which he had raised himself to fame'.[7] The results—pseudo-Scots ballads like

[1] 'Essay on Imitations of the Ancient Ballad' (Lockhart, iv. 32).

[2] K. S. Guthke, 'Die erste Nachwirkung von Herders Volksliedern in England', *Archiv für das Studium der neueren Sprachen*, cxciii (1957), 275.

[3] Ibid. cxciii. 276.

[4] For speculation about the authorship of *Tales of Terror* and the bibliographical confusion which surrounds it, see L. F. Peck, *A Life of Matthew G. Lewis* (Cambridge, Mass., 1961), pp. 132–3, and Morchard Bishop, 'A Terrible Tangle', *TLS*, 19 October 1967, p. 989.

[5] 'Essay on Imitations of the Ancient Ballad' (Lockhart, iv. 74). Scott also recalls the hostility to 'a work in royal octavo . . . by large printing, *driven out*, as it is technically termed, to two volumes, which were sold at a high price'; it selected so freely from the works of other poets that it became known as 'Tales of Plunder' (Lockhart, iv. 75–6).

[6] *Tales of Terror* (London, 1801), p. [1].

[7] 'Essay on Imitations of the Ancient Ballad' (Lockhart, iv. 54–5).

'Glenfinlas, or Lord Ronald's Coronach' and 'The Eve of Saint John', along with his translation of Bürger's 'Der wilde Jäger' —duly appeared in *Tales of Wonder*. Southey too wrote teutonic ballads of the supernatural, such as 'Donica' and 'Rudiger', published in *Poems* (1797) and later anthologized by Lewis. Like Scott, Wordsworth and Coleridge responded enthusiastically to the ballads of Gottfried Bürger; and like Southey, Wordsworth made his own contribution to the ballad of everyday horror. Although the demons and monsters of 'Donica' and 'Rudiger' have no counterpart in Wordsworth's poetry, 'Poor Mary, the Maid of the Inn'—Southey's most famous ballad at the time[1]—provides an obvious parallel for 'The Thorn'. 'Poor Mary' was announced in the *Oracle* during February 1797 as 'a legitimate companion to "ALONZO the *Brave*" ', whose anapaestic rhythm it borrows; but its terrors are not supernatural. Southey has made the transition which is to be central to Wordsworth's ballad experiment, but unlike Wordsworth's, his aims are basically sensational. He begins with the spectacle of a mad woman—

> 'Who is she, the poor maniac, whose wildly fix'd eyes
>   Seem a heart overcharged to express?
> She weeps not, yet often and deeply she sighs,
> She never complains, but her silence implies
>   The composure of settled distress.'

—and ends with the gibbet of her worthless lover:

> 'Where the old abbey stands, on the common hard by
>   His gibbet is now to be seen.
> Not far from the road it engages the eye,
> The traveller beholds it, and thinks with a sigh
>   Of poor Mary the maid of the inn.'[2]

Cheerfully intrepid, Mary braves the imaginary terrors of night in a ruined abbey; in doing so she stumbles on the fact that her lover is a murderer, and returns, unknowingly, with the evidence that incriminates him. Her mind is turned, not by the supernatural, but by grief at their mutual betrayal. Her

---

[1] See *The Life and Correspondence of Robert Southey*, ed. C. C. Southey (6 vols., London, 1849–50), i. 304, and *Selections from the Letters of Robert Southey*, ed. J. W. Warter (4 vols., London, 1856), i. 69–70.

[2] *Oracle*, 11 February 1797.

story anticipates Wordsworth's transference of unbalance and horror to a rustic world—creating what might be called a low-style gothic—and its idiom looks forward to his substitution of the colloquial for the pseudo-antiquarian. But the basic assumptions of the genre are never questioned as they are to be in *Lyrical Ballads*. Where Southey exploits the fashion, Wordsworth challenges it.

11. BÜRGER

'Poor Mary, the Maid of the Inn' declares its debt to Lewis, but the larger debt goes unacknowledged. Southey owes his arresting opening and close to the translation of Bürger's 'Des Pfarrers Tochter von Taubenhain' which had been published shortly before, in the *Monthly Magazine* for April 1796. Of all the supernatural ballad-writing of the 1790s, Bürger's is the most striking, and it was certainly the most influential. Besides 'Des Pfarrers Tochter von Taubenhain', two other ballads by Bürger reached England in translation during the 1790s— 'Lenore' and 'Der wilde Jäger'—and for a short time all three had an unparalleled success. Looking back from 1815, Wordsworth saw in Bürger the natural successor to Percy; while English ballad imitation was 'deservedly disregarded', 'Bürger, and other able writers of Germany, were translating, or imitating these Reliques, and composing, with the aid of inspiration thence derived, poems which are the delight of the German nation.'[1] As no one in England had done, Bürger transformed the traditional ballad into something both novel and contemporaneous. His originality lay in technique rather than theme. The ballads that made him famous did so not because of their subtlety, or their power to move—still less through a recovery of the authentic ballad voice. Each is based on a horror story: 'Des Pfarrers Tochter von Taubenhain' offers seduction followed by infanticide and retribution; the ghostly lover of 'Lenore' returns from the dead to carry his betrothed back to the tomb; (and the callous huntsman of 'Der wilde Jäger' earns eternal punishment from a diabolic hunter.) Yet for all their sensationalism, Bürger's ballad-imitations make

---

[1] 'Essay, Supplementary to the Preface', 1815 (*Prose Works*, iii. 75). Wordsworth bought Bürger's poems in the original German at the same time as Percy's *Reliques*, on his arrival at Hamburg in October 1798 (see *DWJ* i. 31).

compulsive reading. It is not that each has a tenuous claim to morality, depicting the punishment of impiety or crime by supernatural powers.|Nor is it, as one critic has it, that they are 'ghostly in the deepest sense' in their concern with 'eschatological self-encounter'.[1] |The really striking thing about these ballads is quite simply their presentation—their manipulation of pace and narrative control, their galloping rhythms, their onomatopoeic sound effects, their internal and double rhymes.]

The important notice by William Taylor of Norwich, in the *Monthly Magazine* for March 1796, goes a long way towards explaining Bürger's appeal:

Bürger is every where distinguished for manly sentiment and force of style. His extraordinary powers of language are founded on a rejection of the conventional phraseology of regular poetry, in favour of popular forms of expression, caught by the listening artist from the voice of agitated nature./Imitative harmony he pursues almost to excess: the onomatopoeia is his prevailing figure; the interjection, his favourite part of speech: arrangement, rhythm, sound, rime, are always with him, an echo to the sense.)The hurrying vigour of his impetuous diction is unrivalled; yet, it is so natural, even in its sublimity, that his poetry is singularly fitted to become national popular song.[2])

The very terms used by Taylor—'a rejection of the conventional phraseology of regular poetry', 'caught by the listening artist from the voice of agitated nature'—anticipate Wordsworth's 1798 attack on 'the gaudiness and inane phraseology of many modern writers', and his 1800 championing of 'the real language of men in a state of vivid sensation'.[3] Two years before Taylor's notice, Scott's decision to become a ballad-writer had been

hurried into execution, in consequence of a temptation which others, as well as the author, found it difficult to resist. The celebrated ballad of 'Lenoré', by Bürger, was about this time introduced into England . . . The wild character of the tale was such as struck the imagination of all who read it . . . [4]

He goes on to describe the electrifying Edinburgh reading of Taylor's 'Lenore' in 1794 which inspired his own version,

---

[1] See Geoffrey Hartman, 'False Themes and Gentle Minds', *PQ* xlvii (1968), 65.
[2] *Monthly Magazine*, i (March 1796), 118.   [3] *Prose Works*, i. 116, 118.
[4] 'Essay on Imitations of the Ancient Ballad' (Lockhart, iv. 55).

William and Helen.[1] After Taylor's translation had finally appeared in the *Monthly Magazine* in 1796—its publication prompted by the many rival translations that were beginning to appear[2]—Lamb wrote breathlessly to Coleridge: 'Have you read the Ballad called "Leonora," in the second Number of the "Monthly Magazine"? If you have !!!!!!!!!!!!!! There is another fine song, from the same author (Berger), in the 3d No., of scarce inferior merit . . .'[3] Southey thought the second ballad ('Des Pfarrers Tochter von Taubenhain') still better than the first: 'I know no commendation equal to its merit; read it again . . . and read it aloud. The man who wrote that should have been ashamed of Lenora.'[4] One would not expect Southey to be worried by Bürger's sensationalism, but the enthusiasm of a sensitive and discriminating critic like Lamb makes it easy to understand how Wordsworth and Coleridge could have come under its spell.

Wordsworth may well have seen some of the other translations of Bürger that came into circulation between 1796 and 1798;[5] but he must certainly have seen Taylor's version of 'Lenore' in the *Monthly Magazine* for March 1796, followed in April by his rendering of 'Des Pfarrers Tochter von Taubenhain' as 'The Lass of Fair Wone'.[6] By 1800 at least, he also knew Bürger's 'Der wilde Jäger', whether in the original or in Scott's version, 'The Chase' (1796).[7] Bürger's three ballads provided the starting-point for 'The Idiot Boy', 'The Thorn',

[1] See ibid. iv. 56–8, and J. W. Robberds, *A Memoir of the Life and Writings of the Late William Taylor of Norwich*, i. 92. Taylor's translation had circulated in MS. since the early 1790s; see ibid. i. 91–2, as well as Taylor's own *Historic Survey of German Poetry* (3 vols., London, 1830), ii. 51n., and John Aikin's note to his imitation, 'Arthur and Matilda', *Poems* (London, 1791), p. 41n.

[2] See Robberds, i. 101, and *Monthly Magazine* i (March 1796), 135.

[3] 6 July 1796; Lucas, i. 37.

[4] *The Life and Correspondence of Robert Southey*, ed. C. C. Southey, i. 287.

[5] See W. W. Greg, 'English Translations of "Lenore" ', *Modern Quarterly of Language and Literature*, ii, No. 5 (1899), 13–28, and O. F. Emerson, 'The Earliest English Translations of Bürger's Lenore', *Western Reserve University Bulletin*, xviii, No. 3 (1915).

[6] Both ballads are reprinted in Appendix II, pp. 277–88, below. Taylor's translation of 'Lenore'—republished on its own in Edinburgh as a 2nd edn. in 1796, as was 'The Lass of Fair Wone'—also appeared in another version, *Ellenore* (Norwich, 1796).

[7] Scott's translation, published with his 'Lenore' as *The Chase, and William and Helen* (Edinburgh, 1796), was followed by another, *The Wild Huntsman* (Edinburgh, 1797), reprinted as *The Wild Huntsman's Chase* (London, 1798).

and 'Hart-Leap Well' respectively. More important, they
served not merely as sources, but as catalysts. Wordsworth's
initial excitement gave way to awareness of their faults, and his
appreciation, to a statement of alternative values. When he
wrote in the 'Preface' of 1800 that his poetry was distinguished
from 'the popular Poetry of the day' by its stress on 'feeling'
rather than 'situation',[1] Wordsworth was elaborating an earlier
remark apropos of Bürger that 'incidents are among the lowest
allurements of poetry'. Intrigued by Bürger's techniques, he
was also critical of his failure to explore the human heart. In a
letter of late 1798, he told Coleridge:

Bürger is one of those authors whose book I like to have in my hand,
but when I have laid the book down I do not think about him. I
remember a hurry of pleasure, but I have few distinct forms that
people my mind, nor any recollection of delicate or minute feelings
which he has either communicated to me, or taught me to recognize. I do not perceive the presence of character in his personages.
I see everywhere the character of Bürger himself; and even this, I
agree with you, is no mean merit. But yet I wish him sometimes at
least to make me forget himself in his creations. It seems to me, that
in poems descriptive of human nature, however short they may be,
character is absolutely necessary, &c.: incidents are among the
lowest allurements of poetry. Take from Bürger's poems the *incidents*,
which are seldom or ever of his own invention, and still much will
remain; there will remain a manner of relating which is almost
always spirited and lively, and stamped and peculiarized with
genius. Still I do not find those higher beauties which can entitle
him to the name of a *great* poet. . . . Bürger is the poet of the animal
spirits. I love his '*Tra ra la*' dearly; but less of the horn and more of
the lute—and far, far more of the pencil.[2]

For Wordsworth, Bürger offers 'a hurry of pleasure' but no
lasting insight. His verdict implies his own attempts to create
a poetry that extends the reader's sympathies as well as cap-
turing his interest. The ballads of 1798 clearly owe something
to Bürger's spirited 'manner of relating', but they also replace
sheer personality by 'character', or (as Wordsworth put it in a
second letter to Coleridge) 'manners': 'I do not so ardently
desire character in poems like Bürger's, as manners, not tran-

---

[1] *Prose Works*, i. 128.
[2] *EY*, pp. 234–5. Cf. Gray's identification of 'the pencil' with a Shakespearian
humanity and breadth ('The Progress of Poesy', ll. 83–94).

sitory manners reflecting the wearisome unintelligible obliquities of city-life, but manners connected with the permanent objects of nature and partaking of the simplicity of those objects.'[1] These letters, midway between the 1800 'Preface' and the ballads of 1798, suggest the vital interconnection between theory and practice in Wordsworth's poetry.

'The public has been much amused and gratified by a contest for literary fame among the several translators of Leonora, a wild and extravagant, but uncommonly interesting German ballad', observed the *Monthly Magazine* in 1797.[2] Besides the versions by Taylor and Scott, 1796 saw translations by W. R. Spencer, J. T. Stanley, and the poet laureate, Henry James Pye. Most were handsomely produced, some lavishly illustrated (Stanley's very strikingly, by Blake). The competition kept Bürger in the public eye. But there was little attempt to translate the onomatopoeic techniques praised in Taylor's *Monthly Magazine* notice; W. R. Spencer, for instance, comments that

Mr. Burgher has repeatedly used words merely for sound, as 'trap, trap, trap,' for the trotting of an horse; and 'cling, cling, cling,' for the ringing of a door bell. These echoes to the sense, which are strictly 'vox et preterea nihil,' custom may reconcile to a German taste; but, literally adopted in an English version, they would appear more ridiculous than descriptive.[3]

Later the schoolmaster and author Samuel Whyte went further and attacked Bürger's idiom as 'caricature':

The correspondence of sound and sense, for which the German has been distinguished, is, no doubt, a prime ornament of metre, and gives life and spirit of poetic expression; but carried to an extreme, however striking the resemblance, it is the resemblance in caricature, and ceases to be beautiful. The genuine unaffected simplicity of our old English Ballad, depending not on the play of words, but on the conception, would bear translation, and appear with advantage in any language, 'where free to follow nature is the mode;' this is

[1] 27 February 1799; *EY*, p. 255. Cf. Blair's reference to 'those refinements of society . . . which enlarge indeed, and diversify the transactions, but disguise the manners of mankind' (*A Critical Dissertation on the Poems of Ossian*, p. [1]).
[2] *Monthly Magazine*, iii (January 1797), 46.
[3] 'Preface', *Leonora. Translated from the German of Gottfried Augustus Bürgher* (London, 1796).

not the case with the German. The reiteration of *trap, trap, trap*
for the sound of a horse's, or rather the ghost of a horse's feet, and of
cling, cling, cling for that of a door-bell, in Burgher's Poem, is mere
mimickry, adapted to the vulgar ear . . . [1]

The version generally regarded as having won the contest was
Taylor's[2]—a transposition of the German into something
approaching what Whyte calls 'the genuine unaffected simplicity of our old English Ballad'. Even Wordsworth preferred
it to the original.[3] Taylor has adopted the one ballad style—
combining popular vigour with antiquarian licence—that
allows him to incorporate Bürger's exclamatory repetitions and
galloping rhythms, and it is his translation that best captures
the excitement of Lenore's midnight ride to the grave:

> And hurry-skurry forth they go,   *L145*
>   Unheeding wet or dry;
> And horse and rider snort and blow,
>   And sparkling pebbles fly.
>
> How swift the flood, the mead, the wood,
>   Aright, aleft, are gone!
> The bridges thunder as they pass,
>   But earthlie sowne is none.
>
> Tramp, tramp, across the land they speede;
>   Splash, splash, across the see:
> 'Hurrah! the dead can ride apace;
>   Dost feare to ride with mee?'   *L156*
>
> .   .   .   .
>
> Halloo! halloo! away they goe,   *L181*
>   Unheeding wet or drye;
> And horse and rider snort and blowe,
>   And sparkling pebbles flye.

---

[1] *A Miscellany, containing . . . A Critique on Bürger's Leonora* (Dublin, 1799), pp.
170–1.

[2] It was the version chosen for *Tales of Wonder* by M. G. Lewis, who provides a
literal translation of Bürger's opening stanza to demonstrate its unfeasibility; see
Tales of Wonder (2 vols., London, 1801), ii. 469. Wordsworth was to use a stanza-
form based on that of 'Lenore' for 'Ellen Irwin, or the Braes of Kirtle' in *Lyrical
Ballads* (1800); see also the I.F. note (*PW* iii. 443).

[3] See *EY*, pp. 233–4. Wordsworth had been sent the volume of the *Monthly
Magazine* that contained Taylor's translation in early 1797 (see Mary Moorman,
William Wordsworth, p. 309).

How swifte the hill, how swifte the dale,
    Aright, aleft, are gone!
By hedge and tree, by thorpe and towne,
    They gallop, gallop on.

Tramp, tramp, across the land they speede;
    Splash, splash, acrosse the see:
'Hurrah! the dead can ride apace;
    Dost fear to ride with mee?'[1]   L 92

The galloping hoof-beats are there in the rhythm, the landscape
flashes by in swift-moving phrases ('the flood, the mead, the
wood', 'By hedge and tree, by thorpe and towne'). Above all,
the refrain-like exclamations—'Halloo! halloo! away they go',
' "Hurrah! the dead can ride apace . . ." '—maintain the pace
without which our interest would flag.

Wordsworth's changing views mirror those of his period.
Translators and critics had begun by stressing 'Lenore's 'fire
and energy'—'that fire and energy', in Stanley's words, for
which 'the wild and eccentric writings of the Germans' were
famous.[2] But the literary audience which read 'Lenore' was
precisely the one to be worried (as a popular audience would
not have been) by the sensational morality of Bürger's writing.
Spencer represents Lenore's ride to the grave as her punishment for criticizing divine providence, in a moment of impious
despair at her lover's failure to return from the war ('Few
objections can be made to a subject, new, simple, and striking;
and none to a moral, which cannot be too frequently or too
awfully enforced').[3] But for Stanley, this moral was enforced
in an entirely unacceptable way: 'I have often doubted whether
["Lenore"] was not calculated (as far as its effects could extend) to injure the cause of Religion and Morality, by exhibiting a representation of supernatural interference, inconsistent
with our ideas of a just and benevolent Deity.'[4] He duly modifies

(but her soul is forgiven)

---

[1] *Monthly Magazine*, i (March 1796), 137.

[2] 'Preface', *Leonora. A Tale, Translated and Altered from the German of Gottfried
Augustus Bürger* (2nd edn., London, 1796), p. xi.

[3] 'Preface', *Leonora. Translated from the German.*

[4] 'Advertisement', *Leonora. A Tale*, p. vi. *Miss Kitty*, the story of an everyday
elopement, parodies 'Lenore' by contrasting its heroine's fate—the loss of her
dowry—with that of Lenora, who 'for talking somewhat wildly, is dispatched to
that bourne from whence no traveller returns'; *Miss Kitty* (Edinburgh, 1797), p. 29n.

his version to show God in a more favourable light (the ghostly ride becomes a nightmare from which Lenora is woken by the return of her lover, alive and well). But the last word has to go to Samuel Whyte, in 1799. Writing derisively about 'the lesson of patience' which 'Lenore' is said to contain—'the order of nature is subverted; the secrets of the grave prophaned [*sic*], and a tremendous apparatus, as if the fate of nations depended on it, exhibited, for what? To frighten an innocent young maniac, and send her a little before her time to "Heaven" . . .'[1]—he finally puts paid to its fashionable gothicism:

> In truth, the fiction is too violent; it out-herods Herod, and seems merely calculated to keep alive and propagate the exploded notions of ghosts and hobgoblins to the great annoyance of poor children, whose ductile minds are liable to fearful impressions, which by the strongest exertions of reason and good sense are scarcely ever afterwards to be wholly obliterated.[2]

After this, 'Lenore' could never be represented as anything other than a horror-poem for grown-ups. In 1800, Wordsworth himself denounced the 'degrading thirst after outrageous stimulation' which had been the basis of Bürger's popularity; and when he deplores the taste for 'deluges of idle and extravagant stories in verse',[3] one can be sure that he had 'Lenore' in mind.

III. 'THE THREE GRAVES'

Wordsworth's changing attitude to the German ballad is pinpointed in 'The Three Graves', which was begun in early 1797, but taken over and continued by Coleridge during the following spring, and thus spans the crucial year of the ballad experiment.[4] The difference between Wordsworth's and Coleridge's contributions at once emphasizes the change and reveals an underlying continuity. Though contrasting in style and treatment, both concern a curse; and a curse is again to be the sub-

---

[1] *A Miscellany*, p. 164.   [2] Ibid., p. 163.
[3] 1800 'Preface' (*Prose Works*, i. 128).
[4] Only Part II survives in the Racedown Notebook, along with related fragments (see Reed, p. 189n.), but a stub remains to indicate that Part I was also present. The MS. of Parts I and II printed as Coleridge's by E. H. Coleridge is in fact in Dorothy's hand; I am grateful to Robert Woof for this information. See also Reed, pp. 189, 189–90n., 230–1.

ject of Wordsworth's first ballad of spring 1798, 'Goody Blake, and Harry Gill'. Wordsworth's share in 'The Three Graves' (Parts I and II) shows him writing the kind of ballad he was later to denounce: the ballad of the supernatural. At this stage he plays on the qualities that make the supernatural genuinely disquieting—on the disturbing possibility of its intrusion into ordinary life, and the confused borderline between its effects and those of the mind. Part II of 'The Three Graves' centres on a mother's jealous passion for her daughter's lover:

> 'Would ye come here ye maiden vile
> And rob me of my mate',
> And on her child the mother scowled
> The ghastly leer of hate.[1]

Wordsworth's idiom is tinged with fashionable antiquarianism; but this is to be a world, like that of 'Christabel', in which subconscious impulses are released in dramatic confrontations. The mother's curse has chilling authority:

> To him no word the mother said
> But on her knees she fell,
> And fetched her breath while thrice your hand
> Might toll the passing bell.

> 'Thou daughter now above my head
> Whom in my womb I bore,
> May every drop of thy heart's blood
> Be curst for evermore.

> And cursed be the hour when first
> I heard thee wawl and cry,
> And in the churchyard cursed be
> The grave where thou shalt lie.'[2]

Wordsworth creates the emotionally charged atmosphere of the poem economically and without strain. His sophistication lies partly in exploiting the reader's ambivalent attitude to the supernatural—the fact that our disbelief is merely suspended. As the young pair leaves the hall, the mother taunts both them and us:

---

[1] DC MS. 11: *PW* i. 308, ll. 1–4.   [2] Ibid.: *PW* i. 310, ll. 61–72.

'What can an aged mother do?
And what have ye to dread;
A curse is wind, it hath no shape
To haunt your marriage bed.'[1]

We feel otherwise, sensing the power of the irrational and struck
with the lovers' own unstated foreboding. Wordsworth has
made the supernatural a credible extension of morbid states of
mind, as it cannot be in 'Lenore' or 'Des Pfarrers Tochter von
Taubenhain'.

The interest of Part II of 'The Three Graves' lies in its emotional conviction, that of Part I in Wordsworth's debt to
Bürger. The transcript passed on to Coleridge contained stanzas
introducing the central situation and presenting the characters
of the lovers, Edward and Mary, with their friend Ellen. It also
contained the framing device by which we learn the significance of the graves which give the poem its title. The narrative
of Part II is set in the village churchyard, and dramatized as a
sexton's reply to the listening narrator:

BENEATH this thorn when I was young,
    This thorn that blooms so sweet,
We loved to stretch our lazy limbs
    In summer's noon-tide heat.

And hither too the old man came,
    The maiden and her feer,
'Then tell me, Sexton, tell me why
    The toad has harbour here.

'The Thorn is neither dry nor dead,
    But still it blossoms sweet;
Then tell me why all round its roots
    The dock and nettle meet.

'Why here the hemlock, &c. [*sic in MS.*]

'Why these three graves all side by side,
    Beneath the flow'ry thorn
Stretch out so green and dark a length,
    By any foot unworn.'[2]

The graves are those of Ellen, Mary, and her mother; and at
the end of Part II we are told that the spot is a haunted one:

---

[1] DC MS. 11: *PW* i. 311, ll. 121–4.   [2] *CPW* i. 269–70, ll. 1–17.

And 'tis a fearful, fearful tree;
    The ghosts that round it meet,
'Tis they that cut the rind at night,
    Yet still it blossoms sweet.[1]

This is a different kind of horror, and a different approach to the supernatural, from that of the central curse scene. The toads and ghosts originate, not in Wordsworth's imagination, but in Bürger's. William Taylor's *Monthly Magazine* translation of 'Des Pfarrers Tochter von Taubenhain') came into Wordsworth's hands in March 1797 shortly before he is likely to have been at work on 'The Three Graves';[2] and its question-and-answer technique clearly inspired his own device:

BESIDE the parson's bower of yew
    Why strays a troubled spright,
That peaks and pines, and dimly shines
    Thro' curtains of the night?

Why steals along the pond of toads
    A gliding fire so blue,
That lights a spot where grows no grass,
    Where falls no rain nor dew?[3]

The story of seduction and infanticide associated with the spot is Bürger's answer to these questions, and the ballad ends by returning to the bower and pond of the opening stanzas—their macabre significance now understood:

Hard by the bower her gibbet stands:
    Her skull is still to show;
It seems to eye the barren grave,
    Three spans in length below.

That is the spot where grows no grass;
    Where falls no rain nor dew:
Whence steals along the pond of toads
    A hovering fire so blue.

---

[1] *CPW* i. 275, ll. 216–19.
[2] See Reed, p. 194, and Mary Moorman, p. 309.
[3] *Monthly Magazine*, i (April 1796), 223. See also S. M. Parrish, 'Dramatic Technique in the *Lyrical Ballads*', *PMLA* lxxiv (1959), 88–9 (*The Art of the Lyrical Ballads*, pp. 91–3), for Wordsworth's debt to Bürger.

> And nightly, when the ravens come,
> Her ghost is seen to glide;
> Pursues and tries to quench the flame,
> And pines the pool beside.[1]

Wordsworth evidently agreed with the correspondent who wrote admiringly to the *Monthly Magazine* that 'The abruptness of the beginning, and the recurrence to it at the end are unequalled.'[2] In differing forms, the device reappears at start and finish of 'Goody Blake, and Harry Gill', 'The Thorn', and 'The Idiot Boy'. By 1798 it has been adapted to a Wordsworthian purpose; but in 1797 the debt to an alien imagination is clear.

The surprising thing is that when Coleridge took up the unfinished poem in the spring of 1798,[3] he did so not in terms of his own recent achievement in the supernatural ballad, but in terms of Wordsworth's adherence to the everyday. Instead of reflecting the antiquarianism of 'The Ancient Mariner', Parts III and IV of 'The Three Graves' evoke a realistic Somersetshire location and draw on everyday experience; their idiom is that of an intrusive rustic narrator closely related to the garrulous sea-captain of 'The Thorn'. The sexton's role had been minimal in Parts I and II, but Coleridge repeatedly draws attention to his presence, emphasizing his prosaic circumstantiality and his superstitiousness:

> To see a man tread over Graves
> I hold it no good mark:
> 'Tis wicked in the Sun and Moon,
> And bad luck in the dark.
> You see that Grave? The Lord he gives,
> The Lord he takes away!
> Oh Sir! the Child of my old Age
> Lies there, as cold as clay.

---

[1] *Monthly Magazine*, i. 224.   [2] Ibid. ii (September 1796), 603.
[3] See Reed, p. 190n., for the suggestion that Parts I and II were handed over to Coleridge during the summer of 1797. In September 1809, Coleridge refers to having composed 'The Three Graves' 'somewhat more than twelve years ago'; see *CCW* iv: *The Friend*, ed. B. E. Rooke (2 vols., London, 1969), ii. 89. This could suggest that he began work in the summer of 1797, but Parts III and IV reflect the activities of the Alfoxden spring so clearly that the bulk of composition must belong to this period (see Reed, pp. 230–1; and cf. 'The Three Graves', ll. 468–500, 505–17, and *DWJ* i. 14–16).

> Except that Grave, you scarce see one
> That was not dug by me:
> I'd rather dance upon them all
> Than tread upon these Three![1]

In 1809, when his share of 'The Three Graves' appeared in *The Friend*, Coleridge underlined this dramatic element still further: 'The language was intended to be *dramatic*, that is, suited to the narrator, and the metre to correspond to the homeliness of the Diction'. He was already excusing it 'not as the Fragment of a *Poem*, but of a Tale in the common ballad metre'.[2] By 1817, after his *Biographia Literaria* attack on Wordsworth's stylistic experiment, he doubts whether even a dramatic context is 'sufficient to justify the adoption of such a style, in any metrical composition not professedly ludicrous'; the fragment 'is not presented as Poetry, and it is in no way connected with the Author's judgement concerning Poetic diction.'[3] But whatever his later views, Coleridge had entered into the experiment of spring 1798 much more fully than he was prepared to admit.

Nor was the distinction between Coleridge's supernaturalism and Wordsworth's concern with the everyday as clear-cut as it seems to have been in other contexts. Parts I and II of 'The Three Graves' had credited a curse with supernatural power. Parts III and IV illustrate the way in which a curse operates on the minds of its victims: 'Its merits', claimed the 1817 preface, 'are exclusively Pschycological [*sic*].'[4] Coleridge—if one is to believe the 1809 introduction—'was not led to chuse this story from any partiality to tragic, much less, to monstrous events . . . but from finding in it a striking proof of the possible effect on the imagination, from an Idea violently and suddenly imprest on it'.[5] In the story of 'The Three Graves' he found a parallel to the black magic practised among primitive people:

I had been reading Bryan Edwards's account of the effects of the *Oby* Witchcraft on the Negroes in the West Indies, and Hearne's deeply interesting Anecdotes of similar workings on the imagination of the Copper Indians . . . and I conceived the design of shewing

---

[1] *CCW* iv: *The Friend*, ii. 93. [2] *CCW* iv: ibid. ii. 89.
[3] *Sibylline Leaves*, p. 217 (*CPW* i. 268). [4] Ibid., p. 217 (*CPW* i. 268).
[5] CCW iv: *The Friend*, ii. 89.

that instances of this kind are not peculiar to savage or barbarous tribes, and of illustrating the mode in which the mind is affected in these cases, and the progress and symptoms of the morbid action on the fancy from the beginning.[1]

His reading provided him with the studies of melancholy and unbalance on which to base a psychological treatment of the curse theme; he would have had in mind passages such as Edwards's description of the Obeah man's victim, who

falls into a decline, under the incessant horror of impending calamities. The slightest painful sensation in the head, the bowels, or any other part, any casual loss or hurt, confirms his apprehensions, and he believes himself the devoted victim of an invisible and irresistible agency. Sleep, appetite, and cheerfulness, forsake him, his strength decays, his disturbed imagination is haunted without respite, his features wear the settled gloom of despondency: dirt, or any other unwholesome substance, become his only food, he contracts a morbid habit of body, and gradually sinks into the grave.[2]

Transferring these symptoms to a rural setting, Coleridge describes the change in the temperaments of Edward, Mary, and Ellen, and the collapse of their relationships as the curse takes hold of their minds. Another case-history of the same kind —this time taken from Darwin[3]—provided the source for Wordsworth's 'Goody Blake, and Harry Gill', and Coleridge's continuation of 'The Three Graves' perhaps suggests that what he gave Wordsworth in return for his unfinished ballad was an interest in morbid psychology.

Coleridge handles his subject with convincing insight. The gradual erosion of happiness—the wife's inexplicable melancholy, the husband's baffled anger, the friend's uneasy cheerfulness—is disquietingly conveyed. We are shown the troubled relationships of his characters, and their inability to understand or control the experience they undergo. Scenes such as Edward's reluctant return to his comfortless home seem painfully real:

[1] *CCW* iv: *The Friend*, ii. 89.

[2] *The History, Civil and Commercial, of the British Colonies in the West Indies* (2 vols., London, 1793), ii. 91–2. Cf. also Hearne's account of the threats of Indian 'Jugglers' and the effect on their victims (*A Journey from Prince of Wales's Fort in Hudson's Bay, to the Northern Ocean*, pp. 221–2).

[3] See p. 235, below.

Lingering he rais'd his latch at eve
　Tho' tir'd in heart and limb:
He lov'd no other place, and yet
　Home was no home to Him.
One evening he took up a book
　And nothing in it read;
Then flung it down, and groaning cried,
　'O Heaven! that I were dead!'
Mary look'd up into his face,
　And nothing to him said;
She try'd to smile, and on his arm
　Mournfully lean'd her head![1]

The poem seems to reflect Coleridge's own experiences of the Alfoxden spring: not only his pleasure in the companionship of Wordsworth and his sister, but also the latent conflict between his marriage and these new relationships. As in 'Christabel', uncomprehended psychological impulses come to the surface. Edward's 'inward strife' is that of a divided heart ('And Ellen's name and Mary's name/Fast link'd they both together came');[2] and as he grows to fear Ellen's forced mirth and hidden grief, Ellen grows to see in Mary's face the likeness of the woman who has cursed them both (' "Oh Christ! you're like your Mother!—" ').[3] Interwined with the apparent normality of village life, the psychic drama erupts at intervals to deny the common sense of the protagonists themselves: ' "It was a wicked Woman's curse,/Quoth she, and what care I?" '.[4] Coleridge's concern with the subconscious emerges openly in the final scene of Part IV, when Edward's murderous nightmare disturbs the two women as they sit talking peacefully beside him in their holly-bower:

He sate upright; and e're the Dream
　Had had time to depart,
'O God, forgive me! (he exclaim'd)
　'I have torn out her heart!'[5]

The conventional horrors of the supernatural ballad have been outmoded by Coleridge's venture into the realm of abnormal psychology. Like 'Christabel', however, 'The Three Graves'

[1] *CCW* iv: *The Friend*, ii. 94–5.　　　　　[2] *CCW* iv: ibid. ii. 93.
[3] *CCW* iv: ibid. ii. 94.　　　　　　　　[4] *CCW* iv: ibid. ii. 92.
[5] *CCW* iv: ibid. ii. 96.

remained unfinished, exploratory; it broke new ground, but perhaps also touched on areas which Coleridge was unable to resolve in his own experience. It represents an attempt to bring the underlying concerns of the supernatural poems into direct relationship with everyday life, and in this respect reveals in Coleridge an unexpected sympathy with the direction taken by Wordsworth's ballad experiment.

X *The Ballad Experiment of 1798*

> The moving accident is not my trade,
> To freeze the blood I have no ready arts . . .
>   ('Hart-Leap Well', ll. 97–8)

BY 1800, Wordsworth's meditative values were firmly established as the basis of his ballad experiment. Bürger's 'Der
wilde Jäger', a story of violence punished by violence, becomes
'Hart-Leap Well', a tale of silent suffering in which nature
conspires to obliterate human pride in the chase and to mourn
the death of the hunted hart.[1] In 1798, Wordsworth had
responded more straightforwardly to Bürger's ' "*Tra ra la*" ',
but already his own ballads were designed to supply the 'manners connected with the permanent objects of nature and partaking of the simplicity of those objects'[2] which he found lacking
in the supernatural ballad. Wordsworth's experiment produced
some of his most provocative redefinitions. The ballad-reader's
expectations are aroused, disappointed—and redirected towards what were for Wordsworth more significant aspects of
human experience. His achievement is to adapt the ballad to
portraying precisely those states and feelings least susceptible
to narrative presentation. At the same time, he forces us to
reassess the importance of the everyday. While the supernatural
ignores the ordinary world, the mind can transform it, and in
one way or another all the ballads of 1798 concern the workings
of the imagination. 'Goody Blake, and Harry Gill' shows the
power of imagination to enforce humane values. 'The Thorn'
reveals what the imagination can make of a suggestive group of
objects in a landscape, and its difficulty in apprehending the
obscure and inarticulate suffering associated with them. 'The
Idiot Boy' burlesques the ballad of supernatural adventure in
order to establish new priorities—the feelings and experiences
which irradiate the everyday. Written within a few weeks of one

---

[1] See Geoffrey Hartman, *PQ* xlvii (1968), 55–68.   [2] *EY*, p. 255.

another, these ballads show Wordsworth challenging the genre he has adopted—insisting first on writing with a definite 'purpose', then on questioning the very basis of narrative convention, and finally subverting it altogether. The result is a genre capable not simply of expressing Wordsworth's vision, but of modifying and extending the reader's; offered 'Such stores as silent thought can bring', we are shown how to 'find/ A tale in everything' ('Simon Lee', ll. 74, 75–6). The ballads of 1798 are not only technically exhilarating in their own right, but among Wordsworth's most effective statements about the aims and functions of his poetry.

1. 'GOODY BLAKE, AND HARRY GILL'

Wordsworth's comments on 'Goody Blake, and Harry Gill' in the 1800 'Preface' anticipate Coleridge's later remarks about 'The Three Graves':

I wished to draw attention to the truth that the power of the human imagination is sufficient to produce such changes even in our physical nature as might almost appear miraculous. The truth is an important one; the fact (for it is a *fact*) is a valuable illustration of it.[1]

The first of the ballads of spring 1798 grows out of the interest in morbid psychology reflected in Parts III and IV of 'The Three Graves'. Like Coleridge, Wordsworth had been reading Hearne, and a case-history from a contemporary scientific work provides the '*fact*' on which he insists. In early March, he had written to Cottle 'merely to request (which I have very particular reasons for doing) that you would contrive to send me Dr Darwin's Zoönomia *by the first carrier*'.[2] By mid-March, Dorothy writes to Cottle: 'We have received the books for which we are much obliged to you. They have already completely answered the purpose for which William wrote for them.'[3] It is easy to see why this episode from Darwin's *Zoönomia; or, the Laws of Organic Life* (1794–6) captured Wordsworth's interest; like the opening sections of 'The Three

---

[1] *Prose Works*, i. 150.

[2] *EY*, p. 199 (for the date of Wordsworth's letter, see Reed, p. 224n.). Coleridge had met Darwin in 1796 (see Griggs, i. 177) and probably knew *Zoönomia* before 1798; see *The Notebooks of Samuel Taylor Coleridge*, ed. Kathleen Coburn, i. 188n.

[3] *c.* 12 March; *EY*, pp. 214–15 (for the date, see Griggs, i. 399n.).

Graves', it centres on a curse-scene, vivid enough in its own right to offset Darwin's flat reporting:

I received good information of the truth of the following case' which was published a few years ago in the newspapers. A young farmer in Warwickshire, finding his hedges broke, and the sticks carried away during a frosty season, determined to watch for the thief. He lay many cold hours under a hay-stack, and at length an old woman, like a witch in a play, approached, and began to pull up the hedge; he waited till she had tied up her bottle of sticks, and was carrying them off, that he might convict her of the theft, and then springing from his concealment, he seized his prey with violent threats. After some altercation, in which her load was left upon the ground, she kneeled upon her bottle of sticks, and raising her arms to heaven beneath the bright moon then at the full, spoke to the farmer already shivering with cold, 'Heaven grant, that thou never mayest know again the blessing to be warm.' He complained of cold all the next day, and wore an upper coat, and in a few days another, and in a fortnight took to his bed, always saying nothing made him warm, he covered himself with very many blankets, and had a seive over his face, as he lay; and from this one insane idea he kept his bed over twenty years for fear of the cold air, till at length he died.[1]

The circumstantial detail and sudden, casual impressiveness of Darwin's account provided the basis for the central scene of 'Goody Blake, and Harry Gill' almost as they stand. The supernatural may be rationalized, but the small drama retains its power.

What is new in Wordsworth's ballad is a moral context in which to view the confrontation. His version does more than draw attention to the power of the mind over the body; it depicts the imagination as an agent of moral justice. Unlike the innocent trio in 'The Three Graves', Harry suffers because he has been insensible to the suffering of another. Southey's complaint that 'Goody Blake, and Harry Gill' might 'promote the popular superstition of witchcraft'[2] is beside the point, since the poem really concerns hardship. Darwin's 'old woman, like a witch in a play' becomes Goody Blake, living alone in the poorest of counties, and unable to afford local fuel prices ('in

---

[1] *Zoönomia* (2 vols., London, 1794–6), ii (1796), 359.
[2] *Critical Review*, xxiv. 200. Cf. Southey's own version of the theme in 'The Witch' quoted p. 170, above.

that country coals are dear,/For they come far by wind and tide', ll. 31–2).[1] In this context, Harry's policing activities are a form of persecution, and Darwin's empty metaphor ('he seized his prey') is transformed into the stalking and ambush of an unsuspecting victim:

> And fiercely by the arm he took her,
> And by the arm he held her fast,
> And fiercely by the arm he shook her,
> And cried, 'I've caught you then at last!'
> Then Goody, who had nothing said,
> Her bundle from her lap let fall;
> And kneeling on the sticks, she pray'd
> To God that is the judge of all.   (ll. 89–96)

In Darwin's version, the old woman's curse had merely been the last word in an altercation, but Goody's prayer has the authentic speech rhythms of desperation, and her appeal 'To God that is the judge of all' challenges the property values which for Harry had transcended humanity:

> She pray'd, her wither'd hand uprearing,
> While Harry held her by the arm—
> 'God! who art never out of hearing,
> 'O may he never more be warm!'
> The cold, cold moon above her head,
> Thus on her knees did Goody pray,
> Young Harry heard what she had said,
> And icy-cold he turned away.   (ll. 97–104)

The old hand is withered; yet upreared beneath 'The cold, cold moon', it has an eery authority: 'Young Harry heard what she had said . . .' At the start, Harry is an incomprehensible grotesque, his compulsive activity mirrored in the jigging rhythms and jangling onomatopoeia:

> Oh! what's the matter? what's the matter?
> What is't that ails young Harry Gill?
> That evermore his teeth they chatter,
> Chatter, chatter, chatter still.   (ll. 1–4)

[1] In 1795, Dorothy wrote from Racedown that 'The peasants are miserably poor; their cottages are shapeless structures . . . of wood and clay—indeed they are not at all beyond what might be expected in savage life' (*ET*, p. 162).

By the end, the spectacle has taken on cautionary meaning, and Harry's disquiet is as much that of guilt as unbalance: 'Yet still his jaws and teeth they clatter,/Like a loose casement in the wind' (ll. 115–16). The answer to our opening question, 'what's the matter? what's the matter?', lies in the central encounter—unobtrusively yet effectively rewritten to yield Wordsworth's humanitarian lesson: 'Now think, ye farmers all, I pray,/Of Goody Blake and Harry Gill' (ll. 127–8).

The political implications of 'Goody Blake, and Harry Gill' were not lost on Dr. Burney: 'if all the poor are to help themselves, and supply their wants from the possessions of their neighbours, what imaginary wants and real anarchy would it not create?'[1] Wordsworth has subverted a genre which his contemporaries were accustomed to think of as educating the poor not only in virtue, but in acceptance of the status quo. His models would have been the propagandist ballad-tracts of Hannah More's *Cheap Repository* rather than the popular broadside. The prospectus for the *Cheap Repository for Publications on Religious and Moral Subjects*, issued in 1795, anticipates Wordsworth's later reference to his own didactic intentions in writing ballads ('flowers and useful herbs to take place of weeds'):[2]

THE immediate object of this Institution is the circulation of religious and useful Knowledge, as an antidote to the poison continually flowing through the channel of those licentious publications which are vended about our cities, towns, and villages . . .

WHEN it is considered what vast multitudes there are whose reading is in a great measure confined to these corrupt performances . . . it must be obvious that it is become a point of no small consequence to correct so great an evil, which is not likely to be done effectually without condescending to supply tracts equally cheap, and adapted in like manner to the capacity of the common people. And since the poison which is to be counteracted is but too palatable, it is the more material to endeavour that the antidote shall be made pleasant also: a variety of harmless allurements will be used, in order to invite a perusal . . .

BEING well aware that sermons, catechisms, and other grave and religious Tracts may be had from some existing societies, it is not intended to furnish in general from this Institution the same

---

[1] *Monthly Review*, xxix (June 1799), 207.
[2] *MY* i. 248 (see p. 212, above).

kind of didactic pieces. Instructive and entertaining Stories, Lives, Deaths, remarkable Dispensations of Providence, and moral Ballads will form a considerable part of the intended publications . . .[1]

Hannah More's prospectus was printed and available, like her tracts, in Bath—the area where her missionary efforts were concentrated.[2] Wordsworth might well have seen the version printed in the *Monthly Magazine* for January 1797, and he can hardly have avoided coming into contact with the tracts themselves. By early 1796, over two million ballads and tales had been sold, whether to 'the common people' or to their would-be benefactors.[3] 'We shall prefer what is striking, to what is merely didactic', affirmed the 'Plan' in the *Monthly Magazine*;[4] and temperance, industry, or industrial calm, are preached in the guise of eye-catching stories with energetic rhythms and catchy phrasing. In *The Riot: or, Half a loaf is better than no bread* (1795), one worker argues another out of machine-breaking ('I'd rather be hungry than hang'd, I protest');[5] in the same year, *Patient Joe, or, the Newcastle Collier* was rewarded for keeping out of trouble by miraculous escape from a pit disaster. Other self-explanatory titles do their best to promote honesty among the working classes—*The Roguish Miller; or, Nothing got by cheating* (1795), and *The Hampshire Tragedy; shewing how a servant maid first robbed her master, and was afterwards struck dead for telling a lie. A True Story* (1796). Probably the best known of all was Hannah More's temperance tract, *The Carpenter; Or, the Danger of evil company* (1795), narrating a family man's fall from prosperity to drunken poverty; and in its sturdy ballad rhythms—

> THERE was a young West-country man,
>   A Carpenter by trade;
> A skilful wheelwright too was he,
>   And few such Waggons made.

---

[1] Prospectus, *Cheap Repository for Publications on Religious and Moral Subjects* (Bath, 1795), p. [1].

[2] See M. G. Jones, *Hannah More* (Cambridge, 1952), pp. 125–71, for an account of these activities.

[3] See G. H. Spinney, 'Cheap Repository Tracts: Hazard and Marshall Edition', *Library*, 4th ser. xx (1939–40), 295–340, for the origin and history of the project and for the dating of individual ballads.

[4] *Monthly Magazine*, iii (January 1797), 14.

[5] *The Riot* was said to have checked an actual riot near Bath; see William Roberts, *Memoirs of the Life and Correspondence of Mrs. Hannah More* (4 vols., London, 1834), ii. 386.

—one can see where Wordsworth learned his cautionary presentation of Harry Gill ('before' and 'after'):

> Young Harry was a lusty drover,
> And who so stout of limb as he?
> His cheeks were red as ruddy clover,
> His voice was like the voice of three.   (ll. 17–20)

Hannah More's aim, to combine popular appeal with 'religious and useful Knowledge', is matched by Wordsworth's claim for his poems, 'that each of them has a worthy *purpose*'.[1] The important difference is that where Hannah More wished to edify the semi-literate, Wordsworth was asking his literate readers to think about their own code.

The 1800 'Preface' calls 'Goody Blake, and Harry Gill' 'one of the rudest of this collection,' justifying its popular presentation in terms of the 'truth' about the workings of the imagination which it conveys ('I have the satisfaction of knowing that it has been communicated to many hundreds of people who would never have heard of it, had it not been narrated as a Ballad, and in a more impressive metre than is usual in Ballads').[2] But the flamboyance of Wordsworth's writing has behind it a literary impulse as well as a popularizing one. It is surely Bürger's ' "*Tra ra la*" ' which lies behind the onomatopoeic verve and grotesqueness of the opening and closing stanzas of 'Goody Blake, and Harry Gill'. Wordsworth's knowledge of German would have been rudimentary at this stage; he went to Germany in the autumn of 1798 specifically 'to acquire the German language', and only then did he purchase Bürger's *Gedichte* in the original.[3] But it was in March—the month when he was at work on 'Goody Blake, and Harry Gill', 'The Thorn', and probably 'The Idiot Boy'—that the German trip was mooted, and anyone whose interest had been sufficiently aroused by Taylor's account of Bürger in the *Monthly Magazine* had only to turn to one of the translations of 'Lenore' which included the original text.[4] Taylor's praise of 'popular forms of expression, caught by

---

[1] 1800 'Preface' (*Prose Works*, i. 124).   [2] *Prose Works*, i. 150.

[3] See *EY*, p. 213, and *DWJ* i. 31. For a brief discussion of Wordsworth's acquaintance with German literature before the Goslar period, see L. A. Willoughby, 'Wordsworth and Germany', *German Studies Presented to Professor H. G. Fiedler* (Oxford, 1938), pp. 438–42.

[4] Spencer and Stanley had both incorporated texts of the German. In reading

the listening artist from the voice of agitated nature' applies equally to Wordsworth's ballads.[1] Both poets create highly-wrought effects on the basis of a vigorous spoken idiom. As Taylor observes of Bürger, 'the interjection [is] his favourite part of speech', and 'Lenore' is intensified by the rousing cries that reappear in 'The Idiot Boy' (' "Holla, Holla!" '), by exclamations of horror—'Ha sieh! ha sieh! im Augenblick,/Huhu! ein grässlich Wunder!'—or by moments when conventional narrative breaks down under sheer pressure of excitement: 'Und hurre hurre, hop hop hop!/Ging's fort in sausendem Galopp . . .' The onomatopoeic sound effects which were felt to defy translation ('Und horch! und horch! den Pfortenring/ Ganz lose, leise, klinglingling!')[2] go with a deliberate cultivation of the grotesque; the transformation of ghostly rider into skeleton, for instance, is dwelt on with ghoulish relish: 'Zum Schädel, ohne Zopf und Schopf,/Zum nackten Schädel ward sein Kopf . . .'[3] 'Yet still his jaws and teeth they clatter' ('Goody Blake, and Harry Gill', l. 115) has the same outlandishness. This unexpected convergence of English didacticism and German sensationalism in 'Goody Blake, and Harry Gill' is to prove the point of departure for Wordsworth's ballad experiment.

II. 'THE THORN'

Within a matter of days, Wordsworth went on to experiment much more radically with the spirited 'manner of relating' which he admired in Bürger. He seems to have begun without any thought of writing a ballad. The Fenwick Note recalls that the poem 'Arose out of my observing, on the ridge of Quantock Hill, on a stormy day a thorn which I had often passed in calm and bright weather without noticing it,'[4] and Dorothy's *Journal* confirms that on 19 March 'William wrote some lines describing a stunted thorn'.[5] The lines themselves survive in the Alfoxden Notebook:

---

the original, Wordsworth would have had Coleridge's beginner's knowledge of German to help him, as well as the German grammar and dictionary Coleridge owned; see W. W. Beyer, 'Coleridge's Early Knowledge of German', *MP* lii (1954–5), 192–200, and Griggs, i. 435.

[1] See *Monthly Magazine*, i (March 1796), 118, and p. 218, above.

[2] See pp. 221–2, above.

[3] Quotations are from the parallel text in Spencer's *Leonora. Translated from the German.*

[4] I.F. note to 'The Thorn' (*PW* ii. 511).   [5] *DWJ* i. 13.

A summit where the stormy gale
Sweeps through the clouds from vale to vale
A thorn there is which like a stone
With jagged lychens is oergrown
A thorny [*sic*] that wants is [*sic*] thorny points
A toothless thorn with knotted joints
Not higher than a two years child.
It stands upon that spot so wild
Of leaves it has repaired its loss
With heavy tufts of dark green moss
Which from the ground a plenteous crop
Creeps upward to its very top
To bury it for ever-more.[1]

Wordsworth's description is immediately followed by 'A Whirl-Blast from behind the Hill'—another attempt to capture a transient weather-effect among the Quantocks—and has the air of an impressionistic jotting made for its own sake. Asked, as he asks himself at the end of 'A Whirl-Blast', 'This long description why endite?', Wordsworth might well have replied with equal inconsequentiality ('Because it was a pleasant sight').[2] But the Fenwick Note goes on, 'I said to myself, "Cannot I by some invention do as much to make this Thorn prominently an impressive object as the storm has made it to my eyes at this moment". I began the poem accordingly and composed it with great rapidity.'[3] In his 'invention', the thorn, already 'Not higher than a two years child', forms the starting-point for a tale of seduction, infanticide, and madness.

The commonest of all literary associations for a thorn tree were illegitimate birth and child-murder. In Langhorne's *Country Justice*, it is under a thorn that the pitying robber finds the body of an unmarried mother with her new-born child ('Seest Thou afar yon solitary Thorn,/Whose aged *Limbs* the Heath's wild Winds have torn?');[4] and in Richard Merry's

---

[1] DC MS. 14: *PW* ii. 240 app. crit. Cf. 'the lonely thorn . . . with top cut sheer' at the start of Crowe's local poem, *Lewesdon Hill*, and the 'aged Thorn', a symbol of oppressed worth, in Cottle's *Malvern Hills*—the latter returned to Cottle only a week before Wordsworth wrote his own description (see *EY*, p. 214): 'How bent its matted head, by the bleak wind,/That in one current comes . . .' (ll. 41–2).

[2] Ibid.: *PW* ii. 128 app. crit. For the date of 'A Whirl-Blast', see *DWJ* i. 12–13, and Reed, pp. 227–8n.

[3] *PW* ii. 511. De Selincourt prints 'permanently' for 'prominently'.

[4] *The Country Justice*, ii (1775), p. 24 (see p. 145, above).

Pains of Memory (1796), a remorseful seducer recalls: 'There on the chilly grass the babe was born,/Beneath that bending solitary thorn . . .'[1] The Scots ballad known as 'The Cruel Mother' shows how traditional the association would have been:

One of Child's collection

> AND there she's lean'd her back to a thorn,
>   Oh, and alas-a-day! Oh, and alas-a-day!
> And there she has her baby born,
>   Ten thousand times good night, and be wi' thee.
>
> She has houked a grave ayont the sun,
>   Oh, and alas-a-day! Oh, and alas-a-day!
> And there she has buried the sweet babe in,
>   Ten thousand times good night, and be wi' thee.
>
> And she's gane back to her father's ha',
>   Oh, and alas-a-day! Oh, and alas-a-day!
> She's counted the leelest maid o' them a',
>   Ten thousand times good night and be wi' thee.
>
> *   *   *   *   *   *   *   *   *
>
> O look not sae sweet, my bonny babe,
>   Oh, and alas-a-day! Oh, and alas-a-day!
> Gin ze smyle sae ze'll smyle me dead;
>   Ten thousand times good night, and be wi' thee.[2]

One would like to think that the torment of the final stanza comes through in Martha's cry of misery. But although Wordsworth must have known 'The Cruel Mother',[3] there were other and more immediate associations. Already in spring 1797, the haunted bower, gibbet, pond, and grave of Bürger's 'Des Pfarrers Tochter von Taubenhain' had become the haunted graves and thorn of 'The Three Graves'. With 'The Three Graves' once more in mind when Coleridge took it up during the spring of 1798, Wordsworth turned to Bürger for the 'invention' he needed.

---

[1] *The Pains of Memory* (London, 1796), p. 13.
[2] *Ancient and Modern Scottish Songs, Heroic Ballads, etc.*, ed. David Herd (2nd edn., 2 vols., Edinburgh, 1776), ii. 237–8.
[3] It was included by Wordsworth in a common-place book (see *PW* ii. 514), but R. S. Woof, 'The Literary Relations of Wordsworth and Coleridge, 1795–1803' (Doctoral Dissertation, Toronto, 1959), pp. 228–39, argued convincingly for a date of post-1800 for this entry.

Like 'The Thorn', 'Des Pfarrers Tochter von Taubenhain' ('The Lass of Fair Wone', as it became in Taylor's translation) focuses on a spot haunted by past suffering and guilt. 'The parson's bower of yew' is the scene of an infanticide about which Bürger is prepared to be explicit as Wordsworth is not:

> There rending pains and darting throes
>   Assail'd her shuddering frame;
> And from her womb a lovely boy,
>   With wail and weeping came.
>
> Forth from her hair a silver pin
>   With hasty hand she drew,
> And prest against its tender heart,
>   And the sweet babe she slew.
>
> Erst when the act of blood was done,
>   Her soul its guilt abhorr'd:
> 'My Jesus! what has been my deed?
>   Have mercy on me, Lord!'
>
> With bloody nails, beside the pond,
>   Its shallow grave she tore:
> 'There rest in God; there shame and want
>   Thou can'st not suffer more:
>
> Me vengeance waits. My poor, poor child,
>   Thy wound shall bleed afresh,
> When ravens from the gallows tear
>   Thy mother's mould'ring flesh.'[1]

The blend of horror and piety is characteristic—and, as Wordsworth would surely have recognized, disingenuous. For all his pious sentiments, Bürger forces us to dwell on the sensational facts (the murdered infant, the mother's bloody nails, the mouldering flesh on the gibbet), and his interest in the mother's guilt leaves no room for her suffering. Pity is ousted by vicarious interest in violence and pain. Wordsworth plays down the gothicism of his source by transferring it to an everyday setting. The haunted 'pond of toads' and the 'barren grave,/Three spans in length' which figure in Bürger's opening stanzas become part of the Quantock landscape—'a little muddy pond' and a moss-covered mound:

[1] *Monthly Magazine,* i (April 1796), 224.

> And to the left, three yards beyond,
> You see a little muddy pond
> Of water, never dry;
> I've measured it from side to side:
> 'Tis three feet long, and two feet wide.
>
> And close beside this aged thorn,
> There is a fresh and lovely sight,
> A beauteous heap, a hill of moss,
> Just half a foot in height.   (ll. 29–37)[1]

The pond is resolutely prosaic; the mound, no longer a barren grave, is 'fresh and lovely'; and the gibbet, emblem of guilt, has been replaced by the thorn, symbol of suffering. Most important, of all, the skull that seems to eye the grave below becomes a living woman. For the supernatural haunting of Bürger's poem, Wordsworth substitutes something more substantial, and also something that requires a less superficial response— the grief and unbalance of a human being bound to the spot by its tragic associations.

Wordsworth's adaptation of 'The Lass of Fair Wone' raises precisely those questions which his source had evaded. 'The Thorn' is a poem not just about suffering, but about the difficulty of comprehending it, which had been so effectively evoked in *The Borderers*:

> Action is transitory, a step, a blow—
> The motion of a muscle—this way or that,
> 'Tis done—and in the after vacancy
> We wonder at ourselves like men betray'd.
> Suffering is permanent, obscure and dark,
> And has the nature of infinity.[2]

To some extent *The Borderers* had explored as well as stated this central tragic opposition, and in doing so anticipated the study of compulsive behaviour into which Wordsworth converted the spectral hauntings of 'The Lass of Fair Wone'. The

---

[1] The opening stanzas of Bürger's poem are quoted on p. 227, above. The pond itself was not an invention (see *DWJ* i. 16); but Wordsworth's prettified grave-mound, with its 'mossy network' and 'cups, the darlings of the eye,/So deep is their vermilion dye' (ll. 43–4) may recollect the 'fronds of studded moss . . . Begemm'd with scarlet shields, and cups of gold' in Charlotte Smith's 'Apostrophe to an Old Tree', from *Elegiac Sonnets, and Other Poems* (1797), p. 50.

[2] *The Borderers*, MS. B: *PW* i. 188, ll. 1539–44.

woman circling the grave of her illegitimate child in the moonlight is alone in the midst of a village community; like Martha's,
her suffering remains obscure, uncomprehended, viewed from
a distance by the curious villagers. She is both enigmatic ('no
one ever heard her voice'), and surrounded by hearsay: 'in the
church-yard sod her feet have worn/A hollow ring; they say it
is knee-deep—'.[1] Martha too—similarly isolated, similarly
spied upon—becomes a focus for local curiosity:

> 'Now wherefore thus, by day and night,
> 'In rain, in tempest, and in snow,
> 'Thus to the dreary mountain-top
> 'Does this poor woman go?
> 'And why sits she beside the thorn
> 'When the blue day-light's in the sky,
> 'Or when the whirlwind's on the hill,
> 'Or frosty air is keen and still,
> 'And wherefore does she cry?—
> 'Oh wherefore? wherefore? tell me why
> 'Does she repeat that doleful cry?'   (ll. 78–88)

No one knows whether a living child was born to Martha, and
no one can separate her cries of grief from their supernatural
accretions:

> For many a time and oft were heard
> Cries coming from the mountain-head,
> Some plainly living voices were,
> And others, I've heard many swear,
> Were voices of the dead . . .   (ll. 170–4)

Cut off from the human world, Martha has the mad mother's
fellowship with nature: 'And she is known to every star,/And
every wind that blows . . .' (ll. 69–70). We come face to face
with her only once, in a vivid scene which releases the poem's
underlying implications. When the narrator stumbles on her
huddled figure, during a sudden storm, he sees for the first time
the reality of her suffering:

> I looked around, I thought I saw
> A jutting crag, and off I ran,
> Head-foremost, through the driving rain,
> The shelter of the crag to gain,

[1] Ibid.: *PW* i. 143, ll. 388, 394–5 (see p. 141, above).

> And, as I am a man,
> Instead of jutting crag, I found
> A woman seated on the ground.
>
> I did not speak—I saw her face,
> Her face it was enough for me;
> I turned about and heard her cry,
> 'O misery! O misery!'   (ll. 192–202)

Martha is revealed to the narrator as a fellow human being ('And, as I am a *man* . . .'), but at this moment of direct contact, the inevitability of her isolation is most strongly felt. The narrator's instinctive flight—'I saw her face,/Her face it was enough for me'—suggests the difficulty of confronting, still less entering into, misery such as hers.

'The character of the loquacious narrator will sufficiently shew itself in the course of the story', wrote Wordsworth in the 1798 'Advertisement'.[1] This telescope-bearing retailer of local gossip and superstition provides the basis for Wordsworth's experimental narrative. Bürger's device of question and answer becomes an extended display of uncertainty. Woman, thorn, pond, and mound are the fixed points round which the poem revolves; we return to them again and again, yet are never able to clarify their connections or significance. The narrator is as mystified as his questioner: ' "Now wherefore thus . . .?" ', 'I cannot tell; I wish I could . . .'; ' "But wherefore . . .?" ', 'Nay rack your brain—'tis all in vain . .' The sensationalism of 'The Lass of Fair Wone' becomes lurid conjecture, neither confirmed nor denied:

> 'But what's the thorn? and what's the pond?
> 'And what's the hill of moss to her?
> 'And what's the creeping breeze that comes
> 'The little pond to stir?'
> I cannot tell; but some will say
> She hanged her baby on the tree,
> Some say she drowned it in the pond,
> Which is a little step beyond,
> But all and each agree,
> The little babe was buried there,
> Beneath that hill of moss so fair.   (ll. 210–20)

[1] *Prose Works*, i. 117.

'The Thorn' successfully undermines the convention of an omniscient and objective narrator. Bürger gives us the crude facts: Wordsworth filters and distorts them through the imagination of his story-teller. A story, he implies, is not so simple a concept as Bürger had assumed; nor are facts so important in themselves—it is 'the feeling therein developed' that gives them their true significance. The villagers are rebuked by the quaking grave-mound during their quest for circumstantial evidence of Martha's guilt ('And for the little infant's bones/With spades they would have sought', ll. 234–5). And if their question should be left unasked and unanswered, so our questions too are unanswerable: how can we ever know what the thorn means to Martha? Not that her feelings alone (' "O misery! O misery!" ') give the poem its hold on the imagination. The narrator colours the story he tells by his own involvement with it, and the mingled facts and conjectures take their life from the play of his mind.

In 1800, Wordsworth replied to Southey's damning verdict on 'The Thorn' ('he who personates tiresome loquacity, becomes tiresome himself')[1] with an elaborate defence of his narrative method. The note provides an illuminating account of what he had hoped to achieve by his use of the story-teller whose character he describes in such incongruous detail:

The character which I have here introduced speaking is sufficiently common. The Reader will perhaps have a general notion of it, if he has ever known a man, a Captain of a small trading vessel, for example, who being past the middle age of life, had retired upon an annuity or small independent income to some village or country town of which he was not a native, or in which he had not been accustomed to live. Such men, having little to do, become credulous and talkative from indolence; and from the same cause, and other predisposing causes by which it is probable that such men may have been affected, they are prone to superstition. On which account it appeared to me proper to select a character like this to exhibit some of the general laws by which superstition acts upon the mind.[2]

The last sentence of what Jeffrey calls 'this very peculiar description'[3] reveals Wordsworth's purpose in telling his story

---

[1] *Critical Review*, xxiv. 200.   [2] *PW* ii. 512.

[3] For Jeffrey's parody of Wordsworth's defensive circumstantiality—' "Of this piece the reader will necessarily form a very erroneous judgement, unless he is

as he does. 'The Thorn' is not a dramatic monologue designed to be read for what it reveals about the mind of a hypothetical sea-captain.[1] But nor is it a poem concerned solely with the elusive nature of Martha's suffering. Its narrative method reflects Wordsworth's interest in the interplay between the two—in the imaginative processes by which the simple elements of Martha's tragedy take on their sombre impressiveness. The note continues:

> Superstitious men are almost always men of slow faculties and deep feelings; their minds are not loose, but adhesive; they have a reasonable share of imagination, by which word I mean the faculty which produces impressive effects out of simple elements; but they are utterly destitute of fancy, the power by which pleasure and surprise are excited by sudden varieties of situation and by accumulated imagery.[2]

Wordsworth's story-teller lacks the skills of the sophisticated narrator ('the power by which pleasure and surprise are excited'). But, like the stormy weather which had transformed the thorn in Wordsworth's original glimpse, his mind 'produces impressive effects out of simple elements'; and it is this that he has in common with the poet himself.

The 1800 'Preface' deals with the theory of Wordsworth's experiment: his note on 'The Thorn' goes into some of the problems that faced him in putting it into practice. The technical difficulty of substituting feeling for action in a primarily narrative genre is matched by that of conveying a simple narrator's imaginative involvement with his story:

> I had two objects to attain; first, to represent a picture which should not be unimpressive, yet consistent with the character that should describe it; secondly, while I adhered to the style in which such persons describe, to take care that words, which in their minds are impregnated with passion, should likewise convey passion to Readers who are not accustomed to sympathize with men feeling in that manner or using such language. It seemed to me that this might

---

apprised, that it was written by a pale man in a green coat,—sitting cross-legged on an oaken stool,—with a scratch on his nose, and a spelling dictionary on the table" '—see the *Edinburgh Review*, xii (April 1808), 137.

[1] The reverse is persuasively argued by S. M. Parrish in ' "The Thorn": Wordsworth's Dramatic Monologue', *ELH* xxiv (1957), 153–63 (*The Art of the Lyrical Ballads*, pp. 97–112).

[2] *PW* ii. 512.

be done by calling in the assistance of Lyrical and rapid Metre. It was necessary that the Poem, to be natural, should in reality move slowly; yet I hoped, that, by the aid of the metre, to those who should at all enter into the spirit of the Poem, it would appear to move quickly.[1]

Wordsworth's solution—his use of a fast-moving ballad stanza —allowed him to create the illusion of progress while continuing to dwell on Martha's unchanging misery. It also licensed him to draw on the rhythms and repetitions of actual speech. His defence of 'tautology' in 'The Thorn' contains his most central statement about 'the language of passion':

> Words, a Poet's words more particularly, ought to be weighed in the balance of feeling, and not measured by the space which they occupy upon paper. For the Reader cannot be too often reminded that Poetry is passion: it is the history or science of feelings: now every man must know that an attempt is rarely made to communicate impassioned feelings without something of an accompanying consciousness of the inadequateness of our own powers, or the deficiencies of language. During such efforts there will be a craving in the mind, and as long as it is unsatisfied the Speaker will cling to the same words, or words of the same character.[2]

The sea-captain's rambling ineptitude as a story-teller intensifies, rather than weakening, the effect of his tale. His conventional shortcomings become strengths—at once a token of his involvement and a means of involving the reader. When Wordsworth wrote of 'the interest which the mind attaches to words, not only as symbols of the passion, but as *things*, active and efficient, which are of themselves part of the passion',[3] he was invoking the expressive, behaviourist theory of language used by Joseph Priestley to explain the effect of figurative speech—'scarce considered and attended to as *words*, but . . . viewed in the same light as *attitudes*, *gestures*, and *looks*, which are infinitely more expressive of *sentiments* and *feelings* than words can possibly be'.[4] 'The Thorn' enacts the narrator's own fascination with Martha's dimly perceived tragedy, drawing on the processes of communication to mirror those of the imagination. Just as Martha's refrain-like cry becomes cumulatively expressive, so the narrator's garrulousness ends by

---

[1] *PW* ii. 512–13.   [2] *PW* ii. 513.   [3] *PW* ii. 513.
[4] *A Course of Lectures on Oratory and Criticism* (London, 1777), p. 77.

communicating the incommunicable—'Suffering is permanent, obscure and dark,/And has the nature of infinity.'[1]

III. 'THE IDIOT BOY'

'The Idiot Boy' takes Wordsworth's redefinition of ballad narrative a stage further. 'I never wrote anything with so much glee', he remembered, and his pleasure comes through in the poem.[2] The avid ballad-reader of the 1790s is laughed at for his 'degrading thirst after outrageous stimulation'[3] and cajoled into accepting Wordsworth's alternative; as Jeffrey put it, 'All his adventures are of the heart'.[4] Wordsworth's defence of 'The Idiot Boy', writing to John Wilson in 1802, suggests the importance which he attached to his theme:

> I have often applied to Idiots, in my own mind, that sublime expression of scripture that *'their life is hidden with God'* . . . I have indeed often looked upon the conduct of fathers and mothers of the lower classes of society towards Idiots as the great triumph of the human heart.[5]

But in 1798, the blind and passionate attachment of mother-love and the inaccessible joy of idiocy are implied rather than stated. It is through a comical displacement of the supernatural by the everyday that we are taught to recognize their value. The one gothic ballad that Wordsworth could be sure of his readers knowing was 'Lenore', with its midnight race to the grave, its spectral rider, and macabre moral. The opening stanza of 'The Idiot Boy' teasingly echoes the exclamatory refrains of Taylor's *Monthly Magazine* translation—'The moon is bryghte, and blue the nyghte' and 'Halloo! Halloo! away they goe':

> 'Tis eight o'clock,—a clear March night,
> The moon is up—the sky is blue,
> The owlet in the moonlight air,
> He shouts from nobody knows where;
> He lengthens out his lonely shout,
> Halloo! halloo! a long halloo!   (ll. 1–6)[6]

---

[1] *The Borderers*, MS. B: *PW* i. 188, ll. 1543–4.
[2] I.F. note (*PW* ii. 478).   [3] 1800 'Preface' (*Prose Works*, i. 128–30).
[4] *Edinburgh Review*, xxiv (November 1814), 19.
[5] *EY*, p. 357. For John Wilson's letter to Wordsworth, see Mary Wilson Gordon, 'Christopher North', *A Memoir of John Wilson*, i. 39–48.
[6] Cf. the opening of Scott's *Chase*: 'EARL WALTER winds his bugle horn;/To horse, to horse, halloo, halloo!' (p. [1]).

The pastiche of Bürger's ' "*Tra ra la*" ' arouses our expectations only to disappoint them. The excitement of the internal rhyme and the final line anticipate adventure; what we actually get is a mock-epic arming—Betty Foy fiddle-faddling over the most unlikely ballad hero one could imagine, her idiot son: 'But, Betty! what has he to do/With stirrup, saddle, or with rein?'[1] (ll. 20–1), expostulates the narrator. The crisis turns out to be a domestic one, fetching the doctor for a sick neighbour; and Johnny, unbooted and unspurred, is the most cheerfully individual of heroic messengers:

> There is no need of boot or spur,
> There is no need of whip or wand,
> For Johnny has his holly-bough,
> And with a hurly-burly now
> He shakes the green bough in his hand.   (ll. 57–61)

The horse it is that thinks, not Johnny—'And when he thinks his pace is slack' (l. 123). The most spectacular ballad ride of the 1790s is quietly sent up as pony and rider amble out of the poem. Instead of the sound and fury of Lenora's midnight gallop, we have the successive moods of Johnny's mother (pride, anxiety, despair, relief), and the headlong speed of Bürger's narrative is transferred to her frantic pursuit of her missing son.[2] The pace of 'Lenore' derives from action, that of 'The Idiot Boy' from feeling; as Wordsworth wrote later of Bürger, 'incidents are among the lowest allurements of poetry.'[3]

Wordsworth's burlesque of the supernatural ballad is most open in the engaging digression that comes at the climax of Betty's search. A catalogue of imaginary rides parodies the extravagance of the reader's fantasies, and delays the reappearance of Johnny himself—sitting peacefully on his feeding pony, in the moonlight:

> Oh reader! now that I might tell
> What Johnny and his horse are doing!

[1] See also J. E. Jordan on 'The Idiot Boy' as 'rustic mock epic' in 'Wordsworth's Humor', *PMLA* lxxiii (1958), 88–9. Wordsworth's comic method is also discussed by R. F. Storch, 'Wordsworth's Experimental Ballads; the Radical Uses of Intelligence and Comedy', *SEL* xi (1971), 621–39.

[2] For Wordsworth's debt to the verbal patterns used by Taylor's translation, see S. M. Parrish, *PMLA* lxxiv (1959), 87 (*The Art of the Lyrical Ballads*, p. 88).

[3] *EY*, p. 234.

> What they've been doing all this time,
> Oh could I put it into rhyme,
> A most delightful tale pursuing!
>
> Perhaps, and no unlikely thought!
> He with his pony now doth roam
> The cliffs and peaks so high that are,
> To lay his hands upon a star,
> And in his pocket bring it home.
>
> Perhaps he's turned himself about,
> His face unto his horse's tail,
> And still and mute, in wonder lost,
> All like a silent horseman-ghost,
> He travels on along the vale.
>
> And now, perhaps, he's hunting sheep,
> A fierce and dreadful hunter he!
> Yon valley, that's so trim and green,
> In five months' time, should he be seen,
> A desart wilderness will be.
>
> Perhaps, with head and heels on fire,
> And like the very soul of evil,
> He's galloping away, away,
> And so he'll gallop on for aye,
> The bane of all that dread the devil.   (ll. 322–46)[1]

The reader is teased for wanting to be thrilled or scared, and Wordsworth's complaint to the muses when they refuse his plea ('Oh gentle muses! is this kind?/Why will ye thus my suit repel?', ll. 352–3) is a joke at the expense of the reader's imagination as much as the poverty of the everyday. The joke is clinched by the final stanza, when Johnny gives his own topsy-turvy account of the night's adventures:

> 'The cocks did crow to-whoo, to-whoo,
> 'And the sun did shine so cold.'
> —Thus answered Johnny in his glory,
> And that was all his travel's story.   (ll. 460–3)

---

[1] The last stanza ('Perhaps, with head and heels on fire . . .') suggests that Wordsworth knew Blake's frontispiece to Stanley's *Leonora. A Tale*, showing the ghostly horse plunging through the air with its nostrils and hind-hooves flaming.

According to the Fenwick Note, Johnny's words had been 'the foundation of the whole';[1] in reserving them till the end, Wordsworth used them to form the climax not only to his inconsequential story, but to his affirmation of the everyday. Moon and owls have been as marvellous to Johnny as the night's adventures have been terrifying to his mother. By laughing at the supernatural ballad, Wordsworth teaches us to recognize and value the 'delicate and minute feelings', the 'manners', which he found lacking in Bürger's writing.

When Wordsworth criticized Bürger in his letters to Coleridge, the poet he contrasted him with was Burns, and the poem he singled out was 'Tam o'Shanter':

Now I find no manners in Burger; in Burns you have manners everywhere. Tam Shanter I do not deem a character, I question whether there is any individual character in all Burns' writings except his own. But every where you have the presence of human life. The communications that proceed from Burns come to the mind with the life and charm of recognitions.[2]

Unlike 'Lenore', 'Tam o'Shanter' refuses to take its own supernaturalism seriously; gothicism is ousted by comedy, and Tam's helter-skelter ride through the night takes place in a drunken hinterland between fact and fantasy. The 'bogles' Tam fears during his journey are a sign that he has had too much to drink, and the perils he surmounts exist chiefly in his own heated imagination:

> By this time he was cross the ford,
> Where in the snaw the chapman smoor'd;
> And past the birks and meikle stane,
> Where drunken Charlie brak's neck-bane;
> And thro' the whins and by the cairn,
> Where hunters fand the murder'd bairn;
> And near the thorn, aboon the well,
> Where Mungo's mither hang'd hersel.—[3]

---

[1] I.F. note to 'The Idiot Boy' (*PW* ii. 478). Cf. the story about an idiot recorded by Coleridge, in *The Notebooks of Samuel Taylor Coleridge*, ed. Kathleen Coburn, i. 212 and n., and, for another idiot fascinated, like Johnny, by a waterfall, see M. P. Hamilton, 'Wordsworth's Relation to Coleridge's *Osorio*', *SP* xxxiv (1937), 429–32.

[2] 27 February 1799; *EY*, pp. 255–6.

[3] 'Aloway Kirk; or, Tam o'Shanter. A Tale', ll. 81–5, *Edinburgh Magazine*, xiii (March 1791), 244. 'Tam o'Shanter' was also published in the *Edinburgh Herald* for 18 March 1791, and, in April, in Francis Grose's *Antiquities of Scotland* (2 vols., London, 1789–91), ii (1791), 199–201n.

When he stumbles on a real witches' sabbath, the supernatural 'hornpipes, jigs, strathspeys and reels' remain obstinately mundane, and it is no surprise that Tam should be bewitched in another sense by the liveliest of the dancers. His pursuit by an irate young witch after he betrays himself with a cry of ' "Weel done! Cutty Sark!" ' becomes a joke about the time his roving eye landed him in trouble, and the poem ends with a mock-serious admonition against wine and women. 'Tam o'Shanter' has the good humour of the evening's drinking with which it begins, and it is above all life-affirming—as Wordsworth wrote, 'every where you have the presence of human life'. Comic ballads like 'John Gilpin' or Gray's 'A Long Story' cheat and amuse the reader by parodying the sporting hero, or demonstrating how much can be made out of nothing; but 'Tam o'Shanter'—like 'The Idiot Boy'—celebrates while it deflates. Drink makes Tam a hero, a 'rustic adventurer' as Wordsworth calls him—'Inspiring, bold John Barleycorn,/ What dangers thou canst make us scorn!';[1] and although Burns leaves us to think it, drink perhaps creates his adventure as idiocy creates Johnny's, or mother-love, Betty's. Wordsworth's own sympathetic comedy of drunkenness in *The Waggoner* of 1806 gives added understanding to his later defence of 'Tam':

Who, but some impenetrable dunce or narrow-minded puritan in works of art, ever read without delight the picture which [Burns] has drawn of the convivial exaltation of the rustic adventurer, Tam o'Shanter? . . . I pity him who cannot perceive that, in all this, though there was no moral purpose, there is a moral effect.

> 'Kings may be blest, but Tam was glorious,
> 'O'er a' the *ills* of life victorious.'

What a lesson do these words convey of charitable indulgence for the vicious habits of the principal actor in this scene . . . [2]

Wordsworth responds not only to Burns's indulgent sympathy, but to his affectionate glorification of the ordinary man. Tam, 'A bletherin, blusterin, drunken bellum', in his wife's eyes, becomes glorious in his cups—just as Johnny becomes glorious in his topsy-turvy vision: 'Thus answered Johnny in his glory,/ And that was all his travel's story' (ll. 462–3).

[1] ll. 105–6, *Edinburgh Magazine*, xiii. 244.
[2] *A Letter to a Friend of Robert Burns* (*Prose Works*, iii. 124).

'The Idiot Boy's affirmative use of comedy owes much to Burns, but its roots go back to the novel. Wordsworth was reacting against a contemporary taste for 'idle and extravagant stories in verse'[1] much as Cervantes, two hundred years before, had reacted against 'the false and improbable stories recounted in books of chivalry'.[2] Cervantes's readers came increasingly to see that *Don Quixote* went much further than this, and by 1819, Hazlitt could assert that 'There cannot be a greater mistake than to consider Don Quixote as a merely satirical work, or as a vulgar attempt to explode "the long-forgotten order of chivalry". ' For him, Cervantes had anticipated the comedy of feeling: 'The pathos and dignity of the sentiments are often disguised under the ludicrousness of the subject; and provoke laughter when they might well draw tears.'[3] In this light, Don Quixote is the ancestor of saintly fools like Parson Adams or Uncle Toby, in whom extreme simplicity becomes a virtue. As James Beattie wrote in 1776,

the knight of La Mancha, though a ludicrous, was never intended for a contemptible personage. He often moves our pity, he never forfeits our esteem; and his adventures and sentiments are generally interesting: which could not have been the case, if his story had not been natural, and himself endowed with great as well as good qualities.[4]

On one level a comic figure designed to ridicule an outmoded set of chivalric conventions, Don Quixote is also a reminder of values which society is the worse for ignoring. His greatness lies in the lengths to which he goes in applying these values to an obstinately amoral world. For Hazlitt, his madness was a form of insight, a triumphant transcending of reality for the ideal:

The character of Don Quixote himself is one of the most perfect disinterestedness. He is an enthusiast of the most amiable kind; of a nature equally open, gentle, and generous; a lover of truth and

---

[1] 1800 'Preface' (*Prose Works*, i. 128).

[2] *The History and Adventures of the renowned Don Quixote*, trans. Tobias Smollett (2 vols., London, 1755), ii. 466.

[3] *Lectures on the English Comic Writers*, 1819 (Howe, vi. 108). See S. M. Tave, *The Amiable Humorist* (Chicago, 1960), pp. 140–63, for eighteenth-century and Romantic interpretations of Don Quixote.

[4] 'On Laughter and Ludicrous Composition', *Essays* (Edinburgh, 1776), p. 350.

justice; and one who had brooded over the fine dreams of chivalry
and romance, till they had robbed him of himself, and cheated his
brain into a belief of their reality . . . even through the crazed and
battered figure of the knight, the spirit of chivalry shines out with
undiminished lustre . . . [1]

Coleridge too saw Don Quixote as a hero of the imagination,
shaping the world according to an inner vision—'not a man
out of his senses, but a man in whom the imagination and the
pure reason are so powerful as to make him disregard the evidence of sense when it opposed their conclusions'.[2] Both crazed
and inspired, Don Quixote lies behind the paradox of idiocy
and imagination implied in Johnny's words at the end of
'The Idiot Boy'. And as a personage who, though ludicrous, is
never contemptible, he anticipates Wordsworth's celebration
of mother-love in the figure of Betty Foy. For Coleridge, writing unsympathetically in *Biographia Literaria*, 'the idiocy of the
boy is so evenly balanced by the folly of the *mother*, as to present
to the general reader rather a laughable burlesque on the
blindness of anile dotage, than an analytic display of maternal
affection in its ordinary workings'.[3] But the comic tradition to
which Johnny and his mother belong allowed Wordsworth to
write a burlesque that was serious as well as laughable.

Wordsworth's greatest debt to the novel lay in his celebration of the everyday. As James Beattie saw it in 1783,

> Don Quixote occasioned the death of the Old Romance, and
> gave birth to the New. Fiction henceforth divested herself of her
> gigantick size, tremendous aspect, and frantick demeanour; and,
> descending to the level of common life, conversed with man as his
> equal, and as a polite and chearful companion. Not that every
> subsequent Romance-writer adopted the plan, or the manner, of
> Cervantes: but it was from him they learned to avoid extravagance,
> and to imitate nature. And now probability was as much studied, as
> it had been formerly neglected.[4]

Wordsworth's basic complaint about Bürger was his failure

[1] *Lectures on the English Comic Writers* (Howe, vi. 108).
[2] *Specimens of the Table Talk of the Late Samuel Taylor Coleridge*, ed. H. N. Coleridge (2 vols., London, 1835), ii. 87.
[3] Shawcross, ii. 35–6.
[4] 'On Fable and Romance', *Dissertations Moral and Critical* (London, 1783),
p. 564.

'to imitate nature'. In turning to comedy to supply the 'manners' he missed, he was doing what Fielding and Sterne had done before him. Hazlitt's praise of Fielding for his subtly analytic yet apparently casual insight into human nature could equally be applied to the comic realism of 'The Idiot Boy':

The extreme subtlety of observation on the springs of human conduct in ordinary characters, is only equalled by the ingenuity of contrivance in bringing those springs into play, in such a manner as to lay open their smallest irregularity. The detection is always complete, and made with the certainty and skill of a philosophical experiment, and the obviousness and familiarity of a casual observation.[1]

If Fielding showed Wordsworth how comedy might lay bare 'the springs of human conduct in ordinary characters', Sterne showed him how to infuse comic revelation with feeling. Like 'The Idiot Boy', *Tristram Shandy* (1760–7) is designed to disappoint the reader's expectations about narrative ('L—d! said my mother, what is all this story about?');[2] and like Wordsworth, Sterne turns literary assumptions upside down in order to release emotion in an unpromisingly prosaic context. The respective hobby-horses of Uncle Toby and Walter Shandy, or the wooing of Widow Wadman, burlesque the great heroic themes (war, philosophy, love). But through mock-heroic, Sterne reveals the subtler, less heroic qualities of gentleness, affection, and modesty which transfigure the everyday. Uncle Toby's military obsession coexists with unparalleled tenderness of heart, while his simplicity about women implies a precious innocence; and despite being frequently at cross-purposes, the two brothers are united by a bond of unspoken affection. In both Sterne and Wordsworth, feeling is obliquely revealed by the comical incidents which make up the narrative, and both writers end by celebrating the capacity of the ordinary world to yield themes of genuine importance.

Wordsworth's aim in 'The Idiot Boy' was to portray the feelings 'Essential and eternal in the heart' which, as he had written shortly before,

---

[1] *Lectures on the English Comic Writers* (Howe, vi. 113). Cf. Collins's ode, 'The Manners', in which '*Observance*' and knowledge of man's 'native Heart' are associated particularly with the great comic writers.

[2] *The Life and Opinions of Tristram Shandy, Gentleman* (9 vols., London, 1760–7), ix (1767), 145.

> mid the simpler forms of rural life
> Exist more simple in their elements
> And speak a plainer language.[1]

Specifically, 'The Idiot Boy' traces 'the maternal passion through many of its more subtle windings'.[2] Coleridge recorded his perplexity at its method when he objected to Betty Foy as 'an impersonation of an instinct abandoned by judgement'.[3] Like a number of Wordsworth's greatest narrative poems, 'The Idiot Boy' presents love almost as a form of unbalance. In the words used by Coleridge to describe Don Quixote, Betty's love for her child is so powerful that at times it makes her 'disregard the evidence of sense'. Love makes her see Johnny as a hero when he sets out on his mission, and love makes her imagine him the victim of improbable gothic disasters when he fails to return (' "Or him that wicked pony's carried/To the dark cave, the goblins' hall . . ." ', ll. 237–8); and it is love that inspires the contradictory emotions which make up Wordsworth's narrative. 'The Idiot Boy' turns on the conflict between maternal pride, on the one hand, and maternal anxiety, on the other. Sending her son to fetch the doctor gratifies Betty's pride in 'Johnny's wit and Johnny's glory' (l. 136). But it also conflicts with her deepest instinct, concern for his safety and well-being—

> There's not a mother, no not one,
> But when she hears what you have done,
> Oh! Betty she'll be in a fright.   (ll. 24–6)

The narrator's participation—his adoption of Betty's own language and tone—allows us to see what is at stake. This is a real emergency for Betty herself ('What must be done? what will betide?', l. 41), even if it is not the kind of drama the ballad-reader expects, and the decision to dispatch Johnny is momentous. The basis of our sympathetic involvement is Wordsworth's indirect presentation of Betty's feelings, through comedy.[4] Her bustle to get Johnny off and her elaborate

---

[1] 'The Ruined Cottage', MS. B: *PW* v. 380–1, ll. 63–6.
[2] 1800 'Preface' (*Prose Works*, i. 126).   [3] Shawcross, ii. 35.
[4] It is interesting to compare Wordsworth's method with the pathetic realism of a poem like Charlotte Smith's 'Forest Boy' in *Elegiac Sonnets, and Other Poems* (1797), also centring on a mother's love for her child and her anxious wait for his return.

instructions about 'what to follow, what to shun,/ What do, and
what to leave undone' (ll. 64–5) mask an underlying reluctance
to let him go:

> And now that Johnny is just going,
> Though Betty's in a mighty flurry,
> She gently pats the pony's side,
> On which her idiot boy must ride,
> And seems no longer in a hurry.   (ll. 77–81)

The comic rhyme (flurry/hurry) jokes at the contradiction, but
the give-away gesture—'She gently pats the pony's side'—
reveals a tenderness that embraces the pony as well as its real
object, Johnny. Betty's single-minded preoccupation with her
idiot child emerges also from the larger comic reversals. At the
beginning of the central section she is seen nursing her neighbour 'as if in Susan's fate/Her life and soul were buried' (ll.
140–1); but as the night goes by and Johnny fails to return,
good-neighbourliness gives way to mother-love—' "Susan, we
must take care of him,/If he is hurt in life or limb" ' (ll. 199–
200)—and Susan is left to shift for herself. When Betty arrives
at the doctor's, his sleepy and ill-tempered words (' "What,
woman! should I know of him?" ', l. 270) put all other thoughts
out of her head:

> This piteous news so much it shock'd her,
> She quite forgot to send the Doctor,
> To comfort poor old Susan Gale.   (ll. 284–6)

Again, the comic rhyme has a double function. The pattern of
reversals is complete when Susan herself sets out in pursuit, her
sickness cured by fears for mother and child—'And as her mind
grew worse and worse,/Her body it grew better' (ll. 425–6).
We are offered an essentially comic view of feeling, but it is not
an undermining one. When Betty finds her son at last—'She
darts as with a torrent's force,/She almost has o'erturned the
horse' (ll. 384–5)—the strength of her emotion is comically
literalized; but the simile ('as with a torrent's force') reminds us
of its elemental origin. 'The great triumph of the human heart'
is celebrated through comedy, not in spite of it.

   For Betty, the night's inconsequential events are a genuine
adventure. Johnny too has his adventure—not of the heart, but

of the imagination. For his mother, Johnny's idiocy makes him a child specially beloved; 'idiot boy' becomes a term of endearment, associated as it is throughout the poem with her feeling for him ('Him who she loves, her idiot boy'). But for Wordsworth, it means something more. Nowhere in the poem does he state of Johnny that his *'life is hidden with God'*; through fantasy, however, idiocy is redefined as a significant state of imagination. Johnny hunting sheep or galloping away, away, in Wordsworth's teasing digression, is comically incongruous. But the vision of Johnny back to front, 'still and mute, in wonder lost' (l. 334), suggests how he did in fact spend the night—rapt in the marvel of seeing night-time sights and sounds in day-time terms. It also recalls the earlier moment when he rides off beneath a moon 'not more still and mute than he' (l. 91). A mysterious inner life sets him apart, identifying him with the other-worldliness of the moon or the well-being of the curring owlets whose call he echoes with his burring. As the old man of 'Old Man Travelling' is 'insensibly subdued/To settled quiet' (ll. 7–8), so Johnny possesses an enviable, unthinking joy. Impartially good-humoured, he belongs to the benign natural world celebrated elsewhere in Wordsworth's writing during spring 1798. The joy perceived by the Pedlar— 'in all things/He saw one life, & felt that it was joy'[1]—is Johnny's constant state. As he rides away, oblivious of his mother's pride and anxiety, his ecstasy is described in terms that transcend joking indulgence:

> But when the pony moved his legs,
> Oh! then for the poor idiot boy!
> For joy he cannot hold the bridle,
> For joy his head and heels are idle,
> He's idle all for very joy.   (ll. 82–6)

Johnny has a child's delight in the novelty of riding a horse— a novelty suggested by the unidiomatic 'moved his legs', a childishness implied in the comic rhyme (bridle/idle). But the repetition of 'joy' ('For joy', 'For joy', 'for very joy') does more than stress the completeness of his happiness—it appears to define it, in the only words possible. Betty's joy in her child is

---

[1] 'The Ruined Cottage', MS. B: *PW* v. 385, ll. 251–2.

complicated and precarious: Johnny's is the thing itself, absolute, unqualifiable, and impervious.

Betty's successive emotions form the basis of Wordsworth's narrative, but it is through Johnny that 'The Idiot Boy' makes its claim for the value of simple experience. His reply to Betty's questioning at the end of the poem is the crowning inconsequentiality. Yet it does much more than round off a literary burlesque. Johnny responds to what he sees with a freshness of vision which, in taking from owls and moon their familiarity, makes them marvellous:

> And thus to Betty's question, he
> Made answer, like a traveller bold,
> (His very words I give to you,)
> 'The cocks did crow to-whoo, to-whoo,
> 'And the sun did shine so cold.'
> —Thus answered Johnny in his glory,
> And that was all his travel's story.   (ll. 457–63)

His glory is not so much that his life is hidden with God, as that he is vividly in touch with the everyday; as Coleridge said of Wordsworth, his perceptions are '*fresh* and have the dew upon them'.[1] His vision is analogous to the poet's in giving 'the interest of novelty by the modifying colors of imagination'.[2] Johnny's ability to create marvels out of the world around him without recourse to the supernatural perfectly embodies Wordsworth's aim in the *Lyrical Ballads* experiment:

to give the charm of novelty to things of every day, and to excite a feeling analogous to the supernatural, by awakening the mind's attention from the lethargy of custom, and directing it to the loveliness and the wonders of the world before us; an inexhaustible treasure, but for which, in consequence of the film of familiarity and selfish solicitude we have eyes, yet see not, ears that hear not, and hearts that neither feel nor understand.[3]

'The Idiot Boy' makes us see afresh what is familiar, and value fully what is simple in our own experience. Wordsworth's reply to the 'deluges of idle and extravagant stories in verse' put out by his contemporaries was to show what could be done with an idiot and a simple-minded countrywoman—with love, the everyday, and the imagination.

[1] Shawcross, ii. 118.   [2] Ibid. ii. 5.   [3] Ibid. ii. 6.

Conclusion
Peter Bell: *A Manifesto*

WORDSWORTH'S attempt to collaborate with Coleridge on
'The Ancient Mariner' foundered because, in his own words,
'it would have been quite presumptuous in me to do anything
but separate from an undertaking upon which I could only
have been a clog'.[1] The plan for a different kind of collaboration, with Coleridge supplying 'Poems chiefly on supernatural
subjects' and Wordsworth poems on subjects 'taken from common life', seems to have grown out of this failure. *Peter Bell*,
begun in April 1798 and at first intended for *Lyrical Ballads*,[2]
brings the divergence into the open. In issuing a challenge to
Coleridge's supernaturalism, Wordsworth at the same time
offers a defence of his own commitment to the everyday. As he
put it in the 1819 dedication:

> The Poem of Peter Bell, as the Prologue will shew, was composed
> under a belief that the Imagination not only does not require for its
> exercise the intervention of supernatural agency, but that, though
> such agency be excluded, the faculty may be called forth as im-
> periously, and for kindred results of pleasure, by incidents, within
> the compass of poetic probability, in the humblest departments of
> daily life . . . Let this acknowledgement make my peace with the
> lovers of the supernatural . . . [3]

But *Peter Bell* is more than a culminating reaction against the
fashion for supernatural balladry which had proved so fruitful
for Coleridge. It is an attempt to define Wordsworth's personal
vision—the way of seeing things which had made collaboration
on 'The Ancient Mariner' impossible. In the summer of 1798,

---

[1] I.F. note to 'We are seven' (*PW* i. 361).

[2] Begun on 20 April, *Peter Bell* was completed in its original form by *c.* mid-May,
when it was read to Hazlitt (see *DWJ* i. 16, and Reed, p. 233).

[3] *Peter Bell* (London, 1819), pp. iv–v. Gratuitously, Wordsworth addressed his
dedication to Southey rather than Coleridge ('*you* have exhibited most splendid
effects of judicious daring, in the opposite and usual course', ibid., pp. iv–v).

Coleridge (as reported by Hazlitt) was already lamenting the 'something corporeal, a *matter-of-fact-ness*, a clinging to the palpable, or often to the petty' which he later singled out as one of the central defects of Wordsworth's poetry.[1] The issue was not simply that of the supernatural versus the everyday;[2] it was the Coleridgean imagination versus Wordsworth's matter-of-factness. Half-humorously, half-seriously, Wordsworth concedes that beside Coleridge he occupies a hopelessly prosaic world—and then transforms the concession into a special plea for his own imagination.

If the 1798 'Advertisement' is Wordsworth's earliest critical manifesto, the 'Prologue' to *Peter Bell* is his first poetic one—more personal both in application and in tone. Disarmingly, Wordsworth begins by letting us overhear him at play:

> There's something in a flying horse,
> There's something in a huge balloon,
> But through the clouds I'll never float
> Until I have a little Boat
> In shape just like the crescent moon.[3]

But he is being more sophisticated than he seems. The flying horse reminds us that he has a right to the poet's Pegasus, even if his pretensions are undercut by the huge balloon; and the little boat suggests imaginative flight as well as playfulness. Wordsworth's escapism is thoroughly gleeful, and it would be wrong to read the 'Prologue' too solemnly; but the starry voyage is a way of acting out the contrary impulses of withdrawal and involvement—a way of questioning imaginative activity that is also a retreat from reality. Cruising contentedly through the sky, Wordsworth opts temporarily for supra-human calm:

> Away we go, my boat and I,
> Sure never man had such another;

[1] 'My First Acquaintance with Poets' (Howe, xvii. 117); cf. the *Biographia Literaria* complaint about Wordsworth's 'matter-of-factness' (Shawcross, ii. 101 ff.).
[2] See Kathleen Coburn, 'Coleridge and Wordsworth and "the Supernatural" ', *UTQ* xxv (1955–6), 121–30.
[3] MS. 3: *PW* ii. 331, ll. 1–5 and app. crit. Probably belonging to the early summer of 1800, MS. 3 is the first virtually complete MS. of *Peter Bell* to survive; both it and the less complete MS. 2 of 1799 or 1800 must correspond very closely to the fragmentary MS. 1 of April–May 1798; see Reed, pp. 32–3, and, for successive revisions, J. E. Jordan, 'The Hewing of *Peter Bell*', *SEL* vii (1967), 559–603.

> Whether among the winds we strive
> Or deep into the heavens we drive,
> We're both contented with each other.
>
> Away we go, and what care we
> For treasons, tumults, and for wars;
> We are as calm in our delight
> As is the crescent moon so bright
> Among the scattered stars.[1]

But in the last resort it is the world below that claims him, reawakening the commitment of a poet for whom fantasy can only be an interlude:

> Then back again to our green earth,
> What business had I here to roam;
> The world for my remarks and me
> Will not a whit the better be—
> I've left my heart at home.
>
> . . . .
>
> Never did fifty things at once
> Appear so lovely, never, never—
> The woods how sweetly do they ring,
> To hear the earth's sweet murmuring
> Thus could I hang for ever.[2]

Wordsworthian common sense is balanced by the rapturousness of his return to earth; commitment has been humanized, didacticism made a matter of feeling. The ensuing argument between himself and the indignant sky-canoe allows Wordsworth to put the Coleridgean objection—plodding adherence to the everyday—in a comically scolding form:

> 'Out, out, and like a brooding hen
> Beside your sooty hearth-stone cower—
> Go creep along the dirt and pick
> Your way with your good walking stick,
> Just three good miles an hour.'[3]

Wordsworth's 'three good miles an hour', however, reveals not

---

[1] MS 3: *PW* ii. 332, ll. 21–30 and app. crit.
[2] Ibid.: *PW* ii. 333–4, ll. 51–5, 71–5 and app. crit.
[3] Ibid.: *PW* ii. 334, ll. 80/1, app. crit.

so much an earth-bound imagination as an allegiance to the human heart—to the realm of the domestic affections (the sooty hearth-stone), rather than the magical realm offered by the sky-canoe (' "Come to the poet's wild delights . . ." ').[1] Looking down on the earth beneath him, Wordsworth makes the avowal that is central to his stance in *Peter Bell*: 'my heart is touched, I must avow . . . *I feel I am a man.*'[2]

After writing 'The Ruined Cottage' and 'The Idiot Boy', it is not surprising that Wordsworth should choose to represent himself as the poet of the human heart. His tale of a man redeemed through his attempt to steal an ass restates the redemption-theme of 'The Ancient Mariner' in terms that are not merely anti-supernatural, but emphatically humane; the poem's central doctrine is summed up in Peter's final realization that 'The heart of man's a holy thing.'[3] Where Coleridge's Ancient Mariner is alienated from the spiritual world, Peter is alienated from the world of human feeling; shooting the albatross does violence to a cosmic harmony, but beating the ass does violence to human values (love, fidelity, and tenderness). Wordsworth based his poem on a newspaper story 'of an ass being found hanging his head over a canal in a wretched posture. Upon examination a dead body was found in the water, and proved to be the body of its master.'[4] In *Peter Bell*, the episode becomes a parable of brute feeling confronted by human brutality. The 'moral' of 'The Ancient Mariner' fits Wordsworth's poem too ('He prayeth best who loveth best,/ All things both great and small', ll. 647–8); but now it is a capacity for tears that matters, not prayer. Weeping in *Peter Bell* serves as an index of humanity. To start with, Peter is a predator—a bully and a thief; his chief emotions are anger, greed, and fear. The suffering ass, beaten for refusing to abandon the body of its master, is a victim of his life-long abuse of feeling, and an instance of his insensibility to the natural world; this is the Wordsworth who could write in all seriousness: 'I would not strike a flower/As many a man would strike

---

[1] Ibid.: *PW* ii. 334, ll. 80/1, app. crit.
[2] Ibid.: *PW* ii. 334, ll. 68–70 and app. crit. (my italics). In revision, Wordsworth accentuated his point: 'I was lost/Where I have been.'
[3] Ibid.: *PW* ii. 380, l. 1072 and app. crit.
[4] I.F. note to *Peter Bell* (*PW* ii. 527).

his horse.'[1] At the climax of the poem the ass is displaced by the tormenting memory of Peter's sixth wife:

> But more than all his heart is stung
> To think of one, almost a child,
> A sweet and playful Highland Girl
> As light & beauteous as a squirrel,
> As beauteous & as wild.[2]

It is his 'miserable vision' of the broken-hearted Highland Girl—

> crying as she cried
> The very moment that she died,
> 'My mother! Oh! my mother!'[3]

—that prompts Peter's first redeeming tears. His salvation is marked by his ability to feel for the bereaved family to which the ass leads him ('He feels what he for human kind/Had never felt before'),[4] and at the end of the poem we see him helplessly at the mercy of his new capacity for involvement:

> And Peter Bell the ruffian wild
> Sobs loud, he sobs just like a child,
> 'Oh God! I can endure no more.'[5]

Peter Bell is Wordsworth's most doctrinaire celebration of the human heart. For once, one might complain, suffering has been important to him less for its own sake than as a means of proving his thesis about the redemptive effects of feeling; an ass has been maltreated and a family bereaved, all to save a single ruffian. 'A more extraordinary conversion never excited the scorn of the sceptic, in the annals of what is termed Methodism', complained the *Eclectic Review* in 1819.[6] Wordsworth would not have been Methodistically inclined himself, any more than the Unitarian Coleridge would have endorsed the medieval Catholicism of 'The Ancient Mariner'. But the Methodist conversion-narrative—almost a popular art-form in its own right[7]—gave him a contemporary formula for redemption to counter the traditionalism of Coleridge's spiritual voyage. Its

---

[1] MS. JJ: *Prelude*, p. 612.   [2] MS. 3: *PW* ii. 374, ll. 886–90.
[3] Ibid.: *PW* ii. 375, ll. 928–30.   [4] Ibid.: *PW* ii. 380, ll. 1054–5.
[5] Ibid.: *PW* ii. 382, ll. 1118–20.   [6] *Eclectic Review*, xii (July 1819), 6.
[7] See H. F. Mathews, *Methodism and the Education of the People 1791–1851* (London, 1949), pp. 168–9, and cf. also F. C. Gill, *The Romantic Movement and Methodism* (London, 1937), p. 168, where the link with *Peter Bell* is noticed but not developed.

special usefulness lay in the overlap between Methodism
('religion felt') and sentimentalism; the mark of the convert, as
of the man of feeling, was his tears. The role of the hardened
sinner in Evangelical mythology parallels that of Peter—a
hard man won, not to God, but to man; in the words of John
Newton, God

> suffers the natural rebellion and wickedness of their hearts to have
> full scope; while sinners of less note are cut off with little warning,
> these are spared, though sinning with a high hand, and as it were
> studying their own destruction. At length, when all that knew them
> are perhaps expecting to hear that they are made signal instances of
> divine vengeance, the Lord . . . is pleased to pluck them as brands
> out of the fire, and to make them monuments of his mercy, for the
> encouragement of others; they are, beyond expectation, convinced,
> pardoned, and changed.[1]

The more hell-bent the sinner, the greater the impact of his
conversion; hence Wordsworth's insistence on the unregenerate-
ness of Peter's nature, and hence his untroubled sacrifice of
means to ends in the course of saving him. Peter's conversion
takes place under the influence of a Methodist preacher
(' "Repent, repent," he cries aloud,/"God is a God of
Mercy" '),[2] and it follows the pattern of a representative
'testimony'. One of Whitefield's followers, for instance, had
been converted during a sermon preached on the favourite
Methodist text, 'Is not this a brand plucked out of the fire?':

> When this sermon began, I was certainly a dreadful enemy to God,
> and to all that is good; and one of the most profligate and abandoned
> young men living: but by the time it was ended, I was become A
> NEW CREATURE: for, in the first place, I was DEEPLY CONVINCED
> of the great goodness of God towards me all my life; particularly, in
> that he had given his Son to die for me. I had also a far clearer view
> of all my sins; particularly, my base ingratitude towards him.
> These discoveries quite BROKE MY HEART, and caused showers of
> tears to trickle down my cheeks . . . in consequence of which I
> BROKE OFF ALL my evil practices, and FORSOOK ALL my wicked
> and foolish companions, without delay . . . [3]

[1] *An Authentic Narrative of Some Remarkable and Interesting Particulars in the Life
of *********, pp. 6–7 (see p. 26 and n., above).

[2] MS. 3: *PW* ii. 376, ll. 946–7.

[3] *Arminian Magazine*, ii (February 1779), 82–3; the 'testimony' is that of Thomas
Olivers.

Peter too, we are told, 'melted into tears'—

> Sweet tears of hope and tenderness—
> And fast they fell, a plenteous shower;
> His nerves, his sinews seem'd to melt,
> Through all his iron frame was felt
> A gentle, a relaxing power.[1]

—and the language of resurrection is adapted to his awakening humanity ('Nature through a world of death/Breathes into him a second breath')[2] as he is reborn into the Wordsworthian universe of love celebrated elsewhere in the poetry of 1798.

As Coleridge suggests in the first of his autobiographical letters of 1797, the 'testimonies' and 'experiences' of the Evangelical magazines had a special importance to anyone concerned with the individual's inner life:

> I could inform the dullest author how he might write an interesting book—let him relate the events of his own Life with honesty, not disguising the feelings that accompanied them.—I never yet read even a Methodist's 'Experience' in the Gospel Magazine without receiving instruction & amusement . . . [3]

The conversion-narrative was above all an account of subjective experience—of the spiritual events by which an otherwise commonplace life becomes remarkable. This introspectiveness gave Wordsworth the scope for an entirely psychological treatment of the redemption-theme which he had taken over from 'The Ancient Mariner'. Peter's journey of self-discovery focuses on the growing conviction of guilt central to the Methodist 'experiences' summarized by Thomas Jackson in his collected *Lives of Early Methodist Preachers*:

> Their consciences were awakened . . . they felt that they were sinners . . . After many inward conflicts and misgivings, their convictions of guilt, and of the sinfulness of their nature, became more deep and agonizing; and in the extremity of their grief they sought and found relief by faith in Christ . . . In this manner they passed from death unto life.[4]

---

[1] MS. 3: *PW* ii. 377, ll. 961–5.   [2] Ibid.: *PW* ii. 380, ll. 1073–4.
[3] 6 February 1797; Griggs, i. 302.
[4] *The Lives of Early Methodist Preachers*, ed. Thomas Jackson (3rd edn., 6 vols., London, 1865), i. xiii.

In *Peter Bell*, the discovery of the corpse at the climax of Part I is followed in Part II by fresh assaults on Peter's guilty conscience—the doleful, unexplained cry of a small boy searching for his father; the leaf that seems to pursue him, the drops of blood that accuse him from the road. But it takes a final assault to convince Peter of his guilt—the sound of miners rock-blasting beneath the ground. The episode is Wordsworth's counterpart to the apocalyptic rumble which concludes the Ancient Mariner's voyage ('Under the water it rumbled on,/ Still louder and more dread . . .', ll. 579–80), and it at last makes Peter subject to the 'Spirits of the Mind' invoked on his behalf at the start of Part III:

> Then coming from the wayward world,
> That powerful world in which ye dwell,
> Come Spirits of the Mind, & try
> Tonight beneath the moonlight sky
> What may be done with Peter Bell.[1]

Only now does Peter look inward, encountering his past through the partnership of landscape and memory that was always so potent for Wordsworth himself; the things he sees bring vividly to life, in his mind's eye, forgotten episodes of petty theft, pointless cruelty, and finally his betrayal of the Highland Girl. The wraith-like apparition of his former self beside the dying girl ('He sees himself as plain as day')[2] is not simply a traditional portent of death designed to intensify his terror. It signifies the death of the old self, and the birth of the new. When Wordsworth writes 'and now the Spirits of the mind/Are busy with poor Peter Bell',[3] he is announcing the birth of moral consciousness, as well as describing an optical illusion.

Wordsworth's anti-supernaturalism in *Peter Bell* is based on a belief that the experiences which affect the individual most deeply come from within. In *Lyrical Ballads* (1800) he cited it as a defect that Coleridge's Mariner 'does not act, but is continually acted upon';[4] Peter, by contrast, is an active participant

---

[1] MS. 3: *PW* ii. 369, ll. 781–5.
[2] Ibid.: *PW* ii. 375, l. 922 app. crit. Cf. Coleridge's 1805 allusion to this wraith and its causes (*The Notebooks of Samuel Taylor Coleridge*, ii. 2583).
[3] Ibid. *PW* ii. 375, ll. 916–17.
[4] *Lyrical Ballads* (1800), i, notes.

in the drama created by his own imagination. His successive
states of mind—fury, disquiet, terror—are shown to transform
his world as powerfully as could the supernatural; like the sea-
captain of 'The Thorn', Peter has the faculty of producing
impressive effects out of simple elements. Wordsworth's belief
in the efficacy of the imagination as a redemptive force is
central to the poem. His attitude to the 'supernatural' interventions which often figure in Methodist testimonies is explicitly stated at the start of Part III. The story of a pious man
startled at his reading by a ghostly word of admonition formed
on the page before him provokes the comment: 'Let good men
feel the soul of Nature/And see things as they are';[1] it is men
like Peter who deserve to see things as they are not. Wordsworth's aim in *Peter Bell* is not to strip the mind of its mysteries,
and the 'Dread Spirits' which impose on the pious are never
rationalized out of existence. Rather, they are located firmly
in the imagination, becoming a manifestation of its power to
conspire with, or even supersede, the world perceived by the
senses. Wordsworth's allusion to his own experience of such
powers—

> Your presence I have often felt
> In darkness & the stormy night,
> And well I know if need there be
> Ye can put forth your agency,
> Beneath the sweet moonlight.[2]

—links them to the 'Severer interventions, ministry/More
palpable'[3] which he first invokes in Part I of the 1799 *Prelude*,
written only six months later; episodes of boat-stealing or
woodcock-snaring show the natural world interacting in the
same way with a sense of guilt to produce effects that are
permanently educative. The supernatural, Wordsworth implies, bypasses the ordinary world in a way that adds nothing
to it. The imagination, by contrast, invests it with the significance it had lacked to the hardened vagabond of the opening
scenes. At the start of *Peter Bell*,

---

[1] MS. 3: *PW* ii. 368, ll. 764–5. Wordsworth's source for this story is almost
certainly Coleridge, who later claimed to have 'a whole memorandum Book filled
with records of these Phaenomena . . . affording some valuable materials for a
Theory of Perception and its dependence on the memory and Imagination'; see
CCW iv: *The Friend*, ii. 118n.

[2] Ibid.: *PW* ii. 368, ll. 776–80 and app. crit.   [3] *Prelude*, i. 370–1.

> A primrose by a river's brim
> A yellow primrose was to him
> And it was nothing more.[1]

By the end of the poem, the everyday can mean to Peter what the flower of the Immortality Ode means to Wordsworth himself. The 'thoughts that do often lie too deep for tears' are those of the humanized imagination—Wordsworth's theme in *Peter Bell*.

Hazlitt recalls of Wordsworth's famous open-air reading of *Peter Bell* in the summer of 1798 that 'Whatever might be thought of the poem, "his face was as a book where men might read strange matters," and he announced the fate of his hero in prophetic tones.'[2] His description of Wordsworth as he appeared in 1798—the 'convulsive inclination to laughter about the mouth, a good deal at variance with the solemn, stately expression of the rest of his face'[3]—suggests the mixed effect of *Peter Bell* itself. Wordsworth's prophetic seriousness is matched by his playfully self-deprecating method:

> Oh! would that any, friend or foe
> My further labour might prevent;
> On me it cannot easy sit,
> I feel that I am all unfit
> For such high argument.[4]

Like his bungled *in medias res* opening (' "My dearest Sir" cried Mistress Swan,/"You've got at once into the middle" '),[5] his apology has deliberate mock-epic quality; *Peter Bell* is to be a comically individual version of Coleridge's 'high argument'— a ham-fisted treatment of the redemption-theme which makes no claims to rival 'The Ancient Mariner'. Comedy allows Wordsworth to bow out of the contest, while shifting it to an area more favourable to his own talents.[6] His 1800 note on Coleridge's poem complains that 'the events having no necessary connection do not produce each other';[7] in *Peter Bell* this

[1] MS. 3: *PW* ii. 341, ll. 248–50.
[2] 'My First Acquaintance with Poets' (Howe, xvii. 118).
[3] Ibid. (Howe, xvii. 118).   [4] MS. 3: *PW* ii. 369, ll. 786–90 and app. crit.
[5] Ibid.: *PW* ii. 339, ll. 195/6 app. crit.
[6] See also Frederick Garber, 'Wordsworth's Comedy of Redemption', *Anglia*, lxxxiv (1966), 388–97, and R. F. Storch, *SEL* xi (1971), 621–39.
[7] *Lyrical Ballads* (1800), i, notes.

randomness is replaced by a narrative of events mockingly well-engineered. And whereas the Mariner, for Wordsworth, 'has no distinct character', Peter has the robust amorality and the cowardice of a rogue. He is no unwitting sinner, tormented by the spirits of an incomprehensible universe for a crime he does not understand, but a trickster made the butt of his own guilty conscience—a comic inversion of the picaresque adventurer, taken for a ride by the ass he tries to steal. Even religion makes a fool of him ('"Repent, repent"'). Wordsworth's universe is explicable, understood, where Coleridge's is mysterious; Wordsworth's is benign, where Coleridge's brings disproportionate and unknown forces to bear on the erring individual. 'The Ancient Mariner' explores all that is irrational in our experience of the world: *Peter Bell* affirms normality; its laws are stable and its values unambiguous. One poem disturbs, the other reassures; one remains unresolved—its Mariner for ever alone, for ever reliving his guilt—while the other reconciles innocent and guilty in the Wordsworthian community of feeling.

Coleridge wrote of Wordsworth that 'without his depth of feeling and his imaginative power his *sense* would want its vital warmth and peculiarity; and without his strong sense, his *mysticism* would become *sickly*—mere fog, and dimness!'[1] *Peter Bell* triumphantly expresses this balance. A manifesto for the Wordsworthian imagination, it also reveals 'the loveliness and the wonders of the world before us'; its movement is both inward and outward, its values are personal but not solipsistic. The poem's special significance for *Lyrical Ballads* lies in bringing into the open the self-defining struggle for literary identity which is central to the volume. In *Peter Bell*, as in 'Tintern Abbey', creative interaction with another poet makes Wordsworth most fully himself. In their different ways, the two poems are the culminating statement of poetic identity to come out of their period, and both affirm the creed of years to come—that restoration through the dual operation of nature and imagination which is to be Wordsworth's theme in *The Prelude*. *Lyrical Ballads* shows Wordsworth at once encountering tradition and freeing himself from it, as he had to do in order to achieve a permanently enduring poetry of his own.

[1] Shawcross, ii. 114–15.

Appendix I
The Dating of Wordsworth's Contributions to Lyrical Ballads (1798)

1. 'The Female Vagrant': either *c.* 1791, or between August 1973 and April 1794; revised and extended *c.* November 1795 and perhaps spring 1798.

Wordsworth himself suggests that the story of the Female Vagrant goes back to 1791 (see *PW* i. 330), but his evidence is conflicting. The first surviving text forms part of the version of *Salisbury Plain* composed August 1793–April 1794 (MS. 1), and could equally date from this period. The expansion of the woman's story into a version corresponding to that in *Lyrical Ballads* probably belongs to *c.* November 1795 when 'Adventures on Salisbury Plain' was created by extensive revision and the addition of the sailor's story (see *EY*, p. 159). Further revision may have taken place in the spring of 1798, either when Wordsworth was planning publication of *Salisbury Plain* as a whole (see Griggs, i. 400), or when the story of the Female Vagrant was excerpted for publication in *Lyrical Ballads*.

2. 'The Convict': between March and October 1796; probably revised December 1797.

Work on 'The Convict' appears to have been entered in DC MS. 2 at much the same time as the 'Gothic Tale' and 'XVI (a)' and 'XVI (b)', all belonging to the period after Wordsworth's completion of 'Adventures on Salisbury Plain' in March 1796 and before he started work on *The Borderers* in October. Wordsworth's Godwinian attack on the penal system—echoing that of *Salisbury Plain*—was subsequently toned down, probably when 'The Convict' was sent to the *Morning Post* for publication in December 1797.

3. 'Lines written near Richmond, upon the Thames, at Evening': between March and October 1796, but drawing on a sonnet-draft of 1789–90.

Dated 1789 by Wordsworth himself, who associates its composition
with the river Cam (see *PW* i. 324), 'Lines written near Richmond'
is based on a sonnet-draft which clearly reflects the influence of
Bowles; Wordsworth's purchase of *Fourteen Sonnets* belongs to the
Christmas vacation of 1789–90. Draft work for the poem in its later
form is associated in DC MS. 2 with 'The Convict' and 'Address to
the Ocean', both belonging to the period between March and
October 1796. The poem was copied into Cottle's MS. book on 29
March 1797.

4. 'Lines left upon a Seat in a Yew-tree': between *c.* April and June
1797, but perhaps drawing on material from *c.* 1787.

Thematically dependent on *The Borderers* (effectively completed
March 1797), the Yew-tree lines must belong to the following months.
The bulk of composition survives in Mary Hutchinson's hand and
thus dates from before her departure from Racedown in early June
1797, but rough drafts for the concluding section survive only in
Wordsworth's hand and could date from Coleridge's arrival shortly
afterwards. The poem was read to Lamb during his visit of 7–14
July (see Lucas, i. 112). Some lines, probably from the opening
section, may go back to Wordsworth's Hawkshead schooldays (see
PW i. 329).

5. 'Old Man Travelling': between *c.* April and early June 1797;
ll. 15–20 perhaps added early summer 1798.

An offshoot of 'The Old Cumberland Beggar' in its earliest form
('Description of a Beggar'), 'Old Man Travelling' is preserved in
DC MS. 13 and belongs to the months between *c.* April and early
June when Wordsworth was also at work on 'The Ruined Cottage'
(see Reed, pp. 342, 346). The final lines of dialogue appear to have
been added to the fair copy at a different time, and could well
belong to the period when it was decided to include the poem in
Lyrical Ballads.

6. 'Lines written at a small distance from my House': between *c.* 1
and 10 March 1798.

Wordsworth's opening line—'It is the first mild day of March'—
suggests that the poem belongs to the period when Dorothy's
Journal records the beginnings of spring and several pleasant days
(particularly 6, 8, and 10 March).

7. 'Goody Blake, and Harry Gill': between *c.* 7 March and *c.* 13
March 1798.

Probably on 7 March 1798, Wordsworth wrote urgently to Cottle asking for Darwin's *Zoönomia*, which contained his source (see *EY*, p. 199, and Reed, p. 224n.). By *c.* 13 March Dorothy writes that the books sent by Cottle have already completely answered their purpose (see *EY*, pp. 214–15, and Griggs, i. 399). Assuming that 'Goody Blake, and Harry Gill' was composed as rapidly as the other ballads of 1798, this seems likely to imply its completion.

8. 'The Thorn': *c.* 19 March 1798.

Wordsworth's recollection that 'The Thorn' originated in his sight of an actual tree on a stormy day (see *PW* ii. 511) is borne out by Dorothy's *Journal* entry for 19 March 1798 ('William wrote some lines describing a stunted thorn', *DWJ* i. 13) and by the description itself which survives in the Alfoxden Notebook. The I.F. note goes on to record that once Wordsworth had decided on his 'invention', or story, he 'began the poem accordingly, and composed it with great rapidity'.

9. 'The Idiot Boy': *c.* late March 1798.

Wordsworth's opening line—' 'Tis eight o'clock,—a clear March night'—suggests that 'The Idiot Boy' was begun, if not completed, in March 1798. Its burlesque of Bürger's ballad of sensational event makes it likely to follow rather than precede the serious use of Bürger in 'The Thorn', while its comic method points forward to that of *Peter Bell*, begun on 20 April 1798 (see *DWJ* i. 16). The I.F. note records that 'this long poem was composed in the Groves of Alfoxden almost extempore' (*PW* ii. 478), and, like 'The Thorn', it was probably written with some speed.

10. 'Lines written in early spring': *c.* 12 April 1798.

References in the poem itself suggest that primroses and periwinkles were out, and twigs budding. Dorothy's *Journal* records a late and sudden spring. On 24 March, 'The spring continues to advance very slowly' (*DWJ* i. 13) and on 6 April, 'The Spring still advancing very slowly' (*DWJ* i. 14); but on 9 April, 'the larches in the park changed from black to green in two or three days' (*DWJ* i. 15), and on 12 April, 'The Spring advances rapidly, multitudes of primroses, dog-violets, periwinkles, stitchwort' (*DWJ* i. 15).

11. 'Anecdote for Fathers', 'We are seven', 'Simon Lee', 'The Complaint of a forsaken Indian Woman', 'The last of the Flock', 'The Mad Mother': between *c.* early April and *c.* mid-May 1798.

On 12 April Wordsworth wrote to Cottle that he had 'gone on very rapidly adding to [his] stock of poetry' (*EY*, p. 215), and he may well have composed a number of short poems between the ballads of March and beginning *Peter Bell* on 20 April (see *DWJ* i. 16). By 30 April Wordsworth evidently thought of himself as having enough material to make up a volume, since Dorothy writes of one (presumably *Lyrical Ballads*) that is 'nearly ready for publishing' (*EY*, p. 216). Wordsworth's reference on 9 May to having 'lately been busy about another plan' (*EY*, p. 218)—again, presumably *Lyrical Ballads*—may well refer to composition of other poems besides *Peter Bell*, originally also intended for inclusion (see *PW* ii. 527). By the end of May, Cottle had returned to Bristol with the bulk of the volume; Wordsworth is unlikely to have written much between *c*. 16 May, when he left Alfoxden for about a week, and the end of the month. A terminal date of mid-May can be set for the three 'complaints', since Hazlitt heard 'The Mad Mother' and 'The Complaint of a forsaken Indian Woman' on *c*. 21 May, during Wordsworth's absence (see Reed, p. 237); the I.F. note recalls that 'The Complaint of a forsaken Indian Woman' was 'composed for the volume of Lyrical Ballads', and that 'The last of the Flock' was 'Produced at the same time, & for the same purpose' (*PW* ii. 474, 476). This would suggest that all three belong to the period when the plan for *Lyrical Ballads* had taken shape.

12. 'Expostulation and Reply', 'The Tables turned': *c*. 23 May 1798.

The 'Advertisement' of 1798 recalls that the two poems 'arose out of conversation with a friend who was somewhat unreasonably attached to modern books of moral philosophy' (*Prose Works*, i. 117). The friend was Hazlitt, and the conversation itself took place on a walk during Hazlitt's visit of *c*. 20 May to 10 June 1798—probably on 23 May (see Reed, p. 238).

13. 'Tintern Abbey': 11–13 July 1798.

Wordsworth recalls that he began composition on leaving Tintern, and that he completed the poem as he entered Bristol 'after a ramble of 4 or 5 days' (*PW* ii. 517). The date given to 'Tintern Abbey' in its title—13 July 1798—probably refers to its completion. After leaving Bristol on 10 July and spending the night at Tintern, Wordsworth would thus have begun it on 11 July and composed it during the three remaining days of his tour. Elsewhere, Wordsworth remembered it as having taken four days to compose (see *PW* ii. 517), perhaps suggesting that he began it a day earlier; but he is more likely to be reliable in locating the place where he embarked on the poem than in remembering to the day the length of time it took.

Appendix II
Two Ballads by Bürger, translated by William Taylor of Norwich

LENORA.
A Ballad, from Bürger.

AT break of day, with frightful dreams
    Lenora struggled sore:
My William, art thou slaine, say'd she,
    Or dost thou love no more?

He went abroade with Richard's host,
    The Paynim foes to quell;
But he no word to her had writt,
    An he were sick or well.

With sowne of trump, and beat of drum,
    His fellow-soldyers come;
Their helmes bydeckt with oaken boughs,
    They seeke their long'd-for home.

And ev'ry roade and ev'ry lane
    Was full of old and young,
To gaze at the rejoicing band,
    To hail with gladsome toung.

'Thank God!' their wives and children saide,
    'Welcome!' the brides did saye:
But greete or kiss Lenora gave
    To none upon that daye.

She askte of all the passing traine,
    For him she wisht to see:
But none of all the passing traine
    Could tell if lived hee.

And when the soldyers all were bye,
    She tore her raven haire,
And cast herself upon the growne
    In furious despaire.

Her mother ran and lyfte her up,
    And clasped in her arme,
'My child, my child, what dost thou ail?
    God shield thy life from harm!'

'O mother, mother! William's gone!
    What's all besyde to me?
There is no mercye, sure, above!
    All, all were spar'd but hee!'

'Knell downe, thy paternoster saye,
    'Twill calm thy troubled spright:
The Lord is wyse, the Lord is good;
    What hee hath done is right.'

'O mother, mother! say not so;
    Most cruel is my fate:
I prayde, and prayde; but watte avayl'd?
    'Tis now, alas! too late.'

'Our Heavenly Father, if we praye,
    Will help a suff'ring childe:
Go take the holy sacrament;
    So shall thy grief grow milde.'

'O mother, what I feel within,
    No sacrament can staye;
No sacrament can teche the dead
    To bear the sight of daye.'

'May be, among the heathen folk
    Thy William false doth prove,
And puts away his faith and troth,
    And takes another love.

Then wherefore sorrow for his loss?
    Thy moans are all in vain:
And when his soul and body parte,
    His falsehode brings him paine.'

'O mother, mother! gone is gone:
    My hope is all forlorne;
The grave mie onlye safeguarde is—
    O, had I ne'er been borne!

Go out, go out, my lampe of life;
    In grislie darkness die:
There is no mercye, sure, above!
    For ever let me die.'

'Almighty God! O do not judge
    My poor unhappy childe;
She knows not what her lips pronounce,
    Her anguish makes her wilde.

My girl, forget thine earthly woe,
    And think on God and bliss;
For so, at least, shall not thy soule
    Its heavenly bridegroom miss.'

'O mother, mother! what is blisse,
    And what the fiendis celle?
With him 'tis heaven any where,
    Without my William, helle.

'Go out, go out, my lamp of life;
    In endless darkness die:
Without him I must loathe the earth,
    Without him scorne the skye.'

And so despaire did rave and rage
    Athwarte her boiling veins;
Against the Providence of Heaven
    She hurlde her impious strains.

She bet her breaste, and wrung her hands,
    And rollde her tearlesse eye,
From rise of morne, till the pale stars
    Again did freeke the skye.

When harke! abroade she hearde the trampe
    Of nimble-hoofed steed;
She hearde a knighte with clank alighte,
    And climb the staire in speede.

And soon she herde a tinkling hande,
    That twirled at the pin;
And thro' her door, that open'd not,
    These words were breathed in.

'What ho! what ho! thy dore undoe;
    Art watching or asleepe?
My love, dost yet remember mee,
    And dost thou laugh or weep?'

'Ah! William here so late at night!
    Oh! I have watchte and wak'd:
Whence dost thou come? For thy return
    My herte has sorely ak'd.'

'At midnight only we may ride;
   I come o'er land and sea:
I mounted late, but soone I go;
   Aryse, and come with me.'

'O William, enter first my bowre,
   And give me one embrace:
The blasts athwarte the hawthorne hiss;
   Awayte a little space.'

'The blasts athwarte the hawthorn hiss,
   I may not harboure here;
My spurre is sharpe, my courser pawes,
   My houre of flighte is nere.

All as thou lyest upon thy couch,
   Aryse, and mount behinde;
To-night we'le ride a thousand miles,
   The bridal bed to finde.'

'How, ride to-night a thousand miles?
   Thy love thou dost bemocke:
Eleven is the stroke that still
   Rings on within the clocke.'

'Looke up; the moone is bright, and we
   Outstride the earthlie men:
I'll take thee to the bridal bed,
   And night shall end but then.'

'And where is, then, thy house and home;
   And where thy bridal bed?'
'Tis narrow, silent, chilly, dark;
   Far hence I rest my head.'

'And is there any room for mee,
   Wherein that I may creepe?'
'There's room enough for thee and mee,
   Wherein that wee may sleepe.

All as thou ly'st upon thy couch,
   Aryse, no longer stop;
The wedding guests thy coming waite,
   The chamber dore is ope.'

All in her sarke, as there she lay,
   Upon his horse she sprung;
And with her lily hands so pale
   About her William clung.

And hurry-skurry forth they go,
  Unheeding wet or dry;
And horse and rider snort and blow,
  And sparkling pebbles fly.

How swift the flood, the mead, the wood,
  Aright, aleft, are gone!
The bridges thunder as they pass,
  But earthlie sowne is none.

Tramp, tramp, across the land they speede;
  Splash, splash, across the see:
'Hurrah! the dead can ride apace;
  Dost feare to ride with mee?

The moone is bryghte, and blue the nyghte;
  Dost quake the blast to stem?
Dost shudder, mayde, to seeke the dead?'
  'No, no, but what of them?'

How glumlie sownes yon dirgye song!
  Night-ravens flappe the wing.
What knell doth slowlie toll ding-dong?
  The psalmes of death who sing?

It creeps, the swarthie funeral traine,
  The corse is onn the beere;
Like croke of todes from lonely moores,
  The chaunte doth meet the eere.'

'Go, bear her corse when midnight's past,
  With song, and tear, and wayle;
I've gott my wife, I take her home,
  My howre of wedlocke hayl.

Lead forth, O clarke, the chaunting quire,
  To swell our nuptial song:
Come, preaste, and reade the blessing soone;
  For bed, for bed we long.'

They heede his calle, and husht the sowne;
  The biere was seene no more;
And followde him ore feeld and flood
  Yet faster than before.

Halloo! halloo! away they goe,
  Unheeding wet or drye;
And horse and rider snort and blowe,
  And sparkling pebbles flye.

How swifte the hill, how swifte the dale,
  Aright, aleft, are gone!
By hedge and tree, by thorpe and towne,
  They gallop, gallop on.

Tramp, tramp, across the land they speede;
  Splash, splash, acrosse the see;
'Hurrah! the dead can ride apace;
  Dost fear to ride with mee?

Look up, look up, an airy crewe
  In roundel daunces reele:
The moone is bryghte, and blue the nyghte,
  Mayst dimlie see them wheele.

Come to, come to, ye gostlie crew,
  Come to, and follow mee,
And daunce for us the wedding daunce,
  When we in bed shall be.'

And brush, brush, brush, the ghostlie crew
  Come wheeling ore their heads,
All rustling like the wither'd leaves
  That wyde the wirlwind spreads.

Halloo! halloo! away they go,
  Unheeding wet or dry;
And horse and rider snort and blowe,
  And sparkling pebbles flye.

And all that in the moonshyne lay,
  Behynde them fled afar;
And backwarde scudded overhead
  The sky and every star.

Tramp, tramp, across the lande they speede;
  Splash, splash, across the see:
'Hurrah! the dead can ride apace;
  Dost fear to ride with mee?

I weene the cock prepares to crowe;
  The sand will soone be runne:
I snuffe the earlye morning aire;
  Downe, downe! our work is done.

The dead, the dead can ryde apace;
  Oure wed-bed here is fit:
Oure race is ridde, oure journey ore,
  Oure endlesse union knit.'

And lo! an yren-grated gate
    Soon biggens to their viewe:
He crackte his whyppe; the clangynge boltes,
    The doores asunder flewe.

They pass, and 'twas on graves they trode;
    ' 'Tis hither we are bounde:'
And many a tombstone gostlie white
    Lay inn the moonshyne round.

And when hee from his steede alytte,
    His armour, black as cinder,
Did moulder, moulder all awaye,
    As were it made of tinder.

His head became a naked scull;
    Nor haire nor eyne had hee:
His body grew a skeleton,
    Whilome so blythe of blee.

And att his drye and boney heele
    No spur was left to be;
And inn his witherde hande you might
    The scythe and houre-glasse see.

And lo! his steede did thin to smoke,
    And charnel fires outbreathe;
And pal'd, and bleach'd, then vanish'd quite
    The mayde from underneathe.

And hollow howlings hung in aire,
    And shrekes from vaults arose.
Then knew the mayde she mighte no more
    Her living eyes unclose.

But onwarde to the judgement seat,
    Thro' myste and moonlighte dreare,
The gostlie crewe their flyghte persewe,
    And hollowe inn her eare:—

'Be patient; tho' thyne herte should breke,
    Arrayne not Heven's decree;
Thou nowe art of thie bodie refte,
    Thie soule forgiven bee!'

THE LASS OF FAIR WONE.
From the German of Bürger.

BESIDE the parson's bower of yew
  Why strays a troubled spright,
That peaks and pines, and dimly shines
  Thro' curtains of the night?

Why steals along the pond of toads
  A gliding fire so blue,
That lights a spot where grows no grass,
  Where falls no rain nor dew?

The parson's daughter once was good,
  And gentle as the dove,
And young and fair,—and many came
  To win the damsel's love.

High o'er the hamlet, from the hill,
  Beyond the winding stream,
The windows of a stately house
  In sheen of evening gleam,

There dwelt, in riot, rout, and roar,
  A lord so frank and free;
That oft, with inward joy of heart,
  The maid beheld his glee.

Whether he met the dawning day,
  In hunting trim so fine,
Or tapers, sparkling from his hall,
  Beshone the midnight wine.

He sent the maid his picture, girt
  With diamond, pearl, and gold;
And silken-paper, sweet with musk,
  This gentle message told:

'Let go thy sweethearts, one and all;
  Shalt thou be basely woo'd,
That worthy art to gain the heart
  Of youths of noble blood?

The tale I would to thee bewray,
  In secret must be said:
At midnight hour I'll seek thy bower;
  Fair lass, be not afraid.

And when the amorous nightingale
    Sings sweetly to his mate,
I'll pipe my quail-call from the field:
    Be kind, nor make me wait.'

In cap and mantle clad he came,
    At night, with lonely tread;
Unseen, and silent as a mist,
    And hush'd the dogs with bread.

And when the amorous nightingale
    Sung sweetly to his mate,
She heard his quail-call in the field,
    And, ah! ne'er made him wait.

The words he whisper'd were so soft,
    They won her ear and heart:
How soon will she, who loves, believe!
    How deep a lover's art!

No lure, no soothing guise, he spar'd,
    To banish virtuous shame;
He call'd on holy God above,
    As witness to his flame.

He clasp'd her to his breast, and swore
    To be for ever true:
'O yield thee to my wishful arms,
    Thy choice thou shalt not rue.'

And while she strove, he drew her on,
    And led her to the bower
So still, so dim—and round about
    Sweet smelt the beans in flower.

There beat her heart, and heav'd her breast,
    And pleaded every sense;
And there the glowing breath of lust
    Did blast her innocence.

But when the fragrant beans began
    Their sallow blooms to shed,
Her sparkling eyes their lustre lost;
    Her cheek, its roses fled:

And when she saw the pods increase,
    The ruddier cherries strain,
She felt her silken robe grow tight,
    Her waist new weight sustain.

And when the mowers went afield,
  The yellow corn to ted,
She felt her burden stir within,
  And shook with tender dread.

And when the winds of autumn hist
  Along the stubble field;
Then could the damsel's piteous plight
  No longer be conceal'd.

Her sire, a harsh and angry man,
  With furious voice revil'd:
'Hence from my sight! I'll none of thee—
  I harbour not thy child.'

And fast, amid her fluttering hair,
  With clenched fist he gripes,
And seiz'd a leathern thong, and lash'd
  Her side with sounding stripes.

Her lily skin, so soft and white,
  He ribb'd with bloody wales;
And thrust her out, tho' black the night,
  Tho' sleet and storm assails.

Up the harsh rock, on flinty paths,
  The maiden had to roam;
On tottering feet she grop'd her way,
  And sought her lover's home.

'A mother thou has made of me,
  Before thou mad'st a wife:
For this, upon my tender breast,
  These livid stripes are rife:

Behold.' ——— And then, with bitter sobs,
  She sank upon the floor ———
'Make good the evil thou has wrought;
  My injur'd name restore.'

'Poor soul; I'll have thee hous'd and nurs'd;
  Thy terrors I lament.
Stay here; we'll have some further talk ———
  The old one shall repent ———'

'I have no time to rest and wait;
  That saves not my good name:
If thou with honest soul hast sworn,
  O leave me not to shame;

But at the holy altar be
   Our union sanctified;
Before the people and the priest
   Receive me for thy bride.'

'Unequal matches must not blot
   The honours of my line:
Art thou of wealth or rank for me,
   To harbour thee as mine?

What's fit and fair I'll do for thee;
   Shalt yet retain my love ———
Shalt wed my huntsman ——— and we'll then
   Our former transports prove.'

'Thy wicked soul, hard-hearted man,
   May pangs in hell await!
Sure, if not suited for thy bride,
   I was not for thy mate.

Go, seek a spouse of nobler blood,
   Nor God's just judgements dread ———
So shall, ere long, some base-born wretch
   Defile thy marriage-bed. ———

Then, traitor, feel how wretched they
   In hopeless shame immerst;
Then smite thy forehead on the wall,
   While horrid curses burst.

Roll thy dry eyes in wild despair ———
   Unsooth'd thy grinning woe:
Thro' thy pale temples fire the ball,
   And sink to fiends below.'

Collected then, she started up,
   And, thro' the hissing sleet,
Thro' thorn and briar, thro' flood and mire,
   She fled with bleeding feet.

'Where now,' she cry'd, 'my gracious God!
   What refuge have I left?'
And reach'd the garden of her home,
   Of hope in man bereft.

On hand and foot she feebly crawl'd
   Beneath the bower unblest;
Where withering leaves and gathering snow,
   Prepar'd her only rest.

There rending pains and darting throes
  Assail'd her shuddering frame;
And from her womb a lovely boy,
  With wail and weeping came.

Forth from her hair a silver pin
  With hasty hand she drew,
And prest against its tender heart,
  And the sweet babe she slew.

Erst when the act of blood was done,
  Her soul its guilt abhorr'd:
'My Jesus! what has been my deed?
  Have mercy on me, Lord!'

With bloody nails, beside the pond,
  Its shallow grave she tore:
'There rest in God; there shame and want
  Thou can'st not suffer more:

Me vengeance waits. My poor, poor child,
  Thy wound shall bleed afresh,
When ravens from the gallows tear
  Thy mother's mould'ring flesh.'—

Hard by the bower her gibbet stands:
  Her skull is still to show;
It seems to eye the barren grave,
  Three spans in length below.

That is the spot where grows no grass;
  Where falls no rain nor dew:
Whence steals along the pond of toads
  A hovering fire so blue.

And nightly, when the ravens come,
  Her ghost is seen to glide;
Pursues and tries to quench the flame,
  And pines the pool beside.

List of Wordsworth MSS.

from which quotations are drawn

The manuscripts in Dove Cottage Library were renumbered in 1972; the previous numbering appears in square brackets.

DC MS. 2: [4]
'A Ballad': *PW* i. 265–7.
'Dirge.—Sung by a Minstrel': *PW* i. 267–9.
'A Tale' (fragment): *Prose Works*, i. 7–8.
'Her have I often met at Curfew time' (fragment).
Description of a female beggar and her children (fragment).
'On returning to a Cottage' (sonnet draft).
'The Convict': *PW* i. 312–14.
'Gothic Tale' (fragment): *PW* i. 287–92.
'XVI (a)' and 'XVI (b)' (fragments): *PW* i. 292–5.

DC MS. 8:
[Prose 1]
'A Letter to the Bishop of Llandaff: *Prose Works*, i. 31–49.

DC MS. 9: [10]
Windy Brow revisions to *An Evening Walk*.

DC MS. 10: [11]
(Windy Brow Notebook)
Windy Brow revisions to *An Evening Walk*. *Salisbury Plain*, MS. 1.

DC MS. 11: [12]
(Racedown Notebook)
'How rich in front with twilight's tinge impressed' (sonnet draft).
'The Three Graves', Part II: *PW* i. 308–12.

DC MS. 13: [31, 32, 44, 46]
'Yet once again' (fragment): *PW* v. 340. *I* (Pierpoint Morgan Library).
'Description of a Beggar' (Pierpoint Morgan Library).
Baker's Cart lines (fragment): *PW* i. 315–16.
'The Ruined Cottage', MS. A.

DC MS. 14: [19]
(Alfoxden
   Notebook)
	Blank verse fragments: *PW* v. 340. *II. ii*; 341.
	   II. vi.
	Blank verse fragment: *Prelude*, p. 566.
	Description of a thorn (draft): *PW* ii. 240 app.
	   crit.
	'A whirl-blast from behind the Hill'.

DC MS. 16: [18a]	'Discharged Soldier': *Prelude*, iv. 363–504 and pp. 537–8. *Salisbury Plain*, MS. 2.
DC MS. 17: [33]	'The Ruined Cottage', MS. B: *PW* v. 379–99. 'Addendum' to 'The Ruined Cottage': *PW* v. 400–4.
DC MS. 19: [Journal 5]	'Essay on Morals': *Prose Works*, i. 103–4.
DC MS. 23: [15]	*The Borderers*, MS. B. Preface to *The Borderers: Prose Works*, i. 76–80.
DC MS. 34: [37]	*Peter Bell*, MS. 3.

I.F. notes:	transcribed by Dora and Edward Quillinan
	   from notes dictated by Wordsworth to
	   Isabella Fenwick in 1843.

Select Bibliography

ABRAMS, M. H., *The Mirror and the Lamp: Romantic Theory and the Critical Tradition* (New York, 1953).

BROOKS, CLEANTH, 'Wordsworth and Human Suffering: Notes on Two Early Poems', *From Sensibility to Romanticism: Essays Presented to Frederick A. Pottle*, ed. F. W. Hilles and Harold Bloom (New York, 1965), pp. 373–87.

COBURN, KATHLEEN, 'Coleridge and Wordsworth and "the Supernatural"', *UTQ* xxv (1955–6), 121–30.

DANBY, J. F., *The Simple Wordsworth: Studies in the Poems 1797–1807* (London, 1960).

DARLINGTON, BETH, 'Two Early Texts: *A Night-Piece* and *The Discharged Soldier*', *Bicentenary Wordsworth Studies in Memory of John Alban Finch*, ed. Jonathan Wordsworth (Ithaca, N.Y., 1970), pp. 425–48.

FOXON, D. F., 'The Printing of *Lyrical Ballads*, 1798', *Library*, 5th ser. ix (1954), 221–41.

GARBER, FREDERICK, 'Wordsworth's Comedy of Redemption', *Anglia*, lxxxiv (1966), 388–97.

GILL, STEPHEN, 'Wordsworth's Breeches Pocket: Attitudes to the Didactic Poet', *EC* xix (1969), 385–401.

—— 'The Original *Salisbury Plain*: Introduction and Text', *Bicentenary Wordsworth Studies in Memory of John Alban Finch*, ed. Jonathan Wordsworth (Ithaca, N.Y., 1970), pp. 142–79.

—— ' "Adventures on Salisbury Plain" and Wordsworth's Poetry of Protest 1795–97', *SR* xi (1972), 48–65.

GROB, ALAN, 'Wordsworth and Godwin: A Reassessment', *SR* vi (1967), 98–119.

HARTMAN, GEOFFREY, *Wordsworth's Poetry 1787–1814* (New Haven, Conn., and London, 1964).

—— 'Wordsworth, Inscriptions, and Romantic Nature Poetry', *From Sensibility to Romanticism: Essays Presented to Frederick A. Pottle*, ed. F. W. Hilles and Harold Bloom (New York, 1965), pp. 389–413.

—— 'False Themes and Gentle Minds', *PQ* xlvii (1968), 55–68.

JACOBUS, MARY, ' "The Idiot Boy"', *Bicentenary Wordsworth Studies in Memory of John Alban Finch*, ed. Jonathan Wordsworth (Ithaca, N.Y., 1970), pp. 238–65.

—— 'Southey's Debt to *Lyrical Ballads* (1798)', *RES* N.S. xxii (1971), 20–36.

—— '*Peter Bell* the First', *EC* xxiv (1974), 219–42.

JORDAN, J. E., Wordsworth's Humor', *PMLA* lxxiii (1958), 81–93.

—— 'The Hewing of *Peter Bell*', *SEL* vii (1967), 559–603.

—— 'The Novelty of the *Lyrical Ballads*', *Bicentenary Wordsworth Studies in Memory of John Alban Finch*, ed. Jonathan Wordsworth (Ithaca, N.Y., 1970), pp. 340–58.

LANDON, CAROL, 'Wordsworth's Racedown Period: Some Uncertainties Resolved', *Bulletin of the New York Public Library*, lxviii (1964), 100–9.

MAYO, ROBERT, 'The Contemporaneity of the *Lyrical Ballads*', *PMLA* lxix (1954), 486–522.

MOORMAN, MARY, *William Wordsworth: A Biography: The Early Years 1770–1803* (Oxford, 1957).

OSBORN, ROBERT, 'Meaningful Obscurity: The Antecedents and Character of Rivers', *Bicentenary Wordsworth Studies in Memory of John Alban Finch*, ed. Jonathan Wordsworth (Ithaca, N.Y., 1970), pp. 393–424.

PARRISH, S. M., ' "The Thorn": Wordsworth's Dramatic Monologue', *ELH* xxiv (1957), 153–63.

—— 'The Wordsworth–Coleridge Controversy', *PMLA* lxxiii (1958), 367–74.

—— 'Dramatic Technique in the *Lyrical Ballads*', *PMLA* lxxiv (1959), 85–97.

—— *The Art of the Lyrical Ballads* (Cambridge, Mass., 1973).

REED, M. L., 'Wordsworth, Coleridge, and the "Plan" of the *Lyrical Ballads*', *UTQ* xxxiv (1964–5), 238–53.

—— *Wordsworth: The Chronology of the Early Years 1770–1799* (Cambridge, Mass., 1967).

RYSKAMP, CHARLES, 'Wordsworth's *Lyrical Ballads* in Their Time', *From Sensibility to Romanticism: Essays Presented to Frederick A. Pottle*, ed. F. W. Hilles and Harold Bloom (New York, 1965), pp. 357–72.

SHARROCK, ROGER, 'Wordsworth's Revolt against Literature', *EC* iii (1953), 396–412.

—— '*The Borderers*: Wordsworth on the Moral Frontier', *Durham University Journal*, N.S. xxv (1964), 170–83.

SHEATS, P. D., *The Making of Wordsworth's Poetry, 1785–1798* (Cambridge, Mass., 1973).

SMYSER, J. W., 'Coleridge's Use of Wordsworth's Juvenilia', *PMLA* lxv (1950), 419–26.

STORCH, R. F., 'Wordsworth's Experimental Ballads: The Radical Uses of Intelligence and Comedy', *SEL* xi (1971), 621–39.

WHALLEY, GEORGE, 'The Bristol Library Borrowings of Southey and Coleridge, 1793–8', *Library*, 5th ser. iv. (1949–50), 114–32.

WOOF, R. S. 'Wordsworth's Poetry and Stuart's Newspapers: 1797–1803', *SB* xv (1962), 149–89.

—— 'Wordsworth and Coleridge: Some Early Matters', *Bicentenary Wordsworth Studies in Memory of John Alban Finch*, ed. Jonathan Wordsworth (Ithaca, N.Y., 1970), pp. 76–91.

WORDSWORTH, JONATHAN, *The Music of Humanity: a Critical Study of Wordsworth's Ruined Cottage* (London, 1969).

—— 'William Wordsworth 1770–1969', *Proceedings of the British Academy*, lv (1970), 211–28.

Index

'The Lass of Fair Wone', 219, *227–8, 243–4, 284–8*
'Lenore', 218–19 and n., *222–3* and nn., 250, 251 n., *277–83*
Thelwall, John, 36, 51, 67
Thomson, James, 45 and n., 48, 49, 54, 88–9
The Castle of Indolence, 89 n., 148 n.
'Ode on Aeolus's Harp', 69 and n.
The Seasons, 38, *39–44* and nn., 46, 51, 53, 69, 74, 75, 89 n., *105–9*, 138–9
Tickell, Thomas, 'Lucy and Colin', 214

Unwin, Mrs. Mary, 108

Vallon, Annette, 151
Voss, J. H., 169

Wakefield, Gilbert, 63 n.
Wardlaw, Lady Elizabeth, *Hardyknute*, 135, 136 n., 213
Warton, Joseph, 193 n.
'The Dying Indian', 193
'Ode to Fancy', 133–4 and n., 136, 140
Warton, Thomas, sen., 193 n.
Warton, Thomas, jun.
'The Suicide,' 16–17 and n.
'To the River Lodon', 114–15
Watts, Isaac
Divine Songs, 92–3, 100, 101–2
The Psalms of David, 92
Weekly Entertainer, 26 n., 160–1, 164, 185 n.
Whitefield, John, 267
Whyte, Samuel, *A Miscellany*, 221–2, 224
Williams, Helen Maria, 88 n., 187 and n.
Letters Containing a Sketch of the Politics of France, 186–7 and n.
Wilson, John, 10, 250 and n.
Wordsworth, Dorothy, 2, 3, 6, 17, 26 n., 32, 52, 224 n., 231, 234, 236 n., 275, 276
and *An Evening Walk*, 56 n., 61; 'Tintern Abbey', 42, 107–8, 124, 125, 130
Journal, 240, 274, 275
Wordsworth, William
and *Coleridge, collaboration with*, 2, 5–6 and n., 36–7, 224 and n., *228–32* and n., 262; *Coleridge, early meetings*

with, 5 and n., 7, 62 n., *Coleridge, influence of*, 7, 15, 30 n., 35–7 and nn., 38, 47, 59–60, 68, 77, 79, 80, 82–4 *passim, 118–25*; *France, attitude to*, 151–2 and n.; *German, knowledge of*, 239, 239–40 nn.; *Germany, visit to*, 4, 211, 217, 239; *Switzerland, invasion of*, 97 n.; *Wye tour*, 105 and n., 276
and *the ballad experiment*, 159, 205, 209, 211, 212, 214, 216, 220–1, 229, 232, *233–61*; comedy, *250–61* and nn., 263–5, 271–2 and n.; *critical theory*, 7, 8, *188–91* and nn.; 221, 234, 248, 249; *the everyday*, 7, 233, 209, 228, 229, 250, 253, 256–7, 261–5 *passim*, 269–71, 272; *the imagination*, 38, 44, 53, 55–8, 122–7, 133, 233, 235–7, 239, 247–8, 249, 256, 259–61, 263–5, 269–71, 272; *the One Life*, 38, 42, 55, 60–2, 65, 82, 84, 93–5, 96–8 *passim*, 104, *125–130*; *the poetry of suffering*, 133–42, 149–50, 156–9, 166, *170–7*, 182 and n., 183, 244–6, 248–50 *passim*; *'the real language of men'*, 9–10, 184–5, *188–95*, 201, 205, 218, 229; *the supernatural*, 209, 233, 235, 245, 250–3 *passim, 261–5*, 269–71
and *the ballad, broadside*, 212, 237; *the ballad, literary*, 212–17; *the ballad, pseudo-antiquarian*, 135, 136 n. 209, 212–17 *passim*, 225; *the ballad, Scots*, 194, 196–7 and n., 242 and n.; *the ballad, supernatural*, 209, *214–29*, 233, 250–3, 255, 261, 262; *the ballad, traditional*, 194, 196–7 and n., 198 n., 210–12, 221–2, 242 and n.; *the ballad revival*, 209–11 *passim*; *the conversion-narrative*, 266–270 and n. *passim*; dialect poetry, 194–5; *evangelical hymns*, 91–3, 101–102; *Indian poetry*, 189, 191, 193–4 and nn.; *magazine poetry*, 177 and n., *184–8* and nn., 196 and n., 208; *Methodism*, 266–70 and nn.; *the novel*, 255–7; *pastoral*, 167–8 and n.; *pastoral eclogue*, 168–70; *the picturesque*, 107, 110, 110–11 n., 113; *primitivism*, 188–95; *prose reporting*, 160–5; *protest poetry, anti-war*, 142–4, 149–50, 153, 185; *protest poetry, humanitarian*, 7, 134, *142–8*, 152–5, 168–9, 185–6; *the*